EYEWITNESS TRAVEL

ARGENTINA

EYEWITNESS TRAVEL

ARGENTINA

DK

LONDON, NEW YORK,
MELBOURNE, MUNICH AND DELHI
www.dk.com

Managing Editor Aruna Ghose

Editorial Manager Ankita Awasthi

Design Managers Sunita Gahir, Priyanka Thakur

Project Editor Janice Pariat

Project Designer Kavita Saha

Editor Jayashree Menon

Designer Kaberi Hazarika

Senior Cartographic Manager Uma Bhattacharya

Cartographer Alok Pathak

Senior DTP Designer Vinod Harish

Senior Picture Researcher Taiyaba Khatoon

Picture Researchers Sumita Khatwani, Shweta Andrews

Contributors
Wayne Bernhardson, Declan McGarvey, Chris Moss

Photographers
Demetrio Carrasco, Nigel Hicks, Linda Whitwam

Illustrators
Chapel Design and Marketing Ltd, Sanjeev Kumar, Arun Pottirayil, T. Gautam Trivedi

Printed and bound by L. Rex Printing Company Limited, China

14 15 16 17 10 9 8 7 6 5 4 3 2 1

First published in the UK in 2008 by Dorling Kindersley Limited
80 Strand, London WC2R 0RL

Reprinted with revisions 2010, 2012, 2015

Copyright © 2008, 2015 Dorling Kindersley Limited, London

A Penguin Random House Company

MIX
Paper from
responsible sources
FSC™ C018179
www.fsc.org

**The information in this
DK Eyewitness Travel Guide is checked regularly.**

Every effort has been made to ensure that this book is as up-to-date as possible
at the time of going to press. Some details, however, such as telephone numbers,
opening hours, prices, gallery hanging arrangements and travel information, are
liable to change. The publishers cannot accept responsibility for any consequences
arising from the use of this book, nor for any material on third party websites, and
cannot guarantee that any website address in this book will be a suitable source of
travel information. We value the views and suggestions of our readers very highly.
Please write to: Publisher, DK Eyewitness Travel Guides, Dorling Kindersley,
80 Strand, London, WC2R 0RL, UK, or email: travelguides@dk.com.

Front cover main image: Hiking in Parque Nacional Los Glaciares, Patagonia

◀ Lake Viedma, Parque Nacional Los Glaciares, Patagonia

The spectacular Quebrada landscape

Contents

Introducing Argentina

Buenos Aires Area by Area

Brightly painted houses in La Boca,
Buenos Aires

Horse riding in the countryside
outside Tandil

Survival Guide

Mate gourds for sale

A couple perform street tango

Grand old architecture
of Santa Catalina

INTRODUCING ARGENTINA

DISCOVERING ARGENTINA

The following tours have been designed to take in as many of the country's highlights as possible. In a country the size of Argentina long-distance travel is a reality, so internal flights have been recommended on longer tours in order to keep travel time between major stops to a minimum. On the following pages, to start there is a two-day tour of Buenos Aires. Next comes a seven-day tour of South Argentina, with extra suggestions to extend the trip to ten days if desired. Finally, there is a 14-day itinerary taking in some of North Argentina's most magnificent natural highlights. Each itinerary can be followed individually, or combined with another tour. Pick, combine, or faithfully follow – the choice is yours. Booking ahead for major sights is recommended.

Glaciar Perito Moreno
The mighty 2.5-mile (4-km) face of Perito Moreno, the star sight of Parque Nacional Los Glaciares, is best viewed by boat or from the dizzying catwalks on Peninsula Magellanes.

Seven Days in South Argentina

- Boat and hike through the dramatic mountain-lake scenery of **Parque Nacional Nahuel Huapi**, Argentina's oldest national park.

- Trek across the frozen blue ice of **Glaciar Perito Moreno**, one of Argentina's greatest natural wonders.

- Take in the majesty of the Southern Right whale on a wildlife safari to **Reserva Provincial Península Valdés**.

- Marvel at the granite spires of the Fitz Roy massif on a trip to **Parque Nacional Los Glaciares**.

- See some of the biggest dinosaur skeletons ever found on a visit to Trelew's **Museo Paleontológico Egidio Feruglio**.

Key

— Seven Days in South Argentina
— 14 Days in North Argentina

0 km   250
0 miles   250

Iguazú Falls
The sheer splendor and noise of this mighty complex of cataracts and cascades make it North Argentina's must-see destination.

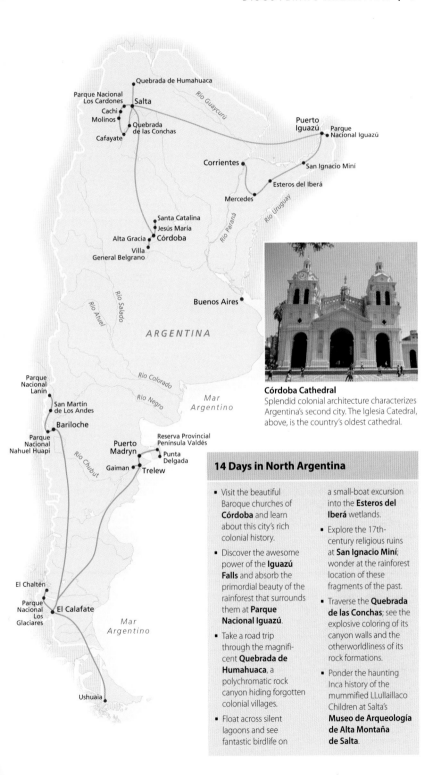

Córdoba Cathedral
Splendid colonial architecture characterizes Argentina's second city. The Iglesia Catedral, above, is the country's oldest cathedral.

14 Days in North Argentina

- Visit the beautiful Baroque churches of **Córdoba** and learn about this city's rich colonial history.

- Discover the awesome power of the **Iguazú Falls** and absorb the primordial beauty of the rainforest that surrounds them at **Parque Nacional Iguazú**.

- Take a road trip through the magnificent **Quebrada de Humahuaca**, a polychromatic rock canyon hiding forgotten colonial villages.

- Float across silent lagoons and see fantastic birdlife on a small-boat excursion into the **Esteros del Iberá** wetlands.

- Explore the 17th-century religious ruins at **San Ignacio Miní**; wonder at the rainforest location of these fragments of the past.

- Traverse the **Quebrada de las Conchas**; see the explosive coloring of its canyon walls and the otherworldliness of its rock formations.

- Ponder the haunting Inca history of the mummified LLullaillaco Children at Salta's **Museo de Arqueología de Alta Montaña de Salta**.

Two Days in Buenos Aires

Argentina's energetic capital combines high culture with entertaining street life. Over 48 hours in Buenos Aires, take in European-style architecture, visit great art museums, and witness the passion of the tango.

- **Arriving** International flights arrive at Aeropuerto Ministro Pistarini (Ezeiza), 22 miles (35 km) from the city center. Shuttle-bus and taxi services link airport and city center.

- **Moving on** Domestic flights depart from the city airport, Aeroparque Jorge Newbery, 10 minutes from downtown. Flying time from Buenos Aires to Bariloche is 2 hrs 20 min.

Buenos Aires's Palacio del Congreso in its historic plaza, seat of the Argentinian government

Day 1

Morning Start at the city's heart, at historic **Plaza de Mayo** (pp66–7). Great buildings front the plaza, led by the pink **Casa Rosada** (p68), from whose balcony Eva Perón once urged revolution. Walk west from the plaza for glorious **Café Tortoni** (p72), the city's oldest café, and Dante-inspired **Palacio Barolo** (p72). Step inside the public lobby here to see sculpted gargoyles and dragons. A city block west, the great dome of the **Palacio del Congreso** (p73) rears above the fountains of **Plaza del Congreso** (p73). From the plaza, hail a cab for the ride along **Avenida 9 Julio** (p74) to the magnificent **Teatro Colón** (pp76–7) and a guided tour of

Street performers entertaining the crowds with passionate renditions of the tango

this ornate opera house. Tour done, head to **Plaza San Martín** (pp92–3) to enjoy a picnic lunch in the city's prettiest plaza.

Afternoon Go north to upscale **Recoleta** (pp99–107), the city's most Parisian district. Peek inside the **Alvear Palace Hotel** (p103) and marvel at the mausoleums of the **Cementerio de la Recoleta** (pp104–5), where the great and powerful of Argentine history lie buried in tombs of marble and bronze. Head to the **MALBA** art museum (p114–15), before concluding with shopping and dining in the streets around **Plaza Serrano** (p119).

Day 2

Morning Start at the Jesuit-founded **Manzana de las Luces** (p70), then walk south along Defensa street to **San Telmo**, once the city's colonial heart. Pass Spanish churches such as **Iglesia del Santisimo Rosario y Convento de Santo Domingo** (p70) and stop at **Plaza Dorrego** (p82) and **Parque Lezama** (p84), whose gardens sweep downwards in the direction of **La Boca**.

Afternoon Take a cab to La Boca's portside: to **El Caminito** (p89), a waterfront street of gaily painted buildings. Watch the tango dancers, then walk to **La Bombonera** (p89), mythic home of Argentina's biggest soccer team. Head back to the waterfront and flag a cab to **Puerto Madero** (p79), a hip docklands district. Round off with a dinner and tango show (p127).

Seven Days in South Argentina

- **Airports** Arrive Aeropuerto San Carlos de Bariloche. Depart Aeropuerto Alte. M. A. Zar, Trelew.

- **Transport** Flights are recommended between major stops (Bariloche, El Calafate, and Trelew) in Argentina's south. Aerolíneas Argentina's Visit Argentina pass offers visitors connections within the region. From major towns, go by road (rental car/local bus) to reach nearby sights, or join an organized tour.

- **Booking ahead** Bariloche: Visit to Parque Nacional Nahuel Huapi; El Calafate: Two visits to Parque Nacional Los Glaciares, El Galpón del Glaciar; Puerto Madryn: Visit to Provincial Península Valdés.

Day 1: Bariloche

Gateway to Argentina's Lake District, **Bariloche** (p242) overlooks haunting **Lago Nahuel Huapi** and is ringed by snowy peaks. Start at the city's **Centro Cívico** and the **Museo de la Patagonia Francisco P. Moreno**. Then take the **Circuito Chico** route out of town, along the lakeshore. Stop for a dip at **Playa Bonita** beach, before continuing on to the **Llao Llao Hotel and Resort**. Dine on the hotel's terrace with views of blue-green lakes and mountains. Return to the city center.

Day 2: Parque Nacional Nahuel Huapi

Join a day tour of **Parque Nacional Nahuel Huapi** *(pp242–3)*. Choose adventure on a road- and boat-trip embracing millennia-old cave paintings at **Isla Victoria** and ancient myrtle woods at **Parque Nacional Los Arrayanes**. Or, opt for waterside tranquility on a visit to the park's lakeside towns, **Villa La Angostura** and **Villa Traful**.

> **To extend your trip...**
> Discover more of Argentina's Lake District on a two-day road trip to pretty **San Martín de Los Andes** *(p240)*. Located on the shore of **Lago Lácar**, it is the springboard for excursions into **Parque Nacional Lanín** *(p241)* and views of majestic **Volcán Lanín**.

Day 3: Bariloche to El Calafate

Journey south to glaciers and icy peaks. Flights arrive at **El Calafate** *(p251)*, which sits on the shore of flame-blue **Lago Argentino** and is a starting base for excursions into **Parque Nacional Los Glaciares** *(p254–5)*. Get to know El Calafate and its environs before heading to the park. Visit the **Museo Regional Municipal El Calafate** before a road trip to nearby estancia **El Galpón del Glaciar**. Here, ride horseback in the shadow of peaks and glaciers.

The beautiful ranchland landscapes around El Calafate

Day 4: Parque Nacional Los Glaciares

Get ready for a day on the big ice. On a day trip from El Calafate, explore the southern sector of this national park *(p258)*, anchoring your excursion on **Glaciar Perito Moreno**, one of Argentina's greatest natural wonders. First, navigate iceberg-strewn lake waters on a boat trip to the glacier's towering front wall. Then, step onto the glacier for a fantastic mini-trek across its blue ice.

Day 5: Parque Nacional Los Glaciares

Explore this national park's dramatic northern sector *(pp256–7)*. Arrive at **El Chaltén** *(p250)* to views of the granite needles of the **Fitz Roy** massif. Make the boat excursion to the icy face of **Glaciar Viedma** *(p257)*, South America's biggest glacier, and then hike to nearby glacial

caves. Or trek one of the shorter trails skirting the forested base of awe-inspiring Mount Fitz Roy. Return to El Calafate.

> **To extend your trip...**
> Depart El Calafate for an overnight stay in the world's southernmost city, **Ushuaia** *(p264)*. Visit the city's old prison at **Museo Marítimo de Ushuaia**. Navigate icy waters on a boat excursion along the **Canal Beagle**.

Day 6: El Calafate to Trelew

From icy glaciers to Atlantic coast: some of the planet's biggest dinosaurs once roamed here, and the excellent **Museo Paleontológico Egidio Feruglio** in Trelew *(p229)* preserves gigantic fossils. Visit the museum or make the short road trip to **Gaiman** *(p229)*, a Welsh settlement; then continue to **Puerto Madryn** *(p229)*. Learn about ocean conservation at Madryn's **Ecocentro**. Enjoy seafood at a beachside restaurant.

Day 7: Reserva Provincial Península Valdés

Spend a day on safari at **Reserva Provincial Península Valdés** *(p230–31)*, a coastal reserve and refuge to abundant marine fauna. Observe the reserve's Big Five – whale, orca, elephant seal, sea lion, and penguin – at wildlife hot spots **Golfo Nuevo**, **Caleta Valdés**, and **Punta Norte**. Lunch at the sheep estancia at **Punta Delgada**. Return to Trelew for a flight to Buenos Aires.

View of Mount Fitz Roy across the clear waters of Laguna Capri

14 Days in North Argentina

- **Airports** Arrive Aeropuerto Internacional, Córdoba. Depart Aeropuerto Internacional, Corrientes.

- **Transport** Flights are recommended between major stops in Argentina's north (Córdoba, Salta, and Puerto Iguazú). Aerolíneas Argentina's Visit Argentina pass offers visitors connections within the region. From major towns, go by road (car rental/local bus services) to reach nearby sights, or join an organized tour.

- **Booking ahead** Winery visit, Estancia Colomé; stay (optional) at Estancia Rincón del Socorro.

Day 1: Córdoba

Córdoba (pp184–5) captured the imagination of early Spanish colonizers and missionaries, and historical buildings ring its Plaza San Martín. Here, wander the cloisters at **Cabildo Independencia 30**; spot the trumpeting angels on the façade of **Iglesia Catedral** (Argentina's oldest cathedral), and admire Peruvian Cuzco-school paintings at the **Museo Histórico Provincial Marqués de Sobremonte**. Afterwards, visit the cluster of Jesuit buildings near the plaza. Head to the **Manzana de Las Luces**, before descending underground to the **Cripta Jesuítica del Noviciado Viejo**.

Day 2: Alta Gracia and Villa General Belgrano

Make the road trip southwest to the small town of **Alta Gracia** (p186), founded by Jesuits in the 17th century. Visit the Jesuit sights, in particular **Iglesia Parroquial Nuestra Señora de la Merced**, whose nave shimmers with Baroque detail. Afterwards, stroll across to the **Museo del Che Guevara**. "El Che" spent much of his childhood in Alta Gracia. This museum conserves the Guevara family home.

Set high in a green valley, **Villa General Belgrano** (p187) is the last stop on the road southwest. Home to a population of German descent, it has a vibrant atmosphere. Enjoy its chocolate shops and jolly beer cellars, then return to Córdoba.

Day 3: Jesús María and Santa Catalina

Follow the Jesuit trail north to **Jesús María** (p188), a sleepy town with 16th-century origins. See sacred relics at the **Museo Jesuítico Nacional de Jesús María** and visit a centuries-old winery. **Santa Catalina** (p190–91), 13 miles (20 km) north, is a Jesuit estancia dating from 1622. A UNESCO site, it is perfectly conserved. Wander its evocative courtyards and workshops before returning to Córdoba.

Day 4: Salta

The scenery takes on new drama at **Salta** (pp196–9), situated at 4,000 ft (1,200 m) above sea level in northwest Argentina. Forested Andean

Hiking the Garganta del Diablo (Devil's Throat) ravine in Quebrada de las Conchas

slopes overlook its colonial Plaza 9 de Julio. On the square, take in the statues of medieval saints at the **Cabildo de Salta**, and don't miss the **Museo de Arqueología de Alta Montaña de Salta**, the resting place of the mummified Llullaillaco Children. On surrounding streets, seek out the exuberant façade of the **Iglesia y Convento San Francisco** and the beautiful **Iglesia y Convento San Bernardo**. The **Museo Casa Uriburu**, meanwhile, is an impeccably conserved family mansion. Dine on regional specialties at a *peña* (folk-music venue).

Day 5: Parque Nacional Los Cardones, Cachi, and Molinos

Climb the Andean foothills west from Salta. The route winds upwards, traversing fertile valleys before turning arid and leveling out at **Parque Nacional Los Cardones** (p195) at almost 12,000 ft (3,650 m) above sea level. Follow the road through the national park, stopping at viewpoints overlooking starkly beautiful cactus forest. A short distance from the park's western border, **Cachi** (p195) appears, a colonial village framed by the eight-peak **Nevado de Cachi**. Admire the cactus-wood altar at Cachi's **Iglesia San José**, and bargain for weavings at the market square. Afterwards, make the short journey south to **Molinos** (p194). Stay overnight at Molinos or at nearby **Estancia Colomé**, a wine estate nestled amid mountainside vineyards. Sip local Torrontés wines before an Andean sunset.

The Palacio de Justicia, one of many fine buildings in Córdoba

Day 6: Cafayate and Quebrada de las Conchas

The road south passes green vineyards en route to **Cafayate** *(p194)*, an adobe village with a winemaking heritage. Enjoy tastings and learn about native cultures at the **Museo de Arqueolgaí Calchaquí**, near the main plaza.

From Cafayate, the loop back to Salta traverses the **Quebrada de las Conchas** *(p194)*. Drink in the polychrome colors of this canyon's towering walls and the eerie rock formations that pock the canyon floor, including **La Garganta del Diablo** (Devil's Throat) and **El Sapo** (The Toad). Arrive at Salta.

Day 7: Quebrada de Humahuaca

Take a day trip to a true natural marvel: the **Quebrada de Humahuaca** *(pp200–4)*, a canyon of awesome size and stunning rock coloration that is populated by ancient villages lost in time. Visit the picturesque village of **Purmamarca**, famed for a multicolored hillside; the mountainside necropolis at **Maimará**. and the pre-Inca fortress at **Tilcara**. Continue through the canyon, stopping at villages **Uquia**, **Humahuaca**, and **Iruya**. Look behind the cactus-wood doors of the 17th-century church at Uquia to discover frescoes of warring angels. Return to Salta.

Day 8: Parque Nacional Iguazú

The landscape shifts deliciously to virgin rainforest at Puerto Iguazú, gateway city to the UNESCO World Heritage Site of **Parque Nacional Iguazú** *(pp176–9)* and the magnificent **Iguazú Falls**. On a day trip to the national park, approach the upper lip of the waterfalls on foot along the **Circuito Superior**, before descending through rainforest to their spray-shrouded base via the **Circuito Inferior**. Then ride the eco-train to the giant **Garganta del Diablo** cataract, and get truly drenched on a powerboat ride to the base of the **Salto San Martín** falls.

The atmospheric ruins of San Ignacio Miní, a centuries-old Jesuit mission

Day 9: Nacional Iguazú: Brazilian side

Cross the international border for panoramic vistas of the Iguazú Falls from their **Brazilian side**. Visitors from some countries will need a visa prior to travel *(see p314)*. Afterwards, return to the forested intimacy of the Argentinian side and trek the **Sendero Macuco**. The roar of the unsighted waterfalls and the chatter of capuchin monkeys accompany this jungle hike.

Day 10: San Ignacio Miní

Discover the ruins of a 17th-century Jesuit mission at **San Ignacio Miní** *(p173)*. Close to the Falls, but a world apart, these orange-stone ruins conserve intact archways, walls, niches and religious statues, set dramatically against the verdant green of the jungle. Stay overnight next to the ruins.

Day 11: Esteros del Iberá

Head to the glassy, silent waters of **Esteros del Iberá** *(pp170–71)*,

Scarlet-headed blackbird, a striking denizen of the reed beds of Esteros del Iberá

the Iberá wetlands: a vast wilderness of marshland, lagoons, waterways, and floating islands. Start your visit at the preserve's gateway village, **Colonia Carlos Pelligrini**, or nearby **Estancia Rincón del Socorro**. Stroll the village's sandy streets, browse native Guaraní handicrafts, and walk the banks of the main **Laguna Iberá**, spying native fauna such as caiman and capybara.

Day 12: Esteros del Iberá

Spend another full day exploring the wetlands. Drift silently across lagoons on a small-boat excursion into the wetlands. Spot abundant wildlife, including songbirds of brilliant plumage. After sunset, don't miss a nocturnal safari of the wetlands. Burrowing owls appear; the eyes of caiman and capybara flash red and green in the pitch black.

Day 13: Mercedes and Corrientes

Make the road trip to gaucho town **Mercedes** *(p169)*. Shop for gaucho ware and visit the shrine to **Gauchito Gil**, a folk saint, at the edge of town. Continue on to Corrientes.

Day 14: Corrientes

End your trip at a little-visited jewel: **Corrientes** *(p172)*, a provincial capital rich in history and set on the banks of the mighty **River Paraná** *(p167)*. Wander its streets and admire 19th-century buildings such as the **Casa de Gobierno**. Dine on the riverbank, with views of forested islands.

Putting Argentina on the Map

Argentina occupies most of the triangular southern tip of South America and shares its borders with Uruguay, Brazil, Paraguay, Bolivia, and Chile. Covering an area of 1.08 million sq miles (2.8 million sq km), it is the eighth-largest country in the world. It is more than 3,100 miles (5,000 km) long following the western frontier down the Andes range, while some 1,900 miles (3,000 km) of Atlantic coastline stretch between Buenos Aires and Tierra del Fuego, an island separated from the continent by the Magellan Strait and shared with Chile. Argentina has a population of 40 million and administratively, it is divided into 23 provinces and a federal district in which stands the bustling capital.

Key

▭ Expressway
▭ Highway
▭ Railroad
▭ International border

0 kilometers   300
0 miles   300

For additional map symbols *see back flap*

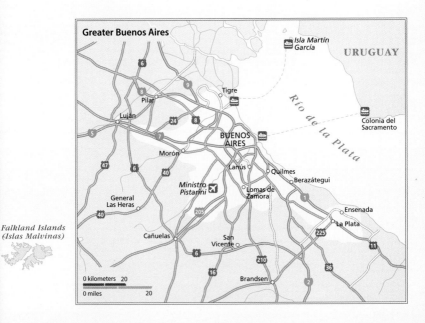

A PORTRAIT OF ARGENTINA

Behind Argentina's European veneer is a colorful, chaotic, and enchanting Latin American nation. Passionate about their music, meat, and politics, the people of the country are fun-loving and friendly. Its breathtaking range of landscapes and distinct historical evolution, both during and since the Spanish conquest, combine to make Argentina the exciting destination it is today.

Bounded by the towering Andes in the west and the waters of the Atlantic to the east, Argentina is the eighth-largest country in the world, second in size only to Brazil in Latin America. About a third of the country's population lives in the bustling capital, Buenos Aires, and its sprawling suburbs. The rest of the country is thinly populated, and lonely swathes of the rural interior, especially in Patagonia, are almost devoid of settlement.

Evidence of the country's Spanish past abounds across Argentina. In the 16th century, Jesuits followed in the wake of the conquistadors, converting natives and building magnificent monuments to their faith. Córdoba, Mendoza, and La Plata most strongly reflect their influence. Following land-grabbing military campaigns in the 1870s and 1880s in the central and southern provinces, many of Argentina's indigenous peoples were wiped out. A wave of immigrants, mainly from Italy and Spain, swept into the country, making it Latin America's most Europeanized nation. The country's history is intricately linked to the five nations with which it shares its borders. The landscapes and peoples of Argentina, however, are utterly distinct, with most *argentinos* bearing a strong sense of national identity.

Guanacos in Parque Nacional Perito Moreno against a backdrop of the Patagonian Andes

◄ People passing a life-size mural on a street in Caminito, Buenos Aires

Land and Conservation

The absence of human settlement in many areas and the abundance of green spaces makes Argentina in many ways a natural paradise. The Pampas grasslands spill endlessly around the capital city, while subtropical forests characterize Argentinian Litoral. The Andean Northwest offers deep ravines weathered by wind and rain, and Patagonia thrills visitors with its magnificent glaciers. The country's 27 national parks and municipal preserves protect a wide range of environments, including ice-fields, deserts, and wetlands.

Visitor center logo, Parque Nacional Chaco

The government has now begun to realize that the booming tourist industry will depend on sustaining this wilderness. For over a century, the country's economy has focused on agriculture, cattle-raising, and sheep-farming, and land in many areas has been damaged by the impact. For example, the plains of Patagonia have been desertified by intensive sheep-farming. The growing of wheat and other grains has replaced the original grasslands of central Argentina, and cash crops such as genetically modified soya and tobacco have replaced the quinoa and amaranth that pre-Columbian farmers planted.

Argentina's growing industrial sector has also had a devastating impact on nature. Native flora and fauna are under threat due to the hydroelectric projects on the Uruguay and Paraná Rivers, and the forestry projects in Misiones and Tierra del Fuego. The World Wide Fund for Nature (WWF) estimates that more than 61,775 sq miles (160,000 sq km) of forest cover were lost between 1980 and 2000. Illegal hunting is a problem in all provinces.

The country's main environmental nongovernmental organization, Vida Silvestre, works with private organizations and philanthropists to create new protected areas and establish sustainable tourism projects. Recent successes have included the temporary shutdown of a Shell refinery in Buenos Aires for inadequate waste-handling procedures, and the creation of Parque Nacional Monte León through the nonprofit Patagonia Land Trust.

The stunning red rocks of Parque Provincial Ischigualasto, a UNESCO World Heritage Site

Gaucho on an estancia near El Calafate, Patagonia

Economy

The Argentinian economy has experienced several booms and melt-downs in the past, and Argentinians have always kept a close watch on economic fluctuations. In the late 1980s, only a few years after the return of democracy, infla-tion soared to 1,000 percent. During the presidency of Carlos Menem in the 1990s, Argentinians thought a new era had been ushered in: the peso was pegged to the dollar, credit was available, and people were able to afford all kinds of luxuries. No one was prepared for what hap-pened in December 2001, when a run on the banks caused the gov-ernment to sequester private savings, and eventually led to the collapse of the peso. Today, as the country experiences a moderate economic revival, confi-dence is gradually returning. The country is one of the biggest and most prestigious beef exporters in the world, and the fifth-largest wine-producer in the world.

Tourism is flourishing and is the third-largest source of the country's income. However, poverty has risen since the 1980s, and crime and security worry most Argentinians, as does the "brain drain." After the 2001 banking disaster, many of Argentina's talented young people left the country, and many have stayed away despite the gradual improvement in affairs back home.

Politics

For the majority of Argentinians, the political arena has been the source of more drama and damage than the worst trials and tribulations of the economy. While there have always been *caudillos* (political-military dictators) in Argentina, almost all Argentinians view the generals who ran the country during the 1976–83 period as tyrants. However, national politics since the military dictatorship has been relatively stable and peaceful, and, while democracy has brought its own set of problems for Argentinians, few would exchange today's elected leaders for the dictators of the past.

Today, the country's government is a representative-democratic, federal, and

Cristina Fernández de Kirchner during the presidential elections

presidential one where-in the president is both the head of state and head of government, complemented by a multiparty system. The country is divided into a federal capital and 23 provinces; the federal government is headed by the president and the bicameral national congress, and the provinces by governors. After winning the popular vote in the October 2007 elections, Argentina's First Lady, Cristina Fernández de Kirchner, became the president of Argentina.

Sports and Arts

Argentina is well ahead of other Latin American countries in terms of sporting prowess and artistic creativity. It is a world-class nation in soccer and several other sports, including tennis, golf, polo, and hockey. At the 2012 Olympics Argentina took home a gold medal in taekwondo, silver in women's field hockey, and bronzes in men's tennis and sailing. An Argentine has also won the US Open Golf Championship. However, it is in soccer that Argentina's passions spill onto the streets. Past legends such as Alfredo di Stefano, Gabriel Batistuta, Mario Kempes, and Diego Maradona are still revered as demi-gods, while Lionel Messi is a current favorite.

Buenos Aires's most important cultural institute, Teatro Colón, is where famous classical music artistes, including pianist Martha Argerich, conductor Daniel Barenboim, and composer Osvaldo Golijov, have performed. While there is always a huge turnout for rock concerts by visiting international bands, many young Argentinians prefer their *rock nacional*. Argentinian pop and rock have been politicized since the 1970s, when the band Sui Generis recorded

Argentinian pop band Miranda at a performance

anti-establishment songs in the midst of the military dictatorship. International critics often point out that there is, through the influence of tango, a melancholy in all Argentinian music. While very few Argentinians actually dance to the famous rhythm, urbanites enjoy Carlos Gardel, the Bing Crosby of Argentinian tango.

After the heady days of the Latin American boom during the middle of the 20th century, few Argentinian writers have won international acclaim. For many, the works of Jorge Luis Borges and Julio Cortázar remain the benchmarks by which all literature must be measured. Nonetheless, Argentinians are avid readers; the annual Feria de Libro in Buenos Aires attracts huge audiences, and the publishing of new books by contemporary writers such as Ana María Shua, Pablo de Santis, and Tomás Eloy Martínez are major events in the cultural calendar.

Cinema is popular in the country. In the last few years, a new school of cinéma verité has developed, which, as well as scooping up prizes in prestigious international film festivals, has given the country a register with which to debate social realities in the post-1983 democratic period.

Lionel Messi playing against the Mexico team

People and society

A nation of immigrants since the 19th century, Argentina is today a cultural melting pot comprising people of Italian, Spanish, Jewish, and French ancestry. Buenos Aires's flamboyant, confident residents, the porteños, enjoy many of the same luxuries and suffer the same stresses as the residents of any major world city. Their city also has certain unique characteristics of its own, such as the enduring melodrama of tango, the booming gastronomic scene, and the insomniac nightlife. Porteños often refer to their ring road, Avenida General Paz, as if it were some kind of frontier, and the less-traveled urban working classes are wont to imagine the provincial heartland as a somewhat untamed, impenetrable, and exotic periphery.

However, those who do venture out of the city limits are often charmed by the myriad pleasures of the interior. In the small towns of Misiones, Chaco, and Corrientes, village life goes on much as it has done for 200 years, with locals gathering at the bar in the plaza, and the year-round rhythms of work and family life broken only by major fiestas. In the Andean plains of the Northwest, vestiges of pre-Columbian life still remain, with

A brightly painted café in Caminito, La Boca

native residents and mestizos (people of mixed European and indigenous ancestry) still playing the panpipes and flutes and wearing ponchos. Far south in Patagonia, visitors will be surprised to meet descendants of Welsh and German settlers.

An essential bonhomie and zest for life have always endured in the Argentinian soul. For the visitor, it is easy to enjoy the endearing qualities of this colorful and thrilling nation, its abundant wildlife, vast landscapes, and friendly people.

An indigenous ceremony taking place in the Neuquén province

Landscape and Wildlife of Argentina

Despite threats to its environment, Argentina still remains one of the richest countries in the world in its variety of flora and fauna. It has over 1,000 species of birds, many of which are unique to the country; 29 sprawling national parks; and a large number of provincial preserves that protect a fascinating array of mammals. It owes its natural wealth to a highly varied topography that covers a range of climatic zones ranging from arid, harsh environments dominated by steppe, salt pans, and soaring Andean peaks to great swathes of grassy plains and wetlands.

View of Mount Fitz Roy in Parque Nacional Los Glaciares

The Pampas Wetlands

Seasonal rainfall across the Pampas in Buenos Aires and Entre Ríos leads to the formation of the channels and vast lagoons of Esteros del Iberá (see pp170–71). It is home to waders and many other bird species.

The wattled jacana, with its huge feet, seems to walk on water. It daintily strides over lily pads and is a discreet wader until it flies and flashes its bright-yellow underwings.

The dorado is king of Río Paraná (see p167). Known for its power, it is the prize catch of anglers in the northeast.

Yacaré thrive in the Iberá wetlands, sharing the banks and islands with capybaras and howler monkeys.

Mountains and *Puna*

At over 8,000 ft (2,400 m) above sea level, the *puna* (montane grasslands) in Argentina's northwestern provinces is a mixture of semi-arid and desert landscapes. On its western edge, it rises to become the Andes range.

The Andean condor has a wingspan of over 9 ft (3 m). It can be seen wheeling on the thermals that form in the crevasses and lagoons of the Andes.

The Royal chinchilla is a rodent found in the high plains. Hunted for its fur, it is an endangered species.

The cardón cactus grows in abundance across the northwest and is protected inside Parque Nacional Los Cardones in the Valles Calchaquíes area (see p195).

The Atlantic Coast

The rugged coastline between Buenos Aires and Cape Horn stretches over 1,900 miles (3,000 km). The cold currents of the South Atlantic are the natural habitat of Southern Right whales, seals, and sea lions, all seen at Península Valdés *(see pp230–31)*. Offshore, petrels and albatrosses patrol the waves.

Magellanic penguins are a common sight along the Patagonian coast. The continent's largest colony is found at Punta Tombo in Chubut *(see p232)*.

The Southern Right whale earned its name as the "right" whale for hunters to kill because it floats after being harpooned. It is now protected in Argentinian waters.

Subtropical Forests

Sizeable protected subtropical forests can be found in Misiones, Corrientes, and Salta. Flora flourishes beneath the dense canopy; the more remote forests provide a habitat for rare species such as harpy eagles and jaguars.

Patagonia

Best known for its vast, semi-arid steppes and glaciers, Patagonia also has forests near the Andes and rich marine wildernesses along its coast. Wildlife includes rare species such as the *huemul* and miniature *pudú* deer.

The *ceibo* is a carmine-red native arboreal bloom, adopted as Argentina's national flower.

The myrtle tree is found all across northern Patagonia. It is a versatile plant, with a warm fawn color.

The Toco toucan is a raucous forest species, seen at dawn or dusk flitting across the canopy in Parque Nacional Iguazú *(see pp176–9)*.

The Magellanic woodpecker is a large, gregarious bird, easily spotted in Parque Nacional Tierra del Fuego in Ushuaia *(see p265)*.

The jaguar is the largest feline in South America. Only a handful are now found in remote corners of protected preserves in the Salta, Jujuy, and Chaco regions.

The *huemul* has been on the endangered list since 1976. It is a shy, solitary woodland deer found mainly in the high Patagonian Andes.

The Peoples of Argentina

Argentina is the most Europeanized of all Latin American nations and the majority of its 40 million people are of mainly Spanish or Italian descent. There are also small but significant British, German, French, Armenian, and Levantine communities, and Argentina has opened its doors to Jewish refugees from Russia and Poland. Official statistics suggest that only 404,000 Argentinians are indigenous, the majority of whom are the Mapuche, although research by the University of Buenos Aires suggests that up to half the population is mestizo.

A shop in Jujuy selling an array of indigenous handicrafts

Indigenous peoples

Few native tribes remain today, compared to the dozens of sizable indigenous groups at the time of the Spanish conquest. While most still live in rural communities, the growing impoverishment of their lands has forced many to migrate to cities.

The Mapuche, estimated to number 250,000, form the country's largest indigenous community. Most of them live in the province of Neuquén.

Mapuche traditional clothing consists of handwoven ponchos and leather belts.

The Guaraní speak a language of the same name and are mostly concentrated in Misiones province in the north of Argentina. There are approximately 10,000 Guaranís in the country.

The Colla community is the main indigenous group in Jujuy province, with an estimated population of 35,000. Their mother tongue is Quechua and they are famous for their colorful handmade clothes.

The Tehuelche were once an important Patagonian tribe. They suffered at the hands of both the Mapuche and the Spanish conquerors. Now, less than 200 people are classified as Tehuelche, though many thousands of mestizos have Tehuelche blood.

The Wichí people number about 25,000, with communities in the provinces of Chaco, Salta, and Formosa. Though Wichí land rights are recognized by law, their territory is under constant threat from developers.

Immigrants

Mass immigration transformed Argentinian society at the end of the 19th century, bringing much-needed cheap labor while at the same time enriching the country's social and cultural scene.

Buenos Aires was the favored disembarking point for European immigrants, and, although conditions were tough for a majority of these people, they continued to come in their thousands.

Animal sacrifices are held to ensure a good harvest for the coming year.

The Italian community in the capital's La Boca area is famous for its tenement buildings painted in primary colors by the first wave of Genoese immigrants. The lively port barrio (neighborhood) still retains something of its original atmosphere.

Germans also form a sizable community. A number of Argentinian towns such as Villa Gesell *(see p154)* were founded by German immigrants, as is apparent from their architecture and street names. Several have retained their native customs, including the Oktoberfest beer festival.

The Jews in Argentina form one of the largest Jewish communities of any country outside Israel. It is estimated to comprise 250,000 people, around 180,000 of whom live in the capital city, which has several synagogues.

Swiss immigrants to Argentina made their homes in towns that nestled in the slopes of the beautiful Andes region. Their architectural influence is still evident today, as can be seen in this Swiss-style hotel in Bariloche *(see p242)*.

The Gaucho: Symbol and Reality

There are macho cowboy figures throughout the Americas, but few are as central to the national culture as the gaucho is to Argentina. The earliest gauchos herded semi-wild Cimarron cattle in the 17th century, often sleeping out in the open pampas and riding into town to trade in leather and tallow. This free-roaming life came to an end when the vast interior was divided up into huge estancias (ranches) in the 19th century. Modern-day gauchos still dress in their traditional garb for major holidays and festivals, and many are first-rate horsemen.

The gaucho and his favorite horse often form a strong lifelong bond

The *asado* is an open-air barbecue for grilling cuts of meat. It is an important community ritual for gauchos and country-dwellers. Here, the griller is grilling *al cuero*, a method of cooking meat with the skin still attached.

Patagonian gauchos, trained for years, are expert shepherds.

Mate is the traditional, rather bitter green tea of Argentina, Paraguay, Uruguay, and southern Brazil. Gauchos sip this concoction during their leisure hours.

The Gaucho Way of Life

The Argentinian estancia is often located far from any major towns or suburbs. Surrounded by largely unpopulated plains or barren hills, it is the classic gaucho homestead, providing them with solitude and freedom, close to the life they once led.

Sheep are the most commonly raised animal on an estancia, bred and sheared for their wool.

Training horses using *boleadoras* (heavily weighted lassos) and breaking in willful colts form part of the daily routine for many gauchos, who are often expert horsemen.

The rhythms of the *milonga*, strummed on a guitar and often accompanied by a "call-and-response" story about some popular local drama, are central to Argentina's rich folk tradition.

Gaucho Festivals

Many towns and cities in the Argentinian interior celebrate their local gaucho and farming heritage with lively parades, folk music concerts, and spectacular equestrian shows. The biggest fiesta in the country is the Día de la Tradición, a festive extravaganza held every November, especially in San Antonio de Areco *(see p149)*.

A gaucho in parade garb and his smartly dressed *china* (female partner) perform a country dance known as the *chacarera*. Originating in the northwest of Argentina, it is a dance of lively rhythms and pantomimic play.

Dancers from the northwest of the country perform a high-spirited *carnavalito* (circle dance) during La Rural *(see p47)*, the annual agricultural fair held in August in Buenos Aires. Here, people celebrate the culture and traditions of the country in the heart of the bustling city.

Gaucho Gear

Gauchos don the full Moorish-influenced costume only for important fiestas. However, their everyday workclothes usually contain a few elements of traditional dress.

The poncho is a simple garment worn usually to keep warm.

The boina is a traditional Basque hat.

Facones are handy for cutting rope, vegetation, and of course meat; they can also be used as weapons.

The rastro is a metal belt decorated with equestrian or patriotic symbols.

Bombachas are loose trousers that have a hint of the Arabian about them.

Tough working boots are replaced by *alpargatas drilles* (sandals) for leisure.

The legend of Juan Moreira

Poster of the film *Juan Moreira*

An outlaw and local folk hero, Juan Moreira is an important figure in Argentina's gaucho history. He fought against the injustice meted out to gauchos as the military advanced across the country's interior during the late 19th century. The plains were fenced off and handed out to Creole aristocrats, and many gauchos were forced into employment as poorly paid peons and foot soldiers fighting in regional battles between landowners. Moreira was murdered by the authorities in 1874. In 1973, Argentinian director Leonard Favio made a celebrated film in his honor.

Boleadoras are heavy ball-lassos, effective for capturing the wild flightless rheas that inhabit the Pampas region.

Religion in Argentina

Argentina's most prominent religion is Christianity, with a large majority of Roman Catholic followers. Native religions were unable to resist the combined force of the Spanish sword and Jesuit teachings, but a certain degree of syncretism took place and a native version of Catholicism evolved, replete with saints, superstitions, and native iconography. Besides traditional religious practices, popular cult or folklore figures such as Difunta Correa, Gauchito Gil, and Ceferino Namuncurá are still venerated throughout the country.

Statues on the façade of Basilica Nuestra Señora de Luján

Christianity

Roman Catholicism is the country's state religion, supported by an article of the Argentinian constitution. This support is both economic and institutional, with the federal state paying salaries to bishops, and with the army setting up special posts for Catholic chaplains. Many schools are also affiliated to the church. The first major Roman Catholic presence in the country was during the period of the Jesuit Missions (1599–1767), which were established in Córdoba and the northeast with their headquarters at Manzana de las Luces in Buenos Aires. The Jesuits, together with Franciscan and Dominican monks, laid the groundwork for the establishment of the Catholic faith as the official religion of the country. Roman Catholicism spread to southern Argentina only at the end of the 19th century. By the 1890s, Salesian missions were active in Patagonia, while Anglican missionaries from the United Kingdom also established an outpost on Canal Beagle.

View of crumbling Jesuit ruins, San Ignacio Miní, Misiones

The Independence movement in the early 19th century, however, was fronted by men fired by secular passions, and the open-door immigration policy that Argentina adopted from the mid-19th century onwards created a tolerant, non-denominational society.

The involvement of Catholic church leaders in the 1955 military coup and in the machinations of the military government between 1976 and 1983 has cast a pall over the religious institution. There have been few left-leaning church leaders in Argentina, and the country has never been a seedbed for revolutionary liberation theology, which focuses on Christ as not only a Redeemer but also a Liberator of the oppressed. The church cannot be said to have fully met its doctrinal promise to represent the poor. Consequently, Catholicism is losing ground to the Mormon church and to evangelical movements in the provinces. Even the election in 2013 of Argentinian Cardinal Jorge Mario Bergoglio as Pope Francis I has not created much of a boom for Catholicism, although the Vatican's yellow and white flag is often now seen. Today, Roman Catholicism is largely an element of Argentina's cultural heritage rather than a national faith.

Judaism

One of Argentina's famous claims is that Buenos Aires, after New York, is the most Jewish city outside Israel. While this is not strictly true, the Jewish community in Argentina is a significant 2 percent of the population and, more importantly, has a cultural presence and political clout disproportionate to mere numbers. Among those who made up the first waves of migration to the rural interior during the late 1880s were groups of *gauchos judíos*

Dome of Templo de la Congregación Israelita, Buenos Aires

(Jewish cowboys). In Buenos Aires, large numbers of Jewish families arrived between 1880 and 1940 to escape the pogroms in Russia and, later, the growing tide of anti-Semitic feeling across central and eastern Europe. After many decades of peaceful coexistence, the bombings of the Israeli Embassy in 1992, killing 29 people and wounding 242, and of the Argentinian-Israeli Mutual Association (AIMA) in 1994, killing 85 people, sent shock waves through the local community. While these acts of terrorism were largely ignored by the international community at the time, post-9/11 they have been attributed to Al-Qaeda.

Pan Altar exhibit, Museo Xul Solar

World Religions

Argentina's constitution guarantees freedom of worship for all. A Muslim minority makes up about 1.5 percent of its population and Buenos Aires's King Fahd Mosque is the biggest in Latin America. The country is also home to other groups, including Mormons, Spiritualists, Jehovah's Witnesses, and Buddhists. A few Buddhist temples in the capital serve the descendants of a Chinese community who migrated to Argentina in the mid-19th century as contract laborers.

Pre-Columbian Beliefs

Although many indigenous groups were wiped out by war and disease during Spanish rule, several groups remain who still practice their traditional beliefs. The Andean Northwest was on the fringes of the Incan empire, and even today mestizo and native communities in Salta and Jujuy pay homage to Pachamama (Earth Mother) and perform pre-Columbian or syncretistic rituals such as Fiesta de Inti Raymi (winter solstice). Some members of the Mbya-Guaraní-speaking tribes of Misiones also follow a belief system that predates the Spanish conquest, with emphasis on the creation of the world by the supreme god, Tupã, dream narratives, and a strong sense of living in harmony with nature's rhythms. Argentina's Mapuche community continues to observe their ancient traditions through storytelling and through *Ngillatún*, a major annual fiesta celebrated at different times according to the local sowing and harvesting calendar.

Gathering of native Mapuche women for *Ngillatún*

Popular Cults

Argentinians venerate a number of unorthodox holy figures and even those who profess to no religion often adopt these as part of the national or regional folklore. The three best-known quasi-saints are Difunta Correa *(see p220)*, a woman who, though deceased, is believed to have continued to breastfeed and nourish her infant son; Gauchito Gil, a Robin Hood figure from Corrientes; and, from the province of Río Negro, Ceferino Namuncurá, son of a Mapuche chief. Ceferino is worshipped across northern Patagonia. Bus drivers often have the Virgin of Luján dangling from their rear-view mirrors alongside the colorful pendants of their soccer teams, and San Cayetano, the saint who cares for poor people, is a figure whose importance ebbs and flows in correlation to the economic realities of the day.

Largest mosque in South America, the King Fahd Mosque, Buenos Aires

Argentinian Tango

Tango has its roots in the bars and bordellos that sprung up around Buenos Aires at the turn of the 20th century. From the cultural melting pot of European immigrants and Africans, a vibrant music and dance form evolved. While early tango was played on flute, violin, and guitar, musicians soon adopted the *bandoneón* (button accordion) for its rhythmic energy and melancholic strains. Tango boomed in Argentina and in Europe in the early 1900s, but declined during the Perón years. Since the 1980s a revival has taken place, and a new tango music scene has emerged, inspired mainly by tango shows.

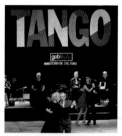

Final of the Tango Metropolitan Championship in Buenos Aires

Tango on the Streets

The age-old tradition of practicing tango on the streets is kept up by professional street performers who don retro gear and show off their flicks and kicks to locals and tourists in Calle Florida, San Telmo, and La Boca.

The upper body is usually stiff, locked in a close embrace in traditional Argentinian tango.

The crowd is usually encouraged to join in and try a few steps with the dancers.

Footwork involves complicated movements and is flexible, quick, and exquisitely choreographed.

Tango postures often reflect machismo culture and traditional societal roles, with the man as the stiff central focus and the woman by turns haughty and provocative, then languid and responsive.

La milonga is both a fast-paced dance style and, informally, the term for a gathering where people listen and dance to tango music. Locals and tourists flock to *milongas* throughout the capital to dance with favored partners or to meet a new one.

Fantasia or show tango is full of clever twirls, exaggerated kicks, and aerial flights of fancy. This is in contrast to the *milonga* style, in which the feet cling to the floor. Fantasia gained popularity during the tango revival in the 1980s.

Tango in Popular Culture

Buenos Aires is sometimes called a "tangopolis" or tango city. Music plays on taxi drivers' radios, graffiti is on the walls, and even films about contemporary issues often include a track of old tango to conjure up the capital city's ineffable melancholy.

Tango in street art is popular and seen in murals and graffiti decorating walls all over Buenos Aires, including this brightly colored relief in the La Boca area.

Tango in film was first used in Rudolph Valentino's *The Four Horsemen of the Apocalypse*, in 1921, to suggest illicit passion.

Tango in pop art is usually portrayed as a colorful and vibrant social experience by Argentinian painters, despite the seeming sobriety of the music. This atmospheric work, *La Milonga 2*, was painted in 2004 by Diego Manuel Rodriguez.

The Best of Tango

Tangueros (tango fans) all have their own halls of fame. Yet everyone accepts that Carlos Gardel was an inspirational pioneer and that Ástor Piazzolla was the last great revolutionary to pick up a baton and lead tango down a new path. *Bandoneón* legend Aníbal Troilo and singer Roberto Goyeneche are up there in the pantheon too.

Carlos Gardel was an enormously popular tango singer during the early 1900s. His death in an airplane crash at the height of his career created an image of a tragic hero. For many music fans, Gardel embodies the soul of Argentinian tango.

Adriana Varela, with her smoky voice, is a popular contemporary tango singer. She is also outspoken about her left-wing leanings.

Ástor Pantaleón Piazzolla is considered the most important tango composer of the late 20th century. His compositions revolutionized traditional tango by adding elements of modern jazz.

Juan Carlos Copes is widely recognized as the greatest dancer of the modern age. He is famed for his performances in the 1980s show *Tango Argentino*.

Music and Dance

Rock nacional, pop, and tango dominate in the country's capital and other urban areas, where middle-class Argentinians stress their fondness for these genres, while *cumbia* and other Latin rhythms are popular among the working classes. Folk music, known in Castellano as *folklore*, enjoys greater popularity in rural parts. *Chacarera* and *zamba*, both dance and musical forms, are popular in the Pampas and Andean high plains respectively, while from the Litoral provinces comes the lively fusion of *chamame*.

Mapuche women playing traditional ceremonial music

Folklore

Built on the rhythms of pre-Columbian indigenous music, *folklore* exhibits Old World influences and has adopted the guitar as a key instrument. It is an umbrella term for the music that combines traditional indigenous elements with the structures or instrumentation of European folk.

Zamba is not to be confused with its homonym, samba. The Argentinian *zamba* is an elegant courting dance during which couples tease and taunt each other using a white handkerchief. Lyrics cover all subjects, from love and the countryside to passionate political protest.

Andean music is synonymous with the sound of pan pipes, *charango* guitars, and flutes, while lyrics praise Pachamama (Earth Mother). Jaime Torres is the country's best-known *charango* virtuoso.

Chamame is a fusion of German *Schottische*, Guaraní ethnic music, Brazilian forms, and Spanish rhythms, and has a notably subtropical feel. Leading exponents include Chango Spasiuk.

Urban Rhythms

In Argentina's major cities there is access to a healthy mix of various genres of music ranging from Western classical and rock to hip-hop, pop, and trance. Urbanites love to listen, and to dance, to tango, *marcha*, *cumbia*, *cuarteto*, pop-influenced *folklore*, and different kinds of rhythms that reflect Latin American and traditional indigenous influences.

Argentinian *cumbia* was originally derived from Colombian *cumbia*. The term used to refer to songs dealing with love and jealousy set to a tinny beat, but in the late 1990s a scene called *cumbia villera* (shanty town) emerged. Well-known bands include Damas Gratis *(right)* and Yerba Brava.

Chacarera is played on the guitar, violin, and *bombo legüero* (drum), and sometimes with an accordion. It is an upbeat country rhythm with a dance akin to a line dance with couples moving in and out of the embrace position. Los Chalchaleros are the best-known performers of this popular genre.

La Nueva Canción is a pan-national movement that emerged in the wake of the successful Cuban Revolution, when Latin American songwriters began to compose protest songs. Argentina's Mercedes Sosa was an early pioneer and over a span of 30 years has become the best-known exponent of the style.

Bombo legüero, an Andean skin drum   A *siku*, pan pipe made of bamboo

Quena, a traditional six-hole bamboo flute

Folklore instruments such as the pan flute and *quena* are the essentials of Andean music, and are often combined with the *charango* and violin. Mapuche folk musicians have their own distinctive instruments, including the *trutruka* (horn) and *kultrun* (hide-drum).

Mapuche Music

Mapuche singer Beatriz Pichi Malen

Although recordings of the musical traditions of the now extinct Tehuelche, Diaguita, and Querandíes cultures are difficult to find, there is still a living Mapuche tradition in Argentina. Artists such as Beatriz Pichi Malen perform songs in *Mapundungun*, the Mapuche tongue, and incorporate native instruments and ancient poetry into their compositions. Mapuche music springs from a tradition of living in close and harmonious contact with nature. Unlike most Western music, it is not codified or written but based on natural melodic patterns and ancestral rhythms that are transmitted orally. Mapuche music influences their poetry, dance, dramatic representations, empirical medicine, as well as religious beliefs.

Rock nacional started in Buenos Aires and Rosario in the 1960s. Although initially incorporating many British rock influences, musicians later explored local musical roots and created a distinctive sound. Santa Fe-born León Gieco *(left)* is a well-loved veteran performer of folk-rock music.

Pop and fusion thrive in Argentina, as young people are able to explore international musicians as well as listen to major local bands such as Divididos and Bersuit Vergarabat. Soda Stereo, led by Gustavo Cerati *(right)*, is the most successful band to emerge in Argentina in the past 30 years.

Art and Literature in Argentina

It is difficult to identify a cohesive "Argentinian" culture prior to Independence; neither the descendants of the Spanish settlers nor the indigenous tribes regarded themselves as belonging to a "nation" in the modern sense. In the 1700s, under the Viceroyalty of the Rió de la Plata whose intentions in the region were purely commercial, Buenos Aires remained a cultural backwater. Only gradually, after Independence and spurred by immigration, a growing middle class, and, later, the explosion of interest in Latin American literature, did Argentina and its vibrant capital begin to export as well as to import arts and culture.

Religious and Indigenous Art

Pre-Hispanic art in what would later become Argentina was mainly produced in the country's northwestern regions, particularly in the valleys of Catamarca and Salta, where the indigenous population developed an array of pottery, metalwork, ceramics, and textiles. Noteworthy is the pottery produced during the La Aguada period (AD 650–900), which usually explored animistic themes through geometric representations of fantastic animals and anthropomorphic avatars of gods and monsters, reminiscent – on a less sophisticated level – of Hindu and Egyptian art. Cave paintings from much earlier epochs have been discovered in several provinces, the most famous being Cueva de las Manos in Patagonia (see p247).

Art in the colonial era was dominated by religious painting – especially of the Cusco School – architecture, and sculpture. The finest works of this period are the altarpieces and pulpits produced by Jesuit sculptors working with indigenous craftsmen. The ruins found in San Ignacio Mini (see p173) are a fine example of this. Jesuit architects such as Andrés Bianchi (1677–1740) built temples, schools, and accommodations in the north of the

Colonial religious painting of the Cusco School

country, the ruins of which still inspire awe for their scale and elegance. The watercolors of German Jesuit Florian Pauke (1719–89) show the everyday life and work of both the indigenous population and European travelers, and are striking for conferring the former with the same dignity and strength of purpose as the latter.

Secular Art

The War of Independence that Argentina waged against Spain had been fueled by the rationalist ideas of the Enlightenment and the French Revolution, so it is no surprise that the country's postcolonial artists largely ignored religious themes. The first major Argentinian artists were the painter and lithographer Carlos Morel (1813–94) and Prilidiano Pueyrredón (1823–70). The latter's *Retrato de Manuelita Rosas* and *The Bath* document the era with great clarity. Cándido López (1840–1902) was a painter and soldier famous for his paintings of the War of the Triple Alliance (1864–70).

Buenos Aires produced few significant artists until the late 19th century, when immigration invigorated the city's cultural scene. Well-known painters include Benito Quinquela Martín (1890–1977) and Fortunato Lacámera (1887–1951).

Modernist styles, mainly French Cubism and Italian Futurism, were imported from Europe's art capitals in the early 20th century. The key artists of this period were Antonio Berni (1905–81) and Xul Solar (1887–1963). Also popular was Florencio Molina Campos (1891–1959), best known for his gaucho caricatures. Major contemporary artists include Antonio Seguí (b.1934), Luis Fernando Benedit (b.1937), and Guillermo Kuitca (b.1961), who is

Painting by Cándido López at Museo Nacional de Bellas Artes, Buenos Aires

widely exhibited and is the most lauded Argentinian artist of his generation.

Independent Voices: 1810–1880

Postcolonial Argentina was, for most of the 19th century, a divided country where the pens of writers and intellectuals were pitted against the swords of provincial *caudillos* in a battle for the support of the population. In the view of writers such as Esteban Echeverría (1805–80) and Domingo Sarmiento (1811–88), the conflict was between European-style civilization (democracy and secularism) and home-grown barbarism (dictatorship and the law of the jungle). Echeverría's and Sarmiento's bête noire was the dictator Juan Manuel de Rosas, whom both writers attack in their best-known works, *El Matadero* (1871) and *Facundo* (1845) respectively.

Gaucho Literature: 1880–1900

José Hernández's (1834–86) verse epic *El Gaucho Martín Fierro* (1872) is highly lauded for its free-spirited hero drawn from rural folk ballads. It is regarded as the greatest expression of the country's national identity. Another key work is Ricardo Güiraldes's (1886–1927) *Don Segundo Sombra* (1926), which casts a skeptical eye on the gaucho myth but still paints a vivid portrait of rural life of the era.

The Moderns: 1900–present day

Partially on its own merits and also drawn along in the slipstream of the boom in interest in Latin American

writing, Argentinian literature has blossomed in the 20th century. Early talents include Uruguay-born Horacio Quiroga (1878–1937), whose collections of short fables made him one of the precursors of magical realism, while Roberto Arlt (1900–1942) is

Puig's *El Beso de la Mujer Araña* on stage

famous for his surreal, violent stories of alienation and despair. Manuel Puig (1932–90) was another influential author who used pop art techniques such as montage to startling effect. His key novels include *El Beso de la Mujer Araña* (1976), which brought him global fame after it was made into a movie and a Broadway musical. Another Argentinian writer whose fame was bolstered by a silver-screen adaptation was Julio Cortázar (1914–84): his story *Las Babas del Diablo* (1959) was the source for Michelangelo Antonioni's movie *Blow-up* (1966).

Movie poster of *Blow-up*

Julio Cortázar's brilliantly structured short stories, along with his experimental novels, have made him one of the most enduringly popular of all Argentinian writers, although he spent most of his life in self-imposed exile, disgusted at the right-wing and authoritarian drift of his homeland. Another politically committed writer was Rodolfo Walsh (1927–77). Regarded as one of the finest and most well-known Latin American journalists, he was shot on the orders of the Argentinian military dictatorship in 1977.

During the second half of the 20th century, the production and publication of women's writing proliferated in Argentina. Heiress Victoria Ocampo (1890–1979) played a leading role in the intellectual life of Buenos Aires during the 1920s and 1930s, working as

a critic and publishing the magazine *Sur*, which provided a platform for local writers as well as translating European writers for Argentinian readers. Protofeminist ideas are evident in the erotically charged writings of poet Alfonsina Storni (1892–1938) and in the anti-patriarchal political works of Latin American playwright and novelist Griselda Gambaro (b.1928).

Other noted contemporary authors include Tomás Eloy Martínez (1934–2010), César Aira (b.1949), and Ricardo Piglia (b.1941). No modern writers, however, have come close to matching the reputation of Jorge Luis Borges (1899–1986), the undisputed master of 20th-century Argentinian letters and one of the most influential writers to emerge since World War II. A prolific poet, essayist, and even film critic, Borges is best known for his two collections of short stories, *Ficciones* and *El Aleph*. As elusive as they are allusive, his brilliant works have influenced many major writers of our time.

Jorge Luis Borges, a 20th-century literary genius and icon

Cinema and Theater

A vibrant dramatic arts scene, especially in Buenos Aires, has existed since the late 1700s, while the Argentinian cinematic tradition dates back to the late 19th century. During the 1920s, the capital was one of the major Latin American centers of film production, a time when theater also peaked with the *sainete criollo* (musical comedy). Although artistic growth was curbed by the military dictatorship from 1978 to 1983, today over 200 films are made in Argentina every year, and the country is also enjoying an exciting and experimental theater boom.

Theater poster on Avenida Corrientes, Buenos Aires

Cinema

The Argentinian film industry boomed between the 1920s and 1950s when tango musicals and gaucho-themed films drew huge audiences. Art-house cinema took off after World War II but was cut short by the dictatorship of 1978–83. Cinema flourished again during the mid-1990s, when a new generation of directors emerged, working with limited budgets to address social issues.

Art house and national cinema of the 1950s and 1960s had directors who responded to the country's turbulent political scene, including Armando Bo, who directed *El Trueno Entre Las Hojas* (1956), Pino Solanas, Leopoldo Torre Nilsson, and Héctor Olivera.

Films on tango and romance in the 1930s and 1940s were very popular. Gaucho and other local themes were often thrown into these movies, which usually featured a beautiful woman and a romantic rival to the lead. In *The Big Broadcast of 1936* (1935), Carlos Gardel played himself – a singer-songwriter.

Theater

The iconic status of Teatro Colón in Buenos Aires is ample evidence of the importance of the dramatic arts in Argentina. Theater peaked in the first decades of the 20th century, when plays began to address national issues and feature gauchos and tango dancers. Corrientes is the Broadway of Argentina; the more serious drama is performed at Teatro General San Martín.

During the early 20th century, Argentinian theater progressed from light musical comedy focused on national issues to more absurdist, social realistic, and grotesque plays. The "neo-grotesque" plays of Griselda Gambaro *(left)* brought together these traditions and gave a voice to women.

In 1981, a powerful cultural movement began against the military dictatorship. The organizers of Teatro Abierto (Open Theater) were a group of writers, actors, and directors, including Roberto Cossa, Osvaldo Dragún, and Carlos Gorostiza, who performed anti-establishment plays.

The brutality of the Dirty War inspired Luis Puenzo's *La Historia Oficial* (1985), which deals with the military junta kidnappings during the 1970s and 1980s. He was the first Argentinian to win an Academy Award for Best Foreign Film.

Foreign Films

Argentinians have catholic tastes when it comes to foreign films, and love Woody Allen and Disney as much as French auteurs or their local cineastes. The films of Spanish director Pedro Almodóvar have a loyal following, particularly in Buenos Aires, as many of them star local actor Cecilia Roth. Argentina has also become a popular location for directors shooting feature films, such as Alan Parker's *Evita* (1996). More recently Brazilian director Walter Salles's *The Motorcycle Diaries* (2004) was enjoyed by Argentinians for its familiar locations and for reminding the world that Che Guevara was one of their compatriots.

Madonna in Alan Parker's popular musical *Evita*

New Argentinian cinema developed in the 1990s, when a group of young directors made films on shoestring budgets, often employing non-actors to give a social realist feel to their stories. The movement was started by Adrián Caetano and Bruno Stagnaro's *Pizza, Birra, Faso* (1998).

Contemporary Argentinian cinema showcases directors who have evolved a subtle, home-grown approach that deals with local subjects. Juan José Campanella's *El Secreto de sus Ojos* won the 2010 Academy Award for Best Foreign Language Film.

Popular theater in the 1980s, in some respects, heralded the return of democracy. La Boca's popular theater troupe Grupo Teatro Catalinas Sur performs plays that offer audiences a grotesque take on modern urban reality with underlying political and social themes.

The latter-day legacy of Teatro Abierto is the thriving off-Corrientes scene, where radical actors perform in small venues. Formerly an underground street theater company, De La Guarda toured their dialogue-free show *Villa Villa* round the world in the late 1990s to huge acclaim.

Architecture

There is no single architectural style that can be called Argentinian. Porteño architects have always borrowed from European styles and the capital is characterized by eclecticism, with French mansards, Art Deco cupolas, and glass-walled skyscrapers. Across the provinces, the most interesting buildings are often small colonial churches and low-slung 19th- and 20th-century town houses which, with their patios and wrought-iron gates, pay homage to Andalucia and the Old World. Occasionally, a Modernist masterpiece or Brutalist warehouse rises in the Pampas, remnants of earlier, wealthier periods in Argentinian rural history.

The ornate Casa Rosada on Plaza de Mayo, Buenos Aires

Early Colonial

Few buildings of the 16th to 18th centuries remain, as most of the fortresses, ranches, and ordinary residences erected then were improvised adobe constructions made of fibrous material.

Iglesia de San Pedro in Salta was built in the 1770s. Its whitewashed adobe and local brick walls, plain façade, and twin bell towers are typical of Spanish colonial churches.

El Zanjón (see p82) in Buenos Aires has arches made of slim, rustic bricks, which can be seen in the remnants of many early civic buildings.

Baroque

Popular in the 18th and mid-19th centuries, the Baroque style was introduced by Jesuit scholars who combined it with Moorish and indigenous elements, giving church exteriors a rich, varied character and imposing façades.

The Iglesia de la Compañía in Córdoba (see p184) is a 17th-century Jesuit-built church with a richly decorated interior. Most noteworthy is the Baroque panel, which is the work of Catamarca-born painter Emilio Caraffa.

Details are picked out in braidlike golden yellow

The church has distinctive terracotta walls

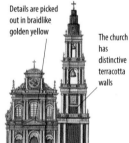

Iglesia y Convento San Francisco in Salta (see p199) was built in 1858, and has a wide and elegant Baroque façade.

Immigrant Architecture

Argentina's architectural eclecticism derives from the native penchant for copying all things European, and also from the fact that many architects are descendants of immigrants. Across the country are dotted British-style railway stations, grand estancias modeled after French rural châteaux, and Bauhaus-influenced urban dwellings.

Truncated dome on the mansard roof

Beaux-arts grandeur of Correo Central

Modernist

Modern styles, including Art Deco, Art Nouveau, and Expressionism, were popular between 1900 and 1940. This new architecture provided tangible proof that Buenos Aires was a cosmopolitan city.

Edificio Kavanagh *(see p95)*, completed in 1936, is a residential tower built along rationalist lines. It is now a national landmark protected by government decree.

— The best apartments have open-air terraces

Palacio Barolo *(see p72)*, commissioned by a local textile magnate, was completed in 1923. This bulbous, 22-story edifice is full of allegorical references to Dante's *Divine Comedy*.

Vernacular Architecture

By taking elements from various traditions and schools, Argentinian architects evolved a native style suited to the country's culture and climate.

Narrow *chorizo* houses allow for dense housing suited to the gridblock layout of the cities.

Contemporary

The predominant model for dwellings and commercial property in Argentina is the mid- to high-rise tower. There has been a surge in skyscrapers over 30 stories tall with gardens, pools, gyms, and social spaces on site.

Torre le Parc, a residential tower located in upscale Palermo, is the ultimate dwelling for television personalities, footballers, and the nouveaux riches.

— The building stands at 51 stories high

— The structure is designed along plain rationalist lines

Estancias in the far south of the country need to be low-slung to cope with the gusting westerly winds.

Museo de Arte Latinoamericano de Buenos Aires *(see pp114–15)* has a striking design that stands out in a neighborhood of high-rise towers. The interior is designed to allow natural light to pour in onto the sculptures and public spaces.

Ersatz Swiss buildings in Bariloche

British-style Puerto Madero docks

German-style chalet, Huapi

Argentina's Equestrian Sports

Although the horse is not indigenous to the country, it has become an intrinsic part of Argentina's national culture and identity. Feats of horsemanship and the traditions that go with equestrian pursuits are taken very seriously in all the provinces. This is most evident in the popularity of equestrian sports, ranging from gauchos competing in sulky races on the Pampas plains to the exciting horse races that take place in Buenos Aires's famous hippodromes. It is in polo, however, that Argentina dominates at an international level. Its polo team has produced some of the top *polistas* (polo players) in the world.

Young rider in a show-jumping competition in Córdoba

Polo

Introduced by English immigrants in the 1800s, polo is one of the most popular equestrian sports in Argentina. Its polo team has been the uninterrupted world champion since 1949 and the annual Argentina Polo Open is one of the world's most important polo competitions.

A player's wrist movement has to be quick and flexible while hitting the ball.

The mallet has a rubber-wrapped grip and a leather thumb sling.

Adolfo Cambiaso is regarded by many to be the best polo player in the world. With his ten-goal handicap (the highest rank possible), good looks, and commercial savvy, he is often referred to as the "David Beckham of polo."

Pato

Argentina's official sport, *pato* is also known as "horseball" and has been practiced since the 17th century. *Pato* is Spanish for "duck" and, originally, games used a live duck inside a basket instead of a ball. The modern version is played with a ball that has six leather handles, which the two teams try to insert into hoops placed on poles located at each end of a field.

A horseball player needs a great deal of practice to skillfully pick up a *pato*. The game requires players to be excellent riders with a great sense of balance and stability. They also need to be able to move swiftly around the field.

The annual Argentinian Pato Championship is usually held in November. Games are played at a number of locations across Buenos Aires province, and the final is held at Campo Argentino de Polo de Palermo (see p113).

Gaucho Sports

Horsemanship is an essential component of the gaucho tradition and lives on in the modern era. There are a number of gaucho sports, the majority of which involve doing dangerous stunts with untamed horses.

The sulky competition is a popular traditional pursuit in the rich Pampas of Buenos Aires province. The sulky refers to the cart that is attached to the horse.

Tradition Day in San Antonio de Areco offers a chance for gauchos to show off their equestrian skills. Various competitions, such as taming wild horses, keep the traditions of rural Argentina alive.

Racing and Show Jumping

Horse racing, known as *el turf*, is hugely popular in the country, and the best race tracks can be found in Buenos Aires. Introduced by immigrant European communities in the 19th century, show-jumping competitions throughout the country attract thousands of enthusiasts.

Argentinian rider Matías Albarracín is a popular contender at show-jumping events. Horse shows are staged at numerous clubs in Buenos Aires and other major cities, and take place weekly from March to December.

The Hipódromo Argentino in Palermo, which can accommodate more than 10,000 spectators, is Argentina's most important turf venue. The biggest draw of the year is the Gran Premio Nacional, held annually in November.

The Argentinian Thoroughbred

Argentina has always had a reputation for breeding top racehorses, a reputation that was bolstered in 2007 when Argentinian-bred Invasor won the Dubai World Cup, the world's richest horse race with prize money of over US$6 million. Argentinian thoroughbreds, a distinct breed of horse, not to be confused with the more general term "purebred," are usually bred for racing, though they may also be used for show jumping, while smaller horses are used for polo. Naturally athletic and with a good temperament and plenty of staying power, Argentinian thoroughbreds are in demand all over the world, with around 200 registered sales in 2006, for example, to destinations all across the world, from Singapore to Sydney.

Argentinian thoroughbred Invasor trains for the Breeders' Cup Classic, Kentucky

Soccer in Argentina

British immigrants brought soccer to Argentina in the late 19th century. The fanaticism for the sport has only grown since then and every schoolboy's dream is to be the next *fútbol* legend. Spare patches of grass in city parks or barren desert in the interior are often used as soccer pitches for impromptu games. However, it is at professional matches that the sport turns into a religion and watching a game featuring one of the First Division clubs is a thrilling experience.

A colorful mural of the popular Boca Juniors soccer team

The first recorded soccer match in Argentina was organized by the Buenos Aires Cricket Club in 1867 and played between two teams of British railroad workers, the White Caps and the Red Caps.

The Alumni sports club team from Buenos Aires's Belgrano district was one of the most important in the early 1900s. They won 10 of the 14 league championships they contested.

The Azteca Stadium in Mexico hosted the FIFA World Cup Final (1986) when Argentina won their second World Cup title.

First Division Clubs

Organized by the Argentinian Football Association (AFA), the First Division is the top category of Argentinian soccer teams. It currently consists of 20 teams who play two single-round tournaments each year. The list shows the longest-standing First Division teams over recent decades.

River Plate's striker Gonzalo Higuain celebrating after scoring a goal in a First Division match

CLUB ATLETICO BOCA JUNIORS (Est.1905)
Stadium: La Bombonera
Capacity: 60,000

CLUB ATLETICO RIVER PLATE (Est.1901)
Stadium: Monumental
Capacity: 66,545

CLUB VÉLEZ SARSFIELD (Est.1910)
Stadium: José Amalfitani
Capacity: 49,540

CLUB SAN LORENZO DE ALMAGRO (Est.1908)
Stadium: Nuevo Gasómetro
Capacity: 43,500

CLUB ATLETICO INDEPENDIENTE (Est.1903)
Stadium: Libertadores de América
Capacity: 52,823

RACING CLUB (Est.1930)
Stadium: Presidente Perón
Capacity: 55,000

Club Newell's Old Boys (Est.1903)
Stadium: El Coloso del Parque
Capacity: 42,000

The offerings of soccer fans decorate the front of the Suizo-Argentina private clinic in Buenos Aires, where the former Argentinian soccer star, Diego Maradona, was hospitalized in 2004. He remained in intensive care for several months as a result of a long period of drug and alcohol abuse which left him fighting for his life.

World Cup Facts

The Argentinian national squad has won two World Cups – in 1978, when they hosted the event and beat Holland, and in 1986, against West Germany. Both victories have been plagued by controversy: in the former it has been claimed that the then military dictatorship paid for Argentina to win against Peru in the semi-finals; in the latter, Argentina beat England 2–1 in the quarter finals, where the first goal was a handball by Diego Maradona. The second goal was a spectacular one-man display, also by Maradona, that shattered England's defence. The team was runner-up in the first tournament, held in 1930 in Uruguay, and in 1990 in Italy.

Fifa World Cup Final (1986)

Argentina jumped to a 2–0 lead after 55 minutes, but West Germany scored two goals to equalize in the last ten minutes. Then, with seven minutes remaining, Jorge Burruchaga scored a brilliant winning goal after receiving a pass from Maradona.

The Argentinian squad, crowned with olive wreaths, celebrates with their gold medals at the 2004 Olympic Games in Athens, Greece. They defeated Paraguay 1–0 in the final match.

Soccer Legends

Over the years, Argentina has produced a pantheon of great players that have outshone others with their skill, agility, and exquisite footwork. These include the soccer player and coach Alfredo di Stefano, the striker Gabriel Batistuta, and the legendary Diego Maradona, who shares with Pele the title of the best soccer player in the world.

Alfredo di Stefano (b.1926), nicknamed Saeta Rubia (Blond Arrow), was a player of immense stamina, versatility, and vision.

Diego Maradona (b.1960) is one of the greatest footballers of all time, despite being embroiled in controversy on and off the pitch.

Oscar Ruggeri (b.1962), nicknamed El Cabezón (Big-Headed One), was one of the most successful defenders to come out of Argentina.

Gabriel Batistuta (b.1969) is a prolific player who, at an international level, is Argentina's all-time highest goal scorer.

Lionel Messi, widely considered to be Maradona's heir apparent, has been crowned FIFA World Player of the Year every year from 2009 through 2012.

ARGENTINA THROUGH THE YEAR

A country that loves fun and celebrations, Argentina has a busy annual calendar, both for its cities and provinces. New Year's Eve is celebrated with fireworks and family reunions, after which many people begin their summer holidays on January 2. Some events are localized, and provincial towns and villages tend to uphold traditions with more enthusiasm than the cities of Buenos Aires, Córdoba, and Rosario. The colorful fiesta of Carnaval is an event of national importance in Gualeguaychú in the Entre Ríos province. The pre-Lent celebrations are still important to the villages of the Andean high plains, where they have been fused with pre-Columbian traditions. The capital loves its festivals, and art and culture extravaganzas are held all year.

Flowers in full bloom during spring in Patagonia

Spring

In central Argentina, the temperate weather conditions of spring make this an excellent time to visit Córdoba, Buenos Aires, and Mendoza. Jacaranda and *ceibo* trees blossom in public parks and plazas, and flocks of migratory birds begin to arrive in the lagoons of the Pampas and the wetlands. Pre-summer storms are possible but not likely to last more than a day. Patagonia is warm and the weather is pleasant in the northern provinces by late spring (mid-October to November), making it the best time to visit Argentina.

September

Eisteddfod *(early Sep)*, Gaiman. This ancient festival of Welsh culture features music, photography, literature, and art.

Fiesta Nacional del Inmigrante *(2nd week of Sep)*, Misiones. Dance, lively music, and exotic dishes pay homage to Argentina's welcoming of immigrants.

Festival Internacional de Buenos Aires *(late Sep–early Oct)*, Buenos Aires. Held every two years, this event is the country's biggest arts festival, featuring prestigious theater, dance, and music acts from all over the world.

October

La Virgen de Luján *(Oct 5)*, Luján. Faithful devotees walk 42 miles (68 km) from the city center to Luján's main basilica to pay homage to the Virgin of Luján, patron saint of Argentina, Uruguay, and Paraguay.

Día de la Raza *(Mon nearest Oct 12)*, across Argentina. This festival officially celebrates the discovery of the Americas by Columbus, although, across the Andean Northwest, activists commemorate the many indigenous peoples massacred by the Spanish colonizers.

Contemporary Dance Festival *(2nd week of Oct)*, Buenos Aires. A week of modern dance events at venues across the capital.

Oktoberfest *(mid-Oct)*, Villa General Belgrano. Córdoba province celebrates its German immigrant heritage with a huge, 11-day-long Munich-style beer festival: expect Bavarian costume, oompah bands, *wurst* and strudel, giant foaming tankards, and, above all, hordes of revelers: attendance often tops 50,000.

Festival Guitarras del Mundo *(mid-Oct)*, Buenos Aires. This is a lively two-week celebration of

An indigenous music band performing on Día de la Raza

the guitar, with an emphasis on world folk traditions.

Casa Foa *(late Oct)*, Buenos Aires. This hugely popular design and architecture exposition is a platform for Argentinian designers, interior decorators, and landscape artists to showcase their work.

November

Día de Todos los Santos *(Nov 1)*, across the Andean Northwest. People gather to decorate graves with tokens and flowers. In some places, traditional folk rhythms are sung.

Día de la Tradición *(weekend nearest Nov 12)*, across Argentina. Gauchos in traditional attire lead horses decorated with silver-buckled bridles in parades.

Abierto Argentino de Polo *(mid-Nov–mid-Dec)*, Buenos Aires. This posh polo event has gained popularity in Argentina over the years.

Creamfields *(late Nov)*, Buenos Aires. The renowned electronic music festival, a staple on the international scene, is the largest such event in Latin America.

Summer

With the whole country on summer holiday, Argentina celebrates the season with a variety of music and produce festivals. Christmas and the arrival of the new year bring their own festivities and family reunions. Carnaval is not as big in Argentina as in Brazil, but is taken seriously in Litoral and the Andean Northwest. Patagonia is warmest in summer but powerful winds roll across the steppes. Many prefer to head farther south to the temperate but relatively wind-free climes of Tierra del Fuego, departure point for cruise tours to Antarctica.

December

El Bolsón Jazz Festival *(early Dec)*, El Bolsón. A festival offering jazz shows in this music-loving town.

Noche Buena *(Dec 24)*, across Argentina. On the "good night," Christmas Eve, most of the

Performers dressed in striking costumes at Carnaval, Gualeguaychú

restaurants and hotels in cities and towns organize theme parties at colorfully decorated venues.

Navidad *(Dec 25)*, across Argentina. On this day, people go to church services in the morning and celebrate with a Christmas lunch. All museums are closed and many bars and restaurants only open in the late afternoon or early evening.

Fin de Año *(Dec 31)*, across Argentina. The new year holiday starts only at noon so the morning is a regular working day.

Meat barbecued during the Año Nuevo celebration

January

Año Nuevo *(Jan 1)*, across Argentina. The new year is welcomed by families and friends who gather and set off fireworks in towns and cities.

Fiesta de la Cereza *(early Jan)*, Santa Cruz. The main fruit-growing farms in this fertile corner of southern Patagonia celebrate with music, dance, and lots of healthy fruits.

February

Carnaval *(Feb)*, Buenos Aires and Gualeguaychú. In the town of Gualeguaychú in the Entre Ríos province, the locals bring color and creative flair to street parades during Carnaval. In different neighborhoods of Buenos Aires, *murga* (bands of street musicians) beat drums and artistes dance to the music in the streets and plazas.

Fiesta de la Pachamama *(Feb 6)*, Purmamarca. With folk concerts, ancient rituals, and mass feasts, indigenous and mestizo groups pay tribute to the important pre-Columbian fertility goddess Pachamama (Earth Mother).

Fiesta del Lúpulo *(late Feb)*, El Bolsón. The country's main hop festival, this is a lively beer-drinking party, extremely popular with the hippies and trekkers who descend on this laid-back town every summer.

Winner of the Wine Queen title at Fiesta de la Vendimia

Fall

Harvests are brought in across the Pampas and fertile highlands, and ripe grapes are gathered in the wine-producing provinces of Mendoza, San Juan, La Rioja, and Salta. The holiday season is over, but most Argentinians make a final trip to the beaches or the tourist spots in the north and south over Easter.

March

Fiesta de la Vendimia *(early Mar)*, Mendoza. Kicking off on the Sunday before the festival proper, the city of Mendoza hosts folk music concerts, local produce fairs, and all manner of grape-themed events. On the following Saturday evening, Parque San Martín hosts a huge gala, with a local beauty contest for the Wine Queen title.

Opera Season *(Mar–Dec)*, Buenos Aires. The reopening of the capital's magnificent opera house, Teatro Colón, is a major event for music lovers and draws many famous singers and world-class orchestras.

St. Patrick's Day *(Mar 17)*, across Argentina. Drinking and dancing, especially at Buenos Aires's Irish-themed bars such as the Shamrock and Kilkenny.

Día Nacional de la Memoria por la Verdad y la Justicia *(Mar 24)*, across Argentina. Victims of the Dirty War are remembered.

Pascua *(Mar/Apr)*, across Argentina. The celebration of Easter Sunday, and its preludes Jueves Santo and Viernes Santo, sees Masses and solemn marches in many towns and villages.

April

Día de las Malvinas *(Apr 2)*, across Argentina. Veterans all over the country honor their comrades who fell in the Malvinas War *(see p58)*.

BAFICI *(mid-Apr)*, Buenos Aires. Latin America's largest independent and international film festival takes over cinemas and other spaces for ten days.

Gala del Fin del Mundo *(late Apr)*, Ushuaia. This music festival offers a series of classical concerts featuring leading national and inter-national performers.

Fería del Libro *(mid-Apr–May)*, Buenos Aires. This three-week book extravaganza for Argentinian and international publishers and guest writers is a public as well as trade event.

Display of contemporary artwork at ArteBA, Buenos Aires

May

Día del Trabajo *(May 1)*, across Argentina. Marches organized by trade unions and protest groups on Labor Day culminate with speeches in plazas.

Fiesta del Algodón *(early May)*, Chaco. Parades and the crowning of the Cotton Queen in the country's cotton capital are the climax of ten days of lively festivities.

ArteBA *(mid-May)*, Buenos Aires. The city's biggest art fair, featuring more than 100 national and international galleries, as well as talks by leading artists.

Día de la Revolución de Mayo *(May 25)*, Buenos Aires. Also known as Día de la Patria, it celebrates the May Revolution of 1810 which ultimately led to independence. In Buenos Aires, grenadier guards march down Avenida de Mayo in the morning and people stop at Café Tortoni *(see p72)* for a coffee and snack. In the evening, a choir performs patriotic songs at the city cathedral.

Buenos Aires military parade celebrates Día de la Revolución de Mayo

Winter

Rain drenches the central provinces, and Patagonia turns bitterly cold. This is, however, the most sublime time to be in the south, as the Southern Right whales swim into Península Valdés and the breeding season begins. The ski season keeps Bariloche and Mendoza busy.

June

Día de la Bandera *(3rd Mon)*, across Argentina. This day commemorates the death anniversary of General Manuel Belgrano, creator of the country's national flag. The white and sky-blue *bandera* (flag) is hoisted and the national anthem sung across the nation.

July

Día de la Independencia *(Jul 9)*, across Argentina. Less important than Día de la Revolución de Mayo, but flags are raised to honor the troops that ousted Spanish control.

Festival Nacional del Poncho *(late Jul)*, Catamarca. This colorful festival features exhibitions displaying beautiful handwoven ponchos, colorful decorated blankets and carpets, tapestries, and other regional textiles. Folk music concerts and lively dances are also held.

August

La Rural *(July–Aug)*, Buenos Aires. A huge three-week agricultural fair, with prize stock displayed proudly by breeders from across the interior provinces. Gauchos dazzle their audiences with equestrian stunts. Local food and organic produce stalls are also an important part of this lively event.

Día de San Cayetano *(Aug 7)*, Buenos Aires. Praying and weeping believers gather at the church of St. Cayetano to ask for help from the patron saint of bread and work and to thank him for favors past. As St. Cayetano Day approaches, the streets fill up with tents around the San Cayetano church.

Festival Buenos Aires Tango *(mid-Aug)*, Buenos Aires. The most important tango festival

People praying in church on Día de San Cayetano

attracts locals and tourists alike. Tango-themed events take over the whole city, from art and photography exhibitions to free dance classes and live shows by major tango stars. The excitement peaks with the World Tango Championships, an international gathering of skilled dancers, couples who don their best and compete at all levels.

Fiesta Nacional de la Nieve *(mid-Aug)*, Bariloche. The new season's snow is welcomed with parades, ski races, and a torch-lit descent of Cerro Catedral. It includes the election of a National Snow Queen.

Día del Libertador General San Martín *(mid-Aug)*, across Argentina. Flags are hoisted and hymns are sung to commemorate the anniversary of Independence hero José San Martín's death.

Public Holidays

Año Nuevo (New Year's Day, Jan 1)

Carnaval (Penultimate Mon and Tue of Feb)

Jueves Santo (Maundy Thursday, Mar/Apr)

Viernes Santo (Good Friday, Mar/Apr)

Día Nacional de la Memoria por la Verdad y la Justicia (Day of Remembrance for Truth and Justice, Mar 24)

Día de las Malvinas (Malvinas War Veterans' Day, Mon nearest Apr 2)

Día del Trabajo (Labor Day, May 1)

Día de la Revolución de Mayo (May Revolution Day, May 25)

Día de la Bandera (Flag Day, 3rd Mon of Jun)

Día de la Independencia (Independence Day, Jul 9)

Día del Libertador General San Martín (General San Martín's Day, 3rd Mon of Aug)

Día de la Raza (Columbus Day, Mon nearest Oct 12)

Inmaculada Concepción de la Virgen María (Immaculate Conception Day, Dec 8)

Noche Buena (Christmas Eve, Dec 24)

Navidad (Christmas Day, Dec 25)

Fin de Año (Dec 31)

Couple participating in the World Tango Championship, Buenos Aires

The Climate of Argentina

Broadly, Argentina's climate can be divided into four types: arid, moderate, cold, and warm. The Andes, Antarctica, the Atlantic Ocean, and the sheer extent of the country also play a major role in determining the country's climate. In Buenos Aires, the *sudestadas* (southeasterly winds) bring torrential rains, while the *pampeano* weather system, influenced by the ocean, can bring electric storms from the western Pampas. The high plains of the Andean Northwest are warm during the day, while Patagonia is subject to powerful winds that rise in the southwest and sweep across the plains unobstructed. The subpolar oceanic climate of Tierra del Fuego makes it windy and wet most of the year.

Climate Zones

- Arid Andean high plains: warm, dry, rainy in the north.
- Arid mountains: sunny, warm, wet summers, cold winters.
- Cold and wet: cold, snowy winters, windy spring.
- Tropical Serrano: long winters, windy, heavy storms.
- Subtropical: very hot, humid summers, mild winters.
- Mild semi-arid: mild summers, severe winters in parts.
- Temperate Serrano: hot summers, seasonal rainfall.
- Arid Patagonia: cool summers, cold winters, frequent storms.

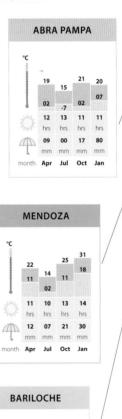

Abra Pa

ABRA PAMPA

°C				
	19	15	21	20
	02	-7	02	07
☀	12 hrs	13 hrs	11 hrs	11 hrs
☂	09 mm	00 mm	17 mm	80 mm
month	Apr	Jul	Oct	Jan

Mendoza

MENDOZA

°C				
	22	14	25	31
	11	02	11	18
☀	11 hrs	10 hrs	13 hrs	14 hrs
☂	12 mm	07 mm	21 mm	30 mm
month	Apr	Jul	Oct	Jan

Neuquén

BARILOCHE

°C				
	13	05	13	21
	02	01	02	08
☀	11 hrs	9 hrs	10 hrs	10 hrs
☂	61 mm	144 mm	41 mm	26 mm
month	Apr	Jul	Oct	Jan

Bariloche

Glaciar Perito Moreno in Parque Nacional Los Glaciares

Patagonia has sunny summers, with long days and cool nights.

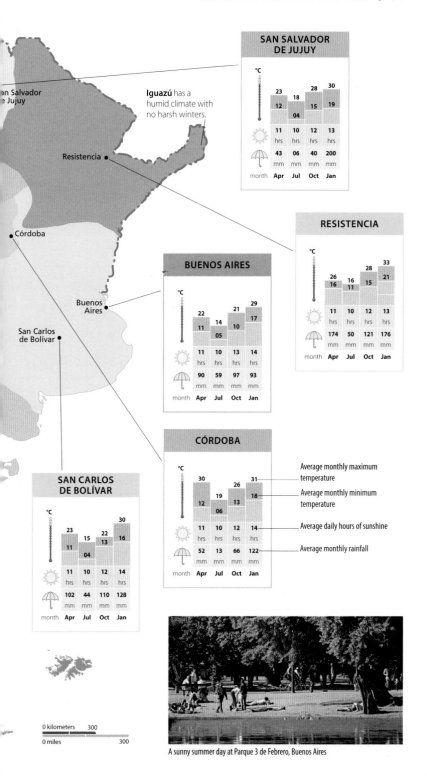

SAN SALVADOR DE JUJUY

°C				
	23	18	28	30
	12		15	19
		04		
☀	11 hrs	10 hrs	12 hrs	13 hrs
☂	43 mm	06 mm	40 mm	200 mm
month	Apr	Jul	Oct	Jan

Iguazú has a humid climate with no harsh winters.

RESISTENCIA

°C				
	26	16	28	33
	16	11	15	21
☀	11 hrs	10 hrs	12 hrs	13 hrs
☂	174 mm	50 mm	121 mm	176 mm
month	Apr	Jul	Oct	Jan

BUENOS AIRES

°C				
	22	14	21	29
	11	10	10	17
		05		
☀	11 hrs	10 hrs	13 hrs	14 hrs
☂	90 mm	59 mm	97 mm	93 mm
month	Apr	Jul	Oct	Jan

CÓRDOBA

°C				
	30	19	26	31
	12	06	13	18
☀	11 hrs	10 hrs	12 hrs	14 hrs
☂	52 mm	13 mm	66 mm	122 mm
month	Apr	Jul	Oct	Jan

Average monthly maximum temperature

Average monthly minimum temperature

Average daily hours of sunshine

Average monthly rainfall

SAN CARLOS DE BOLÍVAR

°C				
	23	15	22	30
	11		13	16
		04		
☀	11 hrs	10 hrs	12 hrs	14 hrs
☂	102 mm	44 mm	110 mm	128 mm
month	Apr	Jul	Oct	Jan

San Salvador de Jujuy

Resistencia

Córdoba

Buenos Aires

San Carlos de Bolívar

0 kilometers 300
0 miles 300

A sunny summer day at Parque 3 de Febrero, Buenos Aires

THE HISTORY OF ARGENTINA

A land of Native American civilizations for millennia, Argentina became a Spanish colonial backwater before transforming itself into one of the world's richest countries by the late 19th century. A study in paradox, it followed this by an era of populist politics, dictatorships, and fluctuating economic cycles. Never losing its vitality, today, while retaining many populist policies and in the face of a volatile economy, it is nevertheless enjoying a robust recovery.

The vast area now known as Argentina was relatively sparsely populated until the period of European colonization in the 16th century. The most densely populated areas were the Litoral northeast and Andean Northwest. In the former, the semi-nomadic Guaraní inhabited large villages, ruled over by male chiefs. They subsisted mainly on manioc, wild game, and maize. In the northwest, a number of distinct sedentary cultures had evolved, each interlinked by trade. Collectively known as the Diaguita, these peoples were conquered and absorbed by the Inca Empire around 1480. Farther south, the Huarpe, who inhabited the Cuyo region, and the Mapuche, in northern Patagonia, had developed settled communities, subsisting on hunting, fishing, and the growing of crops such as corn and quinoa. Other groups were nomadic hunter-gatherers, including the Pampa and the Tehuelche, who roamed the central plains and Patagonian steppe respectively.

Spanish Settlement

Brief explorations into the region were made in the early 1500s by the Spanish and Portuguese, but the first serious attempt by Europeans at settling Argentina came in 1536. Spanish explorer Pedro de Mendoza sailed into the Río de la Plata estuary, founding the settlement of Nuestra Señora Santa María del Buen Aire on its southwestern bank. However, under attack from natives, Mendoza abandoned the region in 1537. Further efforts at settling the country emerged from the central Andes. Spanish conquistadors moved south from the defeated Inca Empire and east from the Chilean frontier, founding settlements such as Santiago del Estero in 1553 and Salta in 1582. By the 1600s, these focused on providing foodstuffs and livestock for the Spanish Viceroy in Lima.

Meanwhile, forced labor and the introduction of European diseases devastated indigenous populations, which dropped by over 90 percent in four generations.

10,000 BC First human settlements appear in Argentina

Detail of rock painting dating from 7000 BC

AD 1520 Ferdinand Magellan makes landfall in Patagonia

AD 1480 Incan armies conquer northwest Argentina

| 15,000 BC | AD 1 | AD 500 | AD 1000 | AD 1500 |

5000 BC First farming settlements appear

AD 1516 Spanish expedition lands in Río de la Plata estuary

AD 1536 Mendoza founds settlement on banks of Río de la Plata

◀ An 18th-century artwork depicting European explorers consorting with indigenous tribes in Argentina

16th-century engraving showing the nascent settlement of Buenos Aires on the banks of Río de la Plata

The Growth of Buenos Aires

In the late 16th century, Spain, threatened by Portuguese ambitions in the region, renewed efforts to settle eastern Argentina, and in 1580 an expeditionary force re-established the port of Buenos Aires. However, in an empire that coveted gold and silver, the new port offered neither and for decades it languished as a colonial backwater. Prosperity came in the 17th century with the smuggling of silver from Upper Peru and then the appearance of Argentina's first estancias (ranches) – the few cattle left behind by Mendoza's aborted expedition had multiplied into thousands on the fertile Pampas.

Apart from consolidating their empire, Spain's main aim was also to spread Roman Catholicism. Jesuits led the effort, founding several missions from 1610 onwards. Exempt from taxation, the missions developed lucrative plantations of yerba mate, used for infusions, and tobacco.

Reform and Discontent

The War of the Spanish Succession (1702–1713) brought the Bourbon dynasty to the Spanish throne and also major changes in Crown policy. In 1768 Spain expelled the Jesuits from its colonies: their protection from taxation represented lost revenue. In 1776, it created the new Viceroyalty of the Río de la Plata, declaring Buenos Aires capital of a territory encompassing Argentina, Uruguay, Paraguay, and Upper Peru. The effect was stunning: Buenos Aires's population boomed with immigrant merchants as it transformed itself into a dynamic commercial center. Interior cities expanded as the capital became an important market for their produce, shipping tobacco and yerba mate from the northeast, wine from the Cuyo region, and cotton from the northwest.

The commercial ascendancy of the new viceroyalty led to strict Crown enforcement of its monopoly over the trading system. This eventually created tensions between *criollos*, American-born Spanish who were

1553–82 Expeditions establish towns in the northwest and Cuyo area

1595 Sale of African slaves begins in Buenos Aires

1630–37 War between the Spanish and Diaguita Indians

1550

1590

1630

1670

1580 Spanish rebuild settlement of Buenos Aires

Jesuit seal

1610 First Jesuit missions established in the northeast

Ruins of the San Ignacio Miní mission

THE HISTORY OF ARGENTINA | 53

mostly pro-free trade, and Spanish-born traditionalists, who defended Spain's monopoly. International events sharpened differences. Wars in North America and Europe saw Great Britain enforce blockades of the Atlantic, disrupting connections between metropole and colonies. With Spanish ships unable to reach the viceroyalty, illegal trade with non-Spanish merchants grew, prompting increasing calls from *criollos* for a loosening of Crown ties. At the same time, the defeat of invading British troops in 1806 and 1807 by Buenos Aires militia forces increased the capital's confidence in its ability to stand alone.

Detail, Fortuny's *Congress of Tucumán*, picturing the Declaration of Independence of Argentina from Spain in 1816

End of Colonial Rule

The overthrow of Bourbon Spain by Napoleon's France in 1808 provoked a final collapse in Crown authority. In the 1810 Revolución de Mayo, *criollos* stripped the Spanish Viceroy of office; in 1816, after an armed struggle led by General José de San Martín, the United Provinces of the River Plate, Argentina's direct forerunner, declared Independence. In their own push for separation, Upper Peru and Paraguay became independent rather than remain part of the former viceroyalty.

Despite Independence, little political harmony existed among the new country's different provinces. Civil war broke out between Unitarists, urbanites who sought to maintain Buenos Aires's authority over the River Plate region, and Federalists, ruralists who desired a decentralized national government with greater provincial autonomy. War ravaged the country for two decades and led to the rise of *caudillos*,

provincial strongmen who led militia forces into battle against the capital. In 1826, a pause in hostilities saw Unitarist Bernardino Rivadavia become the first president of an independent Argentina, but within a year fighting had recommenced. The struggle finally ended in 1835 with the surrender of all political power to Juan Manuel de Rosas.

The Rosas Dictatorship

Federalist by convenience, Rosas had become governor of Buenos Aires in 1829. Sharing the Unitarists' belief in a strong central government, he transformed his Buenos Aires regime into a de facto national government with hegemonic power over the other provinces. Dissent was silenced by censorship and repression by the *mazorca*, Rosas's political police. By the end of his rule the country was an isolated and economically backward country. His brutality had, however, forged national unity – Unitarists and Federalists united to overthrow him in 1852 at Monte Caseros, which allowed for a period of reform and the creation of a functioning, unified state.

Confederation of Argentina's shield

King Philip V, first ruler of the Bourbon dynasty

1768 Spanish Crown orders expulsion of Jesuits

1826 Rivadavia becomes first president of Argentina

1816 Congress of Tucumán declares Independence

1710	1750	1790	1830
1713 War of Spanish Succession ends	**1752** Buenos Aires organizes militia to counter native population threat	**1776** Viceroyalty of the Río de la Plata established. Buenos Aires named capital	**1806–7** Buenos Aires militia army twice defeats British invasion forces	**1816** San Martín defeats Spanish at Battle of Maipú	**1835–52** Rosas dictatorship

Battle of Tuyutí depicting the bloody Triple Alliance War in 1866, by 19th-century artist Cándido López

The Argentinian Boom

The decades that followed Rosas's over-throw saw the ratification of Argentina's federal constitution, which established a strong central government with autono-mous provinces, and the creation of the Argentinian Republic, which came under the rule of a conservative oligarchy. The War of the Triple Alliance (1865–70) against Paraguay created a national army out of the provincial militias.

Along with political stability came expansionism. The government's Conquest of the Desert military campaign against the indigenous population annihilated resis-tance in the Pampas and Patagonia by 1880. Great tracts of land were opened up

A 19th-century painting showing the grand Teatro Colón in Buenos Aires

and foreign investors, responding to European demand, built numerous sheep ranches; wool exports increased tenfold between 1850 and 1880.

Post-1880, foreign investment, trade, and immigration exploded. Railroads built by the British linked rural areas to Buenos Aires and other port cities. Grain farming and ranching turned into fabulous successes, with Argentina becoming the world's primary cereal exporter and the second-largest meat exporter. Prosperity sparked demographic growth: Argentina's popu-lation grew from about 2 million in 1869 to almost 8 million by 1914. Cities embodied the era's ambition. New metropolises sprang up and great public buildings and parks were built. The capital city became synonymous with sophistication: its news-papers gained international prestige; its theaters were vibrant and numerous; its new buildings, such as the Teatro Colón, were monuments to progress.

The boom, however, was fragile and interrupted by a severe financial crisis in 1890 that caused the collapse of the Argentinian currency. Progress also hid

1865–70 War of the Triple Alliance pits Argentina, Brazil, and Uruguay against Paraguay

1878–9 Conquest of the Desert campaign ends indigenous resistance across the Pampas and Patagonia

1880 Buenos Aires becomes Federal Capital

1860	1870	1880	1890

1862 Bartolomé Mitre elected first president of the Argentinian Republic

Bartolomé Mitre

1877 First shipment of frozen beef from Argentina to Europe

1890 Financial crisis leads to the Revolution of 1890

many problems: wealth was poorly distributed and interior provinces had become increasingly distant from Buenos Aires and the Pampas, both economically and socially. Crowding in cities was a problem, and poor health and economic exploitation were common. Such disparities provoked uprisings and demands for greater political representation. In 1916, the newly formed Unión Cívica Radical (Radical Party) won power, marking the advent of popular politics after a century of elite rule.

Juan Perón in front of a portrait of José San Martín

Popular Politics and Militarism

The rise of the Radicals coincided with World War I, a collapse in international grain prices, and recession. Strikes were called and social unrest continued into the 1920s. Inspired by totalitarian Europe, the armed forces began to view Argentina's democracy as flawed, and when the 1929 Wall Street crash unleashed a deeper depression, the military ousted the Radicals in 1930.

Argentina was returned to civilian rule in 1932, with the military backing a succession of conservative governments that became synonymous with fraud. Global recession, meanwhile, pushed unemployment in rural areas up to unprecedented levels, causing thousands of workers to migrate to the big cities. By the outbreak of World War II, Argentina had a new urban working class whose living conditions were desperate. Their plight, and their potential as a social and political force, went unrecognized until the emergence of an obscure army general, Juan Domingo Perón, who went on to become one of the most influential figures in Argentinian history.

The Rise of Perón

Juan Perón gained influence and power between 1943 and 1945 through his alliance with Argentinian labor unions. He became Vice President and Secretary of War in 1945; in the same year he was forced to resign by military opponents. Perón was arrested, but mass demonstrations organized by the trade union federation forced his release. A few days later, he married Eva Duarte. Coming from a poor rural family, she pursued a radio and film career in the capital before meeting the future president at a charity event. Together they changed the course of the country's politics for the next three decades to come.

Military vanguards in the capital city during the 1930s coup

Hipólito Yrigoyen, leader of the Radical Party

1912 The Sáenz Peña Law introduces universal male suffrage

1919 Week-long bloody repression of striking workers earns the nickname Semana Trágica (Tragic Week)

1930 Argentina's first military coup

1943 Second military coup overthrows conservative regime

'00   1910   1920   1930   1940

1916 Radical Party wins national elections

1939–44 Argentina remains neutral for much of World War II

The Peróns and Argentina

In 1946 the election of Juan Domingo Perón as president revolutionized Argentina. Via a populist movement that became known as Peronism, Perón empowered the urban poor and working-class masses by addressing their plight and offering them political participation. He and his charismatic wife Eva Perón, called Evita by supporters, became icons by lifting millions out of misery. In doing so they created a popular power base from which they transformed Argentina: building an authoritarian state able to intervene in all aspects of Argentinian life. The social elite branded the regime totalitarian and Perón a demagogue.

Eva Duarte with Juan Perón in 1945

Juan Perón's first presidential campaign took place in 1946, after he served as Labor Minister in the military dictatorship of the early 1940s. Eva Duarte, affectionately called Evita (little Eva), a famous radio actress whose humble origins gained her popularity with the Argentinian people, played a key role in his victory.

Addressing the crowd at Plaza de Mayo

Central to the Peróns' huge populist appeal was their ability to communicate with audiences. Enormous rallies – some numbering 350,000 – were held in Plaza de Mayo in Buenos Aires in which both Juan Perón and Evita would speak directly to the thronging crowds from the balcony of the presidential palace.

By becoming the champion of the poorer classes or, as she called them, the *descamisados* (shirtless ones), and working to provide them with housing, food, and education via her social-welfare foundation, Evita transformed her celebrity status to adulated, saintlike savior.

LEAL INTERPRETE DE LOS "DESCAMISADOS"

1946 Perón elected president and launches five-year economic plan

1947 Evita embarks on European Rainbow Tour; she wins Argentinian women the right to vote

Eva Perón in Madrid

1949 Peronists remove constitutional ban on presidential re-election

1946

Juan Perón taking the presidential oath

1948

1948 Eva Perón Foundation established for the poor and homeless

1950

Evita marking the fourth anniversary of Perón's government

Trade union support formed the foundation of the Peronist movement. They became state controlled and answerable to Perón, whose setting of a minimum wage, salary increases, and better working conditions guaranteed their unconditional support.

The first five-year economic plan, implemented by Perón in 1946, promoted domestic industrialization and the nationalization of existing industries under foreign control.

Evita's death from cancer in 1952 at the age of 33 was a severe blow to the Peronist cause. In an outpouring of national grief, her grand state funeral extended for over four days.

Perón's regime unraveled after 1952. The economy worsened, repression and censorship increased, and opposition parties and the Catholic Church were attacked. In 1955, Perón gave a speech threatening civil war against his enemies. The military reacted by bombing Plaza de Mayo and forcing Perón into a 16-year exile.

Plaque at Evita's grave in Recoleta Cemetery

1951 Opposition newspaper *La Prensa* brought under Peronist control; Evita bids for position of Vice President

1954 Wave of strikes against government

1955 Juan Perón forced into exile in Paraguay

1952

1954

1952 Perón wins re-election; inflation rises by 30 percent

1953 Perón launches second five-year plan; repression of the rural classes, opposition parties, and Catholic Church

Perón begins exile

Under Perón's Shadow

Post-1955, Argentina became polarized. The military exiled Perón and banned Peronism from the political process. Trade unions, however, remained loyal to the deposed president and worked towards making Argentina ungovernable in his absence. General strikes paralyzed the country. In 1971, with Argentina on the brink of anarchy, the military sanctioned the return of Perón.

Isabel Perón, Argentina's former Vice President

A Society at War

Perón's third presidential term began in 1973 amid spiraling guerrilla activity and a Peronist Party split between left- and right-wing factions. When he died a year later, a hard-right authoritarian regime led by his Vice President and third wife, Isabel Perón, succeeded him. The state-sponsored paramilitary force Triple A targeted left-wing subversives and, at the same time, the military engaged in open warfare with guerrillas. The economy went into freefall and inflation surpassed 1,000 percent. With

Argentina in crisis, the military overthrew the government in 1976 and via the infamous Proceso de Reorganización Nacional, it unleashed upon Argentina a reign of brutality unprecedented in its history. Left-wing guerrilla forces were eliminated in the infamous Guerra Sucia (Dirty War), which exploded into a campaign of terror against the civilian population. Thousands of suspected enemies of the state "disappeared": they were arrested, taken to clandestine concentration camps, tortured, and killed. Thousands more were forced into exile. Practically all dissent was silenced. In 1981, the capital saw its first mass demonstrations since the coup. The regime's market economy had unraveled under high inflation and unemployment, and general strikes again paralyzed the country. As the dictatorship's authority crumbled, it made a desperate attempt to cling to power by appealing to national honor. In 1982 it launched an invasion of the Falkland Islands (Islas Malvinas), subject of a territorial dispute between the United Kingdom and Argentina since 1833. Britain counterinvaded and within 74 days its forces had overwhelmed their Argentinian counterparts. Its political standing shattered, the military returned Argentina to civilian rule.

Democracy and Default

Following national elections the Radical Party was entrusted with the task of bringing reconciliation to a devastated

Protest rally by women whose children disappeared during the armed forces' Dirty War in the 1970s

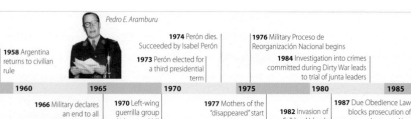

Pedro E. Aramburu

1958 Argentina returns to civilian rule

1966 Military declares an end to all constitutional rule

1970 Left-wing guerrilla group kidnap and kill former president Pedro E. Aramburu

1973 Perón elected for a third presidential term

1974 Perón dies. Succeeded by Isabel Perón

1977 Mothers of the "disappeared" start silent protest

1976 Military Proceso de Reorganización Nacional begins

1982 Invasion of Falkland Islands (Islas Malvinas) defeated

1984 Investigation into crimes committed during Dirty War leads to trial of junta leaders

1987 Due Obedience Law blocks prosecution of lower-ranking officers accused of Dirty War crimes

1960	1965	1970	1975	1980	1985

An airlift taking place during the Falkland Islands (Islas Malvinas) war in 1982

country. However, unable to control a difficult economic situation, which spiraled into hyperinflation, the Radicals were routed in the national elections of 1989. They handed over power to a reinvigorated Peronist Party, led by Carlos Menem. Menem implemented a neoliberal program that emphasized massive privatization and pegged the peso to the dollar at one-to-one. The effect was striking; inflation dropped sharply, but local industry collapsed under foreign competition, provoking recession and record unemployment.

Argentinians turned to Fernando de la Rúa, head of the Radical-backed Alliance. The situation that confronted him, however, was dire. Heavy borrowing during the Menem years had left Argentina with a crippling foreign debt, and the new government was forced to adopt severe measures in order to stave off default. Still the recession deepened, leaving the poor destitute and the middle class struggling. In December 2001, with rumors of default and devaluation at fever point, de la Rúa imposed emergency restrictions on cash withdrawals, preventing Argentinians from withdrawing their savings from banks. For many, it was the last straw. Thousands took to the streets, demanding the government's resignation. After two days of chaos had left 27 dead, de la Rúa resigned. There followed four presidents in 11 days, plus the largest debt default in history – US$150 billion – and a sharp devaluation of the peso in 2003, wiping millions from bank savings.

Post-2003, Argentina has rebounded. A surge in commodity prices prompted an export-driven economy that has grown at over 8 percent per year. Néstor Kirchner's repeals of the Due Obedience Law and of Menem's pardons of Dirty War leaders have won praise from human rights groups and led to new criminal trials. In 2010, Argentina passed a Gay Marriage Law offering same-sex couples equal rights as heterosexuals. Although confidence in a better future remains fragile, Argentina's current political stability, growing tourism industry, and thriving agricultural exports bode well for the country.

Hundreds protest during the economic crisis in 2001, Buenos Aires

1999 Fernando de la Rúa elected president ahead of Peronist candidate

2007 Cristina Fernández de Kirchner wins presidential election

2009 Justicialist Party loses its majority in both houses of Congress

2002 Argentina records biggest debt default in history

2010 Argentina becomes first Latin American country to legalize gay marriage

| 1990 | 1995 | 2000 | 2005 | 2010 | 2015 |

Carlos Menem

1994 Constitutional reform allows Menem to run for re-election and he wins second term

2003 Néstor Kirchner voted in as president

2001 Economic collapse leads to protests

2011 Cristina Fernández de Kirchner wins landslide election and becomes first female Latin American president to be re-elected

BUENOS AIRES AREA BY AREA

Buenos Aires at a Glance

The largest city and port in Argentina, Buenos Aires covers an area of 78 sq miles (203 sq km), fanning out into the Pampas from its location on the western bank of Río de la Plata. The city proper is known as Capital Federal and is home to almost three million people. The capital falls into easily navigable areas. Clustered around Plaza de Mayo are the central barrios of Retiro, San Telmo, and Recoleta. Toward the north are the parklands of Palermo; the old port of La Boca is to the south; while to the west start the grassy plains.

Locator Map

□ Main sightseeing area

AVENIDA CABILDO

AVENIDA PRES. FIGUEROA ALCORTA

AVENIDA DEL LIBERTADOR

PALERMO AND BELGRANO
(See pp108–119)

AVENIDA SANTA FE

AVENIDA CÓRDOBA

RECOLETA
(See pp98–107)

Jardín Japonés *(see pp110–11)* is located in the leafy barrio of Palermo. A quiet retreat from the bustling city, the immaculate gardens feature a large *koi* pond, a *yatsuhashi* (bridge of fortune), *taki* (waterfall), and a variety of flora indigenous to Japan.

Museo Nacional de Bellas Artes *(see p106)* is situated in the Recoleta barrio. In this museum, a large collection of Argentinian fine art sits alongside works by European artists such as Monet and Picasso.

◀ Parque 3 de Febrero, a green oasis in the Palermo district

Galerías Pacífico *(see p95)* is situated on the elegant Calle Florida and is one of the city's most fashionable shopping centers. This grand building is divided into four sectors and has a central cupola with a glass ceiling. Its most dramatic features are the murals added in 1945, painted by renowned Argentinian artists.

0 kilometers   1

0 miles   1

Cabildo de Buenos Aires *(see p69)* is a colonial-era civil edifice built in the 1500s. Its unadorned lines, colonnaded front, and shuttered façade stand in stark contrast to the more ornate buildings around Plaza de Mayo.

PLAZA
N MARTÍN
D RETIRO
e pp90–97)

PLAZA
MAYO AND
CROCENTRO
(See pp64–79)

SAN TELMO
AND
LA BOCA
(See pp80–89)

Plaza Dorrego *(see p82)*, located in the colorful San Telmo barrio, is a lively community area. Lined by cafés and restaurants, the square plays host to street performers and live tango musicians and dancers who encourage audience participation. Over the weekends, the space is taken over by the antique market Feria de San Telmo.

PLAZA DE MAYO AND MICROCENTRO

There has been a *plaza mayor* (town square) at this site since the city's second founding in 1580. During the early years of the Spanish conquest, it would have been both the main marketplace and the political and legislative center. Even now, the Presidential Palace, national bank, and economic ministry line the plaza. When the city established itself as a maritime hub after Independence in 1816, Microcentro became the chief banking and trading district. The narrow crowded streets hark back to the days of Spanish colonization.

Sights at a Glance

Historical Sites, Streets, and Plazas

1. Casa Rosada
2. Banco de la Nación
4. Cabildo de Buenos Aires
8. Manzana de las Luces
9. La City
10. Correo Central
11. Café Tortoni
13. Palacio Barolo
14. Plaza del Congreso
15. Avenida 9 de Julio y Obelisco
19. Plaza Lavalle
20. Palacio de Justicia
22. Palacio de las Aguas Corrientes
25. Puerto Madero

Places of Worship

3. Catedral Metropolitana
7. Iglesia del Santísimo Rosario y Convento de Santo Domingo
17. Templo de la Congregación Israelita

Theaters

12. Teatro Avenida
16. *Teatro Colón pp76–7*
18. Teatro Nacional Cervantes
21. Teatro San Martín

Parks

24. Reserva Ecológica Costanera Sur

Museums

5. Museo de la Ciudad
6. Museo Etnográfico
23. Museo del Bicentenario

0 meters		700
0 yards		700

See also Street Finder maps 1, 2, & 3

◄ Intricate carving on the pink-hued façade of Casa Rosada on Plaza de Mayo

For keys to symbols *see back flap*

Street-by-Street: Plaza de Mayo

The symbolic heart of Buenos Aires, Plaza de Mayo is a welcome open-air space. During Spanish rule, this was an unpaved marketplace and meeting point for sailors, colonial officials, and traders. Today, the square is the city's commercial and administrative center, and has hosted political rallies and music concerts, and even witnessed aerial bombardments. The plaza is dominated by the famous Casa Rosada; at its center is the Pirámide de Mayo, surrounded by towering palm trees. The plaza is flanked by other palatial buildings used mainly for administrative purposes. To the south begins the broad boulevard of Avenida de Mayo.

Ministerio de Economía
This ministry has played a special role in the country's economic history.

❶ ★ Casa Rosada
The Presidential Palace has a bright façade, originally painted with whitewash and oxblood. It also contains the Museo del Bicentenario.

Estatua de Garay

❷ ★ Banco de la Nación
Topped by a huge dome, the biggest in Latin America when the bank was completed in 1943, this was the first building in Argentina to have escalators. It was built by architect Alejandro Bustillo.

Key

— Suggested route

❸ ★ Catedral Metropolitana
Consecrated in 1836, this Neo-Classical church is the resting place of the country's liberator, José de San Martín. A wooden image of Santa María de la Rábida, the patron saint of the Americas, can be seen on the façade.

Pirámide de Mayo
Although it has its origins in the first city plaza traced by founder Juan de Garay in 1580, the plaza takes its current name from the pyramid in the center, which commemorates the Revolución de Mayo of 1810.

Locator Map

Palacio de Gobierno
The City Hall, the headquarters of the mayor of Buenos Aires, is a white Neo-Classical building located beside the Cabildo, from which the Spanish authorities ruled over Argentina.

Manzana de
las Luces

❹ Cabildo de Buenos Aires
Between 1748 and 1821, the city's affairs were managed here, the center of the intellectual debates that led to Argentinian Independence.

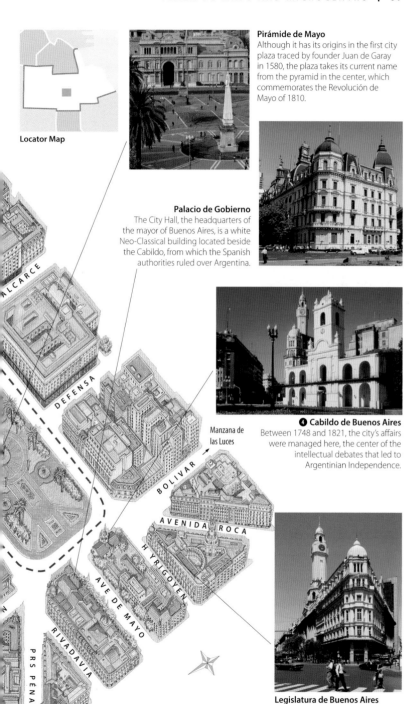

ALCARCE

DEFENSA

BOLIVAR

AVENIDA ROCA

HYRIGOYEN

AVE DE MAYO

RIVADAVIA

PRS PEÑA

0 meters   100
0 yards   100

Legislatura de Buenos Aires
This 1930s building has an octa-gonal tower with five symbolic bells named La Pinta, La Argentina, La Niña, La Porteña, and La Santa María.

The striking Neo-Classical façade of the Casa Rosada

❶ Casa Rosada

Balcarce 50. **City Map** 3 E5. **Tel** (011) 4344-3802. 🚌 24, 28, 29, 152. 🚇 Plaza de Mayo, Catedral. **Open** 10am–6pm Sat, Sun, & hols. 🎥 ♿ 🌐 **casarosada.gov.ar**

Famous as the building from which Eva Perón addressed her adoring supporters, the Casa Rosada (Pink House) has occupied a key role in Argentinian history. Also known as the Presidential Palace, it was built between 1862 and 1885 on the site of the Fuerte Viejo, the city's main fort. The building owes its distinctive pink hue to the blending of lime with oxblood, materials commonly used in construction at that time. Over the years presidents, elected and otherwise, as well as the soccer star Diego Maradona, have used these famous balconies to stir national passions and to demonstrate public support.

The Casa Rosada can be entered from the south side, on Hipólito Yrigoyen, via the **Museo de la Casa Rosada**, which features an interesting collection of photographs and memorabilia documenting the history of the building and the country. The museum has a 17,000-volume library, an archive, and a newspaper and magazine collection. Visitors can also stroll among the exposed colonial catacombs of Fuerte Viejo, which can be seen from the pedestrian mall outside.

❷ Banco de la Nación

Ave Rivadavia 325. **City Map** 3 E5. **Tel** (011) 4347-6000. 🚇 Plaza de Mayo, Catedral. 🚌 24, 28, 29, 74, 111, 140, 152. **Closed** currently closed to the public – call ahead to check for details. ♿ Museo Histórico y Numismático del Banco de la Nación, Mitre 326. **Tel** (011) 4347-6277. **Open** 10am–3pm Mon–Fri. ♿ ✉

Once the country's central bank, the Banco de la Nación is a grand example of the characteristically fortresslike edifices that house Buenos Aires's older banks. Today, it is the headquarters of the country's largest high-street bank, which is still managed by the state, and is open to clients and to the public. Wide marble-floored corridors and ornate decor hark back to the 1940s and 1950s, when the building was erected and when Argentina was enjoying a postwar export boom. The bank's famous architect, Alejandro Bustillo, gave the city many of its most prominent Neo-Classical buildings; these include the elegant Museo Nacional de Bellas Artes and the Palais de Glace (see p106). The Banco de la Nación also houses **Museo Histórico y Numismático del Banco de la Nación** on the

The grand sweep of the Banco de la Nación ceiling

Plaza de Mayo: A flash point of history

As the site of the main colonial fort, a battleground during the English invasions, and a meeting place for pro-Independence leaders,

Mothers of the Disappeared who gather in protest

Buenos Aires's most important plaza has long been a stage for turbulent events. The Peróns (see pp56–7) were perhaps the most adept users of Plaza de Mayo as a popular gathering place: in October 1945 a huge crowd led by Evita gathered to call for the release of her husband Juan Perón from prison. During the Dirty War of 1976–83 military dictators made their pronounce-

ments from the plaza, and in 1982 President Leopoldo Galtieri announced his decision to claim the Falkland Islands (Islas Malvinas). In 2001, following the collapse of the currency, the middle classes joined unions and student protesters at the plaza. Since the late 1970s, the Madres de la Plaza de Mayo march there every Thursday to protest the "disappearance" of their relatives during the Dirty War.

The awe-inspiring Catedral Metropolitana, with its high ceiling and graceful arches

first floor. It contains an excellent display on the Argentinian currency's turbulent history. The magnificent 164-ft- (50-m-) diameter dome on top of the building, only visible to passing helicopters, is the third largest in the world.

❸ Catedral Metropolitana

Ave Rivadavia, cnr San Martín. **City Map** 3 E5. **Tel** (011) 4331-2845. **S** Plaza de Mayo, Catedral. 🚌 24, 29. **Open** 7:30am–6:45pm Mon–Fri, 9am–7pm Sat & Sun. 🚻 church services. 💼 crypt: 11:45am Mon–Sat; art display: 1:45pm Mon–Fri; temple & crypt: 3pm Mon–Sat; children: 3pm Sun. 🔔 8am, 9am, 12:30pm, & 6pm Mon–Fri; 11am & 6pm Sat; 11am, noon, 1pm, & 6pm Sun. ♿ **W catedralbuenosaires.org.ar**

The eighth Roman Catholic church to be built on this site, this Greco-Roman building is the seat of the diocese of Santísima Trinidad in Peru. Built between the 16th and 19th centuries, the Catedral Metropolitana has 12 columns on the façade symbolizing the Apostles, and above these a bas-relief showing Jacob meeting his son Joseph in Egypt. The Baroque interior provides a cool escape from the busy and – in summer – hot plaza outside. The Venetian mosaic floors, silver-plated Rococo altar, and a life-size Christ carved out of native carob wood are

some of its finest features. The mausoleum to the right of the nave contains the remains of Argentinian Independence hero General José de San Martín *(see p53)*.

❹ Cabildo de Buenos Aires

Bolivar/Ave de Mayo. **City Map** 3 E5. **Tel** (011) 4334-1782. **S** Plaza de Mayo, Catedral. 🚌 24, 28, 29. **Open** 10:30am–5pm Wed–Fri, 11:30am–6pm Sat, Sun, & hols. 🏛 🎫 3:30pm Wed–Fri, 12:30pm, 2pm, & 3:30pm Sat, Sun, & hols. **W cabildonacional.gob.ar**

Built between 1725 and 1822, the Cabildo was the first building in Buenos Aires to be constructed completely from bricks. An elegant low-slung colonial-style building, it was the capital's hub of officialdom. Spain erected *cabildos* across

its empire, serving as town halls and administrative seats for the viceroys sent by the court in Madrid. It was chosen as the site for the first few meetings of the liberal intellectuals who would together form the first anti-Spanish junta in 1810.

Despite an attempt to remodel the building in a more Italianate style at the end of the 19th century, the plain, colonnaded front remains in a city where civic architecture is often devoted to Neo-Classical and Francophile pretensions.

The small on-site museum, **Museo Histórico Nacional del Cabildo y de la Revolución de Mayo**, contains the city's first printing presses, objects linked to the English invasions of 1806–7, and a silver and gold shield presented to Buenos Aires in 1807 from the Oruro government in Bolivia.

Colonial arches open into a cobbled courtyard, Cabildo de Buenos Aires

❺ Museo de la Ciudad

Defensa 219. **City Map** 3 E5.
Tel (011) 4343-2123. **S** Plaza de
Mayo, Catedral. **Open** 11am–7pm
Mon–Fri, 10am–8pm Sat, Sun, & hols.
🎫 Mon & Wed free. **W** museo
delaciudad.buenosaires.gob.ar

Located in the heart of the
financial district, the Museo
de la Ciudad is on the first floor
of an elegantly adorned
pharmaceutical building that
was part of the Farmacia de la
Estrella company, created in
1838 by Swiss immigrant
Silvestre Demarchi. His sons
moved it here in the 1890s.
Regarded as one of the most
important chemists in
South America, it is still
operating, selling a
stock of traditional
and homeopathic
medicines on the
ground floor.

The displays in the
museum are rotated
every few months
and are dedicated to
the everyday life of
porteños, the people
who live in Buenos
Aires. They include
aristocratic hats and
combs used in the
19th century and
mate gourds still used by all
tea-sipping Argentinians. The
much-prized art of *fileteado* is
also well showcased. The
building itself is of interest, as
it is one of the few remaining
town houses from the period
when wealthy Argentinians
lived in the center – before

mass removal to Recoleta
following the outbreak of yellow
fever in 1871. One of the rooms
is an excellent reconstruction of
the living quarters of a typical
patrician family of the period.

❻ Museo Etnográfico

Moreno 350. **City Map** 3 E5.
Tel (011) 4345-8196. **S** Catedral,
Bolívar, Plaza de Mayo. **Open** Feb–
Dec: 1–7pm Tue–Fri, 3–7pm Sat &
Sun. **Closed** Jan. 🎫 4pm Sat & Sun.
W museoetnografico.filo.uba.ar

Founded by the scholar Juan B.
Ambrosetti in 1904, this museum
aims to document Argentina's
vast indigenous culture.
It houses ethnographic
items ranging from
masks and cooking
implements used by
the Araucana tribes
that lived in the area
before the arrival of
Europeans, to accounts
of Fuegian natives
transplanted from their
homes at the "end of
the world" to East
London. Exhibits
include pelts from
Bolivia, feathered
headdresses from
Chaco, and bark
from Brazil. Also on display is
jewelry and sculpture of the
Mapuche – the only extant
indigenous society in southern
South America. Many Mapuche
were uprooted from their
Andean settlements in the late
19th century and relocated to
the province of Buenos Aires.

Wooden Maori exhibit from New Zealand, Museo Etnográfico

❼ Iglesia del Santisimo Rosario y Convento de Santo Domingo

Defensa 422. **City Map** 1 E1.
Tel (011) 4331-1668. **S** Bolívar.
🎫 3–7pm Mon–Fri. ✝ 12:30pm
Mon–Fri, 6:30pm Sat, 11am Sun.

Work on this church began in
the mid-18th century, and was
completed 100 years later. It
was built on land acquired by
monks of the Dominican Order
in 1601, soon after their arrival
in Buenos Aires. The area
stretched from Defensa down
to the riverfront, present-day
Paseo Colón, and was at first
given over to vegetable allot-
ments, livestock corrals, and a
primitive chapel.

The church contains some
interesting altars and artworks
from the 17th and 19th centuries. People also come to the
site to visit the mausoleum of
Manuel Belgrano, designer of
the Argentinian national flag. It
is located on the east side near
the entrance and is marked by
an eternal flame. Post-
Independence, the building
was secularized and used as a
museum and observatory. It
was set ablaze by anti-clerical
Peronists in 1955 and later
reconsecrated in 1967.

❽ Manzana de las Luces

Perú 272. **City Map** 3 E5.
Tel (011) 4343-3260. **S** Plaza de
Mayo. 🎫 3pm Mon–Fri; 3pm,
4:30pm, & 6pm Sat & Sun.
W manzanadelasluces.gov.ar
Iglesia de San Ignacio: **Tel** (011) 4331-
2458. **Open** 11am–7pm daily. 🎫
3–6pm Sat & Sun. Colegio Nacional de
Buenos Aires: **Tel** (011) 4331-0733.

While the nickname "Block of
Enlightenment" was only coined
in the 19th century, learning
and liberty have been the
guiding principles of this con-
stellation of buildings for more
than 400 years. The land was
given to the Jesuits by the
Spanish colonial authorities in
1616, who established a church
and school. After being rigorously

The Farmacia de la Estrella that houses the Museo de la Ciudad

The hallowed gates of the Colegio Nacional de Buenos Aires

Fileteado

Characterized by florid garlands and scrolls of bright colors, often including the sky-blue and white hues of the national flag, *fileteado* is a popular art form that is still seen on display in many storefront windows. The compositions sometimes include texts taken from local proverbs and sayings. Banned in the mid-1970s by the military government, who preferred straight lines and right angles – psychological and otherwise – it went underground and is now admired as a truly porteño art form.

A poster in *fileteado* style displaying ornamental scrollwork

remodeled over the centuries, the church that stands today, **Iglesia de San Ignacio**, dates from 1734 and is the oldest in the city. There is also a cinema and a theater here.

Behind the church is the Procuravuria de las Misiones, where the Society of Jesus stored grain and tools for their missions in the northwest. When the Jesuits were expelled from Latin America in 1767, Vertíz, the viceroy of the day, had a school built on the site, the Real Colegio de San Carlos, which educated many of the key players in Argentinian Independence. In 1863, it was renamed as the more secular-sounding **Colegio Nacional de Buenos Aires**, and is still considered the city's most prestigious high school.

❾ La City

City Map 3 E5. 🚇 Catedral, Florida, Perú. Museo Mitre: San Martín 336. **Open** 1–5:30pm Mon–Fri. 🏛 Museo Policial: San Martín 353. **Open** Feb–Dec: 2–6pm Mon–Fri. **Closed** Jan. 🌐 **museomitre.gov.ar**

The Microcentro – a labyrinth of narrow lanes adjacent to Plaza de Mayo, populated by bankers and merchants – is nicknamed La City due to the British influence on Argentina's banking. In the 1980s, when inflation sky-rocketed, money changers plied their trade outside the banks, offering better rates to desperate citizens. With the collapse

of the currency in 2001, the same streets were the target of protesters, who marched banging on pots and pans. There are two small museums in the area – the **Museo Mitre** was the 19th-century residence of Bartolomé Mitre, onetime president and founder of the *La Nación* newspaper, while the **Museo de la Policial** covers the long history of crime and detection in Buenos Aires.

❿ Correo Central

Sarmiento 151. **City Map** 3 E4. **Tel** (011) 4891-9191. 🚇 Leandro N. Alem. **Closed** for construction work.

The Palacio de Correos y Tele-comunicaciones is considered the most imposing of all Buenos Aires's buildings in the French beaux-arts style. The architect, Norbert Maillart, was a French-man, commissioned to build it by President Miguel Juárez in

1888, although the building was only completed 40 years later. Occupying a single block, this elegant palace, now known simply as the Correo Central, symbolized both the increasing wealth of the country and its people, and the particularly important role of Buenos Aires as a port and communications hub.

Sweeping mansard roofs, characterized by two slopes on each of the four sides, long vertical windows, and the south-facing façade, with its four pairs of columns, all echo the classic elements of the style, which became popular in the Americas after the 1893 World's Columbian Exhibition in Chicago. This was held to celebrate the 400th anniversary of Columbus's discovery of the New World. Currently closed for elaborate reconstruction, the Correo is set to reopen as an arts and music space called Centro Cultural Presidente Néstor Kirchner.

The elegant corridors of the Correo Central

⓫ Café Tortoni

Ave de Mayo 825. **City Map** 3 D5.
Tel (011) 4342-4328. **S** Piedras.
Open 8:30am–10:30pm daily.
Closed 25 Dec & 1 Jan. Academia
Nacional del Tango: Ave de Mayo
833. **Tel** (011) 4345-6967.
Open 2:30–7:30pm Mon–Fri.
W cafetortoni.com.ar

Opened in 1858, Café Tortoni
is named after a bohemian
drinking den on the famous
Boulevard des Italiens in Paris
and is probably the oldest and
grandest café in the city. At the
end of the 19th century, its
basement was a popular
meeting place for La Peña, a
group of local writers and artists
led by the painter Benito
Quinquela Martín. Soon many
of the city's greatest young
talents, including Jorge Luis
Borges, Roberto Arlt, and
Alfonsina Storni, as well as
visitors such as Federico García
Lorca and Luigi Pirandello, were
seen nursing a coffee at Tortoni.
A corner of the café, called the
Rincón de los Poetas (Poet's
Corner), harks back to those
days. Tango legend Carlos
Gardel also performed here,
and the café continues to host
tango and jazz concerts.
Statesmen and visiting digni-
taries such as King Juan Carlos
of Spain and Hillary Clinton
have also stopped by.
    The first floor is occupied by
the **Academia Nacional del
Tango**, which has a research
library for tango scholars.
There is also a schedule of
dance classes held here. The
classes cover all levels and

A quiet evening outside the brightly lit Teatro Avenida

operate on a drop-in basis.
The Academia is home to a
self-styled World Tango
Museum that opens daily.

⓬ Teatro Avenida

Ave de Mayo 1220. **City Map** 3 D5.
Tel (011) 4381-0662. **S** Lima.
Open 1–8pm daily.

If it were not for the preemin-
ence of the Teatro Colón (see
pp76–7), this beautiful theater,
reopened in 1994 after almost
being destroyed by a fire,
would get the attention it
deserves. Built along French
beaux-arts lines, with Italianate
elements, the theater has a
magnificent entrance.
    The theater opened in 1908
with a play by Lope de Vega.
This initiated a steady tradition
of performing Spanish zarzuela
(Spanish operetta) works, in
keeping with the Avenida de
Mayo's status as Buenos Aires's
"most Spanish" street – both in
terms of the architecture, which
copies that of the Old World,

and the number of Spanish
tapas bars and restaurants that
lie on or just off the avenue.
Among the Teatro Avenida's
many past glories was a run of
plays by Federico García Lorca,
who lived at Avenida de Mayo
1152 between 1933 and 1934.

⓭ Palacio Barolo

Ave de Mayo 1370. **City Map** 3 D5.
Tel (011) 4381-2425. **S** Saenz Peña.
♦ 4, 5, 6, & 7pm Mon & Thu. **♦ ♦**
W pbarolo.com.ar

Incorporating elements of
Dante's Divine Comedy, the
romantic, Neo-Gothic Palacio
Barolo was built by architect
Mario Palanti. He was
commissioned by Luigi Barolo
– a great admirer of Dante
Alighieri – who arrived from
his native Italy in 1890 and
made money cultivating and
spinning cotton in the
northern province of Chaco.
    In 1919, work began on this
grand 22-story building. It is
328 ft (100 m) high, reflecting
the 100 cantos of the Divine
Comedy, while nine literary
citations carved at the entrance
hall echo the nine infernal
hierarchies. The first 14 floors
of the Palacio are Purgatory,
while the heavens above are
crowned by a spectacular
domed lighthouse. The
number of offices on each floor
equals the stanzas that the
cantos contain. Some of the
details in the building are still
waiting to be decoded, but this
cryptic quality is perhaps what
makes the edifice a true
homage to Dante.

A lively tango show at the landmark Café Tortoni

⑭ Plaza del Congreso

Hipólito Yrigoyen. **City Map** 2 C5.
Ⓢ Congreso. Palacio del Congreso:
Tel (011) 4010-3000 (ext. 3885).
Open for guided tours only, in English
11am & 5pm Mon–Fri.
Ⓦ congreso.gov.ar

Argentina's government is modeled on the bicameral system of the US, and the domed **Palacio del Congreso** shares its architecture with the white Greco-Roman Congress structure in Washington, DC. One of the last buildings of this type to be erected in Buenos Aires before the strong wave of fashionable Francophile architecture took over, the Congreso (as most porteños call the building) is a solid-looking granite-and-marble guardian of Plaza del Congreso to its east. Inaugurated in 1906 and designed by Vittorio Meano, who was also the architect of the Teatro Colón, the building is situated to face the **Casa Rosada** at the other end of the Avenida de Mayo, a symbolic reminder that power does not only belong to presidents but also to the people of the country. Inside the Congreso is a library and several lavish salons, including the famous Salón Azúl (Blue Room), with its colossal allegorical statues and an impressive 4,400 lb (2,000 kg) bronze chandelier beneath the main cupola. The room has been used over the years

Inside the Cámara del Senado (Senate) of the Palacio del Congreso

for presidents lying in state. Out on the plaza, the exuberant centerpiece is the **Monumento a los Dos Congresos**, built to commemorate the first constitutional assembly of 1813 and the Congress of 1816. This imposing statue of the Republic waves a symbolic laurel branch and leans on a plow; below it are two female figures performing the patriotic duties of bearing the national arms and breaking the chains of enslavement.

On the smaller plaza to the east is the far calmer figure of Rodin's *Thinker*, one of the two copies in the Americas, who sits beneath the shade of the leafy jacaranda, *tipa*, and ceibo trees; close by is a statue of Mariano Moreno (1788–1811), a famous and revered Argentinian thinker, lawyer, and journalist, who was also one of the leading lights in the Revolución de Mayo of 1810 *(see p53)*.

Surrounding the Plaza del Congreso is a scattering of interesting buildings, many of which evoke a more luxurious and wealthier past for porteños. One of the grandest, though gradually falling into disrepair, is the **Confitería Molino** (Windmill Café), named for the decorative windmill adorning its façade. Crowds of politicians used to drink their morning coffee here. The impressive **Edificio de la Inmobiliaria**, at the far eastern end of the plaza, adds an Italian and Oriental dash to the eclectic architecture of the barrio.

After the Plaza de Mayo, the Plaza del Congreso, apart from being a popular tourist spot, is one of the regular meeting places for protesters, student political parties, striking unions, and, as the evidence suggests, innovative graffiti artists.

The imposing pillared façade and dome of the Palacio del Congreso

⓯ Avenida 9 de Julio and Obelisco

City Map 3 D4. **S** Carlos Pellegrini, 9 de Julio. 🚌 39, 59, 67.

This 460-ft- (140-m-) wide thoroughfare runs half a mile to the west of the Río de la Plata waterfront and has six lanes in each direction. It was blasted through the center of the city in the 1930s, creating a fitting backdrop for the towering 223-ft (68-m) **Obelisco** that stands at the intersection with Avenida Corrientes.

The magnificent Obelisco was designed by Argentinian architect Alberto Prebisch and was erected in 1936. Each of the monument's four faces illustrates an important event in Argentina's history: the first foundation of Buenos Aires in 1536; the second, more successful, foundation in 1580; the creation of the federal capital in 1880; and the first hoisting of the national flag in San Nicolás church, which once stood at the same spot. The monument is one of the main icons of the city and a venue for cultural activities. It also serves as a gathering spot for sports fans celebrating a win by their favorite team.

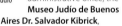

Old Torah at Museo Judío

⓰ Teatro Colón

See pp76–7.

⓱ Templo de la Congregación Israelita

Libertad 769. **City Map** 3 D4. **Tel** (011) 4372-0014. **S** Tribunales. 🚌 29, 39, 109. **Open** 3–5:30pm Tue & Thu. Services: 8am & 6:15pm Sun–Thu, 8am, 6:15pm, & 7:30pm Fri. **W** templolibertad.org.ar Museo Judío de Buenos Aires Dr. Salvador Kibrick: **Tel** same as the synagogue. **Open** 11–6pm Tue–Thu, 11am–5pm Fri. 🎫 📷 call ahead for details.

The foundation stone for this beautiful synagogue was laid in 1897 by the Congregación

Display of costumes at Museo del Instituto Nacional de Estudios de Teatro

Israelita de la Argentina (CIRA), a community organization created by a group of German, French, and British Jews in 1862. The imposing architecture of the building copies the Byzantine-influenced style of 19th-century German synagogues. It is still very much a working temple, and daily services as well as regular bar mitzvahs and marriage ceremonies are held here. The temple also houses, in its administrative office, the **Museo Judío de Buenos Aires Dr. Salvador Kibrick**, which is named after the museum's founder. The displays tell the story of the arrival and settlement of Argentina's sizable Jewish community through paintings, religious art, and artifacts such as altar cloths,

View of the magnificent altar of the Templo de la Congregación Israelita

menorahs, manuscripts, and letters, including one sent by Albert Einstein in 1925 to the Argentinian Jews.

⓲ Teatro Nacional Cervantes

Libertad 815. **City Map** 3 D4. **Tel** (011) 4815-8883. **S** Tribunales. 🚌 29, 39. **Open** Feb–Dec: 10am–9pm Wed–Sun. **Closed** Jan. 🎫 2pm Tue (Spanish only). **W** teatro cervantes.gov.ar Museo del Instituto Nacional de Estudios de Teatro: **Tel** (011) 4815-8885 ext. 179. **Open** noon–6pm Mon–Fri. 🎫 same as the theater. 📷

The only "national" theater to bear that name in the country, the Teatro Nacional Cervantes was once a grand structure. Heavy traffic and pollution has discolored the façade and given the ornate cornices and bas-reliefs an unsightly black sheen. Yet the building still manages to impress – it is built in the Spanish Habsburg Imperial style and takes a cue from the University in Alcalá de Henares in Madrid with its Plateresque elements (a 15th-to 16th-century Spanish art form characterized by much orna-mentation). The interior is decorated with materials imported from Spain, including mirrors from Seville, exquisite tapestries and drapes from Madrid, and tiles from Valencia and Tarragona. The building was given to the city by Spanish actor María Guerrero and her husband Fernando Díaz de

Mendoza, who opened the theater in 1921 with a production of Lope de Vega's *La Dama Boba*. After a few years, mismanagement and poor box-office returns led to bankruptcy, and the building and business were taken over by the government.

In the early decades, plays by great Spanish authors such as Calderón, Tirso de Molina, and Ventura de la Vega were the preferred repertoire, but nowadays the 1,700-seat theater is employed for anything from lively musicals aimed at school audiences to cutting-edge new dramas by emerging authors.

The theater also houses the **Museo del Instituto Nacional de Estudios de Teatro**, which provides a brief yet interesting account of thespian history in Argentina.

⓳ Plaza Lavalle

Bounded by Calles Tucuman & Viamonte. **City Map** 3 D4. **S** Tribunales. 🚌 29, 39, 109.

Honoring Juan Lavalle, who crossed the Andes with the hero of national liberation, José de San Martín, this green, leafy space is a welcome refuge from the surrounding traffic and scurrying young lawyers on their way between their offices and the nearby law courts.

The Palacio de Justicia, home to Argentina's legal system

In the 18th century, this area was still grassed over and was part of the suburbs of the original city; in 1822, the military used the site to build a weapons factory and as a barracks for their artillery.

In 1890, a group of 400 protesters took over the land to stage a demonstration against the presidency of Juarez Celman, and during the ensuing battle with government forces over 150 people were killed.

Around the present-day "plaza" – in fact, there are three other adjacent plazas – are a host of important buildings including the Teatro Colón and the Teatro Nacional Cervantes, as well as the oldest Jewish synagogue, the Templo Libertad, and the Palacio de Justicia, the seat of the Argentinian legal system.

⓴ Palacio de Justicia

Talcahuano 550. **City Map** 3 D4. **S** Tribunales. 🚌 29, 39, 109.

Built during the 1890s, the Greco-Roman Palacio was designed by Norbert Maillart, the architect behind Correo Central (*see p71*) and Colegio Nacional de Buenos Aires. It was inaugurated in 1942 and is home to the nation's scandal-ridden Supreme Court. The Palacio's main hall features *La Justicia*, a statue by the renowned sculptor Rogelio Yrurtia.

The court used to be open to the public but the frequency of marches and protests made the administration limit access around the perimeter of the building.

A shaded path through the leafy environs of the peaceful Plaza Lavalle

⑯ Teatro Colón

Undoubtedly the most elegant edifice on the west side of Avenida 9 de Julio, Teatro Colón is the city's main lyric theater and a world-class center for classical music, ballet, and opera. Work began on the theater in 1880 and it opened its doors in 1908 with a performance of Italian composer Giuseppe Verdi's *Aida*. A succession of architects were involved in the Colón's evolution and they employed a pan-European approach to the building's architecture. Many great artists, from Greek opera singer Maria Callas to German composer Richard Strauss, have performed here. The opulence of the refurbished building combined with fabulous performances makes this the capital's top cultural attraction.

View of the Teatro Colón entrance on Calle Cerrito

Rehearsal Rooms
The many rehearsal spaces include Sala 9 de Julio, which has the same dimensions as the main stage. There is also a mirror-walled room used by the corps de ballet.

Costumes and sets are manufactured in basement work-shops. There are also studios that make shoes and upholstery.

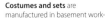

★ Main Hall
The grand hall houses three floors of boxes and accommodates about 3,000 people. The acoustics, modeled after French and Italian opera houses, are world famous.

For hotels and restaurants see pp278–83 and pp288–99

Visiting Artists
Over the years, notable artists have performed here, including the Israeli-based pianist and conductor Daniel Barenboim, who visits his native Argentina to conduct the Teatro Colón's resident orchestra.

★ Soldi's Paintings
Argentinian painter Raúl Soldi was commissioned to paint the dome in the 1960s. It features a host of ethereal dancers, musicians, and opera singers.

The Staircase
The sweeping main staircase is made from white Carrara marble, with Portuguese marble banisters crowned by a pair of handcarved lion heads.

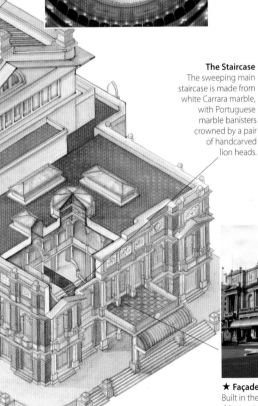

★ Façade on Libertad
Built in the French Renaissance style, this structure has Corinthian and Ionic capitals on the upper floors of the beautiful main entrance.

The Sala Martín Coronado auditorium at Teatro San Martín

❷❶ Teatro San Martín

Ave Corrientes 1530. **City Map** 2 C4. **Tel** (0800) 333-5254, (011) 4374-1385 (guided tours). **S** Uruguay. **Open** box office: 10am–10pm daily. ❂ noon Tue–Fri. **W** complejoteatral.gob.ar
Centro Cultural San Martín: **Tel** (011) 4374-1251. **Open** 8am–10pm.

Built in the 1950s, this state-sponsored arts complex used reinforced concrete in the functional, boxlike style popular at the time. It houses a 1,100-seat theater, two smaller theaters, a cinema, and a photograph gallery. World-class and top-notch local theater companies and major photographic exhibitions fill a busy schedule, while the cinema specializes in art-house retrospectives and screens daring, often obscure archival material. The huge lobby is often given over to free dance shows in the evenings and is a meeting place for students and art-lovers from all over the city.

Over the past few decades, Avenida Corrientes has lost many of its bookshops and is no longer quite the Broadway of Buenos Aires it used to be. This throws into sharper relief the importance of the Teatro San Martín as a well-funded, censor-free milieu for cutting-edge artists. Two companies – the Contemporary Ballet and the Puppeteers Group – are based permanently at the theater. At the rear of the lobby it is possible to walk through to the **Centro Cultural San Martín**, which is, rather confusingly, a

completely separate cultural center, with its own main entrance on Calle Sarmiento. This center is often used by emerging musical artists and aspiring photographers to showcase their talents to the mainstream.

❷❷ Palacio de las Aguas Corrientes

Ave Córdoba 1950. **City Map** 2 C4. **S** Callao, Facultad de Medicina. Museo del Agua y de la Historia Sanitaria: **Tel** (011) 6319-1104. **Open** 9am–1pm Mon–Fri. ❂ 11am Mon.

The Palacio de las Aguas Corrientes (Palace of Running Water), built between 1887 and 1895, is an ostentatious celebration of civic pride and eclectic vitality. Located down Avenida Córdoba, the Palacio is the road's most stunning building. Terracotta tiles were imported from Leeds in Britain,

The vivid façade of the striking Palacio de las Aguas Corrientes

green slate from Sedan in France, and marble from Azúl in the Buenos Aires province. Tall palm trees add to the tropical exuberance of the building, which is decorated with the shields of the various Argentinian provinces. The Palacio once housed the head-quarters of Aguas Argentinas, the firm that evolved out of the old state-run water board during privatization under President Menem's government in the 1980s and 1990s.

Housed within the building is the unusual **Museo del Agua y de la Historia Sanitaria**, which explains the history of water sanitation in Argentina and the world.

Brightly lit exhibits on display in Museo del Bicentenario

❷❸ Museo del Bicentenario

Entrance on Hipólito Yrigoyen & Paseo Colón. **City Map** 3 E5. **Tel** (011) 4344-3802. ❂ 8, 17, 29, 33, 39, 64, 74, 93, 111,130, 152. **Open** Apr–Nov: 10am–6pm Wed–Sun & hols; Dec–Mar: 11am–9pm Wed–Sun & hols. ❂ ❒ **W** museobicentenario.gob.ar

Located within the Casa Rosada in the former Taylor Customs building, this museum commemorates 200 years of Argentina's independence, which was celebrated on May 25, 2010. It was inaugurated a year later by President Cristina Fernández de Kirchner.

The museum, which still has its original red-brick walls, exhibits paintings, personal items, and official possessions that belonged to former Argentine presidents such as Juan Domingo Perón and his wife Eva, as well as photo exhibitions of post-dictatorship leaders including Raúl Alfonsín, Carlos Menem, and the Kirchners. One highlight is the automobile collection, which includes a vehicle that belonged to former president Hipólito Yrigoyen.

The museum also hosts a permanent display of artifacts found during excavations, including parts of the government building, as well as ceramics and animal bones.

㉔ Reserva Ecológica Costanera Sur

Ave Tristán Achaval Rodríguez 1550. **City Map** 3 F4. **Tel** (011) 4893-1588. 99, 2. **Open** Apr–Oct: 8am–4:30pm Tue–Sun; Nov–Mar: 8am–5:30pm Tue–Sun. 10am & 2pm Sat & Sun (Spanish only).

In the 1970s, there was an attempt to reclaim the boglands of the riverside Costanera Sur using the Dutch polder system, which involves the draining and recovering of a water-covered area. When the development ran into difficulties, the land was colonized by tall pampas grass and four lakes were formed, creating an ideal wetland for the wading birds that migrate to the Pampas region each spring. Southern screamers, southern lapwings, coots, wattled jacanas, and flamingos are among the 200 species that can be spotted

A family of black-necked swans, Reserva Ecológica Costanera Sur

at the ecological preserve, formally recognized as such in 1986. Well-marked footpaths wind through the leafy park, drawing joggers, trekkers, and cyclists. Apart from the daily ranger walks, guides lead groups on tours by moonlight every month.

㉕ Puerto Madero

East of Microcentro. **City Map** 3 F5. **Tel** (011) 4515-4600. 152, 111, 109. **puertomadero.com** Buque Museo Fragata Presidente Sarmiento: **Open** 10am–7pm daily. **ara.mil.ar** Coleccion de Arte Amalia Lacroze de Fortabat: **Open** noon–8pm Tue–Sun. 3pm, 5pm. **coleccionfortabat.org.ar**

Built as a result of a competition held to design a new dock at Buenos Aires, Puerto Madero was used to store grain and other perishables during the exports boom of the late 19th century. However, the narrow wharves in this red-brick dockland proved unsuited to larger, more modern

cargo ships, and between 1911 and 1925 another port – Puerto Nuevo – was built a few miles north. For more than 50 years Puerto Madero was left to decay, but in the early 1990s the area was rebuilt and a yacht club, restaurants, and a boutique hotel soon followed. In August 1998, Puerto Madero became Buenos Aires's 47th official barrio. It is unique as the only neighborhood in the city where all the streets are named after women.

Some porteños have criticized the gentrification of Puerto Madero as too elitist and lacking in cultural sites. Worth seeing, however, are Spanish architect Santiago Calatrava's Puente de la Mujer (Woman's Bridge), the **Coleccion de Arte Amalia Lacroze de Fortabat** featuring Argentinian art, and the ship *Presidente Sarmiento*, built in Birkenhead – a British port town famous for its shipbuilding skills – which is now a floating maritime museum named **Buque Museo Fragata Presidente Sarmiento**.

The elegant Puente de la Mujer bridge at the Puerto Madero docks

SAN TELMO AND LA BOCA

The first European to arrive in what is now Buenos Aires, Pedro de Mendoza, made landfall in San Telmo in 1536, and between the 16th and mid-19th centuries this was the main residential district for colonial officials and their staff. La Boca, farther south, rose to prominence in the 19th century, when Genoese settlers began to build their homes along the dockside. Now, the great majority of middle-class

Argentinians choose to live in the smarter northern barrios of Recoleta, Palermo, and Belgrano. Although they may claim that their souls lie in the southern barrios, porteños tend to avoid the run-down La Boca; visitors should exercise caution in these localities. The area is most famous for its colorful zinc shacks and its soccer team, Boca Juniors. Both San Telmo and La Boca lay claim to being the cradle of tango in the 1880s.

Sights at a Glance

Historical Sites, Streets, and Plazas

1 Plaza Dorrego
2 El Zanjón and Casa Mínima
3 Canto al Trabajo
7 Parque Lezama
8 Museo Histórico Nacional
9 El Galpón de Catalinas
10 Museo Histórico de Cera
11 Puente Transbordador Nicolás Avellaneda
12 La Vuelta de Rocha
15 La Bombonera
16 El Caminito

Places of Worship

6 Iglesia Ortodoxa Rusa

Museums

4 Museo de Arte Moderno
5 Museo del Cine Pablo Ducrós Hicken
13 Museo de Bellas Artes de La Boca Benito Quinquela Martín
14 Fundación Proa

See also Street Finder map 1

0 meters 700
0 yards 700

◀ Tango dancers on colorful El Caminito, La Boca

For keys to symbols *see back flap*

The balcony terrace of a lively café overlooking Plaza Dorrego

❶ Plaza Dorrego

Cnr Defensa & Humberto 1°. **City Map** 1 E1. 🚌 24, 29, 126, 130, 152.

A lively and bustling area, Plaza Dorrego is popular with visitors wishing to take time out from walking around the city. It is an ideal place to while away time, lounging over a beer or coffee.

Located in the heart of the San Telmo barrio, this small cobblestoned plaza was formerly the station for carriages and carts passing through the city and is the oldest city square after Plaza de Mayo. Surrounded by beautiful two-storied buildings, many of which have been converted into bars, restaurants, and souvenir shops, it is a lively hub for locals and tourists alike. On weekdays, cafés set up tables in the plaza for people to drink and play cards or chess. On the weekends, the space is taken over by a popular antiques and bric-a-brac market, the **Feria de San Pedro Telmo** (see p124), which claims to be the oldest in the city. It is ideal for browsing although it can get rather crowded.

The houses around Plaza Dorrego and on the neighboring streets were once the homes of patrician families, and many of the antiques on sale are the former fixtures and fittings of these now decaying properties. Bargains are few and far between but keep a look out for old vinyl records, antique *mates*, gramophone players, old ticket machines from the city's buses, the stylish fedora-style *funyi* hats worn by male tango dancers, and examples of *fileteado*, the colorful indigenous porteño art form (see p71).

Plaza Dorrego is also one of the few places in the city, weather permitting, to see informal open-air tango dancing in which tourists and locals participate. The area may sometimes feel like a tourist-trap, but it is popular with bohemian porteños and, out of season, has a genuinely romantic air.

Tango street performers

❷ El Zanjón and Casa Mínima

Defensa 755. **City Map** 1 E1. **Tel** (011) 4361-3002. 🚌 24, 29, 130, 152. **Open** only guided tours. 🎫 📷 El Zanjón: noon, 2pm, & 3pm Mon–Fri (in English), 1–6pm (every 20 mins) Sun; Casa Mínima: 4pm Fri (call in advance). 🌐 **elzanjon.com.ar**

El Zanjón is a restored residence where the living conditions of urban Argentinians can be traced for over three centuries. It is an eclectic mix of an 1830s façade, 18th-century fixtures and fittings, and even older inner walls. During colonial times, a rivulet known as El Zanjón de Granados flowed through this spot and was used to remove sewage. French tiles, African pipes, English china, and other objects have all been found on the site, indicating the cosmopolitan traffic that passed through here.

A two-minute walk away, on Pasaje San Lorenzo, is **Casa Mínima** (Minimal House), an example of the only truly indigenous architectural style to come out of Buenos Aires, the *casa chorizo* (sausage house). These are long, thin dwellings with a narrow frontage and a corridor that stretches about half a block deep. The Casa Mínima was built in the 1880s by freed slaves on a tiny parcel of land granted to them by a benevolent master.

The narrow frontage of the Casa Mínima

The impressive Canto al Trabajo sculpture

❸ Canto al Trabajo

Paseo Colon 800. **City Map** 1 E1.
🚌 24, 29, 126, 130, 152.

Unveiled in 1927, this spectacular bronze sculpture by the famous Argentinian sculptor, Rogelio Yrurtia, was originally located in Plaza Dorrego. It depicts 14 muscular laborers towing a colossal boulder in true Sisyphean style. The sculpture is an allegory of working-class hardship and the dignity of women. The Spanish name means "Ode to Work." Much loved by porteños, the sculpture nonetheless attracted the city's many graffiti artists, and in 1998 an iron fence was erected around the plinth in an attempt to keep them out.

❹ Museo de Arte Moderno

Ave San Juan 350. **City Map** 1 E2. **Tel** (011) 4300-8753. 🚌 29, 64, 86, 130, 152. **Open** 11am–7pm Tue–Fri, 11am–8pm Sat, Sun, & hols. **Closed** Feb. 🏛 Tue free. 📷 5pm Tue, Wed, Fri, & Sun (Spanish only).
🌐 museodeartemoderno.
buenosaires.gob.ar/mam2.htm
Museum of Contemporary Art: **Tel** (011) 5299-2010. **Open** noon–7pm Mon–Fri, 11am–7:30pm Sat & Sun. 📷 5pm Wed–Mon. 🌐 macba.com.ar

Housed in a recycled tobacco depot and opened in 1956, the Museo de Arte Moderno has no permanent collection but rotates a number of exhibitions through the year.
The displays have contained minor works by Renoir and Monet, an assortment of pieces by Matisse, Dali, Miró, and Mondrian, and important pieces by leading Argentinian artists

Xul Solar and Berni. The works of Leon Ferrari and Kenneth Kemble, contemporary Argentinian conceptual artists, are also exhibited. Next door, the **Museum of Contemporary Art (MACBA)**, which opened in 2012, houses collections focused on geometric abstraction; other exhibits feature regional artists and techniques from Brazil and also the US.

❺ Museo del Cine Pablo Ducrós Hicken

Agustín R. Caffarena 49. **City Map** 1 E2. **Tel** (011) 4300-4820. 🚌 29, 64, 86, 130, 152. **Open** 11am–6pm Mon–Wed free. 🚌 📷 🌐 museos.
buenosaires.gob.ar/cine.htm

Named for the film historian who founded the institute in 1971, this museum has exhibition rooms filled with posters, old film reels, and projectors. The collection includes over

2,500 posters that are vivid evocations of the 1930s, 40s, and 50s, the golden era of cinema in the city, and when tango movies were all the rage. There are also posters and stills from the age of silent films and from the 1970s onward, when political dissent began to figure in the discourse of some left-leaning directors. The museum is also considered an important educational and archival center and has a well-stocked library on Argentinian cinema.

Red brick and gray stone façade of Museo del Cine

Finding a *Milonga*

The word *milonga* is possibly of African origin and, while alluding to a type of lively tango beat and a country guitar-based folk genre, it also refers to a salon night in a tango club. Unlike formal shows and classes, *milongas* are aimed at those who have a basic knowledge of tango steps. The basic rules are that men invite women to dance for three musical tracks after which the partners rest; nobody talks during the dance; and only those who know how to tango get up. Although live orchestras are rare these days, there are good *milongas* all over the city. The ideal place to start in San Telmo is the Centro Cultural Torquato Tasso, which hosts *milongas* over the weekend. The Club Gricel and La Viruta are other well-known salons, where classes are combined with the main event.

Tango classes for beginners at Club Gricel

The striking sky-blue onion domes of the Iglesia Ortodoxa Rusa

❻ Iglesia Ortodoxa Rusa

Brasil 315. **City Map** 1 E2. **Tel** (011) 4361-4274. 🚌 10, 29. **Open** varies according to church itinerary. 🕐 3pm, second Sun of month; for tours in English book ahead. 🕐 5pm Sat, 10am Sun. 🌐 **iglesiarusa.org.ar**

Work on the Iglesia Ortodoxa Rusa began in 1901, with a ceremony attended by Argentina's president, Julio A. Roca, and it was completed in 1904. Topped by five onion domes, the church was built using raw materials imported from St. Petersburg in Russia and, even after its completion, Tsar Nicholas II continued to send artworks and other valuables to decorate the interior. As well as a variety of Byzantine works and icons, a painting of the last Russian tsar, by Argentinian artist Carlos Gonzalez Galeano, can also be viewed inside.

The number of domes represents Jesus and the four apostles who were the authors of the four gospels. The sky-blue color and star motifs of the domes are intended to emulate the sky. The chains that hang between them, while unnecessary in Buenos Aires's temperate climate, are employed in Russia to stabilize the cupolas in the event of strong gales.

❼ Parque Lezama

Cnr Brasil & Defensa. **City Map** 1 E2. 🚌 10, 24, 29, 39, 64, 130, 152. **Open** daily.

Many historians claim that this peaceful park is the likely site where Pedro de Mendoza made landfall in Buenos Aires in 1536 while sailing up Río de la Plata. A monument in the corner of the park at Brasil and Defensa records this event as the "first foundation of Buenos Aires," though Mendoza failed to actually establish a city. Between the 17th and 19th centuries, the land belonged to a number of families, some with British connections.

In the 1860s the famed landscape architect José Gregorio Lezama had a private park and botanical gardens laid out here, and many of the soaring *tipa* and palm trees date from this period. In 1894 his estate sold the land to the municipal authorities, and, three years later, the Lezama mansion became the Museo Histórico Nacional. Unlike Parque 3 de Febrero (*see p110*), which is a magnet for tourists, local and international, Parque Lezama is a quiet community area, well used by San Telmo residents. On the weekends especially, elderly porteños can be spotted here playing chess, while families picnic and youngsters play, cycle, and skate around.

Opposite the park, on the corner of Brasil and Almirante Brown, is the famous **Mural Escenográfico Parque Lezama**. In the popular tradition of artists such as Antonio Berni, Quinquela Martín, and Florencio Molina Campos, it celebrates iconic characters of the traditional barrio – the tango dancer, the soccer player, the barrio cop, and the nosy neighbor. Among the well-known faces here are crooner Carlos Gardel, soccer legend Diego Maradona, and button-accordion virtuoso Aníbal Troilo.

Parque Lezama is often the venue for small concerts hosted by local bands as well as a weekend crafts fair organized by artisans, which stretches north along Calle Defensa to Avenida San Juan.

A stroll through the Sunday crafts fair at Parque Lezama

Bells on display at the Museo Histórico Nacional

❽ Museo Histórico Nacional

Defensa 1600. **City Map** 1 E2.
Tel (011) 4307-1182. 🚌 10, 24, 29, 39,
64, 130, 152. **Open** Feb–Dec: noon–
5pm Tue–Fri, 3–6pm Sat, 2–6pm Sun.

Originally called Museo
Histórico de la Capital, Museo
Histórico Nacional was created
by mayor Francisco Seeber in
1889. It is housed in an elegant
Italianate mansion, formerly the
home of the wealthy Lezama
family. The displays present a
concise history of Argentina
from the 16th through to the
19th century. There are 30
rooms that trace, through relics
and paintings, the dramas of the
Jesuit missions and the battles
between the Spanish and indigenous tribes, and between
royalists and republicans.
Finally, the turbulent 19th
century is documented –
this was the period when rival
factions fought over the
newly independent nation.
Donations from living relatives
of important figures from the
Revolución de Mayo and
the Wars of Argentinian
Independence *(see p53)* make
up most of the museum's
excellent collection.
One of the more interesting
exhibits is a series of paintings
produced by Argentinian
painter and soldier Cándido
López *(see p34)* portraying
moving scenes from the war
against Paraguay in the 1870s,
in which he also fought. Oddly
enough, little else is covered
here, and there is nothing to

illustrate the reign of the Péróns,
the social and economic horrors
of the 1970s, or the more recent
financial disasters that threw the
country into disarray.

❾ El Galpón de Catalinas

Ave Benito Perez Galdós 93. **City Map**
1 F3. **Tel** (011) 4300-5707. 🚌 10, 24,
29, 64. 🆆 **catalinasur.com.ar**

Formed in 1982 by artists
from the neighborhood of
La Boca, El Galpón de Catalinas
is open to everyone. This
actors' cooperative has a well-
known theater troupe which
uses a comic, carnivalesque
approach to present an
irreverent, alternative view
of Argentinian history.
The elements of *la murga*
(a local street dance with roots
in Buenos Aires's African
community) are coupled with
iconic Argentinian figures,
including the Péróns, Diego

Maradona and other soccer
stars, church leaders, and
even Buenos Aires waiters.
These elements are thrown
into the dramaturgical melting
pot to create works that are
witty and wild but which also
function as serious historical
commentaries.
Some shows are performed
outdoors, using the amphitheater at Parque Lezama, but
the company's headquarters
remains at this converted
warehouse, where most of
their plays are performed.

❿ Museo Histórico de Cera

Calle del Valle Iberlucea 1261, La Boca.
City Map 1 F4. **Tel** (011) 4301-1497.
🚌 20, 25, 29, 33, 46, 53, 64, 86, 152,
168. **Open** 11:30am–7pm Mon–Fri (to
6pm winter), 11am–8pm Sat, Sun, &
hols (to 6pm winter). 🅿
🆆 **museodecera.com.ar**

The only museum of its kind in
the country, the Museo
Histórico de Cera (Historical
Wax Museum) is located in an
early 20th-century Italian Renaissance style house close to
El Caminito *(see p89)*. Opened in
1980, the museum has since
been recognized as a place of
cultural interest by the city.
The museum delves into La
Boca's history through lifelike
waxwork figures, including a
model of Spanish explorer
Pedro de Mendoza. Also on
display are news clippings,
tango memorabilia, and photographs from the last century.

Raucous live performance at El Galpón de Catalinas

Houses painted in vibrant colors along El Caminito, La Boca ▶

View of boats docked at La Vuelta de Rocha

⓫ Puente Transbordador Nicolás Avellaneda

Ave Pedro de Mendoza, cnr Almirante Brown. **City Map** 1 F4. 🚌 29, 33.

The Puente Transbordador Nicolás Avellaneda is named for the president who governed Argentina between 1874 and 1880. Porteños famously refer to it as "the bridge in La Boca's" and it appears in numerous tango-themed films as an evocative icon of the city. Opened in 1914 by the Ferrocarriles del Sur railroad company, it stands as a reminder of the country's prosperous grain-rich era.

This "transporter bridge" looks as sturdy as when it first opened, but it has in fact not been used since 1940. Gondolas were once suspended from the bridge and towed across the Riachuelo, taking people and goods over the river to the southern suburbs. This function is now fulfilled by the adjacent iron bridge, which, confusingly, bears the same name.

⓬ La Vuelta de Rocha

Calle del Valle Iberlucea y Ave Don Pedro de Mendoza. **City Map** 1 F4. 🚌 29, 33, 152, 159.

It is popularly said that truly to understand tango you need to loiter a while at this street on the elbow of the Riachuelo river. La Vuelta de Rocha (The Corner of Rocha) is a grubby yet picturesque sub-barrio of La Boca that claims to be the cradle of the dance that seduced *fin de siècle* Paris. It also lays claim to an interesting history. Given to the merchant Antonio Rocha in 1635, La Vuelta became a makeshift port. It was here that Admiral Guillermo Brown assembled a small but determined navy to fight in the Independence Wars. Later it was the disembarkation point for thousands of Genoese immigrants and the berth of the *Vapor de la Carrera*, a steamship that once sailed daily to Montevideo and now houses a quaint restaurant and a colorful artisan fair. La Vuelta's steamships and sailors are long gone but the spirit of adventure still lingers.

Display of wares at the crafts market at La Vuelta de Rocha

⓭ Museo de Bellas Artes de La Boca Benito Quinquela Martín

Ave Pedro de Mendoza 1835. **City Map** 1 F4. **Tel** (011) 4301-1080. 🚌 29, 33, 152. **Open** 10am–4pm Mon–Fri. 📷 by prior arrangement. ♿ ✉ 🌐 **museoquinquela.gov.ar**

The building that houses the Museo de Bellas Artes dates back to 1933, when famous Argentinian artist Benito Quinquela Martín (1890–1977) donated a plot of land to the nation. He stipulated that a primary school, a gallery, and a workshop be built on the site.

The museum assumed its current form in 1968 when Martín donated 50 of his watercolors and 27 of his oil paintings to be hung there. The works of other prominent Argentinian artists are also displayed, as well as various objects related to the port's history.

The artist Benito Quinquela Martín

Several of the terraces of the building hold works by well-known Argentinian sculptors, including Rogelio Irurtia and Correa Morales. While many Argentinian artists have been associated with La Boca, which is still a hugely popular bohemian area, the name and reputation of Benito Quinquela Martín towers above them all. His watercolors depict everyday life as it once was on and by the river, and the close relationship between the artist, his work, and his environment is vividly evident in the La Boca that he portrayed.

⓮ Fundación Proa

Ave Pedro de Mendoza 1929. **City Map** 1 F4. **Tel** (011) 4104-1000. 🚌 29, 33, 152, 159, 168. **Open** 11am–7pm Tue–Sun. 📷 🎟 by prior arrangement. ♿ ✉ 🖥 📷 🌐 **proa.org**

Opened in 1996, the Fundación Proa is housed in an elegant Italianate building that dates back to the end of the 19th century. Within the traditional exterior there are three modern floors and a roof terrace, allowing for an extensive and varied year-round program of exhibitions that include painting, sculpture, and photography. Various video installations, concerts, fashion shows, and conferences are also included in the eclectic schedule of events.

Exhibit at Museo de la Pasion Boquense

Several temporary exhibitions are held each year. The primary focus is on 20th-century Latin American art, though not exclusively or dogmatically so. In past years, for example, the museum has exhibited many exciting works ranging from Mexican archaeological finds to contemporary Italian abstract paintings.

Refurbished in 2007, the Fundación Proa now has more spacious exhibition areas and improved facilities. Already considered one of the best art museums in Buenos Aires, this stylish and brilliantly curated gallery is a treasure trove for the culturally minded tourist.

⓯ La Bombonera

Brandsen 805. **City Map** 1 E3. **Tel** (011) 5777-1212. 🚌 29, 33, 152, 159, 168. **Open** 11am–5pm daily. **Closed** restricted on match days. ♿ 📷 Museo de la Pasion Boquense: **Tel** (011) 4362-1100. **Open** 10am–8pm daily. 📷 call to verify. 🌐 **museoboquense.com**

Oddly named La Bombonera (The Chocolate Box), in reference to its particularly compact structure, this soccer stadium was built in 1940 and remodeled in the 1990s by the club's president and city mayor, Mauricio Macri. It has seen many exciting matches and been packed with similarly passionate audiences. When empty, however, it has an eerie stillness and solemnity, like a battlefield devoid of its two armies. Visiting the on-site

museum, the **Museo de la Pasion Boquense**, is infinitely less exciting than going to a match. It does, however, have flashy audio and visual gizmos and statistic-heavy display boards, celebrating Boca Juniors' many trophies and showing a reverence for their former players that borders on idolatry. Modern additions to the museum are *El Diez*, a statue of Diego Maradona, and a 10-ft- (3-m-) high figure of Martín Palermo, the club's highest goal scorer.

⓰ El Caminito

Calle del Valle Iberlucea 1300. **City Map** 1 F4. 🚌 29, 33, 152, 159.

Recognized as Argentina's only open-air museum, El Caminito (Little Lane) is a short pedestrianized street jutting out west from La Vuelta de Rocha. Its name is taken from a tango song reminiscent of a melancholic Shakespearean reflection on the ravages of time, written in 1926 by locals Peñaloza and Filiberto. Although the street is overcrowded with vendors and pamphleteering restaurant staff, its charms have not been entirely obliterated

Empty stands that fill to capacity for matches at La Bombonera

by commercialization. What draws the multitude of photographers and makes El Caminito a staple of glossy coffee-table books are the houses which flank the street and whose corrugated zinc walls and roofs are painted in vivid colors. Blues and yellows, the colors of the Boca Juniors soccer team, predominate. This polychromatic practice was devised by 19th- and early 20th-century Genoese immigrants, who scrounged pots of paint from wherever they could to brighten up their otherwise dismal, and usually overcrowded, slum dwellings. Now the street brims with displays of artworks, handi-crafts, and sculptures.

One of the colorful buildings flanking El Caminito

PLAZA SAN MARTÍN AND RETIRO

It is hard to imagine that this commuter-filled area was once a "retreat" for 17th-century monks. Later, slave markets and military barracks were established here, and huge armies were readied for the Independence Wars in the early 19th century. The proximity of railway stations and passenger and cargo ports made Retiro a natural hub of commerce. Fortunately, Plaza San Martín provides a shaded refuge in the heart of the hustle and bustle. The plaza is lined with the twin splendors of *ombú* trees and the marble homage to San Martín by renowned French sculptor Louis Joseph Daumas.

Sights at a Glance

Historical Sites, Buildings, and Plazas

1. Monumento a los Caídos en Malvinas
2. Palacio San Martín
3. Círculo Militar
4. Palacio Haedo
5. Galerías Pacífico
6. Edificio Kavanagh
7. Torre Monumental
8. Estación Retiro
10. Plaza Embajada de Israel
11. Museo de la Shoá

Museums and Galleries

9. Museo Municipal de Arte Hispanoamericano Isaac Fernández Blanco

| 0 meters | 500 |
| 0 yards | 500 |

See also Street Finder maps 2 & 3

◀ Striking ceiling frescoes at the Galerías Pacífico shopping mall

For keys to symbols *see back flap*

Street-by-Street: Plaza San Martín

Located in the distinguished Retiro barrio, Plaza San Martín is known for its beautiful buildings, which owe a clear debt to French and Italian architecture. Lining the plaza are the famous Círculo Militar, Palacio Haedo, and Palacio San Martín, remnants of the city's prosperous *belle époque* era in the late 19th and early 20th centuries. The area is a commercial hub and offers some of the capital's best shopping. With its grassy lawns and tree-lined avenues, the plaza is a popular outdoor leisure spot with porteños.

❺ ★ Galerías Pacífico
Built in the 1890s, this grand shopping mall is famous for its chic shops and frescoes by leading Argentinian artists.

Centro Naval
This beaux-arts beauty, built in 1914, was meant to reflect the nobility of the naval profession. The wonderfully ornate and striking doors are noteworthy.

Calle Florida
This famous street is celebrated by poets, tango singers, and shoppers alike. It is also home to the Centro Cultural Borges, which houses a theater and cinema.

0 meters 100
0 yards 100

❻ ★ Edificio Kavanagh
Known as a modernist masterpiece, this residential tower block was built in the 1930s. Standing at 395 ft (120 m), it was for a time the tallest building in South America.

❹ Palacio Haedo
Once the residence of the elite Haedo family, this Neo-Gothic palace is now used as the headquarters of the National Parks administration.

Locator Map

❸ Círculo Militar
Built between 1902 and 1914 as the mansion of the aristocratic Paz family, this marble edifice, modeled on palaces in France's Loire Valley, is now owned by the society of retired military officers who bought this grand building in 1938.

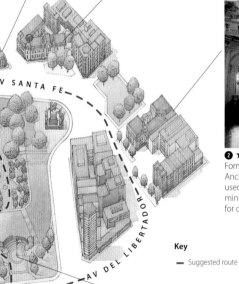

❷ ★ Palacio San Martín
Formerly the palatial home of the wealthy Anchorena family, this opulent structure was used as the headquarters for the foreign ministry between 1936 and 1989. It is still used for ceremonial purposes.

Key

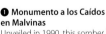
— Suggested route

❶ Monumento a los Caídos en Malvinas
Unveiled in 1990, this somber black wall honors the 649 soldiers who died in the 1982 Falklands conflict.

Estación Retiro

❼ Torre Monumental
This handsome red-brick Palladian clock tower was presented to Buenos Aires by the city's English expatriate community in 1916.

Monumento a los Caídos en Malvinas for soldiers lost in the Falklands War

❶ Monumento a los Caídos en Malvinas

Plaza San Martín. **City Map** 3 E3. **S** Retiro. 🚌 130, 152, 93.

Located at the foot of the grassy slope that leads up to the busy Plaza San Martín, Monumento a los Caídos en Malvinas is a cenotaph made up of 25 somber black marble plaques. Inscribed on them are the names of the 649 Argentinian soldiers, seamen, and airmen who lost their lives in the 1982 conflict (*see p58*). A symbolic eternal flame burns over a map of the South Atlantic islands. Every morning the Argentinian flag is raised, and flies high through the day next to the monument. Soldiers in uniform, from the three branches of the military, perform the changing of the guard every two hours until 6pm.

❷ Palacio San Martín

Arenales 761. **City Map** 3 E3. **Tel** (011) 4819-8092. **S** Retiro, San Martín. 🚌 61, 93, 99, 130, 152. 🕐 2:30pm Wed & Thu.

Formerly known as the Anchorena Palace, Palacio San Martín was built by architect Alejandro Christophersen at the request of Mercedes Castellanos de Anchorena and her sons, once one of the richest land-owning families in the city. Built between 1905 and 1909 in beaux-arts style, the palace is considered one of Argentina's finest historical monuments. It is located opposite Plaza San Martín and made up of three linked houses set around a garden. Architectural features include an imposing gated entrance, fine ironwork, and the ornamental Salón Dorado, modeled on the Hall of Mirrors of the Palace of Versailles. The palace was acquired by the Ministry of Foreign Affairs in 1936. They used it for their headquarters until the offices moved to a building across the road on Calle Esmeralda. The Palacio San Martín is presently used mainly for ceremonies and social events, but it opens for guided tours. The building also houses a good collection of pre-Hispanic American art and, in the garden, a piece of the broken Berlin Wall, gifted by German president Roman Herzog in 1999.

Exquisite stained glass at Palacio San Martín

❸ Círculo Militar

Ave Santa Fe 750. **City Map** 3 D3. **Tel** (011) 4311-1071. **S** Retiro, San Martín. 🚌 61, 93, 99, 130, 152. **Open** for guided tours only. 🕐 3:30pm Thu (English). ♿ 💻 🅆 **circulomilitar. org** Museo de Armas de la Nación: **Open** 1–7pm Mon–Fri.

Formally named Palacio Paz and Palacio Retiro, the Círculo Militar is situated on the south-western side of Plaza San Martín. Covering a plot of over 2.3 sq miles (6 sq km), the structure was built by French architect Louis-Marie Henri Sortais and commissioned by José Camilo Paz, founder of *La Prensa* newspaper.

The elaborate building, which boasts several splendid ballrooms, took 12 years to complete and was not inaugurated until 1914, two years after Paz died. The Hall of Honor, covered in gilded bronze and marble, is now used for conferences. The main façade, on Avenida Santa Fe, was inspired by the Château de Chantilly in France. Since 1938, one wing of the palace has been occupied by an officers' club – the Círculo Militar – and another houses the **Museo de Armas de la Nación**, which has an excellent collection of over 2,000 exhibits relating to the military, including weapons and uniforms, some of which date back to the 12th century.

The extravagant entrance of the Círculo Militar

The interior of Galerías Pacífico topped by beautiful frescoes on its dome

❹ Palacio Haedo

Ave Santa Fe 690. **City Map** 3 E4.
Tel (011) 4311-0303. 🅂 Retiro, San
Martín. 🚌 61, 93, 99, 130, 152.
Open 9:30am–5:30pm Mon–Fri.

Built in 1880, this Neo-Gothic
building was once the grand
residence of the Haedos. They
were one of the handful of
porteño families who amassed
great wealth in the late 19th
century, owing to the boom in
meat exports. The building has
since passed through various
hands, but the current occu-
pant, the Asociación de Parques
Nacionales, has been in
residence since 1942. The
ground floor is open to visitors,
where leaflets on Argentina's
national parks are handed out.
The building also houses the
Biblioteca Francisco P. Moreno.

❺ Galerías Pacífico

Calle Florida 753. **City Map** 3 E4.
Tel (011) 5555-5110. 🅂 Florida.
🚌 6, 93, 130, 152. **Open** 10am–
9pm Mon–Sat, noon–9pm Sun.
🎬 11:30am & 4:30pm Mon–Fri. ♿
🌐 galeriaspacifico.com.ar
Centro Cultural Borges: **Open** 10am–
9pm Mon–Sat, noon–9pm Sun. ✏
♿ 🌐 ccborges.org.ar

Located on Florida, one of the
city's busiest pedestrianized
shopping streets, Galerías
Pacífico (*see p124*) is a handsome shopping mall. Built in

1889 by architects Francisco
Seeber and Emilio Bunge as a
one-stop emporium for the
city's elite, it was reputedly
inspired by the famous Paris
department store Le Bon
Marché. The building was later
taken over by state railroad
offices and became known as
Edificio Pacífico, after the
railroad line that ran through
Argentina to Chile and the
Pacific Coast. In 1945, the
structure was substantially
remodeled and a series of
striking frescoes by
Argentinian muralists Berni,
Castagnino, Colmeiro, and
Urruchúa were added to the
central cupola.

It was not until the early
1990s that the structure
was given an elegant
makeover for its current
function as an upmarket
shopping mall and
home of the **Centro
Cultural Borges** arts
center. Named after
the country's most
famous literary
icon, this active
institute holds
international
painting and
photographic
exhibitions,
along with art
auctions and
experimental
dance and
music shows.

❻ Edificio Kavanagh

Calle Florida 1065. **City Map** 3 E3. 🅂
San Martín, Retiro. 🚌 93 & 152.

This national landmark,
394 ft (120 m) tall, was South
America's tallest building
when it was completed in
1935, as well as the highest
reinforced concrete building
in the world. Edificio Kavanagh
was financed by the Irish
heiress Corina Kavanagh,
who was from a wealthy
ranching family, and who
reputedly used up her entire
inheritance in constructing the
edifice. The imposing tower
features symmetrical setbacks
and gradual surface
reductions, and the
style was hailed as
one of the world's
best examples
of the marriage
between Art Deco,
modernism, and
rationalism. With
integrated air
conditioning
and advanced
plumbing, the
105 apartments
in this tower
represented
the height of
technology
and func-
tionality in
their day.

A view of the monolithic Edificio Kavanagh
from Plaza San Martín

❼ Torre Monumental

Ave del Libertador 49. **City Map** 3 E3. **Tel** (011) 4311-0186. 🚇 Retiro. 🚌 130, 93, 109, 140, 28, 106, 129, 152. **Open** noon–6pm Mon–Fri, 10am–6:30pm Sat, Sun, & hols.

Presented to the nation as part of the centennial celebrations of the Revolución de Mayo in 1810 (see p53) by the Anglo-Argentinian community, Torre de los Ingleses (Tower of the English) was not inaugurated until 1916. Although the official name was changed to Torre Monumental in the wake of the 1982 conflict (see p58), the local residents still know the tower by its original name.

The clock tower was British-designed and nearly all the building material was brought over from England. Built in Palladian style, the tower has ornate reliefs of the British and Argentinian coats of arms above its main entrance. Ascending the tower, the clock's pendulum stands at 128 ft (39 m) and has five bronze bells. Similar to the clock in Westminster Abbey in London, the tower clock also chimes on the quarter-hour. On the tip of the clock tower is the weathercock, which is in the form of an Elizabethan sailing ship. The balcony offers splendid views of the surrounding area, including the park in which the clock tower stands. The building is now used as a tourist office providing information on the museums in Buenos Aires. The gazebo, however, is closed to the public for safety reasons.

Grand main hall of Retiro Mitre on Avenida Ramos Mejía

❽ Estación Retiro

Ave Ramos Mejía 1550. **City Map** 3 E3. **Tel** (011) 4310-0700. 🚇 Retiro. 🚌 130, 106, 108, 129, 152, 93.

Standing beside each other on Avenida Ramos Mejía, three busy railway terminals, Retiro Mitre, Retiro Belgrano, and Retiro San Martín make up the Estación Retiro complex. Of the three, the British-designed Retiro Mitre is the biggest and most architecturally significant. At the time of its construction, it was one of the largest stations in the world. It opened in 1915 and is reminiscent of grand old European stations with a French-style cupola and an English framework.

A plaque on the steel structure reads "Francis Morton & Co. Ltd., Liverpool." The central hall is an impressive space and contains a distinctive light-green circular ticket area. Retiro station used to be the main terminal for services to Córdoba and the Andean Northwest between the 1900s and the late 1940s, when Perón nationalized the British-run rail system at great cost to the state.

Now, a large map near the entrance of the station shows Argentina's once-extensive but now much-depleted rail network. The station serves as a terminal for short-distance trains from Buenos Aires province, including the popular line to the delta town of Tigre (see pp120–21). Next to the Retiro station is the city's large and bustling main bus terminal.

❾ Museo Municipal de Arte Hispanoamericano Isaac Fernández Blanco

Calle Suipacha 1422. **City Map** 3 D3. **Tel** (011) 4327-0272. 🚇 Retiro, General San Martín. 🚌 59, 61, 93. **Open** 2–7pm Tue–Fri, noon–7pm Sat & Sun. 📷 ♿ 4pm Sat & Sun (in Spanish), call for English tour.

Located in a gorgeous 1922 Baroque mansion known as Palacio Noel after its architect Martín Noel, this museum houses a significant collection of Spanish American art, silverware, furniture, and religious artifacts dating from the colonial period to the era of Independence. The museum first opened to the public in 1910 in the home of Isaac Fernández Blanco, a wealthy aristocrat. Opened with Blanco's personal collection of art and artifacts, it was the first such private museum in Argentina. When Fernández Blanco and his family moved out in 1921, he gave over his mansion completely to the museum, and donated it to the city. Until his death in 1928, he continued to buy and donate objects to the collection. In 1947, the museum's collection was moved to its current location in

Jesuit statue exhibit

The distinctive brickwork of the Torre Monumental

Museo Municipal de Arte Hispanoamericano Isaac Fernández Blanco

the Palacio Noel, merging with the Museo Colonial that was already based in the Palacio.

The museum also acquired items from a third municipal museum to add to its exhibits. The original collection has been expanded over the years with a variety of purchases and donations, with the most significant by Celina González Garaño, who donated around 750 items in 1963. The most outstanding items in the museum include more than 100 beautiful antique dolls.

The vast collection of colonial-era silverware is thought to be the most significant of its kind in the world. There is also Luso-Brazilian furniture, porcelain, pretty costumes, decorative arts, and elegant tapestries. The mansion itself is a joy to explore, especially the tranquil Andalusian-style patio which is decorated with ivy and shaded by centenarian trees.

❿ Plaza Embajada de Israel

Calle Arroyo, corner Suipacha. **City Map** 3 D3. **S** Retiro. 🚌 59.

Not much remains on the site of Plaza Embajada de Israel after a truck, driven by a suicide bomber, smashed into the Israeli Embassy. The blast killed 29 people and wounded

hundreds more on March 17, 1992 (see p29). A nearby church and school were also destroyed in the tragic incident. A memorial plaza has been set up near the site – it comprises seven benches and 22 trees planted in rows of two, each standing for the memory of the victims of the blast. Informative plaques explain the details of the horrific event and list the names of the victims in both Hebrew and Spanish. A scarred and ruined embassy wall has been left as it was after the explosion and it stands in stark contrast to the ornate museums around it. At night, the embassy wall is beautifully lit up.

Eichmann exhibit, Museo de la Shoá

⓫ Museo de la Shoá

Montevideo 919. **City Map** 2 C4. **Tel** (011) 4811-3588. 🚌 59. **Open** 11am–7pm Mon–Thu, 11am–4pm Fri. **Closed** Sat & Sun. 🎫 🚫 Spanish only; book ahead. 🌐 **museodelholocausto.org.ar**

Set up by the local Fundación Memoria del Holocausto in 1999, the Museo de la Shoá is dedicated to preserving the memory of people who died in the Holocaust. It traces the background of the Holocaust from prewar Jewish life in Europe and the rise of Nazi power, to the Resistance, the Final Solution, and the survivors' search for a home in the aftermath. Along with the accounts of these tragic events unfolding in Europe, the exhibition also explores the difficult lives of Jewish families in Argentina, and the country's social and political responses to them. The exhibition includes a section on the Nazi war criminals who went into hiding in Argentina. The explanatory texts are in Spanish but the exhibition, including strong visual elements, allows the visitor to follow the stories and incidents through an abundant collection of photographs and an array of historical texts, maps, and other related objects. The museum also has a clear and strong educational agenda on the topics of racism, anti-Semitism, and xenophobia.

Photographs of Jewish victims of the Holocaust, Museo de la Shoá

RECOLETA

Only a street away from the traffic hubs and port depots of Retiro, Recoleta is altogether another world. This area was adopted by upper-class porteños after yellow fever broke out in San Telmo in 1871. Since then it has blossomed into a model of bourgeois refinement with old masters at the Museo Nacional de Bellas Artes and book signings at Centro Cultural Recoleta. Visitors can roam the labyrinth of Cementerio de la Recoleta or watch canines being pampered by hired walkers in the parks. In recent years, a hippy market has established itself in the area and attracts visitors from less wealthy districts, but, for all its newfound democratic appeal, Recoleta shimmers with old-style glamor and appeals as much for its inaccessible wealth as its accessible pleasures.

Sights at a Glance

Historical Sites and Buildings
1. Iglesia de Nuestra Señora del Pilar
2. Centro Cultural Recoleta
3. *Cementerio de la Recoleta (pp104–5)*
4. Café La Biela
5. Alvear Palace Hotel
6. Palais de Glace
8. Biblioteca Nacional

Museums and Galleries
7. Museo Nacional de Bellas Artes
9. Museo Casa de Ricardo Rojas
10. Museo Xul Solar

See also Street Finder maps 2 & 3

◀ One of the many grand mausoleums at Cementerio de la Recoleta

For keys to symbols *see back flap*

Street-by-Street: Recoleta

Recoleta stretches from downtown Buenos Aires to Calle Austria, but its heart is to be found in the cluster of leafy plazas and public buildings that surround the barrio's famous cemetery. The area has grand apartment buildings built in the early 1900s and boasts Café La Biela, one of the smartest and most famous *confiterías* in town. Also located here is the national fine arts museum, a lively cultural center, five-star hotels, and a beautiful old church. The capital's early 20th-century Francophile aspirations are evident in the barrio's architecture and in the name of the best-known green space in the area – Plaza Francia.

❸ ★ Cementerio de la Recoleta
This labyrinthine necropolis is the resting place of many presidents, military heroes, and well-known patrician families.

❶ Iglesia de Nuestra Señora del Pilar
Consecrated in 1732, this Spanish-style church houses a superlative Baroque altar featuring a wrought-silver frontal.

❷ Centro Cultural Recoleta
This sprawling complex, also known as Centro Cultural de Buenos Aires, is dedicated to promoting contemporary Argentinian music, theater, and film.

Café La Biela

Alvear Palace Hotel

❻ Palais de Glace
Opened by the aristocrat Baron de Marchi in the 1920s, the one-time ice rink and ballroom is now an excellent arts-focused exhibition center. Legend has it that tango star Carlos Gardel was shot here by a jealous rival.

❽ Biblioteca Nacional
Designed by three prominent local architects, the Biblioteca Nacional took almost 30 years to complete. When it finally opened in 1992, it was hailed as a Brutalist master-piece. The Peróns' house used to stand at this spot.

Locator Map

Plaza Francia
Surrounded by a French-style residential area, this dramatic monument to Liberty was presented to the nation by France in 1910.

❼ ★ Museo Nacional de Bellas Artes
Formerly a water-pumping station, this Neo-Classical building houses Argentina's most important collection of art. As well as a strong permanent display, there are many temporary exhibitions.

Plaza Intendente Alvear
Named for the mayor who gave the capital a major overhaul a century ago, this sloped plaza is now the site of one of the most popular weekend arts and handicraft markets.

| 0 meters | 100 |
| 0 yards | 100 |

Key

 Suggested route

The exquisite Baroque altar at the Iglesia de Nuestra Señora del Pilar

❶ Iglesia de Nuestra Señora del Pilar

Junín 1904. **City Map** 2 C2. **Tel** (011) 4803-6793. 🚌 10, 17, 60, 92, 110. **Open** varies. ♦ 8am, 11am, & 7:30pm Mon–Fri, 8:30am, 11am, & 7pm Sat, 8.30am, 10am, 11am, noon, 7pm, 8pm, 9pm Sun. 🆆 **basilicadelpilar.org.ar**

Donated to the monks of Recoleta in 1716 by Zaragoza-born entrepreneur Don Juan de Narbona, this church takes its name from Zaragoza's patron saint, Señora del Pilar (Virgin of Pilar). Jesuit architect Andrés Blanqui built it along the lines of a classic Spanish church of the period. Later refinements include an exterior clock made in Britain and Pas-de-Calais ceramic tiles.

The exterior murals are inspired by the work of Spanish painter Fernando Brambilia, an 18th-century specialist in perspective. They show a panoramic view of the river and recount the history of the church as well as the area. Inside is a beautiful Baroque altar, featuring Inca motifs, which was brought along the Camino Real mule-train route from Peru. The church is often open between services, and visitors can wander down into the crypt and see a small but interesting collection of religious art contained in one of the adjoining cloisters.

❷ Centro Cultural Recoleta

Junín 1930. **City Map** 2 C2. **Tel** (011) 4803-1040. 🚌 10, 17, 60, 92, 110. **Open** 1–8pm Tue–Fri, 10am–9pm Sat, Sun, & hols. ♿ 📷 🆆 **centroculturalrecoleta.org/nuevositio**

This complex of buildings dates from the 17th century and is one of the oldest in the city. The plot was donated to the monks of Recoleta in 1716, and Jesuit architects Juan Krauss and Juan Wolf drew up the plans. Andrés Blanqui is thought to have worked on the façade and interiors of the on-site monastery. During the 19th century the building served as an art school founded by liberation hero General Manuel Belgrano, and also as a refuge for the local homeless.

The Recoleta barrio became popular with the middle classes in the 1870s. During this time, the first mayor of Buenos Aires,

Centro Cultural Recoleta, venue of exciting artistic experimentation

Torcuato de Alvear, began a campaign to Europeanize and embellish the city, and this prime chunk of real estate was reclaimed for the barrio. Architect Juan Buschiazzo was responsible for the refurbishment, adding the pavilions, elegant Italianate terraces, and a chapel, which is now an auditorium. After a brief period as a home for the elderly, the complex was remodeled in 1980 and became the Centro Cultural Recoleta (CCR).

The barrio may be ultra-bourgeois, but there is nothing conservative about the schedule of art events that take place at this sprawling cultural center. About 20 galleries are used for stimulating visual arts exhibitions, various theatrical works, and film projections. A number of small dance and theater companies use the CCR as a rehearsal space.

❸ Cementerio de la Recoleta

See pp104–5.

❹ Café La Biela

Ave Quintana 600. **City Map** 2 C2. **Tel** (011) 4804-0449. 🚌 59, 60, 101, 102, 110. **Open** 7–3am daily. ♿ 🆆 **labiela.com**

If it lacks the atmosphere and artistic ghosts of the grand Café Tortoni *(see p72)*, La Biela still has a certain old-world appeal. The terrace could be housed in the streets of Rome or Paris, except

A contemporary installation at the Centro Cultural Recoleta

The Dogs of Recoleta

It is common for wealthy Recoleta families, living in an apartment without the required open space, to hire a *paseador* (a professional dog-walker). Since it became fashionable during the 1970s to own a pure-breed mutt – huskies, chows, and rare breeds are particularly desirable – wealthier porteño families have paid a young, usually male, person to walk their dog. There is great demand for the service, and every employee will happily walk between ten and 25 dogs, looking rather like a maypole at the center of dancing, dueling, and occasionally knotting, ribbons. Recoleta's wide, green spaces and

The glass-roofed L'Orangerie restaurant, Alvear Palace Hotel

Palermo's lovely Parque 3 de Febrero are the preferred rest stops, as they are located close to the dogs' palatial homes and are ideal for a run in the open. Unfortunately, there is little control of dog dirt and, since the scoops are shunned by walkers and well-to-do owners alike, visitors should check carefully before sitting and spreading their picnic on the grass.

A busy afternoon for a local walker

perhaps for the tentacle-like branches of the ancient gum tree that cast a cool, leafy shade. Super-efficient waiters come and go, carrying weighty silver trays of *masitas* (fine pastries) and perfectly machined cups of espresso. There has been a café on this corner since the early 1850s but La Biela became what it is today during the 1950s, when racing-car drivers met here for their post-race drinks. Monochrome photographs hanging on the inside walls hark back to this period. Nowadays it is a favorite for people-watchers, wealthy tourists, and artists who moved into Recoleta before estate prices skyrocketed.

❺ Alvear Palace Hotel

Ave Alvear 1891. **City Map** 3 D2. **Tel** (011) 4808-2100. 🚌 67, 93, 130. ♿ 📶 📱 🌐 alvearpalace.com

Built in 1923, the Alvear is considered by many to be Buenos Aires's only truly grand hotel *(see p279)*. Occupying a city block where the British Embassy used to stand, the grand 16-floor building (five of them are subterranean) is a monument to Francophilia both inside and out. It is a lasting emblem of the city's aspiration to be seen as the "Paris of South America." This

luxury hotel has modernized its facilities by adding a spa and keeping its restaurants at the cutting edge of culinary fashion. Fortunately this has been done without losing any of its romance or sacrificing the impeccable personal service that the richest and most powerful visitors to the city expect. Over the years, these guests have included Spanish kings, Japanese emperors, and American presidents, as well as just about every journalist and media boss from all around the world.

The bars and restaurants are popular and open to the public. The most pleasant is the lovely glass-roofed L'Orangerie, where guests can indulge in a lavish breakfast spread out beneath the streaming rays of the morning sun. Also highly rated is the La Bourgogne restaurant.

Visitors enjoying coffee on the terrace of the bustling Café La Biela

❸ Cementerio de la Recoleta

One of the world's great necropolises, Cementerio de la Recoleta occupies an area of 14 acres (5.5 ha), easily the size of an entire city block. Argentina's first president, Bernardino Rivadavia, commissioned French architect Próspero Catelin to design the cemetery, which opened in 1822. It boasts wide leafy avenues, narrow, marble-walled streets, smart, polished façades, and small, dark alleys. There are more than 6,400 tombs and mausoleums in the cemetery, more than 70 of which are recognized as National Historic Monuments. The architecture is eclectic, ranging from bombastic Greco-Roman mini-palaces to wedding-cake-style experiments in Romanticism to earthy-looking piles of stones.

One of the central tree-lined avenues of the cemetery

Narrow Lanes
These are laid out in a grid fashion, replicating the city beyond, and turning the quiet necropolis into a marble labyrinth – cold, impenetrable, and slightly eerie.

Tomb of Sáenz Peña, a former president.

José Hernández's Tomb
Author of the national poetry epic *Martín Fierro*, Hernández is one of several writers to have a tomb among the rich and powerful. He is laid to rest in an elegant white mausoleum.

VICENTE LOPEZ STREET

Tomb of Bartolomé Mitre, a former president and the founder of *La Nación*.

JUNIN STREET

★ **Eva Perón's Tomb**
A simple black stone affair, the tomb attracts a large number of pilgrims and tourists, all of whom pause to read a plaque with an extract from her famous "I will be millions" speech.

Key
— Suggested route

The many grand tomb structures forming a miniature cityscape

VISITORS' CHECKLIST

Practical Information
Aves Quintana & Junín 1760. **City
Map** 2 C2. 🛈 cnr Ave Quintana
& Junín 1760, (011) 4803-1594.
Open 7am–5:45pm daily. 📷
11am Tue & Thu.

Transport
🚌 17, 61, 62, 67, 92, 93,
& 110.

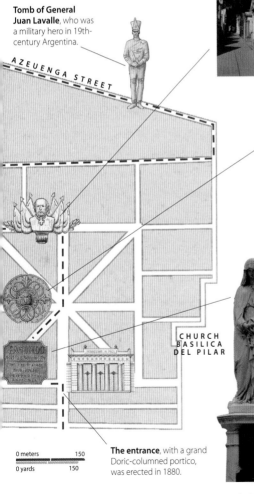

Julio Argentino Roca's Tomb
A general in the army during the 1870s, Roca led the Conquest of the Desert campaign *(see p54)*. He was president of the Argentinian republic from 1880 to 1886 and 1898 to 1904.

Tomb of General Juan Lavalle, who was a military hero in 19th-century Argentina.

AZEUENGA STREET

★ The Paz Family Tomb
José C. Paz was a diplomat, Congressman, and the founder of *La Prensa* newspaper. The family tomb is a grand edifice carved in white stone.

CHURCH
BASILICA
DEL PILAR

Facundo Quiroga's Tomb
Nicknamed "Tiger of the Plains," the assassinated gaucho *caudillo (see p189)* has a tomb adorned by a *dolorosa* (weeping Virgin) carved by Milanese sculptor Antonio Tantardini.

0 meters   150
0 yards   150

The entrance, with a grand Doric-columned portico, was erected in 1880.

❻ Palais de Glace

Posadas 1725. **City Map** 3 D2.
Tel (011) 4804-1163. 🚌 17, 61, 62, 67, 92, 124, 130. **Open** noon–8pm Tue–Fri, 10am–8pm Sat & Sun. 🎦 5pm & 6pm Sat & Sun (book ahead). ♿
🌐 **palaisdeglace.gob.ar**

Officially known as the National Palace of the Arts, the Palais de Glace (Palace of Ice) was inaugurated in 1910. It was initially designed to hold an ice-skating rink, modeled closely on Paris's own Palais de Glace.

The ice-rink idea did not prove popular and in 1915 the palace became a tango ballroom, and during the 1920s it was the city's key party venue. In 1931, the building was donated to the Fine Arts Institute and became an art gallery. From 1954 to 1960 it was used as a television studio for the channel Canal Siete. The palace was later converted back into an art gallery and declared a National Monument in 2004.

The Palais de Glace, with its crowned columns and vaulted dome, can be enjoyed as one of the finest examples of Parisian-style architecture in the city. It is also an important exhibition space for national and inter-national shows which include photography, paintings, and sculpture. The palace hosts the annual Antiques Fair organized by the Association of Friends of the National Museum of Decorative Arts. It is still held in high regard for its historic contribution to tango.

The severe Neo-Classical façade of Museo Nacional de Bellas Artes

❼ Museo Nacional de Bellas Artes

Ave del Libertador 1473. **City Map** 2 C2. **Tel** (011) 5288-9900. 🚌 67, 93, 130. **Open** 12:30–8:30pm Tue–Fri, 9:30am–8:30pm Sat, Sun, & hols. 🎦 12:30pm Tue, Thu, & Fri, 2pm Sat (English). ♿ 📷 🌐 **mnba.org.ar**

In 1932, Argentina's National Fine Arts Museum moved to occupy one of the city's major waterworks facilities, where it has remained ever since. The interior was completely remodeled under the super-vision of Alejandro Bustillo, one of the country's greatest archi-tects. The Neo-Classical façade has changed little since the original facility opened in 1870. Apart from some subsequent expansion and renovation work, the museum, with its spacious and well-lit salons, remains much as it was when President Justo cut the ribbon in 1933.

Currently the museum comprises 34 exhibition rooms divided over three sprawling floors. There are more than 12,000 works in the permanent collection, although only 700 can be displayed at any one time. The specialist art library, also open to the public, contains more than 150,000 volumes.

The collection housed in the Museo Nacional de Bellas Artes is one of the most outstanding in South America. On display are works by many of the canonical figures in art history, including Goya, Rubens, Rembrandt, El Greco, Rodin, Klee, Renoir, Degas, Picasso, and Toulouse-Lautrec. The exhibits also include some of the most famous names in Argentinian art, including Antonio Berni, Xul Solar, Leon Ferrari, Raquel Forner, Prilidiano Pueyrredón, Fernando Fader, and Antonio Seguí, represented by some of their best-known and most influential works. The influences of European art are vividly apparent in the Argentinian works, but the divergences the artists make to illustrate the local viewpoint are interesting. For example, a painter like Berni used the techniques of social realism to specifically portray his own unique criollo (mixed race) environment. The museum is gradually shaking off its reputation as a cautious, hidebound institution. In 2004, it opened its first branch in the Patagonian city of Neuquén, and in 2005 it added a perma-nent display of pre-Columbian art. Audio tours and a well-stocked bookshop have helped make it an excellent modern museum.

Retrato de Manuelita Rosas (1840) by Prilidiano Pueyrredón

The elegant space of the Palais de Glace now used for art exhibitions

❽ Biblioteca Nacional

Agüero 2502. **City Map** 2 B2.
Tel (011) 4808-6000. 🚍 60, 95, 130.
ℹ️ photo ID required for entry.
Open Feb–Dec: 9am–9pm Mon–Fri,
noon–7pm Sat & Sun. **Closed** Jan.
🎬 3pm Mon, Tue, & Thu. ♿ 💻
🌐 bn.gov.ar

One of the largest libraries in the Americas, Argentina's Biblioteca Nacional houses a vast collection exceeding two million volumes. Books, journals, and important historical manuscripts are stored in its huge underground vaults. These include a first edition of *Don Quixote*, the personal literary collection of General Belgrano, and a 1455 Gutenberg Bible. The library's most treasured possessions are books that were printed before 1501. Among these pieces are works by St. Augustine, Dante, and Cicero.

The building itself is none too glamorous; built on the site of the palace where the Peróns lived, it is a T-shaped slab of poured concrete that flaunts its functionality in classic Brutalist style. Architecturally very popular when conceived in the 1960s, the look was slightly dated by the time it finally opened to the public in 1992. The position of library director has been held by novelist José Marmol, historian Paul Groussac, and, most famously, author Jorge Luis Borges, all of whom went blind during their terms.

Literary icon Jorge Luis Borges

❾ Museo Casa de Ricardo Rojas

Calle Charcas 2837. **City Map** 2 B3.
Tel (011) 4824-4038. 🚇 Agüero.
🚍 39, 68, 152. **Open** 11am–7pm
Tue–Sun. 🎬 on request. ♿

This beautiful dwelling, set rather incongruously amid the residential high-rises of Barrio Norte, was the home of the notable writer and pedagogue Ricardo Rojas from 1929 until his death in 1957. The house

The personal library of Ricardo Rojas decorated with Inca symbols

was donated to the country by his widow and opened as a museum in 1958. Rojas remained fascinated by the relationship between pre-Columbian and colonial America, which he conceived as a dialogue as well as a clash of cultures. Built with a mix of Spanish and Inca styles, the house was designed to embody this doctrine. This is particularly evident in the patio and cloisters, where the columns are decorated with various traditional Inca symbols. The façade mimics Casa Histórica in Tucumán city. Rojas's furnishings and household objects have also been well preserved, along with his personal library, which comprises more than 20,000 volumes. The museum is a

fascinating window not only into the mind, but also into the lifestyle of a brilliant writer-scholar.

❿ Museo Xul Solar

Calle Laprida 1212. **City Map** 2 A3.
Tel (011) 4824-3302. 🚇 Agüero. 🚍
39, 68, 152. **Open** noon–8pm Tue–Fri,
noon–7pm Sat. 🎬 4pm Tue–Thu,
3:30pm Sat (by prior arrangement in
English; call ahead to book). ♿ 📧
📷 🌐 xulsolar.org.ar

Once the residence of the 19th-century porteño artist Xul Solar, this 20th-century town house has been converted into the excellent Museo Xul Solar. Described by Jorge Luis Borges as "one of the most singular events of our time," Xul Solar was an eccentric visionary. On display at the museum are his otherwordly paintings, done mainly in watercolor and tempera. His art seems to be a blend of ideas drawn from various sources, such as Hieronymus Bosch, William Blake, and Jules Verne, while at the same time being entirely original. The cryptic landscapes he depicts are inhabited by angels, demons, and jesters, flying reptiles and machines, ladders that lead nowhere, and sphinxes restyled as cave paintings. Solar takes the viewer through a very bizarre looking-glass world.

Apart from these paintings, the museum contains a range of equally bizarre objects from Solar's collection. These include quasi-scientific instruments, masks, and sculptures.

Display of Xul Solar's eccentric artwork at the Museo Xul Solar

PALERMO AND BELGRANO

The sprawling barrios of Palermo and Belgrano boast open spaces filled by parks, a racecourse, and the city zoo. Palermo grew in the late 19th century during the presidency of Sarmiento, who was responsible for the building of Jardín Botánico and Parque 3 de Febrero. Belgrano was named after Manuel Belgrano, the military leader who designed the country's national flag. These barrios are considered superior by most Argentinians for their many urban conveniences and museums, which include MALBA. Their parks are loved by porteños, who come en masse on weekends to walk, jog, or share a round of *mate* on the lawns.

Sights at a Glance

Historical Sites, Buildings, and Plazas

⑩ Hipódromo Argentino de Palermo
⑪ Campo Argentino de Polo de Palermo
⑫ Centro Cultural Islámico Rey Fahd
⑬ La Rural
⑭ Escuela de Mecánica de la Armada (ESMA)
⑮ Las Cañitas
⑰ Belgrano
⑱ Cementerio de la Chacarita
⑲ Plaza Serrano

Parks and Gardens

① Parque 3 de Febrero
③ Jardín Japonés
④ Jardín Zoológico
⑤ Jardín Botánico Carlos Thays

Museums and Galleries

② Museo de Artes Plásticas Eduardo Sívori
⑥ Museo Evita
⑦ *Museo de Arte Latinoamericano de Buenos Aires (MALBA) pp114–15*
⑧ Museo de Arte Popular José Hernández
⑨ Museo Nacional de Arte Decorativo
⑯ Museo Nacional del Hombre
⑳ Museo Argentino de Ciencias Naturales Bernardino Rivadavia

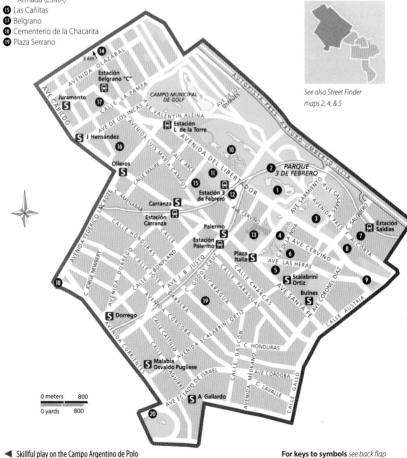

See also Street Finder maps 2, 4, & 5

0 meters 800
0 yards 800

◀ Skilful play on the Campo Argentino de Polo

For keys to symbols *see back flap*

Contemporary art displays at the Museo de Artes Plásticas Eduardo Sívori

❶ Parque 3 de Febrero

Ave Adolfo Berro. **City Map** 5 E2. 🚇 Palermo, Lisando de la Torre. 🅂 Palermo, Plaza Italia. 🚍 10, 34, 36, 37, 67, 130.

The capital's largest and most popular park, Parque 3 de Febrero is also known as the Bosques de Palermo (Palermo Woods). In the 19th century, the land was owned by Argentinian dictator Juan Manuel de Rosas. Following his defeat by General Urquiza in the Battle of Caseros on February 3, 1852, all his land was confiscated and ear-marked for public use. In 1874, the site was converted into a park styled after Paris's Bois de Boulogne and London's Hyde Park and named Parque 3 de Febrero, after the Battle of Caseros. French landscape architect Charles Thays was responsible for the design of the park, as well as that of the nearby Jardín Botánico. It was inaugurated in 1875 by President Nicolás Avellaneda.

Apart from beautifully tended lawns, the park contains a variety of attractions that include a spherical planetarium and the Velódromo Municipal, which was opened in 1951 for the Pan-American Games. Most popular is the Rosedal, a rose garden designed by landscape architect Benito Carrasco, which features about 12,000 rose bushes, a boating lake with pedalos and rowing boats, a wooden bridge, and pergola. The space also has a Poet's Garden, with busts of famous

poets, among them Jorge Luis Borges, Federico García Lorca, and Shakespeare.

Among the monuments in the park are the Monumento a los Españoles, erected as part of the centenary celebrations of the Revolución de Mayo in 1810 (see p53); Auguste Rodin's monument to Sarmiento; and a monument to General Urquiza. Over the weekends the sprawling park gets plenty of joggers, family picnickers, walkers, and bicyclists.

❷ Museo de Artes Plásticas Eduardo Sívori

Bonsai plant at Jardín Japonés

Ave Infanta Isabel 555. **City Map** 5 E2. **Tel** (011) 4774-9452. 🚍 10, 34, 36, 37, 67, 130. **Open** noon–8pm Tue–Fri, 10am–8pm Sat & Sun. 🅰 🅿 free Sat & Wed. 📷 4pm & 5pm Sat (English). 🖥 📷
Ⓦ **museosivori.org.ar**

The Museo de Artes Plásticas Eduardo Sívori houses a diverse and significant collection of over 4,000 pieces of art, among them drawings, paintings, sculptures, and tapestries, dating from the 19th century to the present day. The museum was founded in 1938 as the Museo Municipal de Bellas Artes, Artes Aplicadas y Anexo de Artes Comparadas, but was later renamed for the famous Buenos Aires artist Eduardo Sívori (1847–1918). The museum covers a huge range of styles and media,

including the academic naturalism of Sívori and the Impressionist landscapes of Ramón Silva and Walter de Navazio. Works span the Post-Impressionist and Cubist periods, all the way to Surrealism, Pop Art, and Hyperrealism. The museum moved to its current picturesque home, not far from the Rosedal at Parque 3 de Febrero, in 1995, and now has a small shop, sculpture garden, and café.

❸ Jardín Japonés

Ave Casares & Ave Berro. **City Map** 5 F3. **Tel** (011) 4804-4922. 🚍 10, 34, 36. **Open** 10am–6pm daily. 🅰 📷 11am Sat & Sun (Spanish only). 🅰 🅰
Ⓦ **jardinjapones.org.ar**

These peaceful and carefully maintained gardens were created in 1967 as a gift to the city by its sizable Japanese community. They feature clear man-made lakes and islands. These are crisscrossed by pretty red wooden bridges, such as the curved Puente de la Buena Ventura, leading to the Isla de los Dioses (Island of the Gods). A wealth of flora flourishes here, much of which was imported from Japan, including sakura, ginkgo, and black pines. There are also giant koi carp in the lake, and ducks roaming the gardens. The pagoda houses a

Koi Pond, one of the man-made lakes at the Jardín Japonés

tearoom and a Japanese restaurant, and hosts many exhibitions and events. Within the park is the Campana de la Paz, the bell that is sounded every year to celebrate World Peace Day on September 21.

❹ Jardín Zoológico

Ave Sarmiento & Ave Las Heras. **City Map** 5 E3. **Tel** (011) 4011-9900. 🚇 Palermo. 🅂 Plaza Italia. 🚌 15, 36, 37, 60, 152. **Open** 10am–7pm Tue–Sun. 🚼 free for children under 12. ♿ 🌐 **zoobuenosaires.com.ar**

Located at this site since 1888, this handsome city zoo started out with a total collection of 650 animals and 53 different species. Today, over 2,500 creatures, including 49 reptiles, 89 mammals, and 175 birds, inhabit the 44-acre (18-ha) site. The

One of the elegant greenhouses at the Jardín Botánico

zoo's first director, Eduardo Ladislao Holmberg, played an important role in the design of the park, deciding to house the animals in buildings that reflect their country of origin. This makes for an interesting array of architectural styles, including a reproduction of an Indian temple, a French palace, and a Templo de Vesta with 16 Corinthian columns, as well as a range of sculptures and statues. Among the popular attractions today are a reptilium, an aquarium, and a

Elephants at the Jardín Zoológico

re-creation of a subtropical jungle. The areas are well labeled and the zoo has a strong conservation agenda.

❺ Jardín Botánico Carlos Thays

Santa Fe 3951. **City Map** 5 E4. **Tel** (011) 4831-4527. 🚇 Palermo. 🅂 Plaza Italia. 🚌 15, 36, 37, 60, 152. **Open** 8am–6pm Mon–Fri, 9:30am–6pm Sat & Sun, 11am–6pm hols. 📷 10:30am Fri, 10:30am & 3pm Sat, Sun, & hols. 🌐 **zoobuenosaires.com.ar**

The city's Botanical Gardens, opened in 1898, were designed by famous French landscape architect Charles Thays. He lived in a Tudor-style house in the gardens from 1892 to 1898 while he was the director of parks and public walkways. His house now contains a botanical library. The 17-acre (7-ha) site boasts over 5,500 species of plants from Argentina and around the world, organized by family, origin, and use.

Of the gardens' five greenhouses, the first and most significant was brought over from France from the 1900 Paris Exhibition. Built out of iron and glass in Art Nouveau style, the structure measures 3,000 sq ft (280 sq m), and houses tropical and subtropical species. In addition to its floral riches, the Jardín Botánico has a wealth of public art, including sculptures and monuments. The park is also home to hundreds of abandoned cats.

Juan Manuel de Rosas (1793–1877)

This infamous figure rose to prominence as a leader of the patriotic gaucho armies who fought against the European expeditionary forces, following Argentinian Independence. In 1829, Rosas became governor of Buenos Aires and instigated campaigns to massacre the indigenous peoples of the southern Pampas. Rosas portrayed himself as a man of the people, but with his private paramilitary army, *la mazorca*, he perpetrated countless outrages in

Dictator Juan Manuel de Rosas, who ruled with an iron fist

Argentina and launched invasions of Uruguay and Paraguay. In 1851, he became supreme ruler of the newly created Argentinian Confederation, which plunged into civil war as powerful adversaries rose up against the *rosista* faithful (people whose sympathies lay with Rosas). Rosas was toppled in 1852 and forced into exile, living out the rest of his days as a farmer in Southampton, England. There is not a single street or plaza in Buenos Aires honoring his name, but Rosas is still an icon for many ultra-conservatives.

The beautiful 20th-century building that houses Museo Evita

❻ Museo Evita

Calle Lafinur 2988, Palermo. **City Map** 5 E3. **Tel** (011) 4807-0306. Ⓢ Plaza Italia. 🚌 39, 59, 93. **Open** 11am–7pm Tue–Sun. 🅿 📷 on request. 🖐 limited. 🏠 Ⓦ **museoevita.org**

The museum dedicated to Eva Perón is housed in an early 20th-century mansion that once belonged to the aristo-cratic Carabaza family. The building was converted into a shelter for the homeless in 1948, when it was bought by the Eva Perón Social Aid Foundation. After the fall of the Perón government, it was used for administrative purposes until mid-2002. Opened later that year, the museum is run by the Instituto Nacional Eva Perón, which aims to preserve the legacy of her life and work for the people of Argentina.

The displays trace Eva Perón's life and passions faithfully, while some of the exhibits include items which belonged to the families who once took shelter in the house. However, the most impressive exhibits are Evita's posters, famous photographs, jewelry, and her Dior dresses. One of the most memorable images shows Evita saluting the "shirtless ones" from the balcony of Casa Rosada (see p68). There is also an image of Evita, scrubbed and spotless, amid a crew of grubby miners. Other rare exhibits include magazine articles dating from when she was a radio star in the 1930s.

❼ Museo de Arte Latinoamericano de Buenos Aires (MALBA)

See pp114–15.

❽ Museo de Arte Popular José Hernández

Ave del Libertador 2373, Palermo. **City Map** 5 F3. **Tel** (011) 4803-2384. 🚌 37, 59, 60. **Open** 1–7pm Wed–Fri, 10am–8pm Sat, Sun, & hols. **Closed** 1 Jan, 1 May, Good Friday, & Dec 25. 🅿 Sun free. 📷 by reservation only. 🖥 🏠 Ⓦ **museo hernandez. buenosaires.gob.ar**

Named for José Hernández, the author of *Martín Fierro*, Argentina's first and only national epic, this slightly untidy museum has one of the finest collections of Argentinian popular art, including

Wide wooden doors at Museo de Arte Popular José Hernández

traditional, urban, indigenous, and rural variants. The museum is a salutary reminder that, to understand Argentina and its history, it is necessary to be aware of the importance of its rural heritage and customs.

Housed in an early 20th-century building that was once a hotel, the collection comprises over 8,000 traditional and handmade objects of staggering diversity, showcasing the techniques and materials of both the country's indigenous population and the early colonial settlers.

Among the exhibits are beautifully wrought silverware, masks, musical instruments, and rudimentary weaponry. The pretty patio garden is a great place for a packed lunch.

Interior of Museo Nacional de Arte Decorativo

❾ Museo Nacional de Arte Decorativo

Ave del Libertador 1902, Recoleta. **City Map** 2 B2. **Tel** (011) 4802-6606. 🚌 59, 60, 67, 93. **Open** Jan: 2–7pm Tue–Sat; Feb–Dec: 2–7pm Tue–Sun. 🅿 Tue free. 📷 4:30pm Tue–Sat, 2:30pm Tue–Sun (in English). 🖐 by arrangement. 🅿 🖥 🏠 Ⓦ **mnad.org**

Once home to the wealthy art lover and Chilean diplomat Errázuriz-Alvear, this early 20th-century French-style mansion was declared a listed national monument in 1998. It houses Argentina's only major decorative arts museum, with a collection of over 4,000 objects,

French-style ornate façade of Museo Nacional de Arte Decorativo

ranging from Roman sculptures to contemporary silverware. The bulk of the pieces are of either Oriental or European origin and date from the 16th to the 20th century. Many were donated by Buenos Aires's richest and most celebrated families, including the Errázuriz-Alvears. Among the well-known names whose works are on display are those of Edouard Manet and Auguste Rodin, represented by a portrait and several small sculptures respectively. Temporary exhibitions usually focus on contemporary artisan-type work from Argentina's interior provinces. Although the museum has a varied collection, many prefer just to walk around the beautiful mansion.

Garden sculpture at Museo de Arte Decorativo

❿ Hipódromo Argentino de Palermo

Ave del Libertador 4104, Palermo. **City Map** 5 D2. **Tel** (011) 4778-2800. 🅂 Ministro Carranza. 🚌 130, 160, 166. **Open** varies. ♿ 🚫 📷 🏠 🌐 **palermo.com.ar**

When Buenos Aires's Hipódromo Argentino de Palermo opened its doors in 1876, it had a capacity of only 2,000 people. Today, that has grown to about 100,000. Although its early years were considered its golden days, major races still pull in a large

crowd from across the country. Thought to be one of the best racecourses in the world, the Hipódromo has three tracks, of which two are used for training while the main track is used for competitions. On average, there are ten meetings per month, usually on Mondays, Saturdays, and Sundays. Races start every half-hour. The Hipódromo also hosts what is easily the biggest date on the Argentinian turf calendar, the Gran Premio Nacional in November, which draws massive crowds. The other prominent race, held annually, is the Gran de las Americas. For the best betting, punters should visit the basement of the Neo-Classical Tribuna Oficial, where over 4,000 slot machines are kept. The *belle époque* architecture of the grandstand and manicured gardens adds an elegant touch to this popular sports ground.

⓫ Campo Argentino de Polo de Palermo

Ave del Libertador 4300, Palermo. **City Map** 5 D2. **Tel** (011) 4777-8005. 🅂 Ministro Carranza. 🚌 130, 160, 166. 🚫 ♿ 📷 🌐 **aapolo.com**

Opened in 1928, Campo Argentino de Polo de Palermo is the country's major stadium and one of the best places to see international polo stars, including Adolfo Cambiaso, one of Argentina's top polo players. Also known as Catedral del Polo, the stadium has a capacity of 45,000 spectators and is used for many other purposes, including concerts.

Polo is played in Buenos Aires from September through to December *(see p40)*. The Abierto Argentino de Palermo (Argentinian Open) is contested at the end of the season. Everyone enjoys the tradition of stomping down the divots on the pitch at half-time.

A polo match in progress at the Campo Argentino de Polo de Palermo

❼ Museo de Arte Latinamericano de Buenos Aires (MALBA)

Opened in 2001 to house the art collection of Argentinian connoisseur and philanthropist Eduardo F. Costantini, Museo de Arte Latinoamericano de Buenos Aires (MALBA) is probably the best privately administered art museum in Argentina. The building is a striking example of contemporary architecture, which cleverly combines earth-colored, stone-clad trapezoid shapes. It houses over 500 works of 20th-century Latin American art, including pieces by Frida Kahlo and Fernando Botero, alongside Argentinian masters Antonio Berni, Jorge de la Vega, and Leon Ferrari.

The strikingly contemporary cuboid form of MALBA

★ *Manifestación* (1934)
Argentinian painter Antonio Berni is best known for his slightly grotesque portraits of the urban working classes, as shown in this painting of a protest march.

Temporary exhibition space is used to showcase contemporary art.

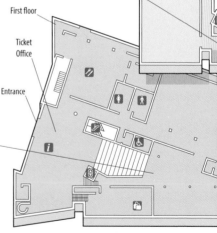

First floor

Ticket Office

Entrance

Atrium
One of the most distinctive features of the museum, the glass walls of the MALBA atrium are specially built to allow natural light to flood the exhibition space.

Siete últimas canciones (1986)
The most successful of the younger generation of Argentinian artists is Guillermo Kuitca, whose abstract works are influenced by design forms in the mass media, cartography, and the theater.

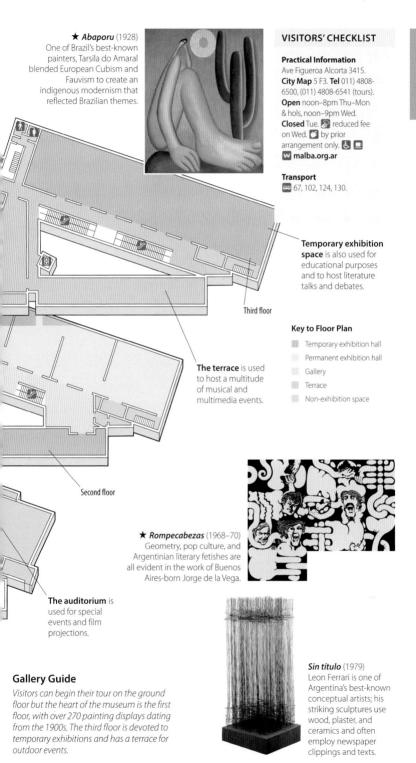

★ *Abaporu* (1928)
One of Brazil's best-known painters, Tarsila do Amaral blended European Cubism and Fauvism to create an indigenous modernism that reflected Brazilian themes.

VISITORS' CHECKLIST

Practical Information
Ave Figueroa Alcorta 3415.
City Map 5 F3. **Tel** 011) 4808-6500, (011) 4808-6541 (tours).
Open noon–8pm Thu–Mon & hols, noon–9pm Wed.
Closed Tue. ♿ reduced fee on Wed. ☐ by prior arrangement only. ♿ ☐
🆆 **malba.org.ar**

Transport
🚌 67, 102, 124, 130.

Temporary exhibition space is also used for educational purposes and to host literature talks and debates.

Third floor

Key to Floor Plan

- Temporary exhibition hall
- Permanent exhibition hall
- Gallery
- Terrace
- Non-exhibition space

The terrace is used to host a multitude of musical and multimedia events.

Second floor

★ *Rompecabezas* (1968–70)
Geometry, pop culture, and Argentinian literary fetishes are all evident in the work of Buenos Aires-born Jorge de la Vega.

The auditorium is used for special events and film projections.

Gallery Guide

Visitors can begin their tour on the ground floor but the heart of the museum is the first floor, with over 270 painting displays dating from the 1900s. The third floor is devoted to temporary exhibitions and has a terrace for outdoor events.

Sin título (1979)
Leon Ferrari is one of Argentina's best-known conceptual artists; his striking sculptures use wood, plaster, and ceramics and often employ newspaper clippings and texts.

The towering minarets of the Centro Cultural Islámico Rey Fahd

center located in the heart of Buenos Aires.

La Rural is a two-week-long agricultural fair that takes place annually in August. It attracts thousands of spectators who come to see a large number of animals, most of which are cattle. Breeders travel from all over Argentina to showcase their livestock.

The showground itself was built by the Sociedad Rural Argentina in the 1870s, and it now also has a modern exhibition hall, which is used for other events and shows.

⓫ Escuela de Mecánica de la Armada (ESMA)

Ave del Libertador 8209. 🚇 Estación Rivadavia. 🚌 29, 60, 130, 160. 🌐 institutomemoria.org.ar

For most Argentinians the acronym "ESMA," short for "Escuela de Mecánica de la Armada" (The Naval Mechanics School), has a grim resonance.

A facility of the Argentinian Navy, it was used as an illegal detention center during the dictatorial rule of the National Reorganization Process which lasted from 1976 to 1983 (see p58). It was here that some of the worst atrocities were committed during the country's military rule. Political prisoners, many of whom were simply teachers or lawyers with left-wing leanings, were brought here, commonly in unmarked Ford Falcons, tortured

⓬ Centro Cultural Islámico Rey Fahd

Ave Intendente Bullrich 55. **City Map** 5 D2. **Tel** (011) 4899-1144. 🚌 15, 36, 37, 60. **Open** 9am–6pm Mon–Fri. 📷 noon Tue, Thu, & Sat. ♿ 🌐 ccislamicoreyfahd.org.ar

Inaugurated in 2000, this cultural center and imposing, modern Gulf-style mosque were designed by Saudi architect Zuhair Faiz on land donated by the former Argentinian president Carlos Menem. The 10-acre (4-ha) site contains the King Fahd Mosque with a 160-ft- (50-m-) high blue-and-white dome and two minarets.

The mosque is the largest in South America, with a colossal prayer room that accommodates more than 1,000 worshipers. It houses schools that conduct Islam and Arabic classes, and has a library and conference and sports facilities. The center's pleasant gardens and water fountains provide a cool retreat from the busy city.

⓭ La Rural

Ave Santa Fe 4201. **City Map** 5 E3. **Tel** (011) 4777-5500. 🚌 15, 36, 37, 60. **Open** only for events.

Named after the most important agricultural event in the Argentinian calendar since the late 19th century, this showground and exhibition space is used as an exporting platform and is a cultural, entrepreneurial, and social

A busy day at the La Rural agricultural fair

and, usually, killed. It is estimated that around 5,000 people were interned at ESMA during the so-called "Dirty War." Most shocking of all were the cases of pregnant women who were detained here, allowed to give birth, then killed so that their children could be given up for adoption to "friends" of the junta.

As part of Argentina's ongoing struggle to come to terms with this dark era, the government has committed itself to the construction of a "Space for Memory and the Promotion and Defence of Human Rights," which is housed within these grounds.

🟕 Las Cañitas

Calle Baez, Arévalo. **City Map** 5 D2. 15, 29, 60, 64, 118.

Named after the sugarcane that used to grow here when the land was part of General Rosas's (see p111) sprawling private estate, Las Cañitas is a fashionable and pricey residential barrio. Although wedged between bustling Belgrano and several lively avenues, including Báez and Arévalo, the streets here are relatively sedate and dead ends keep traffic levels down. During the mid-1990s, ultra-hip restaurants such as Soul Café and

One of the many excellent restaurants in the posh Las Cañitas suburb

Novecento began to appear in the area, setting in motion a spate of exclusive gastronomic openings. Soon they were followed by bars, boutiques, and apartment blocks. Las Cañitas became established as the social hub for the well-heeled and its model of development was copied by Palermo Soho and, later, San Telmo. The Cañitas Creativa street market on Fridays and Saturdays is an attempt to bring culture and craft to the neighborhood, but the accent in the area is mainly on cool clothes and consumerism.

🟖 Museo Nacional del Hombre

Calle 3 de Febrero 1370/8. **City Map** 4 B1. **Tel** (011) 4783-6554. 60. **Open** 10am–6pm Mon–Fri. for groups only, book ahead. inapl.gov.ar

Chané mask, Museo Nacional del Hombre

A small, well-maintained museum, the Museo Nacional del Hombre is part of the Instituto Nacional de Antropología y Pensamiento Latinoamericano, which is dedicated to research in the areas of social anthropology and folklore. The building houses exhibits relating to the prehistory and contemporary status of indigenous South American and Argentinian groups. These peoples include the Mapuche, Tehuelche, Diaguita, and numerous others of the Tierra del Fuego region, many of whom were wiped out by European colonizers.

Among the 5,000 exhibits, some of which are reproductions, are traditional crafts, textiles, musical instruments, masks, and costumes. Noteworthy are the Mapuche silver jewelry and Chané masks, which are made of the native palo borracho tree. The museum shop has a small but excellent crafts selection.

Villa Freud

An oft-repeated claim is that Buenos Aires has more shrinks per capita than any other city on earth. Psychoanalysis first became a prominent feature of intellectual life in the 1920s, and among the many European immigrants were a large number of avant-garde philosophers, academics, and psychiatrists. By the early 1970s, psychoanalysis had established itself as a popular university field.

Sigmund Freud, Austrian neurologist and psychiatrist

In recent decades, television shows portray visits to a psicólogo (psychiatrist) to be as ordinary an experience in the daily life of middle-class porteños as going to a tennis lesson or meeting for a family barbecue. As the area of Palermo around Plaza Güemes is typically middle class and full of psychoanalysts and psychiatrists, it has become known as Villa Freud.

⑰ Belgrano

Northwest of Palermo. 🚇 138, 942. 🚉 Juramento, Belgrano C, Belgrano R. 🚌 60, 65, 114, 118, 152. 🛍 Sat & Sun.

Named after Manuel Belgrano, the Independence hero who designed the national flag, Belgrano was the capital of the Argentinian Republic for a few weeks in 1880. When the authorities in the capital found themselves at odds with the provincial government, it was chosen as a neutral seat of power. These days, the only evidence of this former glory is the town hall, now the **Sarmiento Historical Museum**, and the church of **La Inmaculada Concepción**, known to the locals as La Redonda because of its circular walls. The barrio has a good range of bars, restaurants, and retail outlets and Buenos Aires's only Chinatown is also located here. Belgrano proper is a typical middle-class area, but heading towards Belgrano Residencial beyond Avenida Cramer, the high-rise apartment blocks suddenly give way to cobblestoned streets, private houses, and grand mansions. An English parish church still stands on Cramer, and many houses ape the mock-Tudor style found in England.

Chessboard-tiled dining room at Museo de Arte Español Enrique Larreta

🏛 Museo de Arte Español Enrique Larreta

Ave Juramento 2291. **Tel** (011) 4783-2640. 🚉 Juramento. 🚌 60, 65, 114, 118. **Open** 1–7pm Mon–Fri, 10am–8pm Sat, Sun, & hols. 🎟 Thu free. 📷 5pm Mon–Fri, 4pm & 6pm Sat & Sun. ♿ limited. 📷 🌐 **museo larreta.buenosaires.gob.ar**

San Martín de Tours at Museo de Arte Español

Located in the heart of Belgrano, this museum is housed in the former residence of writer Enrique Larreta (1874–1961). He was an important figure in Argentinian modernism and was nominated for the Nobel Prize in 1941. The house has light-soaked indoor patios and an ornamental garden surrounded by Andalusian fruit trees. The displays include paintings from the Renaissance and Baroque eras, wooden furniture, sculptures, and weaponry collected over several trips Larreta made to Spain to research his 1908 historical novel, *The Glory of Don Ramiro*. There are also several portraits of Larreta himself for which he sat in Paris in 1912. The collection in the museum was substantially augmented in 1997 with 30 paintings and objects from the Museo de Arte Hispanoamericano Isaac Fernández Blanco, including valuable works by Sánchez Coello and Pantoja de la Cruz.

🏛 Museo Casa de Yrurtia

O'Higgins 2390. **Tel** (011) 4781-0385. 🚉 Juramento. 🚌 60, 65. **Open** 11:30am–6pm Wed–Fri, 11:30am–7pm Sat, Sun, & hols. 🎟 Wed free. 📷 3pm Fri, 4:30pm Sat, Sun, & hols. ♿ 📷 📷 🌐 **casadeyrurtia.gov.ar**

Celebrated sculptor Rogelio Yrurtia and his wife, the painter Correa Morales, bequeathed their stylish Neo-Colonial house to the nation in 1942. It opened as a museum in 1949. All the pieces exhibited are from the couple's personal collection and testify to their eclectic tastes. There are sculptures, mostly figurative works in bronze or plaster, and among the paintings are still lifes, landscapes, and portraits by Morales, alongside those of other Argentinian painters such as Martin Malharro, Benito Quinquela Martín, and Octavio Pinto. Standing out among the pieces is *Rue Cortot*, an early Picasso. There is also a collection of Asian domestic porcelain items, and textiles and carpets from Mexico and Bolivia. The furniture is a mix of Victorian English and Second Empire French. The garden is lined with plane trees and grapevines.

The Neo-Colonial façade of Museo Casa de Yrurtia

ⓘ Cementerio de la Chacarita

Ave Guzmán 680 & Federico Lacroze.
City Map 4 A4. **Tel** (011) 4553-9338.
Ⓢ Federico Lacroze. 🚌 39, 45, 71, 93.
Open 8am–6pm daily. 📷 3pm, 2nd &
4th Sat. ♿

Buenos Aires's largest cemetery, though not its most famous or aristocratic, was inaugurated in the wake of the yellow fever epidemic that swept the city in 1871. The plague was so severe it was reported that 576 bodies were buried at Cementerio de la Chacarita during a single day. Since then the necropolis has expanded to 234 acres (95 ha) and is now one of the largest in the world. The cemetery dominates the neighborhood of Chacarita; indeed it is almost a barrio in its own right, having numbered streets and convenient car access. Burials of well-known personalities often draw the media and large crowds to the cemetery. It is the final resting place of many famous Argentinians, though no longer of Juan Perón, who used to be buried here, but whose remains were moved to a family mausoleum in 2006.

The Dinosaur Room at Museo Argentino de Ciencias Naturales

ⓘ Plaza Serrano

Calle Honduras & Borges. **City Map** 5
D4. 🚌 15, 39, 110, 141, 168. 🛍 crafts
market Sat & Sun.

Officially named Plaza Cortázar, Plaza Serrano is the focal point of the fashionable area known as Palermo Viejo or Palermo Soho. Characterized by early 20th-century Spanish-style architecture, this area was once a residential barrio. It is now packed with alternative bars and restaurants serving global cuisine. In the 1990s artists and designers moved into the area to take advantage of low rents, a trend that created a flourishing alternative scene after the economic collapse in 2001.

Located to its north is the area known as Palermo Hollywood, which is now an upmarket nightlife district.

ⓘ Museo Argentino de Ciencias Naturales Bernardino Rivadavia

Ave Angel Gallardo 470. **Tel** (011)
4982-6595. Ⓢ Angel Gallardo. 🚌 65,
97, 105, 112, 124. **Open** 2–7pm daily.
📷 📷 Apr–Nov: Sat, Sun, & hols. ♿
📷 📷 ⓦ macn.secyt.gov.ar

One of the oldest in the country, this museum dates back to 1823 and is the brain-child of Argentina's first president, Bernardino Rivadavia. In 1937, it moved to its current venue, an Italianate building specifically designed and built to house the museum, unusual in a city where most museums were incorporated into various existing structures.

There are over 15 large exhibition spaces, each devoted either to a class of fauna or flora or to a habitat. Fish, mammals, invertebrates, and plant life are all covered, and the squawks and whistles of Argentinian birdlife can be heard in the impressive Sounds of Nature salon.

The star attraction of the venue is the Dinosaur Room, with its reconstructed skeletons, mostly made using bones unearthed in the Patagonian region, where the museum's team of paleontologists continue to carry out research.

The tomb of tango singer Carlos Gardel at Cementerio de la Chacarita

Farther Afield

Located around the capital are a number of interesting towns and suburbs that offer a variety of activities. Gaucho traditions thrive at the Feria de Mataderos, a weekly crafts and bric-a-brac market in the colorful barrio of Mataderos. Beyond this is the riverside town of Tigre, whose Paraná Delta is a hugely popular attraction. The jungle-clad delta houses a complex river system teeming with flora and birdlife. Río de la Plata can easily be crossed by ferry to explore Argentina's Isla Martín García or the UNESCO World Heritage Site of Colonia del Sacramento in Uruguay.

Leather belts sold at the popular artisanal Feria de Mataderos

Key

≋≋≋ Expressway

▬▬▬ Major road

═══ Minor road

Sights at a Glance

❶ Feria de Mataderos
❷ Tigre and the Delta
❸ Isla Martín García
❹ Colonia del Sacramento

❶ Feria de Mataderos

Road map C3. Lisandro de la Torre & Ave de los Corrales, Barrio de Mataderos. **Tel** (011) 4342-9629 (Mon–Fri), (011) 4687-5602 (Sat). 🚌 55, 63, 80, 92, 103, 117, 126, 141, 155, 180. **Open** Jan & Feb: 6pm–1am Sat; Apr–Dec: 11am–8pm Sun. 🔳 feriademataderos.com.ar

Buenos Aires's weekly Feria de Mataderos is a day-long artisans' fair, street party, and gaucho hoedown combined into one. The idea behind the event is to showcase 300 local arts and crafts from Argentina's interior provinces. There is a wide array of items to pick up, including handcrafted *mate* gourds from Misiones and ponchos from Catamarca.

Visitors can also sample traditional regional delicacies such as *locro* (stew), *tamales* (steamed meat parcels), and empanadas (stuffed pastry). Skillful gaucho equestrian feats are performed and a variety of folk music is played, including the lively *chamamé*, an accordion-based folkloric style from the Litoral region. Audience participation is actively encouraged. The Feria de Mataderos attracts a few folk musicians of international renown, such as Victor Heredia and Chango Spasiuk.

❷ Tigre and the Delta

Road map C3. 17 miles (27 km) N of Buenos Aires. 🚶 301,000. 🚇 🚌 60. 🚢 daily. 🔳 tigre.gov.ar

Founded in 1820, Tigre was named for the jaguars hunted in the area by the first European settlers. Its location at the neck of the Paraná Delta made it an important port city, and for decades its quaysides were piled with timber and fruit shipped in from upriver farms and from the islands of the delta itself.

Tigre's port, Puerto de Frutos, holds a daily craft fair which draws thousands of tourists and locals. The city also has quiet, leafy, cobblestoned streets flanked by elegant neo-colonial mansions. The most impressive of them is the imposing Club de la Marina, built in 1876.

Charming though Tigre is, its main appeal is as a jumping-off point for river trips into the

Ferry used to transport visitors in Tigre

Paraná Delta, a diluvial natural labyrinth comprising over 6,500 miles (10,500 km) of canals, rivers, and marshes, as well as countless islands. Many of these river islands are home to small and self-sufficient communities; others are privately owned and built over with smart and exclusive weekend residences, restaurants, watersport centers, and lodgings. The islands can easily be reached by river bus from the Estacíon Fluvial in Tigre or by chartered rides on one of the many boats moored in Puerto de Frutos.

Jacaranda blossoms covering a path at Isla Martín García

❸ Isla Martín García

Road map D3. Río de la Plata. 🏔 150. 🚢 from Tigre, daily.

Although comprising a small area of land, Isla Martín García has been fought over by Spain, Brazil, Portugal, Uruguay, Britain, and France; it was finally conquered by the Argentinian Navy in 1886. The island's fortifications were used as prisons and many A-list political detainees did stretches here, including Presidents Hipólito Yrigoyen and Marcelo T. de Alvear. A thorough account of Isla Martín García's long and violent history is related through the displays in the small **Museo Histórico**, located near the center of the island, close to the old lighthouse. One of the conditions of the

1973 Argentina–Uruguay treaty, which ended the sovereignty squabble, was that the island be converted into a nature preserve. Now, Isla Martín García has a strong reputation among ornithologists, and visitors come for the flora and fauna as much as for the fortifications. There are over 200 species of birds found here, including parrots, woodpeckers, white herons, falcon-like *chimangos*, and snail kites.

❹ Colonia del Sacramento

Road map D3. 🏔 26,000. 🚢 from Puerto Madero.

Founded by the Portuguese in 1680, Colonia del Sacramento is a sleepy coastal Uruguayan town whose Barrio Histórico has been preserved intact since the colonial era. In recognition of this, and to guard against intrusive development, the district was declared a UNESCO World Heritage Site in 1996.

After a century-long fight, the town was ceded by its founders to the Spanish in the late 1770s, who held it until the Independence wars. Portuguese and Spanish influences resulted in the cobblestoned streets, leafy plazas, elegant churches, and stucco-façaded mansions that abound in Barrio Histórico.

Around the town's fig and palm-tree-lined central square, Plaza Mayor, are a number of museums and historical buildings. These include the **Museo Portugués**, with excellent samples of maps on

The serene interior of the Iglesia Matriz, Colonia del Sacramento

the Portuguese voyages of discovery, and the **Museo Municipal**, which houses an array of indigenous artifacts. To the east of the plaza is the Iglesia Matriz, Uruguay's oldest church, with religious artworks that date back over two centuries. Leading off from the square is Calle de los Suspiros (Street of Sighs), one of the region's most-photographed lanes, paved with rough cobblestones and flanked by colonial houses.

Visitors can end their day with a stroll on the beach watching the sunset after a meal at one of the town's excellent restaurants.

🏛 **Museo Portugués**
Casa Historica, Calle de San Pedro, in front of Plaza Mayor.
Open 11:15am–4:45pm daily. 🖼

🏛 **Museo Municipal**
Calle del Comercio, in front of Plaza Mayor. **Open** 11:15am–4:45pm daily. 🖼

One of the picturesque cobblestoned streets in Colonia del Sacramento

SHOPPING IN BUENOS AIRES

Buenos Aires has more upscale malls and smart fashion boutiques than any other city in Latin America. The many great bargains on offer here make the capital a shopper's delight. Leather bags and jackets, silverware, and antiques are the classic purchases for visitors, while handicrafts from across Argentina are available at specialist stores and markets, such as the popular Feria Plaza Francia and Feria de San Pedro Telmo. Even non-fashionistas should take a stroll round Palermo Viejo to see the amazing range of homespun designs and fabrics on show. Buenos Aires is home to thousands of small retailers, ranging from textile outlets in the bustling neighborhoods to stylish delis and wine stores selling boutique products and offering a personalized shopping experience.

Crafts and Gifts

Although the best traditional handicrafts are found in Argentina's interior provinces, where they are locally made, it is definitely worth exploring the craft shops in Buenos Aires. Most souvenir shops cluster around the downtown area, on and off the famous shopping street, Calle Florida. **Kelly's** stocks a wide range of pottery, weavings, *mate* gourds, and all manner of ornaments featuring the Argentinian national colors. **Tierra Adentro** is a smart store for high-end collectibles and native musical instruments. There are beautiful ponchos for sale at **Arte Étnico Argentino**, in Palermo Viejo. For quirky gifts, visit **Calma Chicha**. As well as cowhide cushions, rugs, and leather bags, the shop also specializes in traditional Argentinian crafts with a modern twist. Tango-themed souvenirs are very popular.

An array of items at Feria de San Pedro Telmo, San Telmo barrio

Leather jackets, bags, and ponchos at a gaucho shop

Tango memorabilia is stocked at **Zival's**, an emporium on the corner of Callao and Corrientes. There is a well-established industry in kitsch artwork and, increasingly, tango fashion. For a range of interesting collectibles, including wonderful old posters, T-shirts, and ancient musical scores, visit the **Club de Tango**.

For visitors wishing to purchase original jewelry, there are ornate contemporary silver creations at **María Medici** and more ethnic necklaces and earrings at **Plata Nativa**.

Art and Antiques

There are more than 20 small commercial galleries in the downtown area of Buenos Aires. These include well-established showcases such as the **Ruth Benzacar** gallery and **Fundación Federico Klemm**, and those such as **Galería Rubbers** and **Daniel Abate**, which concentrate on emerging Argentinian painters and sculptors. Located in Palermo is **Elsi del Rio**, another gallery with an eye for promising young artists.

Calle Defensa in San Telmo has a string of antique stores, stocking anything from early 20th-century gramophones to 18th-century statues and original wooden trunks used by early European immigrants. **Mercado de Pulgas** is a dusty flea market in Palermo Viejo that sells clocks, glass soda bottles, ceramic vases, paintings, and even old cars and wooden beds. **Gil Antigüedades** stocks lovely silver-plated *mate* gourds and Victorian clothing, while **HB Antigüedades**, located in an old mansion, displays an array of interesting items that some shoppers may find gaudy.

Fashion

Palermo Viejo is the epicenter of Argentina's haute couture industry, while Recoleta remains the barrio for more traditional fashions. Some designers, such as Martin Churba of **Tramando**, have already made it big on catwalks in Milan and New York; others, such as mid-range designers **Ona Sáez** and **Juana de Arco**, are well-liked by porteños for their chic and urban designs. Popular fashions tend to follow European trends fairly closely, so large shopping malls stock Armani, Louis Vuitton, and other well-known international designers.

For menswear, check out the creations of **Hermanos Estebecorena**, while for cool porteño trends visit **Félix**. Located close by, on Calles Murillo and Scalabrini Ortíz, are several excellent leather shops offering their wares at near-wholesale prices. There are many shops that specialize in children's clothes in the capital, and there are even boutiques that sell haute couture for babies only a couple of months old. **Owoko** in Palermo Viejo is a bright and bubbly emporium, selling pyjamas, dresses, T-shirts, and trendy trousers. A free kids' storybook is given away with every purchase. Another popular clothes shop here is **Cheeky**, which has seasonal collections and purveys a more classic, stylish line in urban gear for young people.

Lingerie and Swimwear

There are numerous high-street stores in Buenos Aires known for selling good-quality lingerie. Even small neighborhood under-wear shops dress their windows in lace and satin finery. The biggest name in the country is **Caro Cuore**, which sells lingerie for women at fairly reasonable prices. The brand has branches in the malls and is stocked by all general retailers.

To cover all bases, from maternity lingerie to something exotic and daring involving lace and fluff, check out **Peter Pan**'s vast selection, especially their strong line in animal-print undies.

For sporty swimwear, there are dozens of excellent sports gear shops located all over the capital, including branches of **Stock Center**. The local fashion retailer, **Salsipuedes**, stocks its own swimming trunks and Al Ver Veras bikinis.

Newspapers, Books, and Music

As in all Argentinian cities, the *kiosko* (newspaper stand) is a popular sight in Buenos Aires. The capital of Latin America's most literate country has a diverse and generally high-quality press. There are

The Ateneo Grand Splendid bookshop

tango *kioskos* in Corrientes, ones that sell law-related books and magazines in the Tribunales area, and posh stands at the airport selling coffee-table books and the latest novels. Newspapers, magazines, and literature can all be obtained at the *kioskos* in Recoleta and Microcentro.

The English-language *Buenos Aires Herald* is sold in many of the centrally located stands. For a wide range of English-language books, visit **Ateneo Grand Splendid** on Avenida Santa Fe and also its branches along Calle Florida. Another good choice is **KEL Ediciones** branch, which is also very popular with English students and teachers.

More sought out by tourists are coffee-table picture books and fancy editions of famous Argentinian classics, such as Borges's poems and short stories and *Martín Fierro* by José Hernández. These are available at branches of **Libros del Pasaje** and **Cúspide**. The former has an outlet in Palermo Viejo and the latter has a branch in the Recoleta Village mall. Zival's is well-known for tango books and also offers an excellent and extensive range of Argentinian tango, folk, jazz, and rock CDs. Branches of **Musimundo**, found throughout the city, are often cheaper for best-selling CDs.

A shop selling a wide range of leather goods, Recoleta

Wine and Food

The boom in delis and wine stores is relatively new, pushed on by the increasing number of wealthy tourists in the city looking for good wines and local products. Travelers not bound for the Mendoza region should definitely explore the wine shops in the capital. For personal service, which includes wine tastings, go to **Ligier**. They also help with organizing overseas shipping. **Winery** is a smart wine supermarket with a range of stock from all regions, while **Lo de Joaquin Alberdi** is more focused on boutique vintages from Mendoza.

There are *panaderías* (bakeries) throughout the city, and most high streets have *dietéticas* (health stores) stocking vitamins, whole-grain biscuits, diet products, and snacks. *Confiterías* (large cafés) and bars sell fresh pastries and sandwiches; the latter delicious at **Pain et Vin**. To try the city's best *medialunas* (sweet croissants), visit **Dos Escudos**.

La Casa del Queso stocks mild, milky cheeses and cured meats from the provinces as well as antipasto, breads, and other bites. **La Fondue: Gourmet Food Shop** also stocks cheeses and other gourmet treats. To try an *alfajor*, the local cookie, visit **Havanna**, which has outlets all across the city.

Stall in popular flea market, Feria de San Pedro Telmo, San Telmo

Markets

The best handicraft markets in Argentina are found in the towns and cities of the interior, especially those where indigenous and mestizo cultures continue to thrive. For those who are limited to buying in the capital, the **Feria Artesanal Plaza Francia** is good for bags, *mate* gear, and jewelry.

The larger **Feria de San Pedro Telmo**, on Plaza Dorrego, stocks tango souvenirs, old vinyl, and low-grade antiques. The Mercado de Pulgas is a great place for a rummage: this huge warehouse is full of rusty old lamps, brass beds, books, and scratched records. Bargains are available for those furnishing houses or aiming at a retro look for a bar or restaurant. Out on the western edge of the capital is the Feria de Mataderos *(see p120)*. At this bustling gaucho-themed flea market, look for works by Florencio Molina Campos, the country's best-known cartoonist. His excellent sketches for the calendars of the Compañia Argentina de Alpargatas are collector's items all over the world.

Shopping Malls

Buenos Aires's oldest shopping center, **Patio Bullrich** stocks exclusive designer wear: Dior, Versace, and Ralph Lauren, as well as beautiful Argentinian couture creations. The grand Galerías Pacífico *(see p95)* was renovated in the late 1990s, and is now a multitiered emporium of high-street fashion outlets, shoe shops, and gift *kioskos*.

Alto Palermo and the larger, more handsome **Abasto** are good for perfumes and health shops. They also house popular local chains such as **Chocolate** and **María Vázquez. Unicenter** is a classic US-style mall, with huge electrical and white goods stores. *Galerías* (small malls) offer less expensive clothes and ornaments, and **Galería Bond Street** off Santa Fe stocks "goth" and alternative fashionwear. Recoleta is also home to the new **Recoleta Mall**, which overlooks the cemetery.

The spacious and elegant interior of the Patio Bullrich shopping mall

DIRECTORY

Crafts and Gifts

Arte Étnico Argentino
El Salvador 4656.
City Map 5 D4.
Tel (011) 4832-0516.

Calma Chicha
Honduras 4909.
City Map 5 D4.
Tel (011) 4831-1818.

Club de Tango
Paraná 123, 5th Floor.
City Map 2 C3.
Tel (011) 4372-7251.

Kelly's
Paraguay 431.
City Map 3 E4.

María Medici
Niceto Vega 4619.
City Map 4 C4.
Tel (011) 4773-2283.

Plata Nativa
Galería Del Sol,
Florida 860.
City Map 3 E4.
Tel (011) 4312-1398.

Tierra Adentro
Arroyo 882.
City Map 3 D3.
Tel (011) 4393-8552.

Zival's
Ave Callao 395.
City Map 2 C4.
Tel (011) 5128-7500.
W zivals.com

Art and Antiques

Daniel Abate
Pasaje Bollini 2170.
City Map 2 C2.
Tel (011) 4804-8247.

Elsi del Rio
Humboldt 1510.
City Map 4 C4.
Tel (011) 4899-0171.

Fundación Federico Klemm
Marcelo T. de Alvear 626.
City Map 3 E4.
Tel (011) 4312-3334.

Galería Rubbers
Alvear 1595.
City Map 3 D3.
Tel (011) 4816-1864.

Gil Antigüedades
Humberto Primo 412.
City Map 1 E2.

HB Antigüedades
Defensa 1016.
City Map 1 E1.
Tel (011) 4361-3325.

Mercado de Pulgas
Niceto Vega & Dorrego,
Colegiales.
City Map 5 D4.

Ruth Benzacar
Florida 1000. **City Map** 3
E4. **Tel** (011) 4313-8480.
W ruthbenzacar.com

Fashion

Cheeky
Abasto, Ave Corrientes
3247. **City Map** 2 A4.
Tel (011) 4959-3549.

Félix
Gurruchaga 1670.
City Map 5 D4.
Tel (011) 4832-2994.

Hermanos Estebecorena
El Salvador 5960.
City Map 4 C3.

Juana de Arco
El Salvador 4762.
City Map 5 D4.

Ona Sáez
Ave Santa Fe 1651.
City Map 1 C3.

Owoko
El Salvador 4694.
City Map 5 D4.
Tel (011) 4831-1259.

Tramando
Rodriguez Peña 1973.
City Map 3 D3.
Tel (011) 4811-0465.

Lingerie and swimwear

Caro Cuore
Galerías Pacifico local 235.
City Map 3 E4.

Peter Pan
Florida 371.
City Map 3 E5.
Tel (011) 4305-1005.

Salsipuedes
Honduras 4814.
City Map 5 D4.

Stock Center
Abasto, Ave Corrientes
3247. **City Map** 2 A4.
Tel (011) 4123-2302.

Newspapers, Books, and Music

Ateneo Grand Splendid
Ave Santa Fe 1860. **City
Map** 2 C3.

Buenos Aires Herald
W buenosairesherald.
com

Cúspide
Santa Fe 1818.
City Map 2 C3.
Tel (011) 4811-6325.
W cuspide.com

KEL Ediciones
Marcelo T de Alvear 1369.
City Map 3 D3.
Tel (011) 4814-3788.
W kelediciones.com

Libros del Pasaje
Thames 1762,
Palermo Viejo.
City Map 5 D4.

Musimundo
Ave Corrientes 1753.
City Map 2 C4.
Tel (011) 4393-8552.
W musimundo.com

Wines and Food

Dos Escudos
Montevideo 1690.
City Map 3 D3.
Tel (011) 4812-2517.

Havanna
Florida 159. **City Map** 3
E5. W havanna.com.ar

La Casa del Queso
Ave Corrientes 3587.
City Map 2 A4.
Tel (011) 4862-4794.

La Fondue: Gourmet Food Shop
Salguero 3069.
City Map 5 F3.
Tel (011) 4806-8958.

Ligier
Ave Santa Fe 790.
City Map 3 E3.
Tel (011) 5353 8060.
W vinotecaligier.com

Lo de Joaquin Alberdi
Borges 1772.
Tel (011) 4832-5329.
City Map 5 D4.

Pain et Vin
Gorriti 5132
City Map 4 C4.
Tel 4832-5654.

Winery
Ave Corrientes 300.
City Map 3 E4.
Tel (011) 4394-2203.
W winery.com.ar

Markets

Feria Artesanal Plaza Francia
Plaza Francia, Recoleta.
City Map 2 C2.

Feria de San Pedro Telmo
Plaza Dorrego, San Telmo.
City Map 1 E1.

Shopping Malls

Abasto
Ave Corrientes 3247.
City Map 2 A4.
Tel (011) 4959-3400.
W abasto-shopping.
com.ar

Alto Palermo
Ave Santa Fe 3253.
City Map 2 A2.
Tel (011) 5777-8000.
W altopalermo.com.ar

Chocolate
Alto Palermo Shopping
Mall. **City Map** 2 A2.
Tel (011) 5777-8072.

Galería Bond Street
Ave Santa Fe 1670.
City Map 2 C3.

María Vázquez
Salguero 3172.
City Map 2 B1.
Tel (011) 5777-6500.

Patio Bullrich
Ave del Libertador 750.
City Map 3 D3.
Tel (011) 4814-7400.
W shoppingbullrich.
com.ar

Recoleta Mall
Vicente López 2050.
City Map 2 C3.
W recoletamall.com.ar

Unicenter
Paraná 3745, Martínez.
City Map 2 C3.
W unicenter.com.ar

ENTERTAINMENT IN BUENOS AIRES

One of the great capitals for arts and leisure, Buenos Aires impresses visitors from across the world with its cultural variety. Porteños have an insatiable appetite for theater, sports, music, and just about any event that brings people together. On a Sunday, strolling around Parque 3 de Febrero, visitors can watch an impromptu soccer match and spot people picnicking under the trees or drinking mate. Visitors can see gauchos competing in equestrian events at Feria de Mataderos, or watch a soccer match at one of the capital's numerous stadiums. The cultural calendar through the year *(see pp44–7)* includes the annual Feria del Libro in April, and February's International Tango Festival which gives everyone an opportunity to test their feet with a few steps of the national dance.

Music poster for a Beatles tribute show on Avenida Corrientes

Entertainment Guides and Tickets

There are myriad sources of entertainment information available in the capital. The well-known London listings magazine **Time Out** has a franchise in Buenos Aires that publishes a visitors' guide twice a year. Every Tuesday to Saturday, the *Buenos Aires Herald (see p123)* publishes a section called getOut! covering both English and Spanish language film, theater, exhibitions, and other entertainment events. Both the major national newspapers, **Clarín** and **La Nación**, also publish entertainment guides on Fridays. For tango fans, the specialist listings magazine **El Tangauta** is available at *kioskos* in the downtown area and covers tango events across the city.

Tickets for a range of entertainment events can be bought at **Ticketmaster** and **Ticketek**. For cheap seats at theaters and shows, there are several branches of **Cartelera Baires** ticket outlets on Calle Lavalle in the city center. For a major sporting event or soccer match, it is advisable to talk to a hotel concierge or contact the local ground agent. **Curiocity** and **Tangol** are both highly recommended local agents who sort out everything from transport to seats, and even ensure security.

Music and Dance

A handful of venues provide stages for major national and international shows for folk rock, UK and US rock stars, and offbeat composers. **Teatro Opera** and **Gran Rex** are good venues for rock, classical, and world music, while **ND Ateneo** and **La Trastienda** are more intimate venues for tango, folk, jazz, and fusion. **Luna Park**, a former boxing arena, is an important venue for *cumbia*, salsa, and other Latin music performances, and shows by international bands. **Notorious**, a smart CD store with a café and restaurant, is a great venue for edgy jazz and virtuoso rock-crossover gigs. **Estadio Obras** in the Nuñez district is de rigueur for alternative rock bands and music festivals, previously featuring Radiohead, Iggy Pop, and the Red Hot Chili Peppers.

Belgrano's **Monumental Stadium** is the main venue for huge crowd-pullers such as U2 and the Rolling Stones, and Argentinian mass-market performers such as Bersuit Vergarabat, Los Piojos, and Soda Stereo. La Boca's La Bombonera *(see p89)*, and various other large soccer grounds have hosted international performers such as the Bee Gees, Peter Gabriel, and Mercedes Sosa. Tickets are not available at the stadiums, as they are merely venues and do not manage the promotional aspects of concerts.

A jazz concert at the popular restaurant Notorious

A tango show in progress in a theater in Buenos Aires

Tango Shows and Classes

The range of tango on show is infinite. For high-quality glitzy shows, head to **La Esquina de Carlos Gardel** or **Piazzolla Tango** in the Abasto neighborhood. **Señor Tango** has been around for years but is a rather corporate affair. **Bar Sur** is a smaller venue and is an ideal place to listen to the singers upclose.

Milongas (see p83) offer a far more authentic tango experience. The **Centro Cultural Torquato Tasso** and **Club Gricel** host events that welcome both diehard dancers and curious visitors. The **Confitería Ideal** is a good place for an atmospheric and aesthetic music and dance experience. This old café holds tango classes for beginners in the afternoon. On Tuesdays and Fridays, there are *milongas* from 11pm with a live band playing under dim lights, and just a handful of couples on a dance floor swirling with tobacco smoke.

Most *milonga* nights are preceded by a tango class. Local agents such as Tangol or Curiocity arrange tango tours for visitors.

Bars and Clubs

Buenos Aires's bars and clubs are an ideal place to while away time, or to meet interesting people from the city. Most of them are open until the early hours, which leaves a lot of time to explore the city's many nightlife options. **Dadá** and **La Cigale** are some well-known places with a vibrant bar scene. Calle Báez in Las Cañitas is mainly known as a popular hangout to check out TV celebrities and soccer stars. For expatriates, **Sugar** and **Casa Bar** are more than convivial. If you want to play the porteño part to perfection, go to Café Tortoni *(see p72)* or Confitería Ideal to try local whiskeys or liqueurs such as Legui or Cynar. To enjoy a drink with Argentinian folk, a good option is to head

Outside Café Tortoni

for Plazoleta Cortazar in Palermo Viejo and cruise down to Avenida Honduras or Borges. Also an excellent place to sip coffee and cognac in the city is Café La Biela *(see pp102–3)* in Recoleta. Some of the coolest nightclubs include **Niceto Club** and **Mandarine** for the stylish crowd, and **El Living**, which draws a more mixed clientele. Visit **Groove** to see authentic *cumbia (see p32)*. Fans of Brazilian samba and dancing can head for **Maluco Beleza** in the Tribunales barrio.

Classical Music and Theater

Many venues listed for music and dance are also sometimes the venues for classical composers and theater groups. Other venues with a classical repertory include Teatro Colón *(see pp76–7)*, Teatro Avenida *(see p72)*, **Auditorio San Rafael** in Nuñez, and the **Catedral de San Isidro**, which is located in San Isidro.

Theater in Buenos Aires is classified as "Corrientes" and "off-Corrientes." The former is lined with huge theaters offering amateur revues that usually feature small-time celebrities. For a more artistic experience, Teatro General San Martín *(see p78)* or Teatro Nacional Cervantes *(see pp74–5)* are good places to stop by. Off-Corrientes venues such as **Espacio Callejón** or **Grupo de Teatro Catalinas Sur** in La Boca also offer a stimulating night out. The latter has been putting on fabulous performances for over 20 years by mixing various European art forms such as opera and *zarzuela*. The biennial **Festival Internacional de Buenos Aires**, held for a fortnight in September, includes a range of national and international theater, dance, and musical performances.

Match between Boca Juniors and River Plate at La Bombonera

Spectator Sports

Major sporting events such as rugby internationals and high-profile race days attract large crowds, while a soccer international or a *clásico* (a derby match between two historic rivals) draws multitudes. Any game between leading soccer teams is unforgettable, while a *superclásico*, a match between Boca Juniors and River Plate, is a clash of national importance. River Plate's Monumental Stadium is big but not very atmospheric, while La Boca's La Bombonera is usually filled with a passionate audience. Other major matches are held at the **Vélez Sarsfield** and **Ferrocarril Oeste**. Marred by violence off the pitch, soccer matches should ideally be attended in the company of locals who are familiar with security arrangements.

Major horse races held at Hipódromo Argentino de Palermo *(see p113)* and **Hipódromo de San Isidro** attract large crowds, as do games at Campo Argentino Polo de Palermo *(see p113)*.

Another popular sport is tennis. Tickets for the Davis Cup and Copa Telmex, and other matches featuring national heroes such as David Nalbandian, Gaston Gaudio, and Guillermo Coria are much sought after. Visitors can buy tickets only at **Asociación Argentina de Tenis**.

Rugby Union is popular in Argentina, especially in Buenos Aires and Tucumán, and there

are several clubs in the northern suburbs of the capital. The competitions are held mainly in Buenos Aires and in Punta del Este. The official website of **Unión Argentina de Rugby** has a schedule of national and international tournaments.

Playing Sports

Porteños are usually active people and most use their local park or the huge green swathe of parks and plazas between Museo de Bellas Artes and Parque 3 de Febrero for jogging and cycling, thanks to the *bicisendas* (bike lanes).

There are gyms all over Buenos Aires; many of the smartest are in five-star hotels and it is easy to get a day pass there. To take a swim, some clubs such as the **Club de Amigos** issue day passes. Many branches of the **Megatlon Gym** chain in the city also have pools. Anyone keen to warm up their equestrian talents, or planning a visit to an estancia or a

cross-country trek, can take a class at **Club Alemán** or **Club Hípico**, both in Palermo. For visitors who prefer an adventurous holiday, the **Renosto Nautica y Deportes** club in San Fernando in Greater Buenos Aires organizes waterskiing and wakeboarding.

Entertainment for Children

The people of Buenos Aires adore children and they are welcomed everywhere. The *heladerías* (ice-cream parlors) in the city are sure to keep children smiling. There is often a circus passing through the capital, and mimes and jugglers, found everywhere in the city, will also keep children occupied. Buenos Aires is proud of its clowns and puppeteers, and to see a free show visit **La Calle de los Titeres** in the Constitución barrio. However, it is advisable to check if the show is aimed only at Spanish-speaking audiences.

Several major venues are designed for children, including the **Museo de los Niños** in the Abasto shopping mall. The museum takes children on tours, introducing them to career options ranging from medicine, construction industries, and fast food. Also popular is the main city zoo, the Jardín Zoológico *(see p111)* which has 89-odd species of mammals. The **Parque de la Costa**, an out-of-town amusement park, can be reached by train through the northern suburbs. Another park located outside the capital is the wildlife park, **Bioparque Temaikén**.

Cyclists at Parque 3 de Febrero in Palermo

DIRECTORY

Entertainment Guides and Tickets

Cartelera Baires
Ave Corrientes 1382.
City Map 3 D4.
Tel (011) 4372-5058.
w cartelerabaires.com

Clarín
w clarin.com.ar

Curiocity
Juncal 2021, Piso 4.
Tel (011) 4803-1113.
w curiocitytravel.com

El Tangauta
w eltanguata.com

La Nación
w lanacion.com.ar

Tangol
Tel (011) 4363-6000.
w tangol.com

Ticketek
Tel (011) 5237-7200.
w ticketek.com.ar

Ticketmaster
Tel (011) 4321-9700.

Time Out
w timeout.com/
buenosaires

Music and Dance

Estadio Obras
Ave del Libertador 7395.
Tel (011) 4702-3223.

Gran Rex
Ave Corrientes 857.
City Map 3 D4.
Tel (011) 4322-8000.

La Trastienda
Balcarce 460.
City Map 1 E1.
Tel (011) 4342-7650.

Luna Park
Bouchard 465.
City Map 3 E4.
Tel (011) 5279-5279.

Monumental Stadium
Ave Figueroa Alcorta
7597. Tel (011) 4789-1200.

ND Ateneo
Paraguay 918.
City Map 3 D4.
Tel (011) 4328-2888.

Notorious
Ave Callao 966.
City Map 2 C4.
Tel (011) 4813-6888.
w notorious.com.ar

Teatro Opera
Ave Corrientes 860.
City Map 3 D4.
Tel (011) 4326-1335.
w operaciti-teatro.
com.ar

Tango Shows and Classes

Bar Sur
Estados Unidos 299.
City Map 1 E1.
Tel (011) 4362-6086.

**Centro Cultural
Torquato Tasso**
Defensa 1575.
City Map 1 E2.
Tel (011) 4307-6506.
w torquatotasso.com.ar

Club Gricel
La Rioja 1180.
Tel (011) 4957-7157.
w clubgriceltango.
com.ar

Confitería Ideal
Suipacha 384.
City Map 3 D4.
Tel (011) 5265-8069.

**La Esquina de Carlos
Gardel**
Carlos Gardel 3200,
Almagro.
Tel (011) 4867-6363.
w esquinacarlos
gardel.com.ar

Piazzolla Tango
Guemes Gallery, Florida
165/San Martín 170.
Tel (011) 4344-8200.
w piazzollatango.com

Señor Tango
Vieytes 1655.
Tel (011) 4303-0231.
w senortango.com.ar

Bars and Clubs

Casa Bar
Rodriguez Peña 1150.
City Map 2 C3.
Tel (011) 4816-2712.

Dadá
San Martín 941.
City Map 3 E4.
Tel (011) 4314-4787.

El Living
Marcelo T. de Alvear 1540.
Tel (011) 4811-4730.

La Cigale
25 de Mayo 597.
City Map 3 E4.
Tel (011) 4893-2332.

Maluco Beleza
Sarmiento 1728.
City Map 2 C4.
Tel (011) 4372-1737.

Groove
Ave Santa Fe 4389.
City Map 5 D3.

Mandarine
Ave Costanera Rafael
Obligado.
Tel (011) 4771-5870.

Niceto Club
w nicetoclub.com

Sugar
Costa Rica 4619.
City Map 5 D4.
Tel (011) 4831-3276.

Classical Music and Theater

Auditorio San Rafael
Ramallo 2606, Nuñez.
w fundacionsanrafael.
com.ar

**Catedral de San
Isidro**
Ave del Libertador 16199.
Tel (011) 4743-0291.

Espacio Callejón
Humahuaca 3759.
Tel (011) 4862-1167.

**Festival Internacional
de Buenos Aires**
w festivaldeteatroba.
gob.ar

**Grupo de Teatro
Catalinas Sur**
Benito Perez Galdós 93.
City Map 1 F3.
w catalinasur.com.ar

Spectator Sports

**Asociación Argentina
de Tenis**
w aat.com.ar

Ferrocarril Oeste
w ferrocarriloeste.
com.ar

**Hipódromo de San
Isidro**
w hipodromosan
isidro.com

**Unión Argentina
de Rugby**
w uar.com.ar

Vélez Sarsfield
Ave Juan B. Justo 9200.
Tel (011) 4641-5663.
w velezsarsfield.
com.ar

Playing Sports

Club Alemán
Ave Corrientes 327.
City Map 5 E1.
Tel (011) 4311-0716.
w clubaleman.com.ar

Club de Amigos
Ave Figueroa Alcorta
3885. City Map 5 F2.
Tel (011) 4801-1213.
w clubdeamigos.
org.ar

Club Hípico
Ave Figueroa
Alcorta 7285.
City Map 5 F2.
Tel (011) 4787-1003.

Megatlon Gym
w megatlon.com

**Renosto Nautica
y Deportes**
Ave del Libertador 2136,
San Fernando.
City Map 2 B2.
Tel (011) 4744-4400.

Entertainment for Children

Bioparque Temaikén
Ruta Provincial 25, Km1,
Escobar.
Tel (03488) 443-6900.
w temaiken.org.ar

La Calle de los Titeres
Ave Caseros 1750.

Museo de los Niños
Ave Corrientes 3247. Tel
(011) 4861-2325.
w museoabasto.
org.ar/

Parque de la Costa
Vivanco 1509.
Tel (011) 4002-6000.
w parquedelacosta.
com

BUENOS AIRES STREET FINDER

The map given below shows the different areas of Buenos Aires covered by the street finder maps – Plaza de Mayo and Microcentro, San Telmo and La Boca, Plaza San Martín and Retiro, Recoleta, and Palermo and Belgrano. The map references given in the text for places of interest, hotels, restaurants,

entertainment venues, and shops refer to these maps. Map references are also given for hotels *(see pp278–283)* and restaurants *(see pp288–299)*. The first figure in the map reference indicates which Street Finder map to turn to, and the letter and number which follow refer to the grid reference on that map.

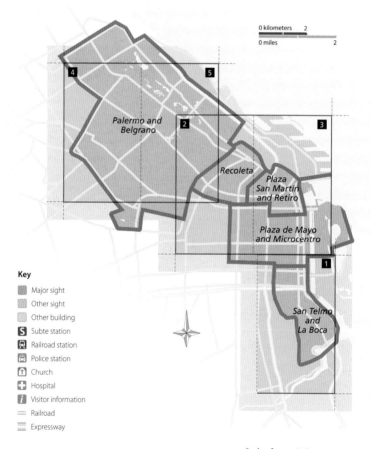

0 kilometers 2
0 miles 2

Key

🟦 Major sight
⬜ Other sight
⬜ Other building
🅂 Subte station
🚉 Railroad station
🚔 Police station
🏛 Church
➕ Hospital
ℹ️ Visitor information
═══ Railroad
▬▬▬ Expressway

Scale of maps 1–5

0 meters 400
0 yards 400

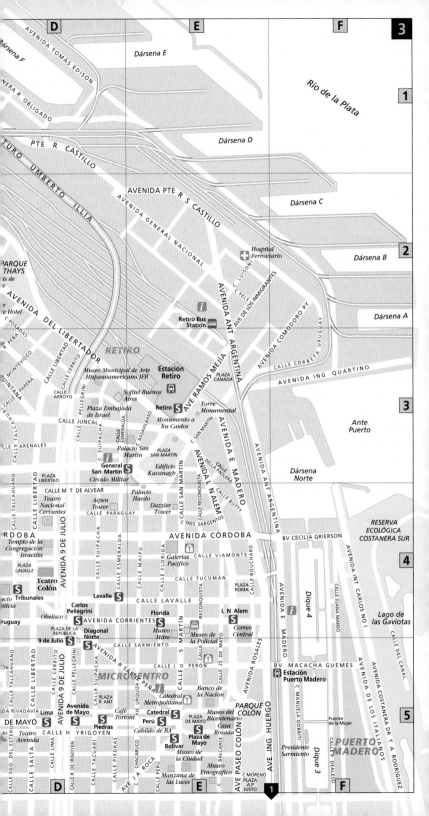

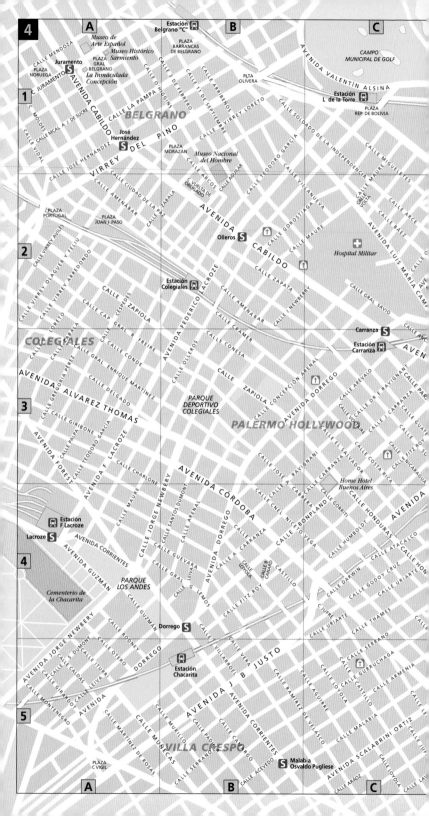

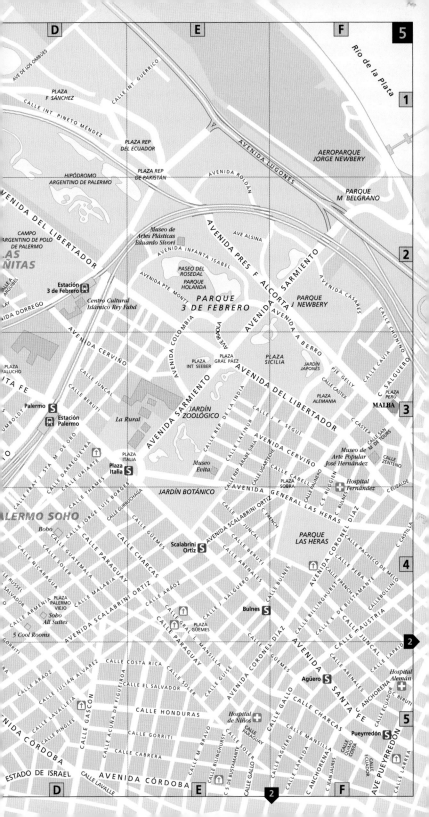

ARGENTINA REGION BY REGION

Argentina at a Glance

By virtue of its sheer size, Argentina has an array of varied and magnificent landforms. The central Pampas is characterized by vast, flat, and fertile grassland, while to the west lie the rugged, snowcapped Andes. The north of Argentina has spectacular waterfalls and subtropical forests, while the south of the country is riddled with rivers, lakes, glaciers, and mountains. Wildlife is plentiful and adventure activities abound, ranging from whale-watching and trekking to white-water rafting and off-road driving. Buenos Aires, Córdoba, Rosario, and Mendoza provide urban counterpoints to Argentina's lonely, wild expanses, offering excellent museums, restaurants, hotels, and shopping opportunities.

CÓRDOBA
THE ANDE
NORTHW
(See pp180–

La R

CUYO AND
WINE COU
(See pp206–

Mendoza

The bodegas of the Mendoza region grow Malbec grapes, which produce the characteris-tic Argentinian red wine, considered among the best in the world. Home to over 1,000 vineyards, Mendoza has a sunny and mild climate through the year.

Neuq

Bariloc

PATAGO
(See pp224

Cueva de las Manos
(see p247) is a UNESCO World Heritage Site in Parque Nacional Francisco P. Moreno. The caves have more than 2,000 magnificent stencilled handprints on the walls made by adults and children, dating back around 9,500 years.

Parque Nacional Los Glaciares
(see pp254–5) is located in the Santa Cruz province. A UNESCO World Heritage Site, the park is divided into two parts – the northern sector consists of Glaciar and Lago Viedma, while the southern sector has the major glaciers Perito Moreno, Upsala, and Spegazzini.

El Calafa

◀ The Cabildo, the oldest colonial building in Salta, in the Andean Northwest

Resistencia

Corrientes

Posadas

ntiago
l Estero

**ARGENTINIAN
LITORAL**
(See pp160–179)

Córdoba

Santa Fe

Concordia

Luis

Rosario

Buenos Aires

La Plata

THE PAMPAS
(See pp140–159)

a Rosa

Mar del Plata

Bahía
Blanca

Necochea

Trelew

omodoro
ivadavia

Gallegos

**TIERRA DEL FUEGO
AND ANTARCTICA**
(See pp260–271)

**Parque Nacional
Iguazú** *(see pp176–9)*, a UNESCO World Heritage Site, has spectacular waterfalls along the Iguazú river surrounded by subtropical rainforest. The star attraction is the 2,300-ft- (700-m-) high Garganta del Diablo waterfall.

Salta *(see pp198–9)*, located at the foothills of the Andes mountains, is the charming capital city of the eponymous province. Considered Argentina's most beautiful city, it is famous for its old-style Spanish colonial architecture and stunning scenery.

0 kilometers   250

0 miles   250

**Catedral de la Inmaculada
Concepción**, located in the city of La Plata *(see pp144–7)* in the Buenos Aires province, is the largest church in Argentina. It is heavily influenced by European Gothic style and has a characteristic red-brick façade.

Elephant seal and penguin colonies dot the icy barrenness of the Tierra del Fuego landscape. This stretch of land is famous for its spectacular scenery, wildlife, and ancient glaciers.

THE PAMPAS

Solitary *ombú* trees, stunning birdlife, and grand estancias are the most visible sights on the rolling grasslands that extend from the Atlantic coast and Río de la Plata in all directions. Settled in the 18th century, the Pampas is the economic heartland of this cattle-raising, farming nation, and the iconic gaucho who oversees this domain remains a heroic archetype for many Argentinians.

The original inhabitants of the Pampas were the Querandí, who lived a semi-sedentary lifestyle on the fertile plains. During the 18th century, the Spanish colonial authorities established a frontier across the region. As the natives were forced out, ranches were established and, by the mid-19th century, wealthy families had divided up most of the land. In the chain of towns around the capital – San Miguel del Monte, Mercedes, and San Antonio de Areco – are some of the most famous estancias in the country. The introduction of new cattle breeds and, later, refrigeration and fencing led to economic booms in the late 19th century and in the 1930s and 40s. The fencing did, however, spell an end for the free-roaming habits of the gauchos. In the 20th century, the Atlantic coast became a place of rest and recreation for wealthy porteños, leading to the rapid growth of coastal towns. These beach resorts, now popular with locals and visitors alike, generate a large amount of revenue for the tourism sector, although the Pampas is the most productive in terms of agriculture and industry. In summer, backpackers and adventurous souls head for the ancient mountain ranges to the south of the province, whose slopes provide an opportunity for many outdoor activities such as mountain biking, rock climbing, and trekking. An array of gaucho activities await visitors who opt to stay at one of the many working estancias scattered in the Pampas, while exclusive tourist ranches offer luxury accommodation.

A row of fishing boats docked at the Mar del Plata port

◄ Female gaucho tending to horses at the Estancia El Ombu de Areco

Exploring the Pampas

The unrelenting plains of the Pampas region offer plenty of opportunity for horseback riding and gaucho activities at the many estancias. Away from the empty spaces, La Plata is a vibrant university city, San Antonio de Areco is a charming colonial town, and Luján houses the country's most important Catholic shrine, La Virgen de Luján. The most popular beach resorts are Mar del Plata, Villa Gesell, Miramar, and Pinamar and Necochea. Heading south, the land begins to roll and, eventually, rise to the green and dramatic mountains of the Sierra de la Ventana and Tandil, which afford an array of outdoor adventure sports.

Stained-glass detail, Catedral de la Inmaculada Concepción, La Plata

Sights at a Glance

Towns and Cities
1 *La Plata pp144–7*
2 Luján
3 San Antonio de Areco
7 Chapadmalal
10 Balcarce
11 Tandil
15 Bahía Blanca
16 Santa Rosa

Resorts
4 Mar del Plata
5 Villa Gesell
6 Pinamar
8 Miramar
9 Necochea

Estancias
14 Estancia Cerro de la Cruz

Parks and Areas of Natural Beauty
12 Sierra de la Ventana
13 Parque Provincial Ernesto Tornquist
17 Parque Nacional Lihué Calel

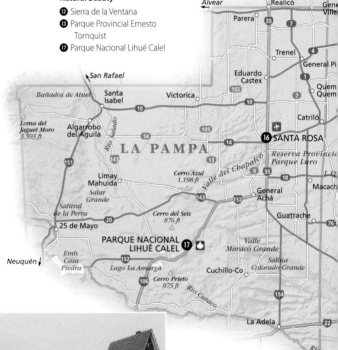

Charming houses near the beach, Pinamar

For keys to symbols *see back flap*

Getting Around

The region can be best explored by car or bus. Ruta Provincial 11 links Buenos Aires to La Plata and also offers great views of the Atlantic coast. Ruta Nacional 2 goes to Mar del Plata, while Ruta Nacional 3 is good for Sierra de la Ventana. Several highways head west across the Pampas towards Mendoza and Neuquén. Travelers need a sturdy car to explore the unmetaled backroads of the Pampas. There are flights between Buenos Aires and Mar del Plata, Bahía Blanca, and Santa Rosa.

View of the slopes of Sierra de la Ventana

Rosario

Río Paraná

178   18   188   21   9

8   Colón   Pergamino

65   General Arenales   SAN ANTONIO DE ARECO   3   12   Campana
L. Mar Chiquita   7   Junín   LUJÁN   Tigre
General Pinto   Lincoln   Mercedes   2   BUENOS AIRES   Berazategui
65   Chivilcoy   5   Lomas de Zamora   1   LA PLATA
68   Bragado   Río Salado   Lobos   11   Verónica
carlos ejedor   9 de Julio   205   Río Samborombón   11
226   Carlos Casares   Saladillo   Arroyos Saladillo   29   Chascomús   Pta. Piedras
huajó   San Carlos de Bolívar   Arroyos Vallimanca   51   Ranchos   3   Castelli   Bahía San Clemente
    Las Flores   Río Salado   57   Dolores   General Lavalle
BUENOS   AIRES   Tapalqué
65   Cerro La China 932 ft   Azul   Rauch   General Guido   11
Cochicó   86   Olavarría   Maipú   Laguna La Argentina   6   PINAMAR
ini   60   General La Madrid   51   74   5   VILLA GESELL
    Arroyos Chapaleofú   3   TANDIL   11   11
76   86   Benito Juárez   74   Sa. del Tandil 1,463 ft   29   Coronel Vidal   L. Mar Chiquita   2
    PARQUE PROVINCIAL ERNESTO TORNQUIST   Adolfo Gonzales Chaves   BALCARCE   10   226   4   MAR DEL PLATA
13   quist   12   SIERRA DE LA VENTANA   85   75   86   Lobería   7   CHAPADMALAL
14   ANCIA CERRO DE LA CRUZ   Tres Arroyos   San Cayetano   88   8   MIRAMAR
HÍA   3   Coronel Dorrego   228   73   9   NECOCHEA
NCA   Monte Hermoso

SOUTH ATLANTIC OCEAN

0 kilometers   100
0 miles   100

Key

- ▬▬▬ Expressway
- ▬▬▬ Highway
- ▬▬▬ Main road
- ▪▪▪▪ Minor road
- ▬▬▬ Railroad
- ▬▬▬ Provincial border
- △ Peak

❶ La Plata

Founded in 1882, the well-organized city of La Plata is the seat of government for Buenos Aires province. Built in under two decades, it is the country's first entirely planned city, earning it the nickname Ciudad Milagro (Miracle City). La Plata boasts several spectacular buildings, world-class museums, and two top-league soccer teams. The city center, planned in detail by French architect Pierre Benoit, consists of 23 plazas connected by broad Parisian-style boulevards lined with trees and impressive public buildings. The city has a rich and vibrant cultural life, mainly due to the three major universities that attract students from all over Argentina.

View of the sparkling white Neo-Classical Palacio de la Legislatura

🏛 Plaza Mariano Moreno

Bounded by Calles 12, 14, 54, & 50.
Catedral de la Inmaculada Concepción Tel (0221) 427-3504.
Open 9am–7pm Mon–Sat, 9am–8pm Sun & hols. 🔲 ♿ **Palacio Municipal Tel** (0221) 429-1000 ext. 291.
Open 9am–5pm Mon–Fri. 🔲🔲

Covering four blocks and located towards the southern side of the city, Plaza Mariano Moreno is a popular public space. It was here that La Plata's foundation stones were laid in 1882, along with a time capsule containing documents that record the event.

The square is lined with remarkable buildings, and foremost among these is the **Catedral de la Inmaculada Concepción**. Located on the southern edge of the plaza, it was inspired by the great Gothic cathedrals of Amiens and Cologne. The cathedral, with its unmistakable reddish brick façade and soaring 370-ft- (112-m-) high twin towers, is deservedly La Plata's most famous landmark. The corner-stone was laid in 1884, and the

church was inaugurated in 1932 to mark La Plata's 50th anniversary. It is the largest structure built in this style in the Americas, with a surface area of 75,350 sq ft (7,000 sq m) and a capacity of 14,000.

Facing the cathedral at the northern end of the square is **Palacio Municipal**. Built in the 1880s in German Renaissance style, the ivory-white complex covers over 150,700 sq ft

The red-brick façade of Catedral de la Inmaculada Concepción

(14,000 sq m), including the gardens. The star attraction is the Salón Dorado (Gold Room) on the first floor, reached via a marble staircase. The floor is made from Slavonic oak and the outstanding bronze chandeliers have 78 lamps apiece. Temporary art exhibitions as well as various civic functions are held here.

🏛 Teatro Argentino

Ave 51, between Calles 9 & 10.
Tel (0221) 429-1745. **Open** 10am–8pm Tue–Sun. 🔲 ♿ 📧 🔲 📷
🌐 **teatroargentino.gba.gov.ar**

Built in 1890, Teatro Argentino is considered the second-greatest opera venue in the country after Teatro Colón (see pp76–7). It became a reputed stage for singers from both home and abroad during the "golden age" of theater in the 1930s and 40s. The curtain fell in 1977 after the building was razed by a fire. It finally reopened in 2000 with an excellent production of Puccini's Tosca. There are now two auditoria: one is dedicated to the classical composer Alberto Ginastera, with a capacity of 2,200; and the other, with space for 300 spectators, is named after tango maestro Ástor Piazzolla, and devoted to chamber music recitals.

🏛 Palacio de la Legislatura

Plaza San Martín. **Tel** (0221) 422-0112.
Open 10am–6pm daily. 🎨 ♿ 🔲
Built in the 1880s, the Neo-Classical Palacio de la Legislatura has three principal points of entry, comprising porticoes held up by four Ionic columns and crowned with sculptural groups. Both the sculptural elements and the reliefs on the façade are allegorical representations of various events from Argentina's history, including the abolition of slavery, the May Revolution, and the Declaration of Independence. The ceiling of the grand Representative's Chamber was decorated by the well-known Argentinian painter Grazziano Mendilaharzu. It depicts a blazing sun, echoing the design of the national flag.

Casa de Gobierno nestled within its leafy garden environs

Pasaje Dardo Rocha

Plaza San Martín, Ave 7 between Calles 49 & 50. **Tel** (0221) 425-1990. **Open** 8am–10pm Tue–Sun. **Closed** Mon.

Now an excellent cultural center, Pasaje Dardo Rocha was once La Plata's railroad station until it was destroyed by fire in 1887, five years after opening. It then endured decades as a makeshift base for various organizations, including the postal service, the regional archives, and even several radio stations. In 1994, the building assumed its current and hopefully permanent role as the best multifunction cultural center in the city. Within the three-story Italianate façade and French-style slated roof there is a small arts cinema and the grand Museo de Arte Contemporáneo Latinoamericano, with its excellent displays. It also has several art galleries that cluster around a beautifully lit, columned central hall.

Casa de Gobierno

Plaza San Martín, Calle 6 between Aves 51 & 53. **Tel** (0221) 429-4185. **Open** 8am–10pm daily.

Located at the northern end of Plaza San Martín, Casa de Gobierno is a Flemish Renaissance-style building, with an impressive mansard roof and dome. It was designed by Belgian architect Julio Doral and construction began in 1882. Among its famous features are the marble staircases, the Salón Dorado (Gold Room), and the sylvan Palm Patio.

Museo de La Plata
See pp146–7.

Paseo del Bosque

Ave 1 & Plaza Rivadavia. **Open** daily.

La Plata's largest municipal park, Paseo del Bosque is an open space covering just over 150 acres (60 ha). Its leafy environs house an old-fashioned zoo with many animals, including rhinos and Patagonian foxes, as well as a botanical garden with examples of Argentina's most emblematic trees, including the *ombú* and the *ceibo*. There is an astronomical observatory that opens mainly in winter to the public. The artificial lake offers rowing boat and pedalo options, while to its west is the open-air theater, Teatro Martín Fierro, with various good productions on offer.

La Plata

1. Plaza Mariano Moreno
2. Teatro Argentino
3. Palacio de la Legislatura
4. Pasaje Dardo Rocha
5. Casa de Gobierno
6. Museo de La Plata
7. Paseo del Bosque

La Plata: Museo de La Plata

The first purpose-built museum in Latin America, opened in 1888, Museo de La Plata is an important showcase for findings as well as an academic hub. Argentina has been the location of many dramatic dinosaur finds, and the museum boasts the original skeleton of a herbivorous *Titanosaurus* and extensive collections of the extinct giant megafauna of the Cenozoic period. Geological and archaeological exhibits, including fantastic animalistic stone sculptures from the Condorhuasi culture of Catamarca, as well as old oil paintings of the huge beasts that used to roam the Pampas, complete the collection.

A saber-toothed-tiger statue at the entrance to the museum

Ethnography Gallery
On display are examples of textiles, weapons, cooking implements, jewelry, and other items used by the country's many indigenous groups. Some were collected by the museum's founder, Francisco P. Moreno.

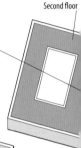
Second floor

Entomology Gallery
The entomology room is filled with various species of beetles, vividly colored butterflies such as the *Papilio thoas thoantides (above)*, and larvae and pupae at every stage of their development.

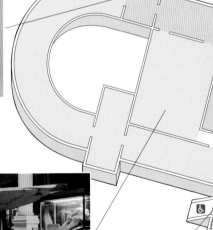

Ticket office

Entrance

★ Jawbones of the Blue Whale
Marine life is a significant part of the zoology display and the gigantic jawbones of the blue whale are a highlight. Also of note are the bird samples collected by naturalist William Henry Hudson in the 19th century.

Circular Entrance Hall
Visitors are welcomed by the sight of a beautiful domed hall, usually flooded with sunlight. The walls are decorated with paintings of the country's native animals.

VISITORS' CHECKLIST

Practical Information
Paseo del Bosque s/n.
Tel (0221) 425-7744.
Open 10am–6pm Tue–Sun.
Closed Jan 1, May 1, Dec 24, 25, & 31. 🅿️ 🎫 9am–2pm Mon–Fri. ♿ 📷
🌐 fcnym.unlp.edu.ar/museo

Transport
🚌 San Marco.

Latin American Archaeology preserves the ancient cultures of Peru and Bolivia.

★ **La Ciénaga Ceramics**
With an extensive and excellent collection, this section showcases the exquisite gray-black ceramics made by the La Ciénaga populations of Catamarca between the 2nd and 5th centuries AD.

Key

- Biological Anthropology
- Ethnography
- Latin American Archaeology
- Northwest Argentinian Archaeology
- Zoology
- Entomology
- Temporary exhibitions
- Egypt Room
- Time and Matter
- Paleontology
- The Earth
- Non-exhibition space

The Time and Matter section aims to archive geological time.

The Earth section offers an interactive approach to the cosmos.

First floor

Gallery Guide

To the right of the entrance hall is the paleontological collection, while the opposite side of the ground floor has zoological and entomological exhibits. The upper floor introduces man's role in the world. Some rooms and exhibits may be temporarily closed due to renovation work.

★ **Paleontology Gallery**
This section documents the country's many fossil findings, including the *Neuquensaurus*, which appeared in Argentina 71 million years ago.

The stunning Basílica Nuestra Señora de Luján

❷ Luján

Road map C3. 45 miles (70 km) W of Buenos Aires. 🚗 110,000. 🚊 🚌 ⓦ lujan.gov.ar

Known as La Capital de la Fe (The Capital of the Faith), Luján owes its existence to a "miracle." In 1630 a terracotta statuette of the Virgin Mary was being transported from Brazil to Peru by ox cart. At the spot where Luján's cathedral now stands, the cart got stuck. Taken as a divine hint that the statue was destined to travel no farther, a chapel was built to house the relic.

Today, Luján attracts some six million pilgrims a year; thousands make the trip from Buenos Aires on foot. There are also excellent restaurants and cafés around the town's central square.

⛪ Basílica Nuestra Señora de Luján

San Martín 51. **Tel** (02323) 420-058. **Open** 7am–8pm daily. ⏰ 10am–5pm Mon–Fri, 10am–6pm Sat & Sun. ♿ ✝ 8am, 10am, 11am, 3pm, 5pm, & 7pm Mon–Sat, hourly 8–11am, 12:30pm, 3:30pm, 5pm, & 7pm Sun. ⓦ basilicadelujan.org.ar

With its 350-ft- (106-m-) high twin spires towering majestically over the Pampas,

Luján's Neo-Gothic cathedral, and the famous relic it protects, is easily the town's biggest draw. Starting out as a small chapel, it was built up between 1887 and 1932, and has ethereal stone details and a circular stained-glass window depicting the Virgin Mary. Around this window are statues of the 12 apostles and the four evangelists. The cathedral can be entered through one of the three huge bronze doors; the terracotta statue of the Virgin Mary is stored behind the altar in the Camarín de la Vírgen.

🏛 Complejo Museográfico Enrique Udaondo

Lezica 917. **Tel** (02323) 420-245. **Open** 12:30–4:30pm Wed, 11:30am–4:30pm Thu & Fri, 10:30am–5:30pm Sat & Sun. ♿ ✆ noon–6pm Wed–Fri. 🖼

There are four museums housed within this complex, which is made up of the former *cabildo* (town hall) and Casa del Virrey (Viceroy's Residence). The principal collection is at the *cabildo*, which was once a prison; famous past inmates here include General Bartolomé

Velocipedo display, Transport Museum

Mitre *(see p54)*. The collection exhibits items related to the area's history, including a range of colonial silverware. The Gaucho Museum has exhibits illuminating the history of the gaucho, while the Transport Museum displays the country's first steam locomotive and the first Argentinian hydroplane to cross the Atlantic. The pavilion nearby has a collection of documents and mementos relating to Argentina's presidents.

Estancia Los Talas

12 miles (20 km) E of Luján. **Tel** (0230) 449-3902. 🖼 ⓦ lostalas.com
More than just another attractive ranch, Los Talas is part of Argentinian history. Built in 1824, it was confiscated by General Manuel de Rosas *(see p111)* in 1840 and returned to the original owners 12 years later, after Rosas's defeat at the Battle of Caseros. Rosas didn't stay at the ranch, but billeted some of his troops there and let his horses graze on the pastures. Now a hotel, the sprawling estancia still retains furnishings and uniforms that date from this volatile epoch. Most extraordinary is its library, one of the most important in the country, comprising over 40,000 volumes. It includes hand-written books from the 13th century, a number of editions printed before 1800, and priceless archives of the works of some of Argentina's most famous influential thinkers.

The lush environs of Complejo Museográfico Enrique Udaondo

Pulpería La Blanqueada at Museo Gauchesco Ricardo Güiraldes

❸ San Antonio de Areco

Road map C3. 70 miles (115 km) NW of Buenos Aires. ⚑ 23,000. ⛴
🎭 Día de la Tradición (weekend nearest to Nov 12). 🖳 **sanantonio deareco.com; caminopampa.com**

For a town increasingly promoted as a tourist destination, San Antonio de Areco has retained almost all of its charm and authenticity. Colonial houses line the leafy roads and working cowboys wear traditional *bombachas* (baggy trousers) and neckerchiefs. The town also has excellent restaurants and is close to some of Argentina's most exclusive estancias.

San Antonio de Areco owes much of its fame to the writer Ricardo Güiraldes *(see p35)*. His 1926 masterpiece, *Don Segundo Sombra*, is set in the area and its eponymous gaucho protagonist is famous in Argentinian literature. Güiraldes's family ranch, La Porteña, is nearby.

Pleasantly quiet for most of the year, the town comes alive in November for the Día de la Tradición, a boisterous festival of country dancing and equestrian stunts celebrating gaucho traditions.

🏛 Museo Gauchesco Ricardo Güiraldes
Caminar Güiraldes s/n. **Tel** (02326) 455-839. **Open** 11am–5pm Wed–Mon. 🎟 🎫 3:30pm Mon–Fri, 12:30pm & 3:30pm Sat, Sun. ♿
🖳 **museoguiraldes.com.ar**

Across a bridge over Río Areco at the northern edge of the town, this museum complex,

which opened in 1938, comprises several open-air and enclosed exhibition spaces. One of the best known is the Pulpería La Blanqueada, a tavern that featured in Güiraldes's *Don Segundo Sombra*. The museum is mostly dedicated to the author, though it also exhibits paintings by several Argentinian and Uruguayan artists. The building itself, with its colonial tiles, trellis windows, and patios bowered with palm trees, is a pleasant place to visit.

🏛 Taller de Platería de Patricio Draghi
Lavalle 387. **Tel** (02326) 454-219. **Open** 10am–12:30pm, 3:30–7pm daily. 🎟 🎫 🖼 🏠

José Draghi is a local silversmith with an international reputation. His workshop and museum are housed in a 19th-century Neo-Classical Italianate mansion. The pieces that Draghi, his sons Patricio and Mariano, and his team manufacture adhere

Silversmiths working at the Taller de Platería de Patricio Draghi

closely to traditional methods and classic designs of gaucho silverware, but also incorporate subtle modern twists. Visitors can watch the making of a range of items including spurs, belt buckles, belts, and stirrups. The in-house museum has two exhibition areas devoted to visual art either inspired by, or directly related to, gaucho themes. Over 180 pieces are on display at any time. Guides explain the history of gaucho silverware and the accessories that a cowboy wears.

Estancia El Ombú
5 miles (8 km) NW of San Antonio de Areco. **Tel** (02326) 492-080. 🎟 ♿
🖳 **estanciaelombu.com**

The *ombú* tree used to be known as the "lighthouse of the pampas," because it was often the only shade gauchos could find when crossing endless grasslands. It is a fitting name for a welcoming estancia that offers guests homemade food, guided horse rides, and even a round of golf. The beautiful main house was built in 1880 for General Ricchieri, whose Italian heritage helped determine the style of the pink-colored, vine-clad palazzo. The park is stunning, dotted with century-old oak trees, araucarias, eucalyptus, and, of course, *ombús*. The ranch also has a collection of old weaponry.

Silver stirrups, Taller y Museo de Platería de Patricio Draghi

Estancia La Bamba
8 miles (13 km) NW of San Antonio de Areco. **Tel** (02326) 454-895. 🎟 ♿
🖳 **labambadeareco.com**

Owned by the Aldao family for several generations, La Bamba is perfect for a taste of traditional gaucho life. Sepia-soaked family photographs line the walls and the rooms are filled with antique French furnishings. There is a reconstructed *pulpería* (small grocery store), and estancia activities such as horse riding are available. La Bamba is also famous for being the backdrop for the legendary Argentinian movie *Camila* (1984).

Cattle grazing on rich pasture near San Antonio de Areco ▶

❹ Mar del Plata

Road map C3. 250 miles (400 km) S of Buenos Aires. ✈ 🚌 📧

Founded in 1874, Mar del Plata is Argentina's seventh-largest city. Its Gothic cathedral, which has some interesting stained-glass windows, was inaugurated in 1905. Originally an important port, the city soon became a popular beach resort, attracting rich porteños from Buenos Aires.

During the 1930s and 40s, many of the resort's luxury residences were built in *pintoresco* style, which drew on European influences ranging from Swiss chalets to mock-Tudor cottages. Most of these houses, however, were demolished in the 1960s to make room for today's generic condos and skyscrapers.

Mar del Plata has long ceased to be a getaway solely for the wealthy. With the 2002 devaluation of the Argentinian peso making international trips prohibitively expensive for middle-class families, there has been a resurgence in the resort's popularity. During the peak season in January and February, the town's population swells to over three million, ensuring that its 11 miles (17 km) of beaches are always crowded. Much of Buenos Aires's entertainment, fashion, and sporting industry moves to Mar del Plata in summer, bringing with them a lively cultural scene. The city's international film festival is held in the off-season in November.

Mar del Plata's cathedral, dedicated to the apostle Peter and the martyred St. Cecilia

🏛 Museo de Arte Contemporáneo de la Provincia de Buenos Aires (MAR)

Ave Felix U. Camet & López de Gomara. **Tel** (0223) 471-6792. **Open** noon–8pm Mon, Tue, & Thu; noon–10pm Fri–Sun. 🅿 🛗 🖶 📷

A new addition to Mar del Plata's culture scene, MAR has introduced an innovative and vibrant approach to contemporary art and culture. Covering an immense 75,000 sq ft (7,000 sq m), the museum is primarily dedicated to pop works by local artistic legends such as Eduardo Gimenez and Marta Minujín, whose outdoor installation of a vast, 36-ft- (11-m-) tall sea lion greeted visitors at MAR's inauguration. The stark, cinder-block-built exterior conceals galleries, an auditorium and art-house cinema, interactive and

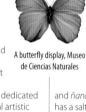

A butterfly display, Museo de Ciencias Naturales

educational facilities, and fun exhibition spaces focusing on Argentinian celebrities; one hugely popular recent display was dedicated to Pope Francis.

🏛 Museo Municipal de Ciencias Naturales Lorenzo Scaglia

Ave Libertad 3099. **Tel** (0223) 473-8791. **Open** 10am–6pm Mon, Wed–Fri; 3–6:30pm Sat. 🅿 📷 (0223) 473-8791. 🛗 🖶 📷 🌐 **mardelplata. gob.ar/museolorenzoscaglia**

Originally founded in 1938, this excellent museum houses the extensive fossil collection of Don Lorenzo Scaglia, who moved to Argentina from Italy in 1877 and settled in Buenos Aires. The museum moved to its current location in 1967. As well as exhibiting fossils from all over the world, the museum has a number of well-organized exhibition spaces devoted to different disciplines within the natural sciences, including geology, paleontology, ornithology, and taxidermy. There is a vast collection of stuffed birds, including *chimangos* and *ñandúes*. The museum also has a salt and freshwater aquarium, where visitors will find small sharks, piranhas, and some of Argentina's most common freshwater species, such as *pacú* and dorados. A trip to the museum can be followed by a meal at one of the fine seafood restaurants clustered around the port area.

A sunny day at the busy seaside resort of Mar del Plata

The exterior of Museo Municipal de Arte Juan Carlos Castagnino

🏛 Museo Municipal de Arte Juan Carlos Castagnino

Colón 1189. **Tel** (0223) 486-1636. **Open** noon–6pm Mon, Wed–Fri; 2–7pm Sat & Sun. 🎟 free Wed. 🛒 💻 📷

Built in 1909, this museum is housed in a striking mock-Anglo-Norman-style mansion of turrets and timbers. Its collection of 450 paintings is dominated by the works of local artist Juan Carlos Castagnino (1908–72). Depicting his hometown in a style that was influenced by European expressionism, while being essentially figurative, Castagnino also produced etchings based on Goya's celebrated "Horrors of War" series. He achieved great fame with his detailed illustrations for a 1962 edition of *Martín Fierro*. The building is noted for its elegant Art Nouveau interior, designed by the famous Belgian decorator Gustavo Serrurier-Bovy. It is a work of art in its own right, packed with playful and extravagant details such as carvings of the five flying ducks over the fireplace. Much of Bovy's work was destroyed during World War II and this museum's collection is one of the few remaining examples of his creations. The furniture in the building is considered some of the finest in the world. Temporary exhibitions, which focus both on local and national artists, are held here all year round.

Castagnino's self-portrait

🏛 Centro Cultural Villa Victoria

Matheu 1851. **Tel** (0223) 492-0569. **Open** 10am–1pm, 5–11pm daily. 🎟 ♿ 💻 📷

A fine writer, intellectual, and critic, Victoria Ocampo influenced most of Argentina's modern literary greats. She was known as an excellent hostess and the soirées she organized at her villa were famous. She is mentioned in Graham Greene's dedication to his well-known novel *The Honorary Consul*. Built by her father as a present to her aunt, the beautiful house was inherited by Ocampo in the 1930s. The writer lived here intermittently until her death in 1979. She bequeathed the building to UNESCO in 1973, although it reverted to municipal control in 1981 when it came to be known as the Centro Cultural Villa Victoria. Surrounded by a sprawling park, the center is well maintained. The building is of architectural interest, constructed from Norwegian wood specially shipped to Buenos Aires in 1911. The wood was then transported by train to Mar del Plata. The big house has 11 bedrooms, but only one of the rooms contains the original antique furnishings. The center now holds a large number of diverse exhibitions, events, and conferences throughout the year.

Fishing trawlers at the harbor in Banquina de Pescadores

🏛 Banquina de Pescadores

South of city center, past Playa Grande.

This working fisherman's wharf teems with activity, brightly painted fishing boats, and the unmistakable smell of fish. The best time to go to Banquina de Pescadores is when the fishermen return at dusk, bringing with them packed crates of bass, squid, and many other seafood delicacies. The dock also has a colony of male sea lions, who have made the port their home and clamor for scraps from the fishermen. Their numbers vary according to the season and, as they are not shy of humans, visitors can get near enough to observe them at close quarters. The port is also known for its excellent seafood restaurants, many of which are dotted around the wharf.

The famous literary retreat Centro Cultural Villa Victoria, Mar del Plata

Sand dunes and pine trees behind the beach in Pinamar

➎ Villa Gesell

Road map D3. 62 miles (100 km) NE of Mar del Plata. 🚉 30,000. ✈ 🚌 ℹ Paseo 107 between Aves 2 & 3, (02255) 478-042. 🎉 Patron Saint (Jul), Beer Festival (Aug). **W** gesell.gov.ar

The beach resort of Gesell was only a dream when Don Carlos Idaho Gesell bought 7 sq miles (18 sq km) of sand dunes on the Atlantic coast in 1931. Here, he built a house for his family, now the Gesell Museum, and protected the dunes by planting several Australian acacia trees. By the 1950s, it had become a fledgling tourist resort, although the town was only officially founded in 1968.

Portrait of Don Carlos Gesell

Now Villa Gesell is filled with lively restaurants, bars, and nightclubs. There is a wide range of hotels, from bed-and-breakfasts to inns and *hospedajes* (lodges). Gesell is popular with youngsters, as there are plenty of beach activities such as quad biking and surfing.

Environs

Just 6 miles (10 km) south of Gesell is **Faro Querandí**, a lighthouse built in 1922. At a height of 180 ft (55 m), with a total of 276 steps, this tower is still in service. About 17 miles (27 km) south, **Parque Natural Pinar del Norte** has ancient woodlands and a dune preserve. The striking expanse of slopes with its complex ecosystem supports diverse grasses and mammals.

➏ Pinamar

Road map D3. 12 miles (20 km) N of Villa Gesell. 🚉 25,000. 🚌 ✈ 🚗 ℹ Ave Shaw 18, (02254) 491-680. **W** pinamar.gov.ar

The resort town of Pinamar is surrounded by fragrant copses of pines planted during the 1940s and 50s. Founded in 1944 by Belgian architect Jorge Bunge, Pinamar was built with a clear vision of urban development. The commercial center has a good handicrafts market.

In the late 1980s, wealthy porteños wanted a smarter resort than Pinamar and so Cariló was founded 4 miles (6 km) away, a pretty village of wooden houses and beach-side bungalows.

➐ Chapadmalal

Road map C3. 14 miles (23 km) S of Mar del Plata. 🚉 2,000. 🚌 **W** chapadmalal.org.ar

An indigenous name meaning "between streams," Chapadmalal is one of the greenest resorts on the Atlantic coast. At the end of the 19th century, the town was known mainly for a ranch owned by founder and first president of the then recently created Nueva Sociedad Rural Argentina, José T. Martínez de Hoz. When he died in 1888, the ranch was divided between his two sons, one of whom built the Estancia Santa Isabel. Most of the hotels here were built when Chapadmalal hosted some events in the 1955 Pan-American Games. Golf and windsurfing are popular activities here.

🏛 **Estancia Santa Isabel**
W santa-isabel.com.ar

One of the greener beach resorts in Argentina, Chapadmalal

For hotels and restaurants see pp278–83 and pp288–99

Rows of tents lining Miramar beach on a sunny day

❽ Miramar

Road map C3. 28 miles (45 km) S of Mar del Plata. 🚗 🚌 *i*
Calle 28, 1086, (02291) 420-190.
W miramarense.com.ar

Well-known as a resort for families and children, Miramar is known as Ciudad de los Niños y de las Bicicletas (City of Children and Bicycles). Popular during the 1980s, it is now somewhat faded and lacks the smart restaurants, trendy bars, pretty houses, and hotels of the resorts to the north. A small surfing community sets up shop every summer to make use of Miramar's extremely powerful wave breaks.

High-rise buildings overshadow the main promenade, but a short walk away is the **Vivero Dunícola Florentino Ameghino**, a group of forested dunes. Here, there is a barbecue area, a small nature museum, a children's playground, and the Bosque Energético (Energy Wood), where an unusual variety of conifers and pines grow.

❾ Necochea

Road map C3. 60 miles (97 km) SW of Miramar. 🚗 🚌 📧 *i* cnr Aves 79 & 2, (02262) 425-983.
W necochea.gov.ar

Residents of towns deep inside the southern Buenos Aires province and northern Patagonia often choose to visit Necochea over Mar del Plata. The waters are cool here, but summer daytime temperatures soar as high as 33° C (91° F). The resort's wide strip of dunes is calmer and more picturesque than the high-rise beachside developments that plague the busier resorts to the north. Half a dozen beaches, pretty woods, a lake, an amphitheater in the **Parque Miguel Lillo**, fossils at Punta Caballido, and the thriving fishing harbor provide entertainment for families. There is ample opportunity for hiking, cycling, dune trips, and rafting on Río Quequén. Windsurfers, jet-skiers, and sailors enjoy the gusting sea breezes off Necochea. Popular among divers is Punta Negra, just 3 miles (5 km) from the center. A little farther up the coast is Cueva del Tigre, famous for its fishing spots.

A small Danish community and a significant Basque community thrive in the town. Some Basque restaurants here specialize in local seafood.

The lush forest in Parque Miguel Lillo, Necochea

❿ Balcarce

Road map C3. 32 miles (52 km) NW of Mar del Plata. 🚍 42,000. 🚌
i Calle 17, 67, (02266) 425-758.
🎉 National Potato Fiesta (Mar).
W sierrasdebalcarce.com.ar

Most Argentinians associate the name of Balcarce with cars, potatoes, and small traditional cookies called *alfajores*. The land around the town is especially good for growing potatoes, grains, and aromatic grasses for the many cattle-rearing farms. This low-key resort town is popular with Buenos Aires families.

The town is famous as being the birthplace of Juan Manuel Fangio, and the **Museo del Automovilismo Juan Manuel Fangio** is a popular tourist site. Along with soccer stars Maradona and Messi and tennis player Guillermo Vilas, Fangio remains a legendary sportsman. He was a record-making Formula 1 driver during the 1950s, the first decade of Formula 1 racing. He won the world championship five times, the same as Michael Schumacher until the latter took his sixth title in 2003. The museum is housed in a century-old building, filled with Fangio

Juan Manuel Fangio in one of his racing cars

memorabilia and a collection of old cars. The most impressive exhibit is located on the top floor – the original Mercedes-Benz Silver Arrow that Fangio drove to victory in 1954.

Also worth visiting in Balcarce are the town hall and cemetery entrance, both of which were designed by architect Francisco Salomone in Art Deco style. The town is also the arena for the annual National Potato Fiesta. Cerro El Triunfo (Triumph Hill), located a mile (2 km) away, is good for walkers and trial motorcyclists.

🏛 **Museo del Automovilismo Juan Manuel Fangio**
Cnr of Dardo Rocha & Mitre.
Tel (02266) 425–540.
Open 10am–7pm daily. 🎫 ♿ 📷
📷 **W** museofangio.com

Horse riding on a sunny evening in the open countryside outside Tandil city

⓫ Tandil

Road map C3. 100 miles (160 km) S of Buenos Aires. 🚠 110,000. 🚌 ℹ️ Ave Espora 1120, (0249) 443-2073. 🆆 tandil.gov.ar

The attractive town of Tandil nestles among Sistema de Tandilia. These are gently undulating granite hills that rise to about 1,800 ft (550 m) above sea level. The town offers weekend breaks to porteños who want a getaway to the hills but cannot travel as far as the Andes. Tandil is extremely popular during Easter, the time when the Stations of the Cross procession takes place. The walk ends at Monte Calvario, a hillock topped by a large cross east of the town. The cobblestoned town center, Plaza Independencia, has been the focal point of life in Tandil ever since the Fuerte Independencia (Fort of

Giant crucifix at the top of Monte Calvario, east of Tandil

Independence) was built on the site in 1823. It was razed 50 years later to make way for the town's expansion. The nearby Neo-Gothic **Templo de la Inmaculada Concepción**, built in 1878, incorporates stones from the fort.

Tandil's **Museo de Bellas Artes**, located south of the plaza, boasts works by local artists as well as a handful of minor pieces by acknowledged Argentinian masters such as Berni and Quinquela Martín. North of Plaza Independencia is another interesting site, the **Museo Tradicionalista**, which has exhibits of photographs and art collected by local families. There is also a good replica of a *pulpería*, a saloon-cum-general store, around which gaucho life revolved.

Tandil has good restaurants and bars, along with a lively nightlife. It is also famous for its cured meats and cheeses. Visitors should head southwest out of town to explore the nearby hills. Cerro El Centinela is the most popular climb, while the higher Sierra Las Animas is more difficult. Horse riding and mountain biking are popular activities.

🏛 **Museo de Bellas Artes**
Chacabuco 367. **Tel** (0249) 443-2067. **Open** 8:30am–12:30pm, 5–9pm Tue–Fri. **Closed** Jan.
🆆 tandil.gov.ar

🏛 **Museo Tradicionalista**
4 de Abril 851. **Tel** (0249) 443-2067. **Open** 4–8pm Tue–Sun. ♿

⓬ Sierra de la Ventana

Road map C3. 20 miles (30 km) NW of Sierra de la Ventana village. 🚉 ℹ️ Ave del Golf s/n, Sierra de la Ventana; (0291) 491-5303. 🅿️
🆆 comarcaturistica.com.ar

The Pampas region is mostly undulating, but the Sierra de la Ventana rises to more than 3,900 ft (1,200 m) above sea level. The range is named after the *ventana* (window), a rock formation on the tallest of its peaks, Cerro de la Ventana. This summit lies within Parque Provincial Ernesto Tornquist.

The range is more rugged than Sistema de Tandilia and is a popular spot for outdoor adventure, drawing hikers, climbers, cyclists, horseback

The "window" formation at the summit of Cerro de la Ventana

riders, as well as casual week-enders. The area is also popular with nature lovers as it supports a large variety of wildlife, which includes foxes, pumas, guanaco, armadillos, and the copper iguana. There are three small villages from which to access the range: Tornquist, Villa Ventana, and Sierra de la Ventana. They are all quiet, laid-back places, but the last has a greater range of services for tourists, as well as a choice of several small hotels.

⓭ Parque Provincial Ernesto Tornquist

Road map C3. 16 miles (25 km) NW of Sierra de la Ventana village.
Tel (0291) 491-0039. 🚐
Open Jan–Feb: 8am–5:30pm daily;
Mar–Dec: 9am–5pm daily.

Covering an area of 26 sq miles (68 sq km), this park offers some of the area's best climbing. It has wrought-iron gates at the entrance, beyond which is a small visitors' center providing useful information on the local ecosystem via audiovisual aids. It houses displays of the area's flora and fauna and a 3-D topographical map. Within the park limits is the 3,700-ft (1,130-m) Cerro de la Ventana, with a well-marked trail leading to the summit. There are also the moderately difficult Cerro Blanco and Claro Oscuro circuits, which offer spectacular views of the area. Numerous short strolls can also be made to waterfalls, the most popular of which is the Garganta del Diablo. The weather can turn unpredictable above 3,300 ft (1,000 m) and it would be best to hire a local guide on the harder treks.

An interesting site within the park is the **Reserva Natural Integral**. This is a strictly controlled area where herds of wild horses can be seen. There are also a number of caves, one of which has ancient paintings on its walls. Birds of prey and common carrion eaters such as *chimangos* and *carranchas* can be seen circling on thermals above the range.

The quiet Estancia Cerro de la Cruz surrounded by greenery

⓮ Estancia Cerro de la Cruz

Road map C3. 2 miles (3 km) E of Sierra de la Ventana village. 🚐 🔾 🔾
Ⓦ **estanciacerrodelacruz.com**

Designed by renowned architect Alejandro Bustillo, this English-style wood-and-stone house is one of the grander estancias in southern Buenos Aires province. The estancia was acquired in 1935 by Argentinian engineer Eduardo Ayerza, who started the first breeding ranch specializing in Polled Hereford cattle in Argentina. During its heyday, the ranch had a separate butler's residence, dormitories for employees, huge barns, and nine silos (warehouses) for storing grains and cereal. Black and white photographs on the inside walls of the main house record these times.

Now open as a five-room hotel, it is popular with nature tourists, golfers, and wealthy hunters who come to this region of Argentina for hunting expeditions.

The Mountains of the Pampas

Long before the cataclysms that brought about the Andes chain, violent geological movements beneath the Pampas forced the land upwards to 1,650–3,600 ft (500–1,100 m) above sea level. The two main ranges are Sierra de la Ventana and Sistema de Tandilia. The former is formed mainly from sedimentary rock dating from the Paleozoic period (570–250 million years ago), and its cool blues and grays make for a striking contrast with the Pampas spread below. The jagged ridges and high peaks mean trekking can be challenging. Sistema de Tandilia is older, with formations dating back to the Precambrian period (4,600–575 million years ago), and has smooth curves, ideal for light treks. Rheas, *chimango* hawks, armadillos, and European hares are common sights on these highlands.

View of the Sierra de la Ventana rising from the Pampas plains

Barber shop kept intact inside Museo del Puerto, Bahía Blanca

⑮ Bahía Blanca

Road map C3. 235 miles (380 km) SW of Tandil. 🚐 301,000. ✈ 🚌 🚉
ℹ Brown 1700, (0291) 481-3993.
🎉 Fiesta de San Silverio (Jun).
ⓦ **bahiablanca.gov.ar**

Known as the Liverpool of Argentina, Bahía Blanca has a history, like the famous English city, that is inseparable from the sea. In 1828, a fortress was established here, principally as a maritime base for defending the southern coast against Brazilian invaders. In 1884, railroads were laid by British firms and Bahía enjoyed a commercial and cultural dynamism that made it unique on this otherwise remote strip of Atlantic coast. Around the same time, 12 miles (20 km) southeast of the city, Puerto Belgrano was created, and today it is the country's largest naval base.

By the end of the 19th century, apart from being a powerful railroad and naval base, Bahía Blanca was booming due to grain and meat exports. When Argentina needed a major cargo port to service the farms of southern Buenos Aires, an Anglo-Argentinian engineer named Don Guillermo White built wharves here which, even today, remain the busiest outside Buenos Aires.

The modern city is no tourist hot spot, but Avenida Alem, with its assortment of European architectural styles and Plaza Rivadavia, makes for a pleasant stroll. Located southwest of the plaza, the Barrio Inglés, with its red-brick semi-detached houses built for railroad workers, reminds visitors of the railroad boom of the 1880s. The main attraction in the city is **Museo del Puerto**, housed in an old customs building, dedicated to the history and evolution of the port. The main exhibition is made up of *tableaux vivans*, mannequins of sailors, dockworkers, barmen, and shopkeepers, who represent "local lifestyles." The museum's archive contains photographs, documents, and recorded oral histories. The entire port quarter is worth visiting on Sundays, when traditional *cantinas* serve steaks and pastas. Every June, *bahienses*, as the locals are known, pay homage to the Italian saint San Silverio, the patron saint of fishermen.

🏛 **Museo del Puerto**
Guillermo Torres 4180. **Tel** (0291) 457-3006. **Open** 8am–1pm Mon–Fri, 4–8pm Sat & Sun. 🈲
ⓦ **bahiablanca.gov.ar**

⑯ Santa Rosa

Road map C3. 75 miles (120 km) NW of Bahía Blanca. 🚐 124,000. ✈ 🚌
ℹ Ave Luro 400, (02954) 424-404.

Founded in 1892 shortly after Argentinian forces had vanquished the native Mapuche settlements, the city of Santa Rosa was originally little more than a handful of estancias, granted to officers who had taken part in the Conquista del Desierto campaign (*see p54*). Today, this friendly city has grown into an important transport hub and has two main urban centers. The relatively newer Centro Cívico is where the government offices and the bus terminal are located. The more interesting area is around Plaza San Martín, where there is a quasi-modernist cathedral, several cafés, and **Museo Provincial de Historia Natural**. The museum's collection of indigenous

Old steering wheel at Museo del Puerto

The Centro Cívico building at Santa Rosa

artifacts is limited, but there are fine examples of Patagonian fauna and some dinosaur fossils that were discovered when the town center was redeveloped in 1994. Santa Rosa is also the base from which to explore the impressive Parque Nacional Lihué Calel.

Environs
Around 23 miles (35 km) south of Santa Rosa is **Reserva Provincial Parque Luro**. A former private estate, the land was once owned by Pedro Luro, a relative of General Roca and son of one of the creators of the resort of Mar del Plata *(see pp152–3)*. The area was taken over by the provincial authorities in 1996. Luro had built a French-style château here called El Castillo, and imported deer from Europe so he could go hunting in grand old European aristocratic style. Today, the preserve is home to many native animals, such as pumas, armadillos, red foxes, wild cats, guanacos, ferrets, and ñandús. It also has exotic species including red deer and wild boar. Guided tours, on foot or on horseback, take visitors around the beautiful château, through thick forests of native trees, and up onto the dunes that surround the green park.

⑰ Parque Nacional Lihué Calel

Road map B3. 140 miles (225 km) SW of Santa Rosa. **Tel** (02952) 436-595. **Open** daily.

Created in 1977, Parque Nacional Lihué Calel covers about 39 sq miles (100 sq km). Meaning "hills of life" in the native Mapuche language, the slopes at Lihué Calel are relatively fertile in comparison to the surrounding plains. This is because the sierras were formed by intense volcanic activity nearly 200 million years ago and retain water provided by scarce rains. The park has an

Guanacos roaming freely in Parque Nacional Lihué Calel

unusual mix of vegetation supporting both ferns and spiked cacti. The most commonly found is the Traitor plant, which is a densely spiked cactus. The park has over 150 bird species, while its pride is the reclusive puma, which is rarely seen. Gray foxes roam freely, especially near campsites, and wild mountain cats, herds of ñandús, guanacos, wild boar, and armadillos can easily be spotted. Venomous snakes such as yarará and coral

Crested Caracara at Lihué Calel

snakes are also found, and it is advisable for visitors to stay away from thick bushes or unexplored paths. Spring is the best time to visit the park; walkers and cyclists can go on self-guided trips to see indigenous cave paintings by the region's first inhabitants or venture on a tougher scramble to the top of the highest peak, the 1,902-ft (580-m) Cerro de la Sociedad Científica. The campground here is free and has showers and barbecues. There is also a service station that houses a slightly old motel, which has some facilities.

The Native Frontier

Spanish viceroys in pre-Independent Argentina were more concerned with protecting the Buenos Aires port and the trade routes to the north than with indigenous populations. Shortly after Independence in 1816, however, the leaders of the newly formed Argentinian Republic turned their attention to the Pampas and Patagonia. The first to wage a military campaign against the indigenous population, in order to acquire their land, was Juan Manuel de Rosas *(see p53)* in southern Argentina in the 1830s. In the 1870s, General Roca, later president, led the Conquista del Desierto *(see p54)*. His campaign moved south beyond Río Negro, vanquishing the Mapuche and Tehuelche and rounding up survivors, who were relocated to central Buenos Aires province. A turning point was the surrender in 1885 of Valentín Sayhueque, an important *cacique* (pre-Columbian tribal chief) and head of the Manzaneros. Today, the Mapuche live in the provinces of Buenos Aires, La Pampa, Neuquén, Río Negro, and Chubut.

General Roca, who led the Conquista del Desierto

ARGENTINIAN LITORAL

Argentina's subtropical northeast Litoral has a landscape dominated by the mighty Ríos Paraná and Uruguay. This region is formed by the provinces of Misiones, Corrientes, Entre Ríos, Formosa, Chaco, and Santa Fe. The area receives a high level of rainfall, which gives rise to lush forests rich in wildlife and flora, huge *embalsados* (floating islands), and acres of wetlands.

The region's original inhabitants were the Guaraní, who, by the 16th century, were living mainly in small agricultural communities. Jesuit missionaries arrived in the 1550s, aiming to evangelize the Guaraní and protect them from Spanish colonial exploitation by building the first of many missions in 1609. In the 19th century, the Litoral served as the battleground for the post-Independence civil war between Unitarios and Federales.

By the 20th century, ranching and grain agriculture were bringing in new income, but at the cost of the environment, prompting the creation of several national parks to counter deforestation. Today, the Litoral's economy remains dependent on farming and forestry, although tourism, driven by natural wonders such as the Iguazú Falls and Esteros del Iberá, is also an important source of income.

The region is a nature lover's paradise, with miles of *yatay* palm forests, wooded marshes, and subtropical jungles. Many national parks serve to protect the area's abundant flora and fauna and offer visitors an opportunity for various outdoor activities ranging from boating and wildlife-watching to camping and trekking. In contrast to the verdant wilderness are the bustling urban centers with their well-preserved colonial buildings and busy calendar of lively folk music festivals and carnival celebrations.

Marsh deer, a common sight in the breathtaking natural preserve Esteros del Iberá

◀ Ruins of the Jesuit mission at San Ignacio Miní, a UNESCO World Heritage Site

Exploring Argentinian Litoral

Stunning natural highlights and historical architecture are the main tourist attractions of the region. Palm-fringed beaches edge the islands and banks of Ríos Paraná and Uruguay. Some of the best beaches can be found at Rosario, Colón, and Gualeguaychú. The region's biggest city, Rosario, brims with museums, galleries, and monumental architecture. Santa Fe and Corrientes have beautifully preserved colonial streets, and San Ignacio Miní houses 300-year-old Jesuit ruins. Off-the-beaten-track destinations include Yapeyú, the birthplace of General San Martín, and Mercedes, gateway to the vast Esteros del Iberá.

Sights at a Glance

Towns and Cities

1 *Rosario pp164–5*
3 Paraná
4 Santa Fe
5 Gualeguaychú
7 Colón
9 Yapeyú
10 Mercedes
12 Corrientes
13 Resistencia

National Parks and Preserves

2 Parque Nacional Pre-Delta
8 Parque Nacional El Palmar
11 *Esteros del Iberá pp170–71*
14 Parque Nacional Chaco
15 Parque Nacional Río Pilcomayo
17 *Parque Nacional Iguazú pp176–9*

Historical Buildings

6 Palacio San José
16 San Ignacio Miní

```
0 kilometers        100
0 miles                      100
```

Cathedral on Plaza Primero de Mayo, Paraná

General Enrique Mosconi

Tartagal

Ingr. Guillermo N. Juárez

Laguna Yerma

Complejo Hídrico R. Teuco-Lag. Yema

FORMO

Gran Chaco

CHACO

Río Gua

Castelli

Tres Isletas

Salta

Preside Roqu

Campo Largo   Sáenz

Las Breñas

General Pinedo   Villa Berthet

Villa Angela

Santa Sylvania

SANTA F

Añatuya

Tostado

Vera

Ceres

San Cristóbal

San Jav

San Justo

Rafaela   Helvecia

Córdoba   **SANTA FE** 4 3 PÁR

Diamante   12

PARQU NACIO PRE-DE

Córdoba   San Lorenzo

ROSAR

Río Cuarto

San Nicolás de Los Arroyos

Melincué

Venado Tuerto

Rufino   *Lag. La Picasa*
Junín

Getting Around

The area's main airports are at Rosario, Corrientes, Resistencia, and Puerto Iguazú. There are regular flights that connect Paraná and Resistencia to Buenos Aires. A reliable option is the long-distance buses that link the main towns and cities. Motorists following the course of Río Paraná via Ruta Provincial 11 and Ruta Nacional 12 should note that main river crossings are via the Rosario–Victoria and Corrientes–Resistencia road bridges, and the Sante Fe–Paraná subfluvial tunnel.

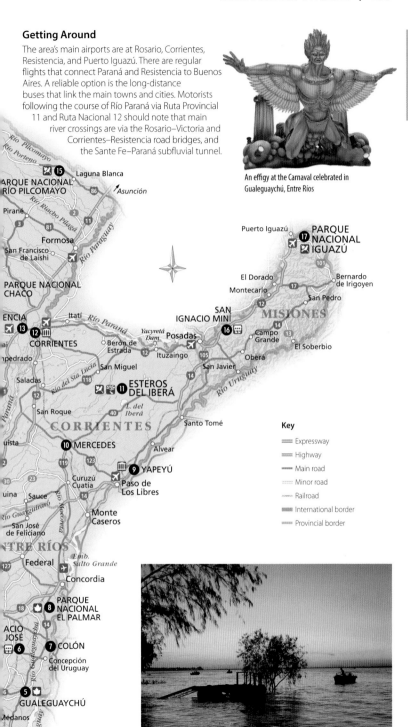

An effigy at the Carnaval celebrated in Gualeguaychú, Entre Ríos

Río Pilcomayo
Río Porteño

🛪 **15** Laguna Blanca
PARQUE NACIONAL
RÍO PILCOMAYO
86 / Asunción

Pirané
Río Riacho Pilagá
2
3 81 11
Formosa
Río Paraguay
San Francisco de Laishi 🛪

Puerto Iguazú 🛪 **17** PARQUE NACIONAL IGUAZÚ 🛪

PARQUE NACIONAL CHACO
101

El Dorado — Bernardo de Irigoyen
Montecarlo
17
San Pedro

ENCIA 🛪 Itatí Río Paraná
13
12 🏛
CORRIENTES
Berón de Estrada
ai
pedrado

SAN IGNACIO MINÍ
16 🏛
12

MISIONES

Yacyretá Dam Posadas 🛪
Campo Grande **14**
13
El Soberbio

Ituzaingó
105
Oberá
San Miguel
San Javier
14

Saladas
Río del Sta. Lucía 118
🛪 🎣 **11** ESTEROS DEL IBERÁ
Río Uruguay

San Roque
40
L. del Iberá
Santo Tomé

Key

uista

10 MERCEDES
119 123
Alvear

🚄 Expressway

30
23
Curuzú Cuatia
🛪 **9** YAPEYÚ
Paso de Los Libres

🚄 Highway

uina
Sauce
Río Guayquiraró
14

🚄 Main road

San José de Feliciano
Monte Caseros

🚄 Minor road

TRE RÍOS
127
Federal
Emb. Salto Grande 🛪

🚄 Railroad

Concordia

🚄 International border

PARQUE NACIONAL EL PALMAR
18 🏕 **8**

🚄 Provincial border

ACIO JOSÉ
🏛 **6**
14
7 COLÓN
Concepción del Uruguay

6
5 🏕
GUALEGUAYCHÚ
Río Uruguay

édanos
Río Gualeguay

View of a beautiful sunset over the Río Paraná, Corrientes

❶ Rosario

Located on the west bank of Río Paraná, Rosario is an industrial powerhouse that enjoys a vibrant cultural scene. This port city first underwent explosive growth at the end of the 19th century, when its surrounding pampas became one of the world's largest grain-producing regions and its port engaged in foreign trade for the first time. Many of the city's impressive constructions date from that period and reflect its Francophile influences. Today, with its architectural heritage, theaters, and museums, Rosario is one of the country's most lively urban destinations.

The majestic Puente Rosario–Victoria over Río Parana

🎨 La Costanera

Ave Belgrano. **Museo de Arte Contemporáneo Rosario (MACRO)** Ave Estanislao López 2250. **Tel** (0341) 480-4981. **Open** 2–8pm Thu–Tue. **Closed** Wed. ♿ 📷 Spanish only. ♿ 📷

Stretching over 6 miles (10 km), Rosario's *costanera* (coast) offers spectacular views of Río Paraná. At its southern end is the pretty **Parque Urquiza**, while a short walk to the north are old grain silos (warehouses). Housed within a brightly painted silo, **Museo de Arte Contemporáneo Rosario (MACRO)** is an outstanding example of the area's vibrant cultural life.

Along the riverfront's northern section are the river beaches of La Florida and Rambla Catalunya. A short stroll north are Costa Alta, a waterfront promenade, and the **Puente Rosario–Victoria**, a suspension bridge linking Rosario with the neighboring province of Entre Ríos.

🏛 Monumento Nacional a la Bandera

Ave Santa Fe 581. **Tel** (0341) 480-2238. **Open** 2–6pm Mon, 9am–6pm Tue–Sun. ♿ 📷 🌐 monumento alabandera.gov.ar

Rosario's Monumento Nacional a la Bandera commemorates the inaugural hoisting of the Argentinian flag by military hero General Manuel Belgrano (1770–1820), on a nearby island in 1812. The work of architect Angel Guido, it is made from unpolished marble. The tower is flanked by patriotic sculptures and bas-reliefs depicting the country's diverse geography. General Belgrano's remains lie in a crypt at the base of the tower, from where a lift climbs towards its summit offering panoramic vistas of the city and river. Guido's design is completed by the **Patio Cívico** (civic courtyard) and the Neo-Classical Propileo (vestibule). On the Avenida Santa Fe side of the vestibule is **Galería de**

Honor a las Banderas, a museum that honors the national flags of the Americas.

🏛 Plaza 25 de Mayo

Aves Córdoba & Buenos Aires.

The city's historical heart, Plaza 25 de Mayo is a pleasantly shaded plaza situated close to the Paraná River coast. At its eastern end stands the Italianate **Basílica Catedral Santuario Nuestra Señora del Rosario**, built in the 19th century. In its crypt is a shrine housing an image of the Virgin Mary brought from Spain in 1773. On the Avenida Santa Fe side of the plaza is the elegant **Museo de Arte Decorativo Firma y Odilo Estévez**, which displays a noteworthy collection of European art from the 17th to the 19th centuries. Other interesting buildings include **Edifício Bola de Nieve**, the city's tallest structure when built in 1907, and Palacio del Correo. **Pasaje Juramento** (Oath Passage), flanked by running water and sculptures by Salta-born artist Lola Mora, links the plaza to the Monumental Nacional.

🏛 Complejo Cultural Parque de España

Sarmiento & Río Paraná. **Tel** (0341) 426-0941/4574. **Open** 7–9pm Tue–Sun (galleries: 10am–1pm, 3–8pm). 🌐 ccpe. org.ar

Located on the coast of the Paraná River, the ambitious Complejo Cultural Parque de España is one of the most modern developments in the city of Rosario. It includes a Cultural Center, a private secondary school, conference and exhibition rooms, a library, and a theater seating more than 500 people. The Cultural Center is a nonprofit institution, dedicated to presenting the most recent Ibero-American art and culture to its visitors.

The attractive Parque de España (Spanish Park) is ideally located by the river, and boasts great views of the Monumento Nacional a la Bandera to the south, and the Rosarian Costanera right up to the Puente Rosario–Victoria to the north.

Museo Histórico Provincial Julio Marc in Parque de la Independencia

🔵 Parque de la Independencia
Bounded by Pellegrini, 27 de Febrero, Moreno y Lagos. 🚻 ♿ 📷 🏛
Museo de la Ciudad Boulevard Oroño 2300. **Tel** (0341) 480-8665. **Open** 9am–3pm Mon–Fri, 2–7pm Sat, Sun, & hols, however hours may vary seasonally and according to budget; call in advance or check online. 🕐 Spanish only. ♿ 📷 🏛
W museodelaciudad.org.ar
Museo Historico Provincial Julio Marc Avenue del Museo. **Tel** (0341) 472-1457. **Open** 9am–7pm Tue–Fri, 3–8pm Sat, Sun, & hols. 📷

The grand Parque de la Independencia is Rosario's largest and most beautiful green space. Its many attractions include an ornamental rose garden, a lake, soccer stadium, and two museums.

Museo de la Ciudad has exhibits on the city's social and political history and the **Museo Histórico Provincial Julio Marc** houses historical displays from pre-Columbian times onward.

🏛 Museo Municipal de Bellas Artes Juan B. Castagnino
Ave Pellegrini 2202. **Tel** (0341) 480-2542. **Open** 2–8pm Wed–Mon. **Closed** Tue. 📷 under 12s free. 🕐 varies (call in advance). ♿ 🏛
W museocastagnino.org.ar

Inaugurated in 1937, this exceptional museum was the culmination of an initiative by Rosarino progressives to transform their city into a cultural capital and banish the city's reputation as the "Chicago Argentino," earned for its port

industry, mafia activity, and numerous red-light areas.
Spanning two floors, the museum houses mainly modern Argentinian art from the 19th century to the present day. There are works by great Argentinian artists such as Benito Quinquella Martín and Rosarino artist Antonio Berni. European art from the 17th century onward is also displayed. The museum's main attraction lies in the curators' decision to eschew any kind of thematic or chronological organization and place contemporary pieces alongside more traditional works in a dynamic and unpredictable mixture of forms.

Rosario

① La Costanera
② Monumento Nacional a la Bandera
③ Plaza 25 de Mayo
④ Complejo Cultural Parque de España
⑤ Parque de la Independencia
⑥ Museo Municipal de Bellas Artes Juan B. Costagnino

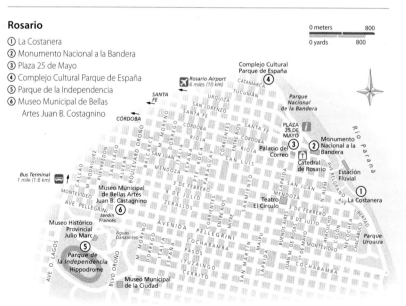

0 meters 800
0 yards 800

❷ Parque Nacional Pre-Delta

Road map C2. 62 miles (100 km) N of Rosario. 🛈 25 de Mayo 389, Diamante; (0343) 498-3535. **Open** 7:30am–7:30pm daily. ⚠

Created in 1992, Parque Nacional Pre-Delta protects 10 sq miles (26 sq km) of subtropical wetlands. The landscape is a mosaic of marshland, floating islands, lakes, and drainage channels. The islands, edged by lush forests, are marked at their centers by deep, almost permanently inundated depressions. These form lagoons that harbor the park's main botanical feature, the *irupé*, the giant Victoria water lily, which sits on the water's surface like a floating bowl.

Myriad bird species, including the ringed kingfisher, which is the park's symbol, and numerous large wading birds are easily sighted. Other animals include the semi-aquatic capybara, *coipu*, and a population of broad-nosed caiman. As only a fraction of the park is accessible by foot, there are boat excursions that embark from the park's entry point at **La Jaula**. The longest one navigates the narrow water channels to **Isla Las Mangas**, where there is a hiking trail that leads to **Laguna Los Baños**. This lake is often covered with *irupés*.

Colorful ringed kingfisher

View of a water channel, Parque Nacional Pre-Delta

❸ Paraná

Road map C2. 84 miles (136 km) N of Rosario. 🚉 238,000. 🚂 🚌 🛈 Ave Buenos Aires 132, (0343) 423-0183. 📅 Festival Provincial del Mate (Feb). 🌐 **turismoparana.gov.ar**

A historic destination, Paraná is home to fine 19th-century architecture and long stretches of river beaches. It was declared capital of the Argentinian Confederation in 1854, and on its main square, Plaza Primero de Mayo, stands the old **Antiguo Senado de la Confederación**, the nation's then seat of government. Ornamented by classic Italianate fountains and *yatay* palms, the plaza is fronted by **Palacio Municipal**, **Escuela Normal Paraná**, and the **Catedral Municipal**. A few blocks east from the plaza is the **Museo Histórico Martiniano Leguizamón**, named after the gaucho who fought for the rights of the indigenous people. North of the plaza, **Parque Urquiza** descends the bank of

Río Paraná towards palm-fringed beaches. Boats to the facing islands depart from the river's waterfront.

🏛 **Museo Histórico Martiniano Leguizamón**
Laprida y Buenos Aires. **Tel** (0343) 420-7869. **Open** 8am–12:30pm, 3–8pm Tue-Fri; 9am–noon, 3–7pm Sat; 9am–noon Sun.

❹ Santa Fe

Road map C2. 104 miles (167 km) N of Rosario. 🚉 370,000. 🚂 🚌 🛈 Belgrano 2910 (in bus station), (0342) 457-4124, (0342) 457-4128. 🌐 **santafeturismo.gov.ar**

Steeped in history, Santa Fe also has a spectacular architectural heritage. Its most important buildings cluster around Plaza 25 de Mayo. The whitewashed façade of the Jesuit-built **Iglesia Nuestra Señora de los Milagros** conceals a lavish interior that contains a painting of the Immaculate Virgin from 1634 by Cavaillé-Coll. Dominating the square's southern end, the beautiful **Casa de Gobierno** was built on the site of the colonial *cabildo* where the Argentinian Constitution was signed in 1853.

South of the square is **Iglesia y Convento de San Francisco**, built between 1662 and 1695, with a beautifully conserved interior. A stroll away from the church is **Museo Histórico Provincial Brigadier General Estanislao López**, which functions within a colonial house. Its variety of exhibits includes antique, ornate *mate* gourds and unique displays on the 19th-century struggle between Unitarios and the Urquiza-led Federalists.

🏛 **Iglesia y Convento de San Francisco**
Amenábar 2257. **Tel** (0342) 459-3303. **Open** 8:30am–6:30pm daily.

🏛 **Museo Histórico Provincial Brigadier General Estanislao López**
San Martín 1490. **Tel** (0342) 457-3529. **Open** 8:30am–7pm Tue-Fri, 3:30–6:30pm Sat, Sun, & hols. 🚫 📷 Tue–Fri.
🌐 **museobrigadierlopez.gob.ar**

The elegant façade of Catedral Municipal, Paraná

The Paraná River System

The great Río Paraná is the longest river in Argentina and the second longest in all of South America. This mighty waterway flows 2,479 miles (3,990 km) from its source in tropical Brazil to its mouth at the temperate Atlantic, draining an area of more than 380,000 sq miles (100,000 sq km). On its course through Argentina, it forms a natural border with Paraguay before snaking southwest, marking the western limit of Argentina's islandlike Litoral region. In its far south, the river forms the Paraná Delta, a floodplain and great labyrinth of drainage channels, wetlands, and river islands. A subtropical microhabitat at the heart of a temperate zone, the junglelike delta forms a dramatic contrast with the arable pampas that surround it.

The Yacyretá Dam is a huge hydroelectric project completed in 1994. It is reported to be affecting the water flow and level of the region's two biggest natural spectacles: Esteros del Iberá and the Iguazú Falls.

Wildlife is rich along the Paraná riverbanks, and the delta supports a wide variety of fauna. Mammals found here include otters, capybaras, and deer; among the many reptiles are caiman, turtles, and snakes; and birdlife includes herons, storks, coots, and kites.

Santa Fe is located at water level and is prone to flooding, at great cost to human life.

Fishing provides sustenance for numerous communities along the river. Species such as *surubí sábalo* and dorado are also exploited for their commercial value.

The Paraná Delta is an alluvial basin of silty channels and humid, densely vegetated islands. The delta starts to form between Santa Fe and Rosario. Its gateway is the town of Tigre *(see pp120–21)*, near Buenos Aires.

Map labels: Resistencia, Corrientes, MISIONES, Posadas, Río Paraná, Río Uruguay, Río Aguapey, Esteros del Iberá, Mercedes, CORRIENTES, SANTA FE, Paso de los Libres, Río Salado, Río Paraná, Federal, Santa Fe, Concordia, ENTRE RÍOS, Paraná, Río Gualeguay, Río Uruguay, Rosario, Tigre, Buenos Aires, Río de la Plata

0 kilometers 150
0 miles 150

➎ Gualeguaychú

Road map C2. 140 miles (226 km) SE of Paraná. 🚍 100,000. 🚌 🛈 Plazoleta de los Artesanos, Paseo del Puerto; (03446) 423-668. 🚢 Sat. 🎭 Carnaval (Jan & Feb).
w gualeguaychuturismo.com

Derived from the Guaraní phrase for "river of the large jaguar," Gualeguaychú sits on the bank of its namesake river, a tributary of Río Uruguay. It is most famous for its Carnaval, when thousands of revelers descend on this small town to enjoy the country's biggest and most extravagant summer celebration. Festivities center around the **Corsódromo**, an open parade ground overlooking Gualeguaychú's old railroad line and train station.

Outside of Carnaval, the town attracts visitors for its river beaches, which stretch over 12 miles (20 km). **Parque Urquiza**, across the river, has some of the most popular beaches. Also noteworthy is the town's colonial architecture; two immaculately restored early 1800s abodes, **Azotea de Lapalma** and **Solar de los Haedo**, are open to the public as museums. **Instituto Magnasco**, Gualeguaychú's main cultural space, houses many local artworks and historical artifacts.

🏛 **Azotea de Lapalma**
San Luis y Jujuy. **Tel** (03446) 437-028. **Open** varies (call in advance). **Closed** Sun, Mon, & Tue. 🎭 🎦 by prior arrangement (Spanish only).

🏛 **Solar de los Haedo**
San José y Rivadavia. **Tel** (03446) 437-036. **Closed** Sun, Mon, & Tue. 🎭 🎦 by prior arrangement (Spanish only).

The grand reception hall at General Urquiza's Palacio San José

➏ Palacio San José

Road map C2. Ruta Provincial 39, Km 128. **Tel** (03442) 432-620. **Open** 8am–7pm Mon–Fri, 9am–6pm Sat, Sun, & hols. 🎭 🎦 Spanish only.
w palaciosanjose.com.ar

Some 70 miles (110 km) north of Gualeguaychú, this Italianate palace is best reached by car, or by taxi from Concepción del Uruguay. Built between 1848 and 1860, it was an architectural statement of power and influence for regional *caudillo* and Federalist leader, General Justo José Urquiza (1801–70). A national monument, the palace sits in forested countryside and is recognizable by the watchtowers at either end of its pink, arcaded façade. Surrounded by magnificent ornamental gardens, the palace is built around two courtyards. Rooms include the richly decorated Sala de los Espejos,

where the General entertained guests, and the Sala de Tragedia, Urquiza's bedroom, where he was assassinated in 1870. Outbuildings include a private chapel, notable for its frescoes and altar. Also set within the gardens is a large artificial lake.

➐ Colón

Road map C2. 180 miles (290 km) SE of Paraná. 🚍 22,000. 🚌 🛈 Ave Costanera y Gouchón, (03447) 421-233. 🎭 Fiesta Nacional de Artesanías (Feb). **w** colon.gov.ar

A picturesque settlement on the western bank of Río Uruguay, the little town of Colón is the perfect venue for a relaxing break. Its riverside setting facilitates a variety of activities, including swimming, boating, and lounging in the thermal waters of its public spa. Its balustraded riverfront stretches 6 miles (10 km) and overlooks, at its northern and southern reaches, long sections of sandy, palm-fringed beaches. Boats to the facing river islands depart regularly from the waterfront. The

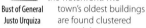
Bust of General Justo Urquiza

town's oldest buildings are found clustered around the port area. Here, **Estación Fluvial**, Colón's railroad station, is an elegant, Italianate construction encircled by tall *yatay* palms. Several more historical buildings front Plaza San Martín and the main Avenida 12 de Abríl. On the avenue, **Teatro Centenario** is a well-restored theater, dating back to 1925.

A relaxing day at the beach on the banks of Río Uruguay

Towering *yatay* palm protected at Parque Nacional El Palmar

❽ Parque Nacional El Palmar

Road map C2. 31 miles (50 km) N of Colón. 🛈 Ruta Nacional 14, Ubajay (03447) 493-053.
Open daily. 🛱 🛱 🖳 🏕 🛆
W elpalmarapn.com.ar

Covering an area of 33 sq miles (85 sq km), Parque Nacional El Palmar was created in 1965 to conserve the *yatay* palm, which once covered most of the Entre Ríos and Corrientes provinces. These tall, slender trees were in danger of extinction from mass clearing for farming and forestry in the early 20th century. The park also protects large swathes of marshland and gallery forest.

The park is home to myriad fauna, including reptiles such as the *tegu* lizard and the ostrich-like *ñandú*. The wetlands and gallery forests are a refuge for herons, kingfishers, and woodpeckers, while otters and capybaras inhabit the park's riverbanks. Hiking trails criss-cross the park, which is also traversable by car.

❾ Yapeyú

Road map D2. 245 miles (395 km) SE of Corrientes. 🚈 3,000. 🛈
Sargento Cabrán & Gregoria Matorra (03772) 493-198. **W** todoyapeyu.com.ar

Founded as a base in 1626 by Jesuits seeking to convert the indigenous Guaraní, Yapeyú is better known to Argentinians as the birthplace of revered Independence hero General José de San Martín (*see p53*). At the eastern edge of the main Plaza San Martín is **Templete Sanmartiniano**, which preserves the ruins of the small fort where the liberator spent his childhood. To the south of the plaza is **Museo de Cultura Jesuítica Guillermo Furlong**, which sits atop the Jesuit mission's red sandstone foundations. It houses Jesuit artifacts and wooden panels detailing the history of the region. At the southern end of town is **Museo Sanmartiniano**, displaying weaponry that belonged to the San Martíns.

🏛 **Museo de Cultura Jesuítica Guillermo Furlong**
Sargento Cabral & Romero. **Open** 8am–noon & 2–6pm Mon–Fri.

🏛 **Museo Sanmartiniano**
Ave Libertador s/n. **Open** 8am–4pm daily. 🛱

Wooden horse display, Museo Jesuítica

❿ Mercedes

Road map C2. 167 miles (270 km) SE of Corrientes. 🚈 35,000. 🚌 🛈
Sarmiento 650, (03773) 1541-2216.
🎭 Fiesta del Chamamé (Nov).
W mercedescorrientes.gov.ar

A gateway to the stunning Esteros del Iberá (*see pp170–71*), Mercedes is a sleepy town with lovely 19th-century streets and distinctive adobe buildings. The town's single museum is housed within the **Casa de la Cultura**. Exhibits here include bayoneted rifles recovered from 19th-century civil war battlegrounds. Mercedes has several shops, such as **Manos Corrientes**, that sell exquisite gaucho ware. A 6-mile (9-km) drive west of town is a roadside shrine to local saint-hero Gauchito Gil.

🏛 **Casa de la Cultura**
Parque Mitre. **Open** Dec–Mar: 4–8pm daily; Apr–Nov: 8am–noon, 2–6pm daily.

The Legend of Gauchito Gil

Popular saint Gauchito Gil was a deserter from a 19th-century provincial war. On escaping to the mountains, he became a Robin Hood-type figure who stole from rich landowners to give to the poor. His legend was sealed on his capture, where at his hanging he is said to have whispered to his executioner, "When you go home you will find your son dying. Pray for my intercession, for the blood of an innocent can perform miracles." The hangman returned home to find his son in agony. After the child's recovery, he erected a cross hung with a red ribbon in honor of Gauchito. Today, this site is a ribbon-festooned, candle-adorned shrine covered with messages beseeching the intercession of Gauchito. Such is Argentina's reverence for this popular saint, who is not recognized by the Vatican, that each January on the anniversary of Gil's hanging, up to 100,000 pilgrims visit the shrine.

Gaucho Antonio Gil's shrine where pilgrims tie red ribbons

⓫ Esteros del Iberá

Covering over 5,200 sq miles (13,700 sq km), the stunning Iberá wetlands are a biologically diverse wilderness of water, marshland, and islands. The reserve derives its name from the Guaraní for "shining waters," hinting at the clear-water lagoons that occupy 25 percent of its surface area. Water from these lagoons seeps into a network of narrow channels, each flanked by marshland and *embalsados* (floating islands). Guides steer boats along the channels, allowing visitors to observe a subtropical wildlife that includes over 350 bird species and numerous reptiles and mammals.

Visitors on a walkway accompanied by a guide

Caiman
Two species of caiman inhabit the preserve: the black caiman *(above)*, and the smaller broad-nosed caiman. They can be found lounging on the banks of *embalsados*.

Capybara
Weighing about 155 lb (70 kg), capybaras are the world's largest rodents. Ubiquitous within the preserve, they live in large groups on the banks of lagoons.

Marshlands at the edge of lagoons are the habitat of reclusive mammals such as the marsh deer.

Mburucuyá
Eros de Santa Lucía

Bella Vista
118
Santa Rosa

Concepción

Eros del Batel

C O R R I E N T E

Laguna Trin

Laç Fern

Río Corrientes

40

123

Mercedes

Curuzú Cuatia

Key

═══ Main road

─── Minor road

─ ─ Park boundary

Black Howler Monkey
Usually seen only through binoculars, these noisy primates inhabit the canopy of the preserve's forests. Their "howl" is more like a deafening roar, and can be heard from quite a distance away.

★ Laguna Iberá

The preserve's most-visited lake is easily accessible by trips on boats and horseback and nocturnal safaris. These explore its marshland, floating islands, and water channels, as well as the abundant wildlife they harbor.

★ Colonia Carlos Pellegrini

This charming and quiet village of sandy streets, artisans' shops, and adobe buildings fronts the banks of Laguna Iberá and is where most lodging options can be found. Boat and horse-riding excursions head daily from here into the wetlands.

The Birds of Esteros del Iberá

A haven for over 350 bird species, the preserve is an ornithological paradise. Among the most brightly colored are the scarlet-headed blackbird, yellow-billed cardinal, and vermilion flycatcher. Tall wading birds include numerous species of heron, stork, and limpkin. Biggest of all is the jabiru stork, the tallest stork in the Americas. Birds of prey include the ground-dwelling crested caracara. The savanna hawk is commonly seen gliding over the preserve's savanna, home also to the greater rhea.

Estancia Rincón del Socorro

One of several upscale estancias in or bordering the preserve, Rincón del Socorro (see pp310) is a beautifully restored tourist ranch owned by conservationist and former North Face clothing magnate Douglas Tompkins.

A couple of nesting jabiru storks

⓬ Corrientes

Road map C1. 168 miles (270 km) NW
of Mercedes. ⚐ 350,000. ✈ ➡ 🛈
Costanera General San Martín 245,
(0379) 464-504. ➡ Sat & Sun. 🎭
Carnaval (Jan). ⓦ **corrientes.com.ar**

With a history stretching back to
1558, Corrientes was founded
on the eastern bank of Río
Paraná as a staging post
between Asunción, Paraguay,
and Buenos Aires. It was a major
battleground in the 19th century in the struggle between
Unitarios and Federalists, and
also from 1865 to 1870, during
the War of Triple Alliance against
Paraguay *(see p54)*.

Today Corrientes possesses an
extraordinary wealth of colonial
and 19th-century architecture.
Its well-conserved historical
center lies roughly between
streets 9 de Julio, Buenos Aires,
Mendoza, and Avenida
Costanera. Housed in a lovely
colonial-era building, **Museo
de Artesanía Tradicional
Folklórica** exhibits native crafts.
A plethora of 19th-century
buildings includes **Casa de
Gobierno**, whose pink exterior
is an eclectic mix of architectural styles. Three blocks
north, Avenida Costanera is a
riverside promenade which
offers great views of Río Paraná.

🏛 **Museo de Artesanía
Tradicional Folklórica**
F. J. de la Quintana 905. **Tel** (03783)
475- 945. **Open** 7–8pm Mon–Fri, 9am–
noon, 4–7pm Sat. 🎫 Spanish only. 📷

Shady promenade of Avenida Costanera
in Corrientes

The green wetland at the Parque Nacional Chaco

⓭ Resistencia

Road map C1. 12 miles (19 km) W of
Corrientes. ⚐ 350,000. ✈ ➡ 🛈
Julio Roca 20, Plaza 25 de Mayo,
(03722) 458-289. ➡ Fri & Sun. 🎭
Bienal Internacional de Escultura (Jul).
ⓦ **mr.gov.ar**

Known as Ciudad de las
Esculturas (City of Sculptures),
the lovely town of Resistencia
has more than 400 sculptures
that adorn its streets and parks.
The city is also known for its
Bienal Internacional de
Escultura, a festival in
which international
sculptors transform
the city's Plaza 25
de Mayo into an
open-air studio.
Among Resistencia's
main attractions
are its museums.
**Museo del Hombre
Chaqueño Ertivio
Acosta** houses
artifacts from the native Wichí,
Toba, and Mocoví communities.
El Fogón de los Arrieros is a
museum and art gallery; its
eclectic displays include a
painting by well-known artist,
Raúl Soldi, and boxing gloves
that belonged to former world
champion Carlos Monzón.

Wooden wheel at El Fogón
de los Arrieros

🏛 **Museo del Hombre Chaqueño
Ertivio Acosta**
J. B. Justo 280. **Tel** (03624) 453-005.
Open 8am–noon, 3–7pm Mon–Fri; may
vary seasonally. 🎭 🎫 Spanish only.
ⓦ **museodelhombrechaco.com.ar**

🏛 **El Fogón de los Arrieros**
Brown 350. **Tel** (03722) 426-418.
Open 8am–7pm Mon–Fri,
9am–12:30pm Sat. 🎭

⓮ Parque Nacional Chaco

Road map C1. 69 miles (112 km) E of
Resistencia. ➡ 🛈 Captán Solari,
(03725) 499-161. **Open** 6am–7pm
daily. 🎭 ⛰ ⓦ **parquesnacionales.
gob.ar**

Created in 1954, Parque
Nacional Chaco is a protected
area of exceptional biodiversity.
Covering 58 sq miles (150 sq
km), it conserves residual forests
of the *quebracho* tree, which
once covered the entire
western part of Chaco.
The *quebracho*,
which produces
large tannin yields
and durable
hardwood, had
declined due to
farming and forestry.
The park also
protects swamp,
palm savanna, and
gallery forest. These
diverse habitats provide refuge
for an extraordinary array of
wildlife that includes an estimated 341 bird species. The
most easily spotted are wading
birds such as jacanas, herons,
and jabiru storks. Howler
monkeys, often heard rather
than seen, inhabit the forest
canopy, while other large
reclusive species include the
giant anteater, maned wolf, and
puma. Following rainfall, the
paw marks of big predators can
be spotted on trails. Reptiles
include the commonly sighted
broad-nosed caiman. Bird-
watching and hiking are the
main activities on offer here. A
variety of trails start from the

park's reception area. The 3-mile (5-km) trek to the **Carpincho** and **Yacaré** lagoons provides excellent bird-watching opportunities. A single road, often impassable during the wet season (November–March), provides vehicle access through to the *quebracho* forests.

⑮ Parque Nacional Río Pilcomayo

Road map C1. 224 miles (360 km) N of Resistencia. 🚌 Resistencia to Laguna Blanca via Formosa. 🛈 Ave Pueyrredón & RN86, Laguna Blanca; (03718) 470-045. **Open** daily. ⚠
🌐 **parquesnacionales. gob.ar**

Bounded to its north by Río Pilcomayo, Argentina's river border with Paraguay, this 185-sq-mile (490-sq-km) park shares much of the flora and fauna found in Parque Nacional Chaco. However, it contains more, and larger, bodies of water. The park's main highlights are the beautiful **Laguna Blanca** and **Esteros Poi**, both of which are reachable by foot and vehicle trails.

The park's biggest lake, Laguna Blanca, is edged by forests alive with noisy howler monkeys, toco toucans, and pretty ringed kingfishers. The park has a myriad of other animals, including elusive mammals such as the maned wolf, which is also the park's symbol, and the graceful ocelot. The lake is a popular bathing spot, despite the presence at its shoreline of broad-nosed caiman and capybara, neither of which bite. It is advisable, however, to swim with shoes on. Visitors are also advised not to feed the fish. To the west of the lake, the Esteros Poi marshland is inhabited by wading birds such as herons, jabiru storks, and jacanas.

Apart from Resistencia, the nearest major town to Parque Nacional Río Pilcomayo is Formosa, 112 miles (180 km) north in the Formosa province.

Elusive maned wolf found in the Parque Nacional Río Pilcomayo

Taxis and *remises* (licensed mini-cabs) run regularly from Formosa to the park entrance. The towns of Laguna Naick-Neck and Laguna Blanca sit near its southern limit. The latter is linked to Formosa by bus and has better tourist facilities. The small town is also the location for the park's administrative headquarters.

Ringed kingfisher at Laguna Blanca

⑯ San Ignacio Miní

Road map D1. 230 miles (370 km) E of Corrientes. 🚹 6,200. 🚌 from Corrientes. 🛈 Ave Sarmiento, access from San Ignacio, (03764) 349-833.
🌐 **misiones-sanignacio.com.ar**

A UNESCO World Heritage Site, the Jesuit ruins at San Ignacio Miní are the most stunning and extensive of the six ruins that remain from the Jesuit-Guaraní missions founded in the region in the 17th century.

The entrance of the site, the **Centro de Interpretación**, has themed rooms which depict the story of the mission from its founding to its eventual decline following the Jesuits' expulsion from the New World in 1767 by the Spanish colonial authorities. It also has a few exhibits that touch on Guaraní life. A short grassy path leads to the ruins among which lies a large and still clearly recognizable central plaza. Dominating the plaza is the mission's imposing red-sandstone church designed by Italian architect Juan Brasanelli in a sophisticated style known as Guaraní Baroque. Its lavishly gilded interior no longer exists and the roof has long since crumbled away, but its magnificent portal, adorned with bas-reliefs sculpted by skilled Guaraní artists, stands as a testament to the building's original splendor. In a second square adjacent to the church are the Jesuit priests' quarters, together with the remains of a cemetery, libraries, dining rooms, and a kitchen.

The ancient ruins occupy nearly six blocks of the village of San Ignacio, which has a wide range of accommodation and restaurant options. There are also sound and light shows that recount the area's rich history.

🏛 Centro de Interpretación
Alberdi s/n. **Tel** (03752) 470-186.
Open 7am–7pm daily. 🎟

The Jesuit ruins of San Ignacio Miní, founded in the 17th century

A panoramic view of the magnificent horseshoe-shaped Iguazú Falls ▶

⑰ Parque Nacional Iguazú

A UNESCO World Heritage Site, the subtropical rainforest of Parque Nacional Iguazú provides the setting for one of the world's great natural wonders, the mighty Iguazú Falls. Iguazú derives its name from the Guaraní word for "big water," a fitting description for a series of cataracts that stretches 2 miles (3 km) and comprises over 250 individual waterfalls. Once a source of legend for the Guaraní people, the falls retain an awe-inspiring, primordial beauty for visitors. Most arrive on day trips from nearby Puerto Iguazú, exploring the park via a network of catwalks and trails.

Visitors taking a walk along the Circuito Inferior

★ **Garganta del Diablo**
At 262 ft (80 m) high, Garganta del Diablo (Devil's Throat) is the biggest and most spectacular of the cataracts. Catwalks cross extremely close to its waters.

Map of Iguazú Falls

Estación Garganta del Diablo

Key

— Road
- - Trail
— Railroad
- ⋅ - International border

Río Iguazú Superior

Puerto Canoas Restaurant

BRAZIL

Isla San Martín

Circuito Superior

Circuito Inferior

ARGENTINA

Tropical das Cataratas Hotel

Sendero Macuco

Río Iguazú Inferior

Viejo Hotel Cataratas

Área de Recepción

General Service Area

Amphitheater

Sheraton International Hotel

Train Station

0 meters   100
0 yards   100

Tren Ecológico de la Selva
This train leaves from the Area de Recepción, stopping at Estación Cataratas for Circuito Superior and Circuito Inferior before heading to Estación Garganta del Diablo.

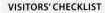

★ **Salto San Martín**
The second largest after Garganta del Diablo, this magnificent waterfall is best viewed from Isla San Martín.

Powerboat trips
Inflatable boats depart from Circuito Inferior, taking visitors on exciting rides to the foot of Salto San Martín.

★ **Wildlife**
Refuge to over 430 bird species and 70 types of mammals, the Paranaense rainforest abounds with colorful animal life.

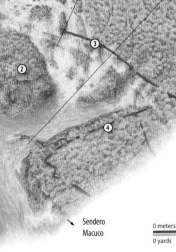

Sendero Macuco

0 meters 50
0 yards 50

KEY

① **Tropical das Cataratas** offers luxury accommodation as well as awe-inspiring views of the falls.

② **Isla San Martín**

③ **Circuito Superior**

④ **Circuito Inferior**

Exploring Parque Nacional Iguazú

Although exploring the breathtaking Parque Nacional Iguazú involves traversing dense rainforest, the task is made easier by an eco-train that runs the length of its crowning feature, the magnificent Iguazú Falls, and by a network of walkways that lead both along the top and to the base of the tumbling cataracts. Other trails head away from the water into the jungle, where tropical birds and capuchin monkeys can be observed. For thrill-seekers, excursions include powerboat trips to the foot of the falls, a salutary and soaking reminder of the awesome power and inventiveness of nature.

The foaming Salto Bossetti seen from Circuito Superior

Key

▬▬▬ Major road

═══ Minor road

■ ▪ International border

--- Park boundary

Ciudad del Este

Foz do Iguaçu

BRAZIL

Foz do Iguaçu International Airport

Puerto Iguazú

Río Iguazú

PARAGUAY

Río Paraná

ARGENTINA

Area de Recepción

Garganta del Diablo

0 kilometers 5

0 miles 5

Iguazú International Airport

Area de Recepción

165 ft (50 m) from park entrance. **Tel** (03757) 491-469. **Open** 8am–6pm daily.

All visits to Parque Nacional Iguazú start at the Area de Recepción. Here, the Centro de Interpretación Yvirá Retá has displays on the park's abundant flora and fauna as well as the human history of the greater Atlantic rainforest which the park helps to protect. It also has exhibits showing the devastating effects of farming and logging on the forest.

From the Area de Recepción, the falls are approached via the **Tren Ecológico de la Selva**, a propane-powered eco-train, or via the **Sendero Verde** (Green Trail), an easy 20-minute walk through tropical forest filled with birdlife. Both routes lead to

the **Estación Cataratas** train station, from which point it is a short stroll to the Circuito Superior and Circuito Inferior trails and the thunderous roar and spray of the cataracts.

Wildlife displays within the Centro de Interpretación

Circuito Superior and Circuito Inferior

from Estación Cataratas.

arranged at park entrance.

Circuito Superior only.

An hour-long trail that runs along the upper lip of the falls, Circuito Superior (Upper Circuit) affords spectacular views of the waterfalls framed by verdant jungle, tumbling into a swirling abyss of bubbling white water. Dazzling rainbows formed in the spray thrown up by the crashing water arch across the river and the falls.

Circuito Inferior (Lower Circuit) is also an hour-long walk, and includes steep stairs. It crosses the dripping rainforest to the foot of several cataracts, allowing visitors to observe the forest and falls from much closer quarters. Boats depart from a jetty on the Circuito Inferior for **Isla San Martín**, a rocky, forested island that offers stunning views of the falls, all the way to Garganta del Diablo (Devil's Throat).

Garganta del Diablo

🚻 📷 arranged at park entrance. ♿

The biggest and most jaw-dropping of all the falls, the Garganta del Diablo waterfall is reachable only by taking the eco-train to its final destination, **Estación Garganta del Diablo**. From the station, a 1.4-mile (2.2-km) walkway cuts across the Upper Río Iguazú and jungle river islands before approaching almost to the lip of the 260-ft- (80-m-) high horseshoe-shaped cataract. The walk takes about 2 hours and it is advisable to wear waterproof clothing and bring plastic bags to protect cameras from the vapor that rises from the waterfall.

Sendero Macuco

📷 arranged at park entrance.

Compared to the busy Circuito Superior and Circuito Inferior trails, Sendero Macuco (Macuco Trail) is a quieter, less trodden track. It leads away from the waterfalls into the surrounding jungle of tall *lapacho* and *palo rosa* trees, where several species of fauna, including myriad birds and butterflies, coatimundis and capuchin monkeys can be observed. The 3-hour-long trail ends at a small rock pool located at the base of the beautiful **Salto Arrechea** waterfall. The pool is a good place for swimming.

An awe-inspiring view of the spectacular Garganta del Diablo

Boat Excursions

Tel (03757) 491-469. 📷 arranged at Area de Recepción.

There are several options for boat excursions within the park. **Aventura Naútica** is a 12-minute powerboat trip along the Lower Iguazú River to the base of the 230-ft- (70-m-) high Salto San Martín waterfall. The hour-long **Gran Aventura** leads to the same destination, after an open-truck drive via the Sendero Yacaratia jungle track, and a 4-mile (6-km) powerboat ride, which includes a mile (2 km) of rapids. Departing from the Estación Garganta del Diablo, the **Paseo Ecológico** is a gentle boat journey that glides alongside the gallery forests of the Upper Iguazú River. Tour operator **Jungle Explorer** runs each of these excursions.

Brazilian Side

Open Dec–Mar: 9am–6pm daily; Apr–Nov: 9am–5pm daily. 🚻 🅿 📷
ⓦ **cataratasdoiguacu.com.br**

Offering panoramic vistas of the Garganta del Diablo, the Brazilian side of the falls is a short distance away. A trip can include a visit to Parque dos Aves Foz Tropicana, which has rare bird species. For a longer stay on the Brazilian side, the city of **Foz do Iguaçu** has numerous hotel options. Brazilian immigration rules require some nationalities, including citizens of the US, Canada, Japan, and Australia, to obtain a visa prior to travel.

The Wildlife of Parque Nacional Iguazú

A haven for some 430 bird and over 70 mammal species, Parque Nacional Iguazú boasts extraordinary biodiversity. Though much of its fauna, including the giant anteater, the piglike tapir, and the powerful jaguar, is reclusive, a diverse range of wildlife can be spotted along the trails. Most visible are coatimundis, raccoon-like creatures that approach visitors for food. The jungle canopy is home to chattering capuchin monkeys, which descend to the forest floor to forage and can be observed from the Macuco Trail. Kaleidoscopically colored butterflies abound: the beautiful heliconius, its jet-black wings emblazoned with yellow and red flashes, is ubiquitous. Reptiles include caiman and the often-sighted iguana. Birdlife is also abundant. Great dusky swifts nest on rock faces behind the falls and dart in and out of the vapor kicked up by the tumbling water. Predatory kites can be seen gliding high in the sky and jungle trails are enlivened by exotically plumaged toucans (best observed early in the morning), parrots, trogons, caciques, and other tropical birds. Wading birds fish in streams and at the top of the falls.

Capuchin monkey, usually found in the canopy of the park's forests

Coatimundi, one of the most commonly spotted mammals in the park

CÓRDOBA AND THE ANDEAN NORTHWEST

Varied and distinctive, the landscape of this region is marked by deep canyons stratified into all the colors of the rainbow, huge salt lakes shimmering with pink flamingos, and prairies baked by the intense heat of the subtropical sun. With a tangible pre-Columbian and colonial past, the Northwest boasts well-preserved landmarks set amid spectacular desert and mountain scenery.

The pre-conquest settlers of this region were the Aymara, Quechua, Comechingones, and Sanavirones. With the arrival of the Spanish conquistadors in the 1500s, some tribes were displaced and many rendered extinct. The Jesuit priests, who followed the colonizers in the 16th century, played a leading role in the development of the towns of Santiago del Estero, Tucumán, Córdoba, Salta, and Jujuy as major administrative, cultural, and religious centers.

Today, the region is still thrillingly Andean; the influence of the Aymara- and Quechua-speaking people from Jujuy – their folk music, beautiful textiles, and cuisine – extends down into the more mestizo societies of Tucumán and Salta.

The land and its guardian Pachamama (Earth Mother) are also central to the local mind-set. Agriculture and livestock provide most of the area's income, coupled with a growing tourism industry.

Much of the region's beauty can be experienced on road journeys through the Cafayate and Humahuaca *quebradas* (ravines). Most cities have a well-preserved Jesuit heritage with colonial churches, convents, and civic edifices that give them an old-world feel. The south of the province is considered by many to be Argentina's second wine region, after Mendoza, and a source of delicious semisweet Torrontés wines as well as some exceptional red varietals produced by local boutique wineries.

Finca La Rosa, converted from a *bodega* into a wine-themed hotel and spa, Cafayate

◀ Arid Andean foothills with the mountains rising behind, Parque Nacional Los Cardones

Exploring Córdoba and the Andean Northwest

The region's eponymous capital Córdoba is a popular university town, characterized by beautiful old colonial buildings. Beyond the city, heading west, the roads invariably zigzag into the Andean foothills and on to the high passes of the Argentina-Chile border. To the east lie the grassy plains of Santiago del Estero and to the north, the scrublands of Jujuy and the tropical jungle in Salta. The scenery while traveling to quiet villages and towns such as San Salvador de Jujuy, Cafayate, and Cachi is breathtaking, especially against the backdrop of the canyons of the Quebrada de Humahuaca.

Sights at a Glance

Towns and Cities

1 *Córdoba pp184–5*
2 Alta Gracia
3 Villa General Belgrano
5 Cosquín
6 La Cumbre
7 Jesús María
9 La Rioja
11 San Fernando del Valle de Catamarca
12 Santiago del Estero
13 Termas de Río Hondo
14 San Miguel de Tucumán
15 Tafí del Valle
17 Cafayate
19 Molinos
20 Cachi
22 *Salta pp196–9*
25 Yavi

National Parks

4 Parque Nacional Quebrada del Condorito
10 Parque Nacional Talampaya
21 Parque Nacional Los Cardones
24 Monumento Natural Laguna de los Pozuelos
26 Parque Nacional Calilegua
27 Parque Nacional El Rey

Sites of Interest

8 *Santa Catalina pp190–91*
16 Quilmes
18 Quebrada de las Conchas
23 *Quebrada de Humahuaca pp200–4*

MONUMENTO 🗺 NATURAL LAGUNA 24 DE LOS POZUELOS

Cerro Panizos 17,152 ft — Abra Pampa

JUJU

QUEBRADA HUMAHUAC

San Salvador de J

PARQUE NACIONAL 🏞 LOS CARDONES 21
43 CACHI 20 🍴
MOLINOS 19
40
Volcán Antofalla 20,013 ft QUEBRADA DE LAS CONCHAS
Antofagasta de la Sierra CAFAYATE 17
QUILMES 16 🏨
Paso de San Francisco 15,775 ft TAFÍ DEL VALLE
CATAMARCA TUCU
Cerro Palca 17,263 ft Monter
Mte.Pissis 22,578 ft 60 Belén Aguilare
46
Cerro Bonete 22,175 ft Tinogasta Saujil La M
76 SAN FERNANDO DEL VALLE DE 1 CATAMARCA
Villa San José de Vinchina Famatina Ancas
Villa Castelli 75 ✈
Villa Unión LA RIOJA 9 🏨
40 76
10 🍴 LA RIOJA
PARQUE NACIONAL Patquía TALAMPAYA
Chami
Olta
38
Malanzán
29
Chepes
PARQUE NAC QUEB DEL COND

A view of *Cerro de Siete Colores* (Hill of Seven Colors), Purmamarca

For keys to symbols *see back flap*

Museo Histórico Provincial Marqués de Sobremonte, Córdoba

Getting Around

The area's main airports, San Miguel de Tucumán and Salta, have regular flights that connect the cities to Buenos Aires. Better options, however, are long-distance buses or hiring a car to explore the Andean Northwest region. Ruta Nacional 9, the old Camino Real, connects Córdoba to Quebrada de Humahuaca, while Ruta Provincial 40 winds near Quebrada de las Conchas. It is advisable to drive with particular care as the roads can be rough in the Andean foothills.

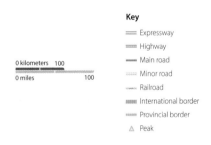

Key

▬▬▬	Expressway
▬▬▬	Highway
▬▬▬	Main road
▬▬▬	Minor road
⌐⌐⌐	Railroad
▪▪▪▪	International border
▪▪▪▪	Provincial border
△	Peak

0 kilometers 100

0 miles 100

Rows of handicraft stalls at Tilcara, Quebrada de Humahuaca

❶ Córdoba

Set in a wide valley in the central sierras, Argentina's second city is a bustling modern metropolis and university town. Founded in 1573, the city boasts some of the country's most impressive colonial architecture, including the "Jesuit Block," all of which has been carefully preserved. With a population that is predominantly of Italian descent, Córdoba has a reputation for warm hospitality and strong civic pride. It's an important commercial and industrial center, and its proximity to the mountains makes for a pleasant stopover between Buenos Aires and the Andean Northwest.

Statue of José San Martín in Plaza San Martín

🚏 Plaza San Martín
Cnr Buenos Aires & San Jerónimo.
Cabildo Independencia 30
Tel (0351) 433-2758. **Open** 9:30am–12:30pm, 3–6pm Mon–Fri; 9:30am–1pm, 3–7pm Sat, Sun, & hols.
Iglesia Catedral Tel (0351) 422-3446.
Open 9am–12:30pm, 4:30–8pm daily.

Since its founding, this single block has been the focal point of Córdoba city. Adorned with Italianate cast-iron fountains, acacias, palm trees, and native *palo borracho* and *lapacho* trees, it is a subtropical refuge from the city. The plaza features a monument to liberation hero José San Martín. Loved by the locals, it is a popular venue for strolls. The **Cabildo**

Independencia 30, formerly the colonial headquarters, sits on the western side of the plaza. The original building was erected here at the end of the 16th century, functioning at various times as prison, law courts, and police station, as well as provincial parliament. The present building dates from the 1780s; elegant arches decorate the white façade, while antique lamps hang over the vaulted colonnade supported by slender pillars.

The **Iglesia Catedral** was built in 1782 and is the country's oldest cathedral. Part Baroque, part Neo-Classical, the church has towers that are notable for the angelic trumpet-players wearing the exotic garb of the Guaraní craftsmen who sculpted them. Inside, rococo features and a floor of Valencian tiles enliven the somber atmosphere. A silver tabernacle is housed in a side-chapel to the left of the 19th-century main altar.

Also overlooking the square are the Banco Nación; the remains of the colonial mansion of the city's first bishop, Manuel Mercadillo; and Museo Gregorio Funes, which houses a collection of Catholic artifacts and holds art exhibitions.

Córdoba

① Plaza San Martín
② Museo Histórico Provincial Marqués de Sobremonte
③ Cripta Jesuítica del Noviciado Viejo
④ Museo Municipal de Bellas Artes Dr. Genaro Peréz
⑤ Museo Histórico de la Universidad Nacional de Córdoba

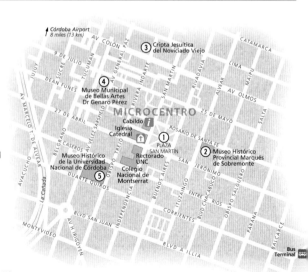

0 meters 300
0 yards 300

For keys to symbols *see back flap*

🏛 Museo Histórico Provincial Marqués de Sobremonte

Rosario de Santa Fe 218.
Tel (0351) 433-1661. **Open** 9:30am–2:30pm Mon–Fri.

The superb 18th-century building that houses this museum was once the city's largest colonial residence, home of the Governor-General of Córdoba, Marqués de Sobremonte, between 1784 and 1798. He was largely responsible for modernizing the city's sanitation. While only a few of the items on display in the museum belonged to the Marqués, most are from the same period. These include some wonderful paintings in the style of the Peruvian Cusco School, some of which have been restored and seem to glow ethereally in the light. The cedarwood altarpiece in the Capilla Azul (Blue Chapel) and the religious paintings in the adjoining room compete for attention with various secular displays of pharmaceutical products, musical instruments, and home furnishings.

🕳 Cripta Jesuítica del Noviciado Viejo

Cnr, Rivera Indarte & Ave Colón.
Tel (0351) 434-1228. **Open** 10am–4pm Mon–Fri.

Unearthed in 1989, this underground site was a Jesuit novitiate in the 1600s and 1700s, until the Society of Jesus was expelled from Argentina in 1773. The remnants of the original brickwork can be seen in fragments on the walls. The three original naves carved into the rock are used to house cultural exhibitions and conferences. Good acoustics also enable theatrical performances here.

🏛 Museo Municipal de Bellas Artes Dr. Genaro Pérez

Ave General Paz 33. **Tel** (0351) 434-1646. **Open** 10am–8pm Tue–Sun. 🆆 **museogenaroperez. wordpress.com**

Dedicated to Argentinian works of the 18th and 19th centuries, this municipal art gallery is

The stylish exterior of Museo Municipal de Bellas Artes

located in a lovely 19th-century mansion built in the French style by its owner, Dr. Tomás Garzón. Many of the paintings hail from the local Cordobesa School, whose leading practitioner was Genaro Pérez (1807–54).

Many of the works are influenced by the French Impressionists, with a focus on the landscapes of the sierras and portraits of local politicians and aristocrats. There is also a collection of art from the 1880s and the 1920s, the former characterized by social realism, and the latter by European Cubism and Surrealism.

Antique guitar at Museo Histórico

🕳 Museo Histórico de la Universidad Nacional de Córdoba

Obispo Trejo 242. **Tel** (0351) 433-2075. **Open** 9am–6:30pm Mon–Sat. 🆆 **museosdecordoba.com.ar**
Iglesia de la Compañía **Open** 8am–1pm, 5–8pm Tue–Sun. 🚻 noon, 8pm.

Granted by the colonial rulers to the Jesuits in 1583, this complex is also called Manzana de los Jesuitas (Jesuit Block). From here the Society of Jesus oversaw their mission to convert native peoples across central and northwestern Argentina, as well as the administration of their farming and agricultural interests. The complex, along with five Jesuit estancias in the province, was recognized by UNESCO as a World Heritage Site in 2000.

Iglesia de la Compañía was built in 1640 and is the country's oldest surviving Jesuit temple. The interior and exterior are

simple, almost rustic in their lack of adornment, while the nave has panels depicting the trials of the Jesuits. The most striking elements of the church are the Cusco altarpiece and the elaborate pulpit. A doorway marked Puerta del Cielo (Gateway to Heaven) provides access to the Capilla Doméstica. This small space is a model of artisanal church decoration, featuring bamboo and raw-hide panels painted using vegetable pigments.

South of the church is the **Rectorado de la Universidad Nacional de Córdoba (UNC)**. Dating from 1621, this is Argentina's oldest university. Shaded patios, bougainvillea, and well-stocked libraries make this a pleasant place of study. The **Colegio Nacional de Monserrat** located nearby is another Jesuit edifice. An earlier school, located outside the city, was founded in 1687, but was transferred to the present site in 1782, after the Jesuit priests had been expelled. An all-male school until 1998, it still enjoys a reputation as an elite center of learning. The neo-colonial shell is embellished with majolica tiling, ornate door-ways, and window grilles.

The grand Cusco altarpiece at Iglesia de la Compañía

The altar and pews of Iglesia Parroquial Nuestra Señora de la Merced

❷ Alta Gracia

Road map B2. 25 miles (40 km) SW of Córdoba. 🗺 43,000. 🚌 ℹ️ (0347) 428-128. 🌐 **altagracia.gov.ar**

In the prosperous agricultural belt of the Calmuchita Valley is the small, historic town of Alta Gracia. It was founded by the Jesuits on land granted to them in the 17th century by the colonial government. The Jesuits built a large ranch, part of a network of similar sites developed to help fund the Universidad Nacional de Córdoba, one of Latin America's oldest universities. The Alta Gracia estancia, which fell into disuse after the Jesuits' expulsion in 1773, was named a UNESCO World Heritage Site in 2000. It is now the **Museo Histórico Casa del Virrey Liniers**.

Alta Gracia came into prominence in the 1920s and 30s when it attracted wealthy Argentinians in search of fresh air and second homes. The most famous of these were the families of Ernesto Che Guevara and Spanish composer Manuel de Falla.

To the north of the city is the Tajamar, an artificial lake built by the Jesuits in 1653 and probably the first of its kind in the Americas. Located here is the town's clock tower, built in 1938 to commemorate Alta Gracia's 350th anniversary.

Religious painting, Museo Liniers

🏛 Iglesia Parroquial Nuestra Señora de la Merced

Plaza Manuel Solares. **Tel** (03547) 421-303. 🕐 Jan–Feb: 9:30am–8pm Tue–Sun & hols; Mar–Dec: 9am–1pm, 3–7pm Tue–Fri, 9:30am–12:30pm, 3:30–6:30pm Sat, Sun, & hols. 🕐 Jan–Feb: 8pm Mon–Sat, 10am Sun; Mar–Dec: 6pm Mon–Sat, 10am & 6pm Sun. 🌐 **museoliniers.org.ar**

Designed by Andrés Blanqui, this is one of Argentina's finest extant churches of the late Italian Baroque style. Its curved outer walls resemble a cross, and the highly ornamented interior has a carved wooden pulpit and a columned altar.

🏛 Museo Manuel de Falla

Pellegrini 1011. **Tel** (03547) 429-292. **Open** Jan–Feb: 9am–8pm daily; Mar–Dec: 2–6:30pm Mon, 9am–6:30pm Tue–Sun. 🌐 free Wed. 🌐 call ahead. 🌐 **altagracia.gov.ar/cultura**

Fleeing the Franco regime in 1939, Manuel de Falla, one of Spain's greatest modern composers, lived in Argentina until his death in 1946. From 1942 onwards he lived in Alta Gracia in a small house which has been converted into this excellent museum.

The Museo Manuel de Falla re-creates the composer's life, showcasing his music and various musical influences with exhibits that include his library, his piano, and his personal letters. Although Manuel de Falla chose to live in Alta Gracia because of its reputation for fresh mountain air, one of the displays is the machine used to roll his cigarettes. Piano and chamber music recitals are occasionally held in the concert hall in the garden.

🏛 Museo del Che Guevara

Avellaneda 501. **Tel** (03547) 428-579. **Open** Jan–Feb: 9am–8pm daily; Mar–Dec: 2–6:30pm Mon, 9am–6:30pm Tue–Sun. 🌐 free Wed. 🌐 by prior arrangement. 🦽 limited. 🌐 **altagracia.gov.ar/museos/che**

Known as Villa Beatriz, this pretty mock-Tudor house was one of several dwellings occupied by the Guevara family during the 1930s. In 2001, it was reopened as a museum, or more as a shrine, dedicated to the revolutionary Che Guevara.

Although they do not provide an in-depth analysis of his life and ideals, the displays feature an interesting collection of family photos, Cuban bank notes, school report cards, letters from Che to his favorite aunt, and editions of books by authors favored by the adolescent Guevara, including Freud, Baudelaire, Pablo Neruda, and Jules Verne.

Home of Spanish composer Manuel de Falla, now a museum

❸ Villa General Belgrano

Road map B2. 55 miles (89km) SW of Córdoba. 🜨 5,000. 🚌 ℹ️ Julio A. Roca 168, (03546) 461-215. **Open** 8:30am–8:30pm daily. 🎪 Oktoberfest Beer Festival (Oct). 🌐 **vgb.gov.ar/turismovgb**

Founded in the 1930s, Villa General Belgrano is one of Argentina's top holiday resorts. A significant percentage of the population is descended from the surviving crew of the *Admiral Graf Spee*, the German pocket battleship scuttled off the Uruguayan coast in 1939. A monument to the crew stands in Plazoleta Graf Spee.

The town's main thoroughfare, Avenida Julio Roca, is lined with beer cellars and souvenir shops; the former purveying authentic German food and drink, the latter, an assortment of tourist merchandise. With its chocolate shops, Lutheran chapels, and strains of oom-pah music, Villa Belgrano still preserves a vibrant Germanic atmosphere, especially when it explodes into life in October with the increasingly popular annual beer festival.

❹ Parque Nacional Quebrada del Condorito

Road map B2. 53 miles (85 km) SW of Córdoba. 🚌 ℹ️ Fundación Cóndor, (03541) 433-371. **Open** 24hrs daily (visitor center: 9am–4pm Mon–Fri, 8am–8pm Sat, Sun, & hols). 📷 call ahead. 🚻 🏕️ by prior arrangement. 🌐 **condoritoapn.com.ar**

Covering an area of 16 sq miles (41 sq km), Parque Nacional Quebrada del Condorito is one of the few places in the world where condors can be seen in their natural habitat. The park surrounds a deep, misty gorge that cuts through the hills of the Pampa de Achala. The ravines form an ideal breeding ground for condors, and adult birds with wing spans of over 10 ft (3 m) can be seen

A pleasant midsummer view of the meandering Río Cosquín

circling majestically overhead. Numerous trails, some arduous and slippery, wind down the steep canyon and alongside the river at the bottom. There is a wide variety of flora and fauna that can be found along the way, including giant ferns and rare white gentians, wild cats, foxes, indigenous rodents, and several types of snake, none of which are venomous.

The majestic condor

❺ Cosquín

Road map B2. 40 miles (63 km) NW of Córdoba. 🜨 19,000. 🚌 ℹ️ Cosquín San Martín 590, (03541) 454-644. 🎪 Festival Nacional de Folklore (Jan). 🌐 **cosquinturismo.gob.ar**

Dating back to colonial times, Cosquín is one of the oldest settlements in the region. This town is built on the banks of the river of the same name and in the shadow of the 4,150-ft (1,260-m) El Pan de Azúcar. The summit of this sugar-loaf mountain affords great views of the sierras. It can be reached by *aerosilla* (chairlift) from the well-signposted lower station located at the foot of the hill.

Cosquín's fame rests on its unofficial status as Argentina's folklore capital. The Festival Nacional de Folklore, held annually in January in Plaza Próspero Molina, draws many folk and classical musicians, dance troupes, and fans from around Argentina and beyond.

The town's best year-round visitor attraction is Museo Camín Cosquín, on the RN38, which displays local archaeological and paleontological finds, including fossils, semiprecious stones, jewelry, and ceramics crafted by the area's pre-Hispanic inhabitants.

The Boyhood of Ernesto Guevara

The revolutionary Che as a young man

It was because four-year-old Ernesto Guevara suffered from asthma that his family left behind the muggy climate of Rosario for the drier air of Alta Gracia in 1932. Although he never shook off the asthma, his childhood was both happy and active and he excelled at sports. The young Ernesto's mind was no less agile. He competed in local chess tournaments from a young age and plundered his father's library for literary treasures ranging from Jack London to Sigmund Freud. For the adult Che, life would only become richer. He left Córdoba to study medicine at the University of Buenos Aires in 1947, before embarking on the first of his well-chronicled cross-country journeys in 1949. His radicalism dates from here; the restlessness and travel-hunger of a boy who read London and Verne long before he touched Marx and Trotsky was already present.

The faded exterior of the once-exclusive Hotel Edén at La Falda

❻ La Cumbre

Road map B2. 59 miles (95 km) N of Córdoba. 🏠 7,000. 🚌 ℹ️ Ave Caraffa 300, (03548) 452-966. 🌐 alacumbre.com

The name La Cumbre (The Summit) was given to this town because it was the last and highest stop on the old British-built railroad line that began from Córdoba city. The trains stopped chuffing up the hill a long time ago, but La Cumbre's timbered mock-Tudor cottages, lovely manicured lawns, and the famous golf club still testify to the long-standing Anglo-Saxon presence. La Cumbre is a laid-back town known for its trout fishing spots and horseback riding. It has also become synonymous with adventure sports such as hang gliding and paragliding. Competitions are held here annually in March. Some of the best views of the surrounding Punilla Valley can be had from the climb up to the Cristo Redentor statue on Cerro Viarapa.

Environs
Just 8 miles (13 km) south of La Cumbre, **La Falda** is a larger town and another good base for outdoor pursuits. Visitors can tour the interiors of the town's once exclusive Hotel Edén, which closed in the 1960s; in its heyday it welcomed royalty, presidents, and a former patents clerk named Albert Einstein.

❼ Jesús María

Road map C2. 32 miles (51 km) N of Córdoba. 🏠 21,000. 🚌 ℹ️ Jesús María, Acmafuerte 451, (03525) 443-773. 🎭 Fiesta Nacional de Doma y Folklore (Jan).

Founded in the 16th century, the sleepy market town of Jesús María was once an important link in the chain of agricultural estancias built by the Jesuits to feed and fund the University of Córdoba. Most of the town's historical buildings date from the mid-1700s. In 1946 the old church, convent, *bodega*, and residences were converted into **Museo Jesuítico Nacional de Jesús María**. The museum contains archaeological finds and sacred relics. The famous Jesuit winery can also be visited. It was here, so the story goes, that the first colonial wine served to the Spanish royal family was produced.

In January the town's population temporarily swells to over 200,000 when it plays host to one of Argentina's most popular gaucho and folk festivals, the Fiesta Nacional de Doma y Folklore. Lasting ten days, this fiesta combines extremely daring feats of horsemanship with improvised folk singing that doubles as a commentary on the rodeo action.

🏛 Museo Jesuítico Nacional de Jesús María
Pedro de Oñate s/n. **Tel** (03525) 420-126. **Open** 8am–7pm Tue–Fri, 10am–noon, 2–6pm Sat & Sun (Oct–Mar: 3–7pm). 🎭 Tue free. 📷 on request. 🌐 estanciajesusmaria.org

The Museo Jesuítico Nacional de Jesús María

❽ Santa Catalina
See pp190–91.

A gaucho textile display at Museo Folklórico in La Rioja

❾ La Rioja

Road map B2. 290 miles (467 km) NW of Córdoba. 🏠 150,000. 🚍 🚌 ℹ️ La Rioja, Yrigoyen 91, (0800) 999-5300. 🌐 municipiolarioja.gov.ar

Located at the foot of the granite Velasco Sierras, La Rioja is the capital city of the namesake province. Founded in 1591 by Juan Ramírez de Velasco, it has been struck regularly by major earthquakes over the intervening centuries, the most destructive of which was in 1894. The city was an unremarkable agricultural outpost until the 1970s, when industrialization sparked a population surge. Although a pleasant city to visit most of the year, it is uncomfortable during the summer months when temperatures regularly exceed 40° C (104° F). The best time to visit is in spring, when the climate is relatively cool and the parched air is perfumed by the multitude of blossoms on the jacaranda and orange trees. Due to these blooms, La Rioja has often been referred to as La Ciudad de los Naranjos (the City of Oranges). Around Plaza 25 de Mayo, the city's main

Stunning red cliffs at Parque Nacional Talampaya, weathered by millennia of wind and rain

square, is the neo-colonial government building, Casa de Gobierno, and to the south, **Catedral San Nicolás de Bari**, which contains a 17th-century image of the saint, carved from walnut wood. **Iglesia Santo Domingo**, one block east of the plaza, dates from 1623 and is said to be the oldest building in Argentina. Its highlights include the carob-wood doors, carved by indigenous artisans in the 17th century. Located west of the plaza, **Museo Folklórico** is a superbly organized reconstruction of a Victorian Riojano dwelling, packed with hand-carved furnishings and gaucho gear. It also has a display on local myths and legends.

⛪ Iglesia Santo Domingo
Lamadrid 111. **Open** 9am–12:30pm, 6–10pm Mon–Sat; mornings only Sun.

🏛 Museo Folklórico
Pelagio B Luna 811. **Tel** (03822) 428-500. **Open** 9am–1pm, 4–8pm Tue–Fri, 9am–1pm Sat & Sun.

Statue of San Martín at La Rioja's Plaza 25 de Mayo

❿ Parque Nacional Talampaya

Road map B2. 135 miles (216 km) SW of La Rioja. **🛈** L. N. Acem s/n, (03825) 470-356. **🚌 Open** May–Sep: 8:30am–5:30pm daily; Oct–Apr: 8am–6pm daily. **w** tampalaya.gov.ar

Designated a national park by President Menem in 1997, Parque Nacional Talampaya is also a UNESCO World Heritage Site. Its name comes from the indigenous words *ktala* (the local *tala* bush), and *ampaya* (dry riverbed). The park covers an area of 97 sq miles (251 sq km) and contains some of Argentina's most amazing natural features, including

sheer sandstone cliffs that soar up to 590 ft (180 m) from the plain. Millions of years of torrential rain and dry, gritty winds have sculpted the cliffs into fantastic shapes, their anthropomorphic qualities earning them imaginative nicknames such as The Monk and The Three Kings. Apart from the rock formations, guides can also point visitors towards pre-Columbian glyphs scratched into the cliff faces and patches of rare flora. Condors and eagles glide majestically overhead. Apart from the wind and the occasional bird cry, the predominant sound is one of silence.

The Legend of Facundo Quiroga

One of the most famed and feared of Argentina's early 19th-century gaucho chieftains, Juan Facundo Quiroga (1790–1835) was born into a poor family of cattle breeders. He was nicknamed "the tiger of the plains" by his friends and enemies alike. Quiroga fought briefly in the revolutionary wars before rising quickly to the head of the Andean provincial armies. When his de facto military rule came under threat from the Centralist forces of President Rivadavia, who had established a "Unitarian"

19th-century lithograph of Quiroga greeted by supporters

constitution in 1826, Quiroga led his Federalist army through a series of victories and defeats until finally beating the Centralist army in Salta. In 1934, while en route to Buenos Aires after a mission in the northern provinces, he was ambushed and murdered by gunmen. Facundo's lasting fame owes as much to his biographer, writer and statesman Domingo Sarmiento, as to his own infamous achievements.

❽ Santa Catalina

A UNESCO World Heritage Site, this Jesuit estancia was founded in 1622. It became an important agricultural and sheepfarming establishment, yet its most important function was as the provider of thousands of mules for cargo trains traveling along the Camino Real between Buenos Aires and Alto Perú (now Bolivia). The extensive site contained workshops, a smithy, a carpentry, two flour mills, and a reservoir; there were also residences for priests, native laborers, and slaves. Its soaring main church is one of the best examples of colonial Baroque in the country. While it is now administered by the state in accordance with a presidential decree, Santa Catalina remains the private property of the Díaz family.

Corridor characterized by plain brick walls and curved ceiling

Rear Courtyard
The rear patio is surrounded by workshops and possibly residences for laborers, though slaves were housed in a building apart from the main complex.

★ **Central Courtyard**
The grandest of the three main patios, this is enclosed by a vaulted gallery and has a central fountain. Cloisters and workshops occupy the rooms along the sides.

★ **Altar**
Above the main wooden altar stands a gilded retablo (altarpiece) housing an image of Saint Catherine (Santa Catalina). Other wooden statues include one of the Señor de la Humilidad y la Paciencia, and another of the crucified Christ.

The cemetery is where priests and workers were buried, some of whom had spent their entire life at the estancia.

Front Courtyard
A quiet and plain patio, the front courtyard would have been used by the Jesuit priests to receive deliveries from the neighboring towns as well as for non-ecclesiastical gatherings.

★ **Church Façade**
The high and elegant white façade has two towers and curved pediments framing the doorway, typical of the Baroque school of architecture.

Statue of Virgen del Valle, Catedral de Nuestra Señora del Valle

❶ San Fernando del Valle de Catamarca

Road map B2. 96 miles (154 km) NE of La Rioja. 🗷 141,000. ✈ 🚌 ℹ Ave Gral. Roca 50, Manzana de Turismo, (0383) 445-5308. 🗷 National Poncho Festival (Jul).
Ⓦ turismocatamarca.gob.ar

Founded in 1683, San Fernando del Valle de Catamarca, usually called just Catamarca, is the capital of the San Fernando province. It is a quiet town that has a number of sights worth seeing, though it is advisable to keep away during the area's hot summer months.

The city's nucleus is its main square, Plaza 25 de Mayo, designed by French landscaper Charles Thays. The palm, orange, and *palo borracho* trees provide welcome shade from the blistering afternoon sun. On the western side of the square is the 19th-century Neo-Classical **Catedral de Nuestra Señora del Valle**. Under its brick-red terracotta façade, it houses, in an elaborate antechamber, one of the country's most venerated religious relics: the diamond-crowned statue of the Virgen del Valle. She is said to have "appeared" to locals in the 19th century, and her graven image now attracts thousands of pilgrims on the saint's feast day in December.

Catamarca's lively annual National Poncho Festival, held traditionally in July, also draws a large number of people, including the cream of folkloric talent from all across the country. The city also serves as an ideal base for those who wish to explore the province's rugged and lovely unspoiled backcountry.

🏛 **Catedral de Nuestra Señora del Valle**
Plaza 25 de Mayo. **Open** 7am–noon, 5–8pm daily.

❷ Santiago del Estero

Road map C1. 130 miles (210 km) NE of Catamarca. 🗷 245,000. 🚌 ✈ ℹ Libertad 417 (0385) 4213-253.
Ⓦ sde.gov.ar

Founded in 1553, Santiago del Estero is Argentina's oldest city. It was once full of attractive colonial architecture, most of which has been damaged by natural causes or razed to make way for new buildings.

There are, however, a few sites worth visiting, including the Neo-Classical **Catedral**, built in 1867 on the site of the former 16th-century structure. It contains a variety of ancient relics of saints. The **Provincial History Museum**, set in a grand 18th-century town house, is also a fascinating place to explore.

Santiago del Estero has a strong musical tradition. It was the birthplace of the *chacarera*, one of Argentina's most exuberant folkloric styles, which developed in the mid-19th century *(see pp33)*. Another folk rhythm and dance here is the *zamba*, and there are regular concerts by top-notch performers coming from across Argentina.

The Neo-Classical exterior of the Catedral, Santiago del Estero

❸ Termas de Río Hondo

Road map B1. 40 miles (65 km) NW of Santiago del Estero. 🗷 27,000. 🚌 ℹ Sarmiento 343, (03858) 421-768.
Ⓦ lastermasderiohondo.gov.ar/informacion.php

Located on the banks of Río Dulce (Sweet River), Termas de Río Hondo is South America's biggest spa town, packed in the high season with visitors "taking the cure." The spring waters, rich in minerals, gush out of every hotel tap and fill several public baths across town. The waters are said to be particularly effective against rheumatism and hypertension.

A pool filled with spring water in a spa hotel, Termas de Río Hondo

The Hall of Independence at the Casa Histórica de la Independencia

⓮ San Miguel de Tucumán

Road map B1. 98 miles (158 km) NW of Santiago del Estero. ⛰ 530,000. ✈ 🚌 🛈 24 De Septiembre 484, (0381) 430-3644.

The biggest and economically most important town in northwest Argentina, San Miguel de Tucumán is located in the Rió Salí Valley, to the east of the towering Sierra de Aconquija. Usually known simply as Tucumán, the town is a hectic, relatively thriving metropolis, with a youthful population and vibrant nightlife. The city has played a key role in Argentinian history – it was here, on July 9, 1816, that Argentina declared her independence from the Spanish crown. The room in which the fateful *démarche* was delivered can be visited at the **Casa Histórica de la Independencia**. The house, with a series of creeper-draped patios and whitewashed colonnades, was originally built in the late 1700s, but was razed to the ground in the late 19th century. It was replaced by a replica in the 1940s. A sound-and-light show in the garden re-enacts the story of how independence was declared.

Plaza Independencia is the focal point of San Miguel de Tucumán, with native trees, a large pool, fountains, and a statue representing Liberty. Located nearby is **Museo Folklórico**, housing a wide collection of *mate* ware, textiles, and traditional musical instruments.

🏛 **Casa Histórica de la Independencia**
Congreso 141. **Tel** (0381) 431-0826. **Open** 10am–6pm daily. Sound-and-Light Show: 8:30pm Fri–Wed. 🔊
🌐 museocasahistorica.org.ar

⓯ Tafí del Valle

Road map B1. 66 miles (107 km) W of Tucumán. ⛰ 4,500. 🚌 🛈 Los Faroles s/n.
🌐 tucumanturismo.gov.ar

Peruvian pelican, Casa Histórica de la Independencia

A popular weekend getaway during the blistering summer months, Tafí del Valle is a small town. It is located significantly higher than Tucumán, making it cooler with average summer temperatures of 12º C (54º F). The road taking travelers up from the sticky lowlands winds through forests and lemon orchards, and up into the pleasant highlands. Sunny but bearable weather is guaranteed all year round, making Tafí del Valle an ideal base for hiking, fishing, and horseback-riding trips. Trails snake their way up the surrounding peaks, which include Cerro El Matadero and Cerro Pabellón, both topping 10,000 ft (3,000 m).

The town has a number of hotels, restaurants, and adventure tourism agencies around the central plaza.

⓰ Quilmes

Road map B1. 110 miles (177 km) NW of Tucumán. 🚌 **Open** daily, subject to staffing: check ahead by calling (0381) 430-3644. 🔊 📷 ♿ limited. 🔊

One of the most important and best preserved archaeological sites in Argentina, the Quilmes ruins are the last vestiges of a city founded by the pre-Incan tribe of the same name in the 9th century AD. It was originally intended to be a bulwark against Inca incursions. The population peaked here in the 17th century, at close to 6,000. The settlement had by then held out for around 150 years against attacks by the better-armed Spanish conquerors.

The ruins have been expertly excavated and preserved – stone walls, terraces, and even entire buildings can be seen, and the effect of walking through them is haunting. The excellent on-site museum displays tools and weaponry excavated in the area. The Hotel Ruinas de Quilmes is located at the foot of the ruins.

The excavated Quilmes ruins dating back to the 9th century AD

⓱ Cafayate

Road map B1. 140 miles (225 km) NW of Tucumán. 🚍 12,000. 🚌 ℹ️ San Martín 26, (03868) 422-442/422-223. 🎭 Folk Festival (Mar). 🌐 turismosalta.gov.ar

Considered one of the prettiest towns in Argentina, Cafayate is a natural stopover for anyone touring the Valles Calchaquíes or traveling between Quilmes, Tucumán, and Salta. Cafayate was settled at the beginning of the 18th century by Franciscan missionaries. They made use of the two rivers passing through, Río Chuschas and Río Loro Huasi, to create indigenous farming reserves. Cafayate was officially founded in 1840, and soon after, a number of *bodegas* were established on the slopes that rise gradually around the edges of town.

With the tranquil ambience of a village, Cafayate today has restaurants, museums, and a few colonial mansions. Southwest of the main plaza is **Museo Arqueológico Rodolfo Bravo**, whose ceramic and urn displays tell the story of the area's native inhabitants. The nearby **Museo de la Vid y del Vino** displays a variety of wine-related relics.

The vineyards of Cafayate are exceptional, the grandest being Finca La Rosa. Now the **Patios de Cafayate Hotel y Spa**, La Rosa was established in 1892. Surrounded by vineyards and geraniums and rose bushes, this colonial-style ranch is a classic

The huge monolith El Obelisco at Quebrada de las Conchas

Argentinian aristocratic estancia. It also has a wine-themed spa and a stylish swimming pool.

🏛 **Museo Arqueológico Rodolfo Bravo**
Colón 191. **Tel** (03868) 421-054. **Open** 11am–7pm daily (worth calling ahead).

🏛 **Museo de la Vid y del Vino**
Ave Güemes s/n. **Open** 10am–7:30pm Tue–Sun & hols. 🅿️
🌐 museodelavidyelvino.gov.ar

🏨 **Patios de Cafayate Hotel y Spa**
RN 40 & RN 68, Salta. **Tel** (03868) 422-229. 🌐 patiosdecafayate.com

⓲ Quebrada de las Conchas

Road map B1. 12 miles (20 km) N of Cafayate. 🚌

The Quebrada de Humahuaca (*see pp200–4*) wears the UNESCO World Heritage Site title, but for many travelers in northwestern Argentina the red-rock ravine of Las Conchas ("the shells") is just as memorable. The towering walls of the ravine are an explosion of scarlet and crimson, rust, and vermilion. Río Conchas flows through the valley floor, but only a narrow strip of land is fertile.

Wind and storm showers over the years have led to erosion, leaving behind surreal rock formations. Some outstanding ones have been given nicknames, such as the gigantic Los Médanos (The Dunes) and El Obelisco. A huge ravine on the east side is known as La Garganta del Diablo (The Devil's Throat), while a solitary rock is named El Sapo (The Toad).

Ruta Nacional 68 runs through this ravine, connecting Cafayate with Salta. Along the route, locals sell handicrafts, such as ceramics.

⓳ Molinos

Road map B1. 155 miles (250 km) N of Cafayate. 🚍 4,000. 🚌 🎭 Virgin of the Candelaria (Feb).

Founded in the mid-17th century, Molinos (Mills) was a feudal estate producing corn-flour, wheatflour, alfalfa, peppers, and wine until Argentinian Independence in 1816. Most visitors only pass through this remote hamlet on a drive through the Valles Calchaquíes. However, the town's colonial, 18th-century **Iglesia San Pedro Nolasco de Molinos** is well worth a visit. A small preserve nearby gives protection to native *vicuña*.

The dramatic landscape of cactus-clad slopes around the town is ideal for riding and trekking. Around 6 miles (10 km)

Fermentation tanks in one of Cafayate's many *bodegas*

A Spanish-style parish church built in the 1600s, Molinos

away from town is the Estancia Colomé, a huge vineyard and agricultural estate owned by Swiss businessman Douglas Hess. It has an art gallery, a smart restaurant, a good library, and an open-air pool with sweeping views of the beautiful surrounding mountains.

⑳ Cachi

Road map B1. 85 miles (136 km) N of Cafayate. 🏔 4,000. 🚌 ℹ️ Ave Guemes & Benjamin Solillas, (03868) 491-902. 🎭 Fiesta de San José (Mar).

Founded in the 18th century, Cachi is a quiet village with a rustic atmosphere, retaining only a few original adobe properties from that period. This picturesque village, known for its pretty plaza lined with palms and orange trees, sits at the foot of the towering, snowcapped Nevado del Cachi which stands at 20,932 ft (6,380 m). The small **Museo Arqueológico Pío Pablo Díaz** to the east of the plaza has displays of items used by the origi-nal inhabitants of Valles Calchaquíes. Also worth a visit is the extensively restored **Iglesia San José**, north of the main plaza, with a classic white façade, wooden floor, and remarkable cactus-wood altar. Small shops around the town center sell local crafts that include ceramics and ponchos with lovely designs.

At 7,480 ft (2,280 m) above sea level, Cachi's microclimate is pleasant for most of the year. The rainfall it receives keeps the maize terraces, vineyards, and plantations of peppers and legumes green and healthy. A drive to the nearby hamlet of Cachi Adentro offers lovely views of farmlands interspersed with carpets of red pepper fields drying in the sun.

🏛 **Museo Arqueológico Pío Pablo Díaz**
Juan Calchaquí s/n. **Tel** (03868) 491-080. **Open** 10am–7pm Mon–Fri, 10am–6pm Sat, 11am–2pm Sun. **Closed** public hols.

The 16-ft (5-m) tall *cardones* at the Parque Nacional Los Cardones

㉑ Parque Nacional Los Cardones

Road map B1. 16 miles (25 km) N of Cafayate. 🚌 ℹ️ Ave San Martín s/n, (03868) 496-005. **Open** daily. 🌐 **parquesnacionales.gov.ar**

Created in 1996, the 158-acre (64-ha) Parque Nacional Los Cardones protects the *cardón* cacti that cover this dusty valley, as well as other species of flora that are suited to the arid climate. The preserve was established to protect the *cardones*, which were widely being used for firewood or to make furniture. Although

Wooden shovel, Museo Arqueológico

some of the gigantic cacti can reach heights of 16 ft (5 m), these plants grow only a few millimeters every year. They are found between 8,858 ft (2,700 m) and 18,044 ft (5,500 m) above sea level.

Rare bird species such as the endemic Steinbach's canastero and the little-known Zimmer's tapaculo can be spotted throughout the park, along with condors, falcons, and numerous species of tyrant and finch. Parque Nacional Los Cardones is also an important paleontological site, containing traces of dinosaur footprints dating from more than 70 million years ago.

The Wines of Salta

There has been winemaking in the scattered oases of the province of Salta since the days of the Spanish conquest. In the 17th century, winemakers in the area supplied priests and monks, who needed wine for mass. Today, there are *terroirs* at a variety of altitudes, ranging from 5,577 ft (1,700 m) in Cafayate and 6,561 ft (2,000 m) in Yacochuya Comarca de la Viña to 7,874 ft (2,400 m) in Colomé. Benefiting from long hours of sunshine and fast-flowing streams fed by rains that wash off the high peaks to the west, the vineyards of Salta are some of the most visually striking in the world. Cabernet Sauvignon and Malbec grapes prosper here, as do Chardonnay and Chenin. A small number of vineyards are also succeeding with Tannat, a grape more often associated with Uruguay. The most famous varietal from Salta is the aromatic Torrontés white, a wine that has fallen out of favor in Europe but thrives in this region. Its success has made the wine Argentina's most popular after Malbec.

Grapes ready to be picked at a *bodega*

❷ Street-by-Street: Salta

Many of Salta's well-preserved colonial gems are centered around Plaza 9 de Julio and a short stroll takes visitors down streets lined with churches and civic buildings, as well as handsome 18th- and 19th-century town houses. When the town was founded in 1582, the plaza was sited here to provide an outpost with strategic views over the surrounding plain. Natural moats, long since covered over in the *microcentro*, were another factor that made the city an attractive settlement. The main cathedral, *cabildo*, and the city's cultural center are all on the plaza, and the most striking church, Iglesia San Francisco, is two blocks east.

★ Catedral Basílica de Salta
This Neo-Classical cathedral dates from 1882, the third centenary of the city.

Museo de Arqueología de Alta Montaña de Salta
An ancient mummy discovered in the Andes, a ceramics collection, and Carnaval masks are the highlights of this museum dedicated to pre-Columbian cultures of the Northwest.

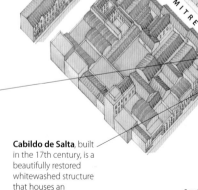

Casa de Gobierno
Now a cultural center that goes by the grand name of Casa Cultural América, this striking building, built in 1913 in the French style, was once the headquarters of the provincial government.

Cabildo de Salta, built in the 17th century, is a beautifully restored whitewashed structure that houses an eclectic collection of religious art and archaeological finds.

| 0 meters | | 50 |
| 0 yards | | 50 |

★ **Iglesia y Convento San Francisco**
Salta's most iconic church, built between the mid-18th and mid-19th centuries, is a grandiose exercise in exuberant Italianate Neo-Classicism. It houses images of Señora de las Nieves (Our Lady of the Snow) and San Pedro de Alcántara, attributed to Spanish sculptor and architect Alonso Cano.

VISITORS' CHECKLIST

Practical Information
Road Map B1. 995 miles (1600 km) NW of Buenos Aires. 464,000. Buenos Aires 93, (0800) 222-2752, (0387) 431-0950. Culture Festival (Apr). Casa de Gobierno: Mitre 23, Plaza 9 de Julio, (0387) 431-7327. Museo Casa Uriburu: Caseros 417, (0387) 421-8174. **Open** 9:30am–6pm Tue–Fri, 9am–1:30pm Sat. El Solar del Convento: Caseros 444, (0387) 421-5124.
turismosalta.gov.ar

Transport

Convento de San Bernardo

Key
— Suggested route

Museo Casa Uriburu
One of the finest neo-colonial edifices in Salta, this late 18th-century house boasts period furnishings formerly used by the powerful Uriburu family.

El Solar del Convento, once a Jesuit convent, is now a restaurant serving regional specialties (see p294).

★ **Plaza 9 de Julio**
Bordered by elegant *recovas* (arcades), this plaza is Salta's social hub and a great spot for people-watching over coffee.

DEAN FUNES
CASEROS
CÓRDOBA
BUENOS AIRES
GENERAL ALVARADO
ERDI

Exploring Salta

Founded in 1582, Salta is derived from the Diaguita word *sagta*, which means "beautiful." With its dramatic Andean backdrop, its array of well-preserved colonial and neo-colonial buildings, and its thriving cultural and gastronomic scene, it is a city that lives up to its name. As well as being the ideal base from which to explore its namesake province, Salta provides a range of interesting things to see and experience. A large number of the city's most beautiful and historically important buildings are clustered around Plaza 9 de Julio. Salta has excellent restaurants and lively *peñas* (folk music venues) where many regional delicacies can be sampled, such as the delicious *empanadas salteñas* and *locro* stew.

A cluster of sidewalk cafés lining the streets of Salta

🏛 Plaza 9 de Julio

Bounded by Calles Caseros, España, Mitre, & Zuviría.

One of the most attractive and best-maintained town squares in the country, Plaza 9 de Julio is Salta's center and the most logical place from which to start exploring the city. The middle section of the square comprises plenty of greenery in the form of palm and *tipa* trees, as well as fountains, benches, and a lovely 19th-century bandstand. It is bordered on all sides by elegant *recovas*, perfect for sipping a coffee and watching the city's ebb and flow.

The northern end of the plaza is dominated by the cream-colored **Catedral Basílica de Salta**. Originally a Neo-Gothic structure, it was built by Italian architects in 1882 to mark the city's third centenary, and later remodeled in the Neo-Classical style. Some eye-catching frescoes adorn the interior walls.

🏛 Cabildo de Salta

Caseros 549. **Tel** (0387) 421-5340. **Open** 9:30am–1:30pm, 3:30–8:30pm Tue–Sun, 4:30–8:30pm Sat. 🎫 📷 11am, 12:30pm, 5pm, & 7pm. ♿ 🖥 📷 🖥 **museonor.gov.ar/cabildo** **Museo Histórico del Norte Tel** same as the Cabildo. **Open** 9am–6pm Tue–Fri, 9am–1:30pm Sat & Sun.

On the southern side of Plaza 9 de Julio, the white-façaded Cabildo de Salta was originally built in the early 17th century and is the oldest surviving colonial structure in the city. The *cabildo* was extensively, and rather clumsily, reconfigured in 1780, resulting in two rows of arches that do not line up.

Inside the *cabildo* is the **Museo Histórico del Norte**, which exhibits various artifacts from the pre-Columbian, colonial, and 19th-century epochs, including coins, archaeological finds, architectural blueprints, and colonial furniture. Noteworthy is the superb 18th-century wooden pulpit depicting saints Augustine, Jerome, Ambrose, and Aquinas. Temporary exhibitions are held regularly and showcase the work of contemporary artists from the region. Workshops and activities for children also take place here.

🏛 Museo de Arqueología de Alta Montaña de Salta

Mitre 77. **Tel** (0387) 437-0592. **Open** 11am–7:30pm Tue–Sun. 📷 free Wed. 📷 prior arrangement only. ♿ 🖥 📷 🖥 **maam.gob.ar**

Dedicated to cultures and peoples found in high-altitude locations, this is one of the best museums of its kind in the country. It was set up by the provincial government in order to exhibit the Llullaillaco Children. These three Inca infants were found in 1999, preserved in ice near the peak of Mount Llullaillaco, the highest peak in the Salta province. They were buried in the 1400s just prior to the Spanish conquest and a natural process of mummification left them perfectly preserved. The permanent collection includes over 150

The elegant arches and shaded courtyard of Cabildo de Salta

The striking Iglesia y Convento San Francisco

for a building that was completed piecemeal over several centuries, the overall effect is a pleasing one of harmony and balance, of Latino exuberance tempered by Latinist rigor.

🏛 Iglesia y Convento San Bernardo

Calle Caseros 73. **Tel** (0387) 431-0092. **Open** 9am–noon, 4–6pm Mon–Sat, 8–10:30am Sun. 🅿 🚻 8–10:30am Sun. 🆆 saltalalinda.gov.ar

The oldest surviving ecclesiastical complex in Salta, Iglesia y Convento San Bernardo is considered one of the most beautiful religious buildings in the country. This is still a Carmelite nunnery and thus closed to the public, except for occasional matins. It was originally intended to be a hospital dedicated to Saint Andrew. The earliest parts of the building date from the late 16th century. In 1846, both the patron saint and the function were switched and it became a monastery. Several

Carved rococo door at the Iglesia y Convento San Bernardo

earthquakes and the late 19th-century enthusiasm for "improvement" meant that the structure has been much altered over the centuries. However, the dark, intricate rococo doors that are still in place were carved from walnut wood by indigenous craftsmen in 1762 and installed in 1845.

The site is still evocative: the building is set against the foothills of the Andean mountains, with simple lime-washed walls bathed in soft light falling from lamps in wrought-iron fittings.

artifacts that were buried with the children, originally intended to accompany them into the next world, but now on display to the public.

Temporary exhibitions at the museum illuminate other aspects of indigenous culture, with a particular focus on pre-Hispanic textiles and tapestries – objects of primary importance in a culture that never developed alphabetical writing. Other activities at the museum include workshops on archaeology, multimedia storytelling sessions for kids, and classes in Andean dance.

🏛 Iglesia y Convento San Francisco

Calle Córdoba 15. **Tel** (0387) 431-0830. **Open** 10:30am–12:30pm, 4:30–6:30pm Tue–Fri, 10:30am–12:30pm Sat. 🅿 🚻 🚻 9am & 8pm Mon–Sat, 9am, 11:30am, & 8pm Sun. 🆆 saltalalinda.gov.ar

Probably Salta's best-known landmark, this spectacular church endures as one of the finest examples of both Neo-Classical and colonial architecture in the country. The main building and convent date from the mid-18th century, while the façade, with its Latin inscriptions and eclectic symbols, and the atrium are the work of Italian architect Luigi Giorgi and were completed in 1870. A statue of Saint Francis, his habit flowing and his arms folded within it, stands in the courtyard, while the slender tower dominates the city's skyline. Miraculously,

Train to the Clouds

Designed by US engineer Richard Fontaine Maury, this famous route connects north Argentina with the mining regions of Chile. Although the line was inaugurated in 1948, the train assumed its current, purely touristic, function in the 1970s. The train leaves once a week from General Belgrano station in Salta, taking passengers on a 280-mile (450-km), 15-hour round trip that includes 29 bridges, 13 viaducts, and countless breathtaking vistas and heart-stopping moments. Salta's Tren a las Nubes (Train to the Clouds) is not a metaphorical conceit – it is entirely descriptive. The highest and last of the viaducts, La Polvorilla, launches into thin air at 13,850 ft (4,220 m) above sea level and takes the train above as well as through the cloud line, giving passengers the impression of being on some kind of otherworldly, celestial express.

Salta's Tren a las Nubes passing over Polvorilla viaduct

㉓ Quebrada de Humahuaca

The magnificent Quebrada de Humahuaca is a geological marvel, a canyon steeped in Argentinian history. As the road rises beyond Purmamarca, the technicolor strata of the walls of the Río Grande Valley are revealed. At dawn and sunset, shades of rose, emerald, violet, and every hue of yellow and brown can be seen glowing on the rocky surface. Adding human warmth to this beautiful landscape is a cluster of towns that hold fiercely to native traditions. The indigenous communities pay homage to the Pachamama of their ancestors and every festival is celebrated with a colorful carnival parade and wonderful folk concerts.

Shops selling traditional clothes and crafts, Tilcara

★ Tilcara
The liveliest of the *quebrada* towns, Tilcara is the site of an important *pucará* (pre-Columbian fortification) that was discovered in 1903 and reconstructed in the 1950s.

Maimará is a charming village nestling next to a hill known as Painter's Palette.

Posta de Hornillos
The restored site was once the residence of General Belgrano during the independence struggle.

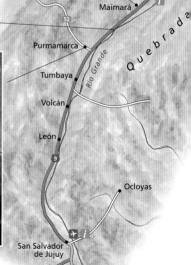

J U J U Y

El Aguilar

Huacale

Tilcara

Maimará

Purmamarca

Tumbaya

Volcán

León

Ocloyas

San Salvador de Jujuy

Salta

Río Grande

Quebrada

★ Purmamarca
Apart from the multihued rock strata on *Cerro de Siete Colores* (Hill of Seven Colors), this town is also famous for its artisanal markets.

For hotels and restaurants see pp278–83 and pp288–99

La Quiaca

bra Pampa

Potrero

Tres Cruces

Pueblo
Viejo

Iruya

Iturbe

Humahuaca

ura

Key

Expressway

Highway

Minor road

VISITORS' CHECKLIST

Practical Information
Road map B1.
78 miles (125 km) N of San
Salvador de Jujuy.
 San Salvador de Jujuy:
Gorriti 295, (0388) 422-1326;
Tilcara: Belgrano 590, (0388) 495-
5720. All Souls' Day (Nov 1),
Day of the Dead (Nov 2).
turismo.jujuy.gov.ar

Transport

Iruya
This well-preserved hamlet with
cobblestoned streets has a timeless
feel and is an excellent base for
taking walks into the beautiful
surrounding countryside.

★ **Humahuaca**
With adobe houses and whitewashed walls, Humahuaca is the most
populated settlement in the valley. Well worth visiting are the Iglesia
de la Candelaria, the *cabildo*, and the excellent handicraft stores.

0 km   20
0 miles   20

Uquia
This quiet village is noted for
its Cusco School paintings of
arcabuceros – angels armed with
Spanish weapons – on display
in its 17th-century church, Iglesia
de San Francisco de Paula.

Exploring Quebrada de Humahuaca

The easiest way to explore the stunning *quebrada* landscape is to drive along Ruta Nacional 9, which runs from the picture-postcard village of Purmamarca to the junction for the idyllic hamlet of Iruya. The road up is flanked by the towering walls of the massive multicolored gorge and the drive is especially beautiful in the mornings and evenings when the western side is soaked by sunrise and the eastern wall is hit by sunset, bringing out the flaming orange and vermilion of the mountains. To see man-made wonders along this ancient route – whitewashed colonial chapels, lush fields of quinoa, and alpaca farms – take detours to the villages of Tilcara, Uquia, Maimará, and Humahuaca.

Cerro de Siete Colores under a blue sky in Purmamarca

San Salvador de Jujuy

75 miles (121 km) N of Salta. 240,000. Gorriti 295, (0388) 422-1326. turismo.jujuy.gov.ar

Museo Histórico Provincial Juan Lavalle Lavalle 256. **Tel** (0388) 422-1355. **Open** 8am–noon, 4–8pm Mon–Sat. 10am, 11:30am, 5pm, & 6:30pm.

The capital of Jujuy province, San Salvador de Jujuy is the highest provincial capital in the country. Located 4,166 ft (1,270 m) above sea level, and flanked by Ríos Grande and Xibi Xibi, the city enjoys a temperate climate. Founded in 1593, Jujuy was destroyed and rebuilt several times due to wars and earthquakes. The city's history can best be traced through its churches that are scattered around the central Plaza General Belgrano.

To the west stands the **Catedral**, which was built in 1606. Among its treasures is the Baroque pulpit, designed by local artisans in the 18th century. Its carvings, which depict Biblical subjects such as Jacob's Ladder, are richly detailed and show both the skill of the craftsmen and the enduring eloquence of religious art.

Two blocks west of the plaza is the neo-colonial **Iglesia San Francisco**, which was built between 1925 and 1927. It is best known for its Spanish Baroque pulpit, which was carved by 18th-century Bolivian

Grand interior of the Iglesia San Francisco in San Salvador

craftsmen. South of the main plaza is **Museo Histórico Provincial Juan Lavalle**, which houses colonial paintings and artifacts. Its claim to fame, however, is its reputation as a crime scene. General Juan Lavalle was assassinated here during Argentina's civil wars in the 1840s. The hole through which the lethal bullet passed is still visible. Three blocks west of the museum is the 18th-century **Capilla de Santa Bárbara**, with an outstanding collection of religious paintings.

Quiet for most of the year, Jujuy offers little apart from leisurely strolls through its cobblestoned streets. It is an excellent base from which to explore the province's remote areas including the two cloud forest national parks, Calilegua *(see p205)* and the less accessible Barítu.

Purmamarca

40 miles (65 km) NW of Jujuy. 2,100. Rivadavia and Jujuy.

The picturesque village of Purmamarca nestles at the base of the gorge of the same name. It owes its fame to the hill that overlooks it, **Cerro de Siete Colores** (Hill of Seven Colors). The contrasting shades of the rock's strata range from grimy orange to psychedelic purple and are at their glittering best just after sunrise. A signposted route takes visitors to a viewing point just outside the village.

Posta de Hornillos

45 miles (73 km) NW of Jujuy. **Open** 9am–6pm Wed–Mon.

Built in 1772, this wonderfully evocative adobe-walled building was once a stop-off point on the route that connected the colonial viceroyalties of Upper Peru (now Bolivia) and Río de la Plata. In 1979, it was converted into a museum and its 19 rooms display old furniture, weapons of war, costumes, and historical documents from the 18th and 19th centuries. Its other claim to fame is that General Belgrano rested here after defeating the Spanish in the battles of Tucumán and Salta in 1813.

A view of tombs and crosses set against the breathtaking backdrop of the *quebrada*, Maimará

Maimará
47 miles (76 km) N of San Salvador de Jujuy. ⛰ 2,000.

Overlooked by the beautiful multicolored rock formations of the *quebrada*, the village of Maimará is best known for its man-made stoneworks. The extraordinarily diverse range of tombs and crosses found in its cemetery form a chaotic hillside necropolis. The different colored tombs are decorated with bright bouquets of paper flowers.

Tilcara
52 miles (84 km) NW of Jujuy. ⛰ 5,640. ➡ ℹ Lavalle s/n, (0388) 495-5720. 🎭 Fiesta de la Pachamama (Aug). ⛰ **Museo Arqueológico Doctor Eduardo Casanova** Belgrano 445, Plaza Alvarez Prado. **Tel** (0388) 495-5006. **Open** 9am–noon, 2–6pm daily. 🏛 **Museo Irureta de Bellas Artes** Cnr, Belgrano & Bolívar. **Tel** (0388) 495-5124. **Open** 10am–1pm, 3–6pm daily. 📷

Dominated by the dramatic mountains that surround it, Tilcara is a tiny village with a pleasant, easy-going air. It is quiet for most of the year, although it attracts a large number of visitors when the annual Pachamama festival is celebrated. For centuries, the town has been a hub of crafts-men and artists and many galleries and workshops remain active today.

Housed in a lovely colonial building, **Museo Arqueológico Doctor Eduardo Casanova** has a collection of pre-Columbian artifacts from across Latin America including ceramics, menhirs, and even a mummy. There are over 5,000 pieces in the permanent collection and two salons hold temporary exhibitions all year.

In Museo Ernesto Soto Avendaño, the rooms are dedicated to the sculptor who created Monumento a la Independencia de Humahuaca.

The small **Museo Irureta de Bellas Artes** displays over 100 engravings, paintings, and sculptures by modern Argentinian artists. Works of Hugo Irureta, the sculptor who founded the museum, are also displayed. Located close by is Museo José Antonio Terry, whose exhibition space is dedicated to the painter who

Sculpture at Museo Arqueológico Doctor Eduardo Casanova

was born in Buenos Aires, but spent most of his working life in Tilcara. Here he produced oil paintings depicting landscapes and local personalities. Tilcara's most popular attraction is an open-air Inca "museum," the Pucará de Tilcara. This hilltop fortress, situated half a mile (1 km) away from town, predates the arrival of the Incas by up to five centuries. It was first excavated in 1903 and has been restored and preserved since the 1950s under the auspices of the University of Buenos Aires. The old fortress, which includes a botanical garden of native flora, mostly cacti, affords wonderful views of the *quebrada*.

Uquia
62 miles (100 km) N of San Salvador de Jujuy. ⛰ 315. **Iglesia San Francisco de Padua Open** 10am–noon, 2–4pm daily.

Set against a backdrop of red-rock mountains and lush *quebracho* trees, Uquia is a picturesque village centered around a delightful square and a pretty church. The 17th-century **Iglesia de San Francisco de Paula** and its tower are painted in spotless white with bright green doors. The church is famous for its unusual paintings of "warring angels" from Collao in Bolivia.

The whitewashed façade of Museo Ernesto Soto Avendaño, Tilcara

The picturesque Humahuaca nestled in the Andean hills

Humahuaca

78 miles (125 km) N of Jujuy. 🚌 12,000. 🚌 **Iglesia de la Candelaria y San Antonio** Buenos Aires 383. **Open** 9:30am–noon & 4–7pm Mon–Fri.
🌐 **ciudadhumahuaca.com**

Founded in 1591, Humahuaca is the largest town between San Salvador de Jujuy and the Bolivian border. It has a picturesque town center, and its narrow, roughly paved streets and rustic adobe houses are classically Andean.

The town's star attraction is **Iglesia de la Candelaria y San Antonio**, also a National Historical Monument. This striking white church was built by the Jesuits toward the end of the 17th century, and has undergone extensive restoration after it was largely destroyed by an earthquake in 1873. The interior is richly ornamented, with two rococo altarpieces depicting various Biblical events. Other artworks in the church include the series called *The Twelve Prophets*, completed in 1764 by well-known Cusco School artist Marcos Sapaca.

The handicraft shops in town, well-stocked with souvenirs, and the tiny folk music venues are highly popular with tourists. Humahuaca is also a good base from which to explore the haunting landscapes of Puna Jujeña, an area of wild highland, lagoons filled with pink flamingos, and tiny mud-brick hamlets.

Iruya

44 miles (70 km) N of Humahuaca. 🚌 1,200. 🚌 🌐 **iruyaonline.com**

Overlooking the river of the same name, Iruya is a beautiful Andean hamlet located 9,120 ft (2,780 m) above sea level. Time seems to pass slowly here, and the fortified walls, cobblestoned streets, and whitewashed adobe dwellings are much as they have always been.

The village's focal point is its church, the colonial **Iglesia de Nuestra Señora del Rosario y San Roque**. Here, on the first Sunday of October, the feast of Our Lady of the Rosary is held, a surreal procession of masked figures that blends elements from Easter festivals and pre-conquest animistic rituals.

View of Iglesia de Nuestra Señora del Rosario y San Roque

㉔ Monumento Natural Laguna de los Pozuelos

Road map B1. 30 miles (48km) NW of Iruya. **Tel** (03887) 491-349. 🚌 ℹ️ Macedonio Gras 141, Abra Pampa, (0388) 491-349. **Open** 8am–3pm daily. 🅰️ by prior arrangement.

Situated in a natural basin between Sierra de Cochinoca and Sierra de Rinconada, this remote wildlife preserve rises 11,810 ft (3,600 m) above sea level. Spread over an area of 58 sq miles (153 sq km), the park is one of the most important wetlands in South America.

Although it has shrunk in recent years after a few dry summers, the park's lagoon still takes up about half the total area. It is the habitat of large flocks of Andean flamingos and numerous other species of wildfowl including teals and avocets. Shy *ñandús* (lesser rheas) can also be spotted scuttling away for cover. The best way to observe these birds at close quarters is by walking through the park from its entrance rather than driving. The park can be accessed at any time but it is advisable to drop in at the *guardería* (ranger station), which is located on the south side of the lake, for a chat with the knowledgeable and welcoming *guardaparques* (park rangers).

㉕ Yavi

Road map B1. 195 miles (314 km) N of Jujuy. 🚌 300. 🚌

Another sleepy high-plains hamlet of sloping cobblestoned streets and adobe houses, Yavi also seems to have given modernity the slip. The village dates from the late 17th century when nobleman Juan Fernández Campero, the first Marqués del Valle del Tojo in Spain, married into the area's landholding family. In 1708, Spain's King Phillip V named him Marqués of Tojo, a unique honor in colonial Argentina. The well-preserved 18th-century family home, **Casa del Marqués de**

Sweeping view of towering peaks covered in verdant *yunga* forest, Parque Nacional Calilegua

Tojo, still stands and is now an interesting museum exhibiting some of the ruling dynasty's memorabilia.

Standing next to it is a 17th-century church, **Iglesia de Nuestra Señora del Rosario y San Francisco**. Behind its whitewashed façade are the region's best-preserved colonial interiors, complete with a wonderfully ornate Baroque pulpit. The interior would be even more impressive had not some of the church's treasures been looted during the border disputes with Chile in the late 1970s. The windows are perhaps the most unusual feature, as their panes are made of wafer-thin onyx, casting a surreal, yellow-orange glow over the nave.

The 18th-century Casa del Marqués de Tojo, now a museum

㉖ Parque Nacional Calilegua

Road map B1. 75 miles (120 km) NE of Jujuy. **Tel** (03886) 422-046. 🚌
Open 9am–6pm daily. 🗓 🅰
🌐 parquesnacionales.gob.ar

Comprising over 290 sq miles (763 sq km) of subtropical *yunga* forests, lakes, and rivers, Parque Nacional Calilegua is the largest of the national parks in northwest Argentina. Thanks to its easy accessibility, it is also the most visited. The park is the setting for Gerald Durrell's popular 1960s book *The Whispering Land*. Parque Nacional Calilegua is easy to navigate with many trails that weave through dense and tangled cloud forest, often leading above the tree line and to the drier prairies of the high *puna*. As well as diverse flora, which changes according to the altitude and humidity, brown eagles, condors, and northern *huemul* deer can also be seen. Jaguars and pumas roam the forests, though both species have a well-founded fear of humans. Mornings and evenings are the best times to see these animals. Visitors can hire guides and also find useful maps and information at the park's entrance.

㉗ Parque Nacional El Rey

Road map C1. 155 miles (250 km) SE of Jujuy. **Tel** (03487) 4312-683. 🚌
Open 9am–dusk Mon–Sat. 🅰
🌐 parquesnacionales.gob.ar

Created in 1948, Parque Nacional El Rey is one of three cloud forest parks in northwest Argentina, the others being Calilegua and Baritú to the north. It rises to an average of 2,950 ft (900 m) above sea level and the peaks are usually enveloped in thick cloud, keeping most of the plant life lush and green even in the drier months. Previously a private estate, the park now protects 155 sq miles (408 sq km) of *yunga* forests. Strikingly diverse in both flora and fauna, El Rey is home to a number of endangered mammals including jaguars and pumas.

Toucan in Parque Nacional El Rey

The avian population, totalling over 150 species, is more visible and includes the emblematic giant toucan and several species of parrot and eagle. Numerous footpaths and one major vehicle trail snake around the park from the visitor center. The best trail for bird-watchers is the 8-mile (13-km) Senda Pozo Verde, which climbs through the bird-filled forest to a small, beautiful lake.

CUYO AND THE WINE COUNTRY

Known as the wine cellar of Argentina, Cuyo is noted for a landscape dominated by plains covered with acres of lush vineyards. To the west of the province are the towering Andes, which give way to the fertile wine-producing valleys. Heading east, the landscape changes dramatically to one of sand dunes and rocky desert formations shaped by the region's dry and dusty Zonda wind.

The original inhabitants of the Cuyo region were the Huarpe people, colonized by Chile's Captain-General Garcia de Mendoza in the late 1500s. Although Cuyo was administratively under Chile and was a flourishing region, it was isolated from Santiago de Chile by the snows of the Andes for months on end. This encouraged a self-sufficiency that survived even after the area became part of independent Argentina.

The region is a vital energy storehouse as most of the country's petroleum and natural gas reserves are found here. Its main economic activity, however, is agriculture, most notably viticulture. Meltwater from the snowcapped Andean peaks flows into canals that irrigate the region's many vineyards. Mendoza alone contributes 70 percent of Argentina's wine production, and the world-class Malbec is the region's specialty. Cuyo's wines in turn are driving its tourism sector, which also offers a wide array of outdoor activities that attract locals and visitors from around the world. These range from mountain-climbing and white-water rafting in summer to skiing at Las Leñas in winter. The region's cities have good museums, sprawling parks, and verdant plazas, as well as quality restaurants and accommodation options. Growing areas of interest, however, lie in the fossil-rich deserts and dramatic canyon country of Ischigualasto and Las Quijadas, both emblematic of Argentina's impressive achievements in paleontology.

Rows of wooden wine barrels in the cellar of Zapata Agrelo winery, Luján de Cuyo

◄ The magnificent El Hongo balancing rocks at Parque Provincial Ischigualasto, San Juan

Exploring Cuyo and the Wine Country

Cuyo is a year-round destination, and the city of Mendoza is the best base from which to explore the region due to its easy access to wineries and proximity to sights such as Parque Provincial Aconcagua. Highlights to the north and east, such as the dramatic Parque Provincial Ischigualasto and Parque Nacional Sierra de las Quijadas, and sights in and around Malargüe, are about a day's drive away. Many activities, such as hiking and climbing, take place at Aconcagua, along with rafting and kayaking on Río Mendoza arranged by tour operators from Mendoza. Skiing is also popular at Los Penitentes and Las Leñas. Wineries are open to visitors most of the year.

Round concretions found at Parque Provincial Ischigualasto

Sights at a Glance

Towns and Cities

1. *Mendoza pp210–13*
3. Uspallata
7. San Juan
8. San José de Jáchal
9. Pismanta
11. San Agustín del Valle Fértil
13. San Luis
14. San Rafael
15. Malargüe

Tours

2. *Mendoza Winery Tour pp214–51*

National and Provincial Parks

6. Parque Provincial Aconcagua
10. Parque Provincial Ischigualasto
12. Parque Nacional Sierra de las Quijadas

Ski Resorts

4. Los Penitentes
16. Las Leñas

Sites of Interest

5. Cristo Redentor

For keys to symbols *see back flap*

Getting Around

Cuyo has a good network of highways, and while they are mostly paved, drivers should be careful on the two-lane roads as they can be dangerous, especially around blind curves. A rental car is ideal for visiting scattered sights within a compact area such as Mendoza and its vicinity. Hiring a car and driver for the day, however, can be cheaper and more convenient, especially for visiting wineries. Buses are reliable for intercity travel as they are frequent and comfortable.

Old bottling equipment at Bodega La Rural

Key

=== Expressway
=== Highway
--- Major road
····· Minor road
~~~ Railroad
▪▪▪ International border
--- Provincial border
△ Peak

0 kilometers 100

0 miles 100

View of Laguna de Horcones, Aconcagua

❶ Mendoza

Lying at the base of the eastern Andes, Mendoza was devastated by the 1861 earthquake. Extensively rebuilt, it now has lush landscaped plazas decorated with striking tilework, murals, statuary, and fountains. The heart of the country's wine industry, the city is an ideal base from which to explore many excellent *bodegas* (wineries) that dot the area. It draws a large number of foreign tourists through the year, especially during the city's wine harvest festival in March. Even during the winter months, Mendoza gets visitors who enjoy the clear, mild days and go skiing in the nearby Andes.

A bustling sidewalk café in Mendoza city

🎞 Plaza Independencia

Espejo, Chile, Rivadavia & Patricias Mendocinas. 🚌 ⛴ Sat & Sun.
Museo Municipal de Arte Moderno
Tel (0261) 425-7279. **Open** 9am–8pm Tue–Fri, 2–8pm Sat, Sun, & hols. 🎫
🎫♿📷📹
🅦 ciudaddemendoza.gov.ar

Occupying the city's geographical center, Plaza Independencia is Mendoza's modern hub. Shaded by syca-mores and acacias, it hosts a weekend crafts fair and live concerts. It is also the site of Teatro Quintanilla, a live theater venue, the subterranean **Museo Municipal de Arte Moderno**, and the prestigious 1920s Plaza Hotel, which has been refurbished by the Hyatt chain.

🎞 Plaza España

Ave España & Montevideo. 🚌 ♿
Built by traditional artisans from Spain in the 1940s, Plaza España is the most colorful and visually dramatic of all Mendoza's plazas. It has lacquered tile murals and geometric Moorish designs on its fountains and benches. The murals reflect themes from Argentinian and Spanish literature and history, including the famous *Don Quixote*, the gaucho classic *Martín Fierro*, Columbus's voyage, and the Spanish missionaries of Argentina.

Spanish-style tiled murals at Plaza España

🎞 Plaza Italia

Montevideo & 25 de Mayo. 🚌
Densely planted with palms and conifers around a central fountain and studded with statuary on Roman themes, Plaza Italia, once called Plaza Lima, honors Mendoza's Italian immigrants and their heritage. Argentinian sculptor Luis Perlotti created the Etruscan-style wolf that symbolizes the founding of Rome. Even the grapes that produce Mendoza's wines get their symbolic tribute here.

Mendoza

① Plaza Independencia
② Plaza España
③ Plaza Italia
④ Plaza Chile
⑤ Plaza San Martín
⑥ Parque Bernardo O'Higgins

Mendoza Airport
4 miles (6 km)

Templo de San Francisco
Museo del Área Fundacional

BELTRÁN
ALBERDI
URQUIZA
BARCALA
AVE GODOY CRUZ
GRAL. PAZ
AVENIDA LAS HERAS
SALTA
9 DE JULIO
SAN MARTÍN
CORRIENTES
MONTE CASEROS
CÓRDOBA
LA RIOJA
SAN LUIS
ENTRE RIOS
ITUZAINGÓ
⑥ Parque Bernardo O'Higgins
Basílica de San Francisco
PLAZA CHILE ④
NECOCHEA
GUTIÉRREZ
ESPEJO
JULIO A. ROCA
ZAPATA
PATRICIAS MENDOCINAS
GRAL.
PLAZA SAN MARTÍN ⑤
BUENOS AIRES
⑦ PLAZA ITALIA
LAVALLE SARMIENTO
SAN JUAN
CATAMARCA
GARIBALDI
SAAVEDRA
CNEL. RODRÍGUEZ
25 DE MAYO
BELGRANO
PERÚ
CHILE
RIVADAVIA
MONTEVIDEO
① Museo Municipal de Arte Moderno
PLAZA INDEPENDENCIA
③ PLAZA ITALIA
② PLAZA ESPAÑA
SAN LORENZO
AVE COLÓN
AVE ZAPATA
SAN MARTÍN
GRAL. SAN MARTÍN
Hospital Central
AVENIDA ALEM
LÓPEZ B.
AV. GOB. VIDELA
ALBERDI
QUAY
MALLEN
Bus Terminal
Parque San Martín
VILLANUEVA
AVE BELGRANO
ZAPATA
AVENIDA MOLINA PEDRO
Centro Cívico
Museo de Bellas Artes Emiliano Guiñazú
Chacras de Coria
Canal Cacique Guaymallén

0 meters 800
0 yards 800

⚏ Plaza Chile

Gutiérrez & 25 de Mayo. 🚌

Shaded by a large *aguaribay* tree, Plaza Chile is centered around a monument dedicated to the friendship between Argentina and Chile. Created by Chilean sculptor Lorenzo Domínguez, it shows Argentinian Independence hero, José de San Martín, and Chile's liberator, Bernardo O'Higgins, together. The plaza gained its name in recognition of Chile's assistance after the 1861 earthquake. Mendoza welcomes Chileans to celebrate their mid-September Independence days here.

⚏ Plaza San Martín

Ave España & Gutiérrez. 🚌 ♿
Basílica de San Francisco Ave España and Necochea. **Open** 8am–12:30pm, 5–8:30pm daily.

Before crossing the Andes to Chile, Independence hero José de San Martín spent extended periods in Mendoza. This plaza, earlier known as Plaza Cobo, commemorates that fact with an equestrian statue, a replica of one that stands in Buenos Aires's namesake plaza. Across the street, the Neo-Classical **Basílica de San Francisco** contains the image of Nuestra Señora del Carmen de Cuyo, the patron saint of San Martín's Army of the Andes. There is also a mausoleum with the remains of his family. Despite the devastating earthquakes of 1861 and 1927, the basilica still stands immaculate.

❂ Parque Bernardo O'Higgins

Ituzaingó & Buenos Aires. 🚌
♿ **Museo del Área Fundacional** Alberdi 571. **Tel** (0261) 425-6927. **Open** 8am–8pm Tue–Sat, 3–8pm Sun. 🎫 🚫 ♿ 📷 🏛
W ciudaddemendoza.gov.ar

At the eastern edge of downtown Mendoza, Parque Bernardo O'Higgins is a greenbelt that stretches north for several blocks to the city's original site, where **Museo del Área Fundacional** covers the excavated foundations of the colonial *cabildo* (town hall). The museum is also notable for its indigenous Huarpe artifacts,

The Museo del Área Fundacional in Parque Bernardo O'Higgins

an impressive set of historical dioramas, and a collection of historical photographs. In addition to the museum, the park also has an aquarium. Nearby are the crumbling ruins of the 18th-century **Templo de San Francisco**, nearly leveled in the 1861 earthquake that spurred the city's relocation to the southwest.

❂ Parque San Martín

Ave Emilio Civit & Ave Boulogne Sur Mer. 🚌

In the 19th century, French architect Charles Thays left a legacy of magnificently landscaped public parks and private properties throughout the country. None, however, surpasses Mendoza's Parque San Martín, crowned by **Cerro de la Gloria**. Atop its summit, Uruguayan sculptor Juan M. Ferrari's *Monumento al Ejercito Libertador* pays homage to San Martín's Army of the Andes.

The iron-filigree gates at the park's main entrance lead to a diverse woodland, punctuated by a rose garden, horse track, zoo, and museums. Other sights include a Greek-style

theater, which is the main venue for the fall wine festival, and the **Estadio Islas Malvinas**, which hosted the 1978 World Cup matches.

Chacras de Coria

Besares. 🚌 🏠 Sat & Sun.
Museo Provincial de Bellas Artes Emiliano Guiñazú San Martín 3651, Mayor Drummond, Luján de Cuyo. **Tel** (0261) 496-0224. **Open** 8:30am–6pm Tue–Fri, 2–7pm Sat & Sun. 📷

Only 15 minutes away from downtown Mendoza, the leafy suburb of Chacras de Coria was once the capital's kitchen garden and orchard. Many of its dirt roads still survive, but over the years it has morphed into a gourmet ghetto of fancy restaurants and wine bars. The central Plaza Geronimo Espejo is the site of an art and antiques fair every Sunday. Chacras is also home to the **Museo Provincial de Bellas Artes Emiliano Guiñazú**, a fine arts museum in an erstwhile summer residence surrounded by gardens.

View from Cerro de la Gloria in Parque San Martín

For hotels and restaurants see pp278–83 and pp288–99

The Wines of Mendoza

The province of Mendoza is the locus of Argentina's wine industry and produces more than 80 percent of the country's wine. In colonial times, Mendoza's first vines arrived from neighboring Chile and spread along the Andean front range. From the late 19th century, European – especially Italian – immigration spurred production for Argentina's growing urban market, in what is now the world's sixth-biggest wine producer. From the 1970s, Argentina began to produce fine wines for export. Since then, burgeoning foreign investment has accelerated the process. Dozens of *bodegas* are open for tours, tasting, and dining. Several wineries have their own guesthouses as well.

Neatly arranged wooden casks at Bodega La Rural

The Grape Growing Process

The production of Mendoza's wine is aided by the area's altitude and climate, which is temperate and semi-arid, offering plenty of sunlight and little rainfall. However, the height of the Andes can cause climatic features, such as the withering Zonda wind, to be more destructive than on the plains.

High altitudes receive increased ultraviolet light, improving grape color by enhancing tannins and pigments; the altitude also concentrates grape sugars, making the wine complex and intense.

Irrigation takes place through an elaborate system of dams and canals that are fed by the region's many rivers, including Río Mendoza. These rivers carry the melting snows of the Andes mountain range.

Vineyards remain healthy and free from fungal diseases due to the high altitudes that ensure good air circulation.

Good Producers and Vintages

- Luigi Bosca – *Luigi Bosca Malbec Reserva 2007, Luigi Bosca Syrah Reserva 2005*
- Bodega Terrazas de los Andes – *Malbec 2007*
- Bodegas Caro – *Amancaya Malbec* and *Cabernet Sauvignon 2005*
- Bodega Catena Zapata – *Malbec 2008*
- Rutini – *Rutini Cabernet Malbec 2011*
- Alta Vista – *Alta Vista Malbec Mendoza Premium 2004*

Hail nets are common over Mendoza vineyards. Due to the heat and high altitude, electrical storms are frequent in summer and can bring destructive hail at any time. Many growers reduce their risk with scattered vineyards, but some take the additional, but labor-intensive, precaution of protective netting for their grapes.

The Making of Mendoza Wine

Mendoza wineries produce countless varietals and blends, including international standards such as Cabernet Sauvignon, Pinot Noir, and Chardonnay. Their signature wines are the deep red Malbec and the dry white Torrontés.

Torrontés, probably a cross between an American and eastern Mediterranean grape, is Argentina's characteristic white grape, and produces a dry but fruity wine.

Malbec grapes were once abundant in southwest France but responded better to Argentina's arid west. The bluish-black, thin-skinned, and soft-pulp grape reaches its highest development in Maipú in Mendoza.

Newly harvested grapes first undergo a sorting process and are crushed lightly to bring them in to contact with selected yeasts. Fermentation then happens in temperature-controlled stainless steel tanks.

Wine is among the country's premier exports and has recently doubled in volume and quality. Malbec is the most popular and recognized varietal, alongside others such as Syrah, Merlot, and Chardonnay.

Fiesta Nacional de la Vendimia

This wine harvest festival is Mendoza's single biggest event, with nearly 50,000 tourists crowding the city. It takes place on the first full weekend of March. The festival begins with the Blessing of the Fruits ceremony and ends with fireworks at the Teatro Griego.

The harvest festival, held since 1936, begins with the grape gathering in January and February. It culminates in March when people line the streets to watch the Harvest Queen parade.

Teatro Griego in Mendoza's Parque San Martín is the venue for the Harvest Queen competition. The complex holds about 22,000 people and thousands more view the events from the surrounding hills.

❷ Mendoza Winery Tour

Although much of the Mendoza wine route is suburban, southern Luján's sycamore-studded landscape opens onto vast vineyards with Andean panoramas, while the snow-covered Cordón del Plata provides a spectacular backdrop to the poplar-lined roads of Uco Valley. Some *bodegas* are intimate boutiques while others are massive, isolated monuments. Some have long local histories, others house art galleries and excellent gourmet restaurants. Nearly all, however, have opened their doors for tours and tasting.

⑩ Bodegas Salentein
Set in the heights of Tunuyán, Bodegas Salentein is famous for its architecture, wines, Killka restaurant *(see p296)*, accommodations, and fine art space.

⑨ Cavas Wine Lodge
Set amongst its own modestly sized vineyards, Cavas Wine Lodge offers premium accommodations *(see p281)*, and has its own outdoor swimming pool, a restaurant, and a book-lined living room. It also hosts occasional cultural events.

⑦ Chandon
Located on Luján's outskirts, Chandon is one of the first foreign vintners to operate in Argentina. This French-operated *bodega* has produced sparkling wines and others since 1959.

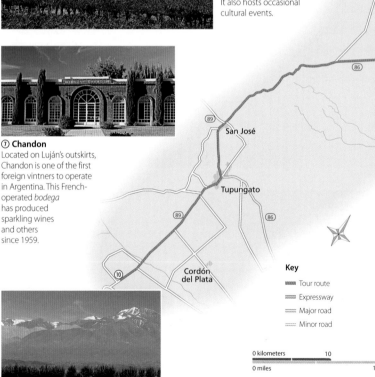

San José

Tupungato

Cordón del Plata

Key

▬▬ Tour route
═══ Expressway
──── Major road
╌╌╌ Minor road

0 kilometers   10

0 miles   10

⑧ Catena Zapata
Rising high above the lush vineyard, Catena Zapata's Mayan pyramid structure makes it Mendoza's most attention-grabbing winery. The varietals and blends are just as remarkable.

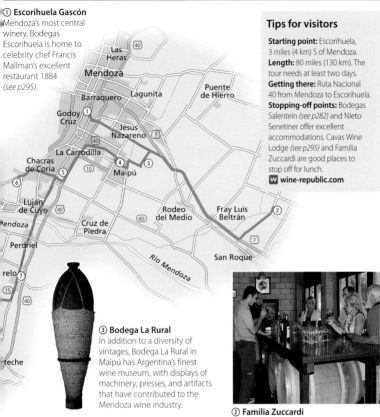

① Escorihuela Gascón
Mendoza's most central winery, Bodegas Escorihuela is home to celebrity chef Francis Mallman's excellent restaurant 1884 (see p295).

Las Heras

Mendoza

Barraquero

Godoy Cruz

Lagunita

Puente de Hierro

Jesús Nazareno

La Carrodilla

Chacras de Coria

Maipú

Luján de Cuyo

Mendoza

Cruz de Piedra

Rodeo del Medio

Fray Luis Beltrán

San Roque

Perdriel

Río Mendoza

relo

teche

Tips for visitors

Starting point: Escorihuela, 3 miles (4 km) S of Mendoza.
Length: 80 miles (130 km). The tour needs at least two days.
Getting there: Ruta Nacional 40 from Mendoza to Escorihuela.
Stopping-off points: Bodegas Salentein (see p282) and Nieto Senetiner offer excellent accommodations. Cavas Wine Lodge (see p295) and Familia Zuccardi are good places to stop off for lunch.
W wine-republic.com

③ Bodega La Rural
In addition to a diversity of vintages, Bodega La Rural in Maipú has Argentina's finest wine museum, with displays of machinery, presses, and artifacts that have contributed to the Mendoza wine industry.

② Familia Zuccardi
Located to the east of Maipú, Familia Zuccardi hosts a wine tasting fair in November. This gathering is the biggest event at any Mendoza winery.

④ López
Created in the late 19th century, this modernized *bodega* is still managed by the third and fourth generations of the founding López family. It produces some less common vintages such as Pinot Noir and Sémillon.

⑥ Nieto Senetiner
Situated within secluded, manicured grounds in Luján, the stylish conglomerate-owned Nieto Senetiner, complete with guesthouse, more closely resembles a boutique winery.

⑤ Bodega y Cavas de Weinert
Founded in 1975 and located in Luján de Cuyo, the unique Cavas de Weinert arranges tours exploring the restored historic cellars filled with huge oak casks.

❸ Uspallata

Road map B2. 89 miles (140 km) NW of Mendoza. 🚻 3,284. 🚌 ℹ junction of Ruta Nacional 7 and Ruta Provincial 52, (0261) 413-2101.

At the headwaters of Río Mendoza, Uspallata, the biggest settlement between Gran Mendoza and the border, occupies a scenic valley. Its resemblance to Central Asian highlands is so striking that the location was chosen for the 1997 movie *Seven Years In Tibet*, starring Brad Pitt.

While Uspallata has only a few sights to explore, several rafting and kayaking companies offer trips on the sediment-clogged Río Mendoza *(see p308)*. Though it lacks difficult rapids, it gets big waves during the spring runoff, which is the best time for a good kayaking and rafting experience.

Environs

The surrounding countryside along Ruta Provincial 52 and other nearby roads has a cluster of interesting historic sights. About 1.2 miles (2 km) west of Uspallata stand the **Bóvedas Históricas Uspallata**, white-washed domed kilns that date from the 17th century. They were used for metallurgy even in pre-Columbian times. A short distance to the northeast, there are several beautiful pre-Columbian petroglyphs and a shrine to the Mapuche "saint" Ceferino Namuncurá *(see p29)* at the lava outcrop of **Cerro Tunduqueral**. Another route to Mendoza continues via a zigzag road past the hot springs of **Villavicencio**, which have been

A Los Penitentes ski resort in summer

closed for many years because of a legal dispute. This route was the same taken by Independence hero José de San Martín's Army of the Andes and also Charles Darwin a couple of decades later. To the north, along Ruta Provincial 39 toward Calingasta, the **Comunidad Huarpe Guaytamari** is an indigenous outpost with a llama farm and handicrafts market.

❹ Los Penitentes

Road map B2. Ruta Internacional 7, Km 163. ℹ Ski Center (0261) 425-5511. 🚌 🚻 🚌 🚻 🌐 penitentes. com.ar

From Uspallata, rugged roads to the west give way to spectacular scenery all the way to Los Penitentes. At 8,464 ft (2,580 m) above sea level, Los Penitentes is the best skiing option for Mendoza-based visitors. Better known as Villa Los Penitentes, the village is filled with several brightly

painted ski resorts. Set against the backdrop of the Andes mountain range are 26 snow-dust tracks, ideal for both professional and amateur skiers. The town is also a base for Aconcagua-bound hikers and climbers. Modern ski-lifts run at weekends during selected months for visitors to enjoy the fabulous valley and mountain views.

❺ Cristo Redentor

Road map B2. Ruta Nacional 7, near Las Cuevas. 🚌 🚻 🚌 🚻 🌐 cristoredentorchiar.galeon.com

After Argentina and Chile resolved one of their countless border differences in 1902, the two countries, under the auspices of British King Edward VII, signed a pact to determine the Andean boundary between them. As part of the pact, they installed a 26-ft (8-m) statue of Christ, 13,779 ft (4,200 m) above sea level. The statue was made by Uruguayan sculptor Mateo Alonso using metal from cannons and other weapons. The road to the saddle where the statue stands is a vertiginous zigzag that yields spectacular panoramas of the Río Mendoza Valley.

Cristo Redentor statue on the Chile border

For many years, the old route to Cristo used to be the main international highway. It has since been superseded by a tunnel, but tour buses and private cars still transport visitors to the statue.

However, the road is open only between January and March; the rest of the year it is closed due to heavy snowfall. When the road is open, most tours go up to the 17,817-ft (5,430-m) **Cerro Tolosa**, where climbers train to scale Aconcagua.

Domed kilns used to smelt metal, Bóvedas Históricas Uspallata

Spectacular backdrop of Laguna de Horcones, Parque Provincial Aconcagua

❻ Parque Provincial Aconcagua

Road map B2. 115 miles (185 km) W of Mendoza. 🚌 **ℹ** Ranger station, Horcones, (0261) 156-210118. 🏛 Permits: Mendoza, (0261) 425-8751. **Open** 8am–6pm daily (for entry). 🎿 🛶 ⛰ **W** aconcagua.mendoza.gov.ar

One of the country's best-known parks, Parque Provincial Aconcagua contains one of the world's highest summits. At 22,841 ft (6,962 m), **Cerro Aconcagua** has been the goal of many novice mountaineers as, unlike Mount Everest and other famous peaks, it enjoys easy access and requires no technical climbing skills. By the traditional northwest route, the "Roof of the Americas" is relatively a low-difficulty climb. This does not mean that it is easy; prospective summiteers must be in good physical condition to deal with oxygen deficits, not to mention extreme weather conditions. On other, more technical routes, the issue is even more clear-cut: more than 100 climbers have died on Aconcagua and a professional guide is imperative for non-mountaineers.

Fortunately, Aconcagua has more to offer than just its summit. From its visitor center, only 2 miles (4 km) north of the highway, day-trippers can take a short hike to **Laguna de Horcones** (Horcones Lake) for spectacular views. Another option is to go ahead to Confluencia, an intermediate camp for trekking to **Plaza Francia** and to **Plaza de Mulas**. In three days, backpackers can reach Plaza Francia, the 14,763-ft (4,500-m) base camp for Pared Sur, Aconcagua's difficult south face. In a week, they can reach and return from Plaza de Mulas, where most mountaineers start their final climb to the summit. Here, backpackers should be prepared for summer gridlock and competition for campsites. It is mandatory for hikers to have permits for every walk beyond Horcones and to have an ascent permit to continue beyond Plaza de Mulas. The **Glaciar Polaco** route, about 9 miles (15 km) east of Los Penitentes, is longer and slightly less difficult than the south face.

Unlike many national parks, Aconcagua has relatively little to offer other than its spectacular scenery. This is one of the Andes' most barren sectors, with little vegetation and few mammals. Some visitors may spot the Andean condor, which came close to extinction due to hunting, circling on the thermals.

About 4 miles (7 km) west of Los Penitentes is **Puente del Inca**, which takes its name from a natural bridge over Río Mendoza. This geological curiosity, formed by an ancient petrifying process, was once visited by Charles Darwin. Puente del Inca is home to the **Cementerio de los Andinistas**, an Aconcagua climbers' cemetery. The area has street stalls selling souvenirs.

🏠 **Puente del Inca**
Ruta Nacional 7, Km 175. 🎿 🛶 ⛰

Natural rock formation at Puente del Inca

Organic vineyard in the Mendoza Valley, with the Andes rising beyond ▶

The sunlit patio of Casa Natal de Sarmiento in San Juan

❼ San Juan

Road map B2. 102 miles (165 km) N of Mendoza. 🏙 115,566. ✈ 🚌 🔥 Sarmiento 24 Sur, (0264) 421-0004. 🅦 **sanjuanlaestrelladelosandes.com**

The city of San Juan is nestled in the valley of Río San Juan. The city has played a key role in Argentinian history as the birthplace of the cosmopolitan author, diplomat, educator, and former president, Domingo F. Sarmiento. It is also the place where populist Juan Domingo Perón entered the public eye during the relief efforts of Argentina's worst earthquake in 1944. With hardly a building more than a century old, San Juan is a young and modern city. Its wine industry and the **Casa Natal de Sarmiento** are the town's main tourist attractions. Declared a national monument in 1911, Casa Natal de Sarmiento is a typical colonial house with spacious sunlit interiors built around a large patio. Damaged in the violent earthquake on January 15, 1944, it has been restored many times.

🏛 **Casa Natal de Sarmiento**
Sarmiento 21 Sur. **Tel** (0264) 422-4603. **Open** spring/summer: 9am–8:30pm Mon–Fri, 9am–3pm Sat, Sun, & hols; fall/winter: 9am–7:30pm Mon–Fri, 10am–4pm Sat, 10am–6pm Sun & hols. 🅦 **casanatalsarmiento. com.ar**

The Difunta Correa

About 37 miles (60 km) east of San Juan's provincial capital is the popular Difunta Correa shrine at Vallecito village. According to one of the legends, Deolinda Correa, a young widow, died of thirst while following her conscript husband during the 19th-century civil wars. Her baby, however, survived at her breast. Despite doubts that she ever existed, this "miracle" made her a popular "saint." Today, at Easter and other times, the sprawling shrine attracts thousands of pilgrims, who leave tokens of gratitude – ranging from models of modest houses to antique automobiles in mint condition – for various favors granted.

Miniature roadside shrines to the Difunta Correa

❽ San José de Jáchal

Road map B2. 96 miles (155 km) N of San Juan. 🏙 10,901. 🚌 🔥 San Martín 622, (02647) 420-003, ext. 311. 🎭 Fiesta de la Tradición (Nov).

A gaucho town, Jáchal is known for hand-woven blankets and ponchos but it is more famous as a base for exploring the surrounding villages, the high Andes, and white-water rafting in the town's river. The major attraction is the 19th-century **Iglesia San José**, a national historical monument that houses Cristo Negro, a unique image of the crucified Christ.

Environs
About 14 miles (23 km) east of Jáchal, Huaco is the site of the adobe tomb of *gauchesco* poet, Buenaventura Luna. To the west, Ruta Nacional 150 leads over the Cuesta del Viento to the hamlet of Rodeo, the starting point for rafting down Río Jáchal.

🏠 **Iglesia San José**
San Juan. **Open** daily.

A thermal bath under an open sky in Pismanta

❾ Pismanta

Road map B2. 116 miles (187 km) NW of San Juan, Ruta Nacional 150. 🚌 from San Juan to Jáchal. 🅦 **hoteltermaspismanta.com.ar**

From Jáchal, Ruta Nacional 150 leads southwest to the modest hot-spring oasis of Pismanta, where the hotel has a good restaurant and enormous hot baths that are also open to non-guests.

La Esfinge (The Sphinx) rock formation at Parque Provincial Ischigualasto

The highway continues to the 15,680-ft (4,780-m) **Paso de Agua Negra**, the highest pass between Argentina and Chile. Open from December to March, it is one of the best places to see the *penitentes*, conical snow formations resembling hooded monks.

⑩ Parque Provincial Ischigualasto

Road map B2. 202 miles (325 km) NE of San Juan. 🚌 from San Juan. 🚏 25 de Mayo y Las Heras, San Juan, (0264) 422-7372. **Open** museum & park: Apr–Sep: 8am–4pm; Oct–Mar: 8am–5pm. 🎫 inclusive of museum price. 🚻 ♿ 🚻 🏪 🎥 **w** ischigualasto.gob.ar

Less colorful than the red sandstone canyons of Sierra de las Quijadas *(see p222)* and the desert parks of the Andean Northwest, the Triassic sediments and volcanic ash of Ischigualasto have brought about some of the top dinosaur discoveries of recent decades. In a country where paleontologists have not received the widespread recognition they deserve, the park, also known as the Valley of the Moon, is slowly changing the situation. With impressive exhibits and informative tours, it has now become an imperative stop-off for both specialists and visitors in general.

Since its designation as a UNESCO World Heritage Site, together with Parque Nacional Talampaya *(see p189)* across the provincial border in La Rioja, the park has opened a branch of the Universidad Nacional de San Juan's **Museo de Historia**

Natural. Housed in a high-ceilinged warehouse adapted as a museum, its lifesize models of *Eoraptor lunensis*, *Herrerasaurus ischigualastensis*, and other dinosaurs that roamed the earth up to 228 million years ago are the starting point for informative backcountry tours. University students explain in Spanish the process of reconstructing the skeletons before leading 2-hour landforms such as La Esfinge (The Sphinx) and El Hongo (The Mushroom).

Due to the terrible summer heat, most animals are nocturnal but visitors may be able to see the Patagonian hares, rheas, red foxes, armadillos, pumas, and the rarely spotted condors. The main plant varieties found are four kinds of cactus, native *brea* trees, and *jarilla* shrubs.

Visitors touring the backcountry must either have their own vehicles or arrive with a private operator from San Agustín del Valle Fértil. Rare wet weather can make the

Dinosaur display at the museum in Parque Provincial Ischigualasto

road for the 24-mile (40-km) circuit inaccessible. Most of these tours visit the park in the morning and Talampaya in the afternoon before heading back to San Agustín.

In addition to the vehicle tour, visitors can also take a 3-hour hike to the 5,734-ft (1,748-m) summit of the barrow-like **Cerro Morado** for panoramic views of Ischigualasto and north to Talampaya. Best done in the morning, the hike necessitates hiring a guide at the park ranger station at the entrance.

Pre-Columbian petroglyphs at Piedra Pintada

⑪ San Agustín del Valle Fértil

Road map B2. 250 km (400 miles) NE of San Juan. 🏔 3,889. 🚌 🚏 General Acha 52, (0264) 642-0104. 🎉 Founding of San Agustín (Apr). **w** sanjuanlaestrelladelosandes.com

Unlike the blazing deserts to its north and south, the cozy oasis of San Agustín del Valle Fértil (Fertile Valley) enjoys a verdant woodland setting at the base of Sierra de la Huerta. The place is filled with wide maize fields, a pasture for goats, and olive groves. Improved highways and visitor services have made it the best place for travelers to arrange tours to Ischigualasto in San Juan and Talampaya across the provincial border in La Rioja.

A cluster of archaeological sites nearby includes pre-Columbian petroglyphs at **Piedra Pintada**, just across Río Seco. Another highlight of the town is **Parque Provincial Valle Fértil**, a large roadless area in the enticing mountains to the west and southwest.

⑫ Parque Nacional Sierra de las Quijadas

Road map B2. 104 miles (167 km) SE of San Juan. 🚌 from San Juan & San Luis. 🛈 Ecuador 735, (02652) 445-141; ranger station at park entrance. **Open** 8am–5pm daily. 🅿 🛈 only Spanish. 🚻 🅰 🆆 **parques nacionales.gov.ar**

The enormous orange-red sandstone canyons of Parque Nacional Sierra de las Quijadas get far fewer visitors than their spectacular scenery merits. A treasurehouse for paleontologists, this impressive network of canyons is part of a northern paleontological circuit that includes San Juan's Ischigualasto (see p221) and La Rioja's Talampaya (see p189).

About 120 million years ago, in the Cretaceous period, pterosaurs (flying reptiles) roamed the area freely. A half-hour hike from the park's entrance leads to the **Loma del Pterodaustro**, a fossil-field of dinosaur remains.

A gravel road leading up a narrow sedimentary canyon emerges onto the spectacular panoramas of the **Potrero de la Aguada**, which is located about 5 miles (8 km) from the park entrance. This is a veritable maze of small canyons leading to a dry lake bed. Much photographed, the majestic Aguada is best enjoyed during sunset when it takes on a fiery orange color. Guided descents into the canyons take about 3 or 4 hours. For less ambitious hikers, there is a relatively easy nature trail that skirts the canyon rim while passing cacti, aloes, and shrubs. A more ambitious hike follows the canyon rim south for about half an hour, and has better views from higher cliffs.

In addition to its natural appeal, Las Quijadas also has numerous archaeological sites. Between the park entrance and Aguada, the recently excavated **Hornillos Huarpes**, ovens where the park's pre-Columbian peoples fired their ceramics, is a sight of interest.

⑬ San Luis

Road map B2. 174 miles (280 km) E of Mendoza. 👥 152,198. ✈ 🚌 🛈 Ave Illia & Junín, (0266) 442-3479. 🆆 **sanluis.gov.ar**

Calling itself the Gateway to Cuyo, San Luis is a tidy provincial capital whose colonial grid contains attractive public spaces such as **Plaza Pringles**. This is the center of the city, dominated by the Neo-Classical **Iglesia Catedral** with its twin bell towers and elaborately sculpted pediment. To the northwest is Avenida Illia,

Moorish-style Iglesia de Santo Domingo

a restaurant and bar district. Four blocks south, also impressively landscaped, is **Plaza Independencia**, the city's other central square and home to **Palacio de Gobierno**, the provincial government house. Opposite the plaza is **Iglesia de Santo Domingo**, a 17th-century church built in Moorish style.

Environs
Only 12 miles (20 km) northeast of San Luis is the hill station of **Potrero de los Funes**, where the capital's residents take a break with watersports or horse riding in the nearly roadless Sierra de San Luis.

🛈 **Iglesia Catedral**
Pringles and Rivadavia.
Tel (0266) 442-4414. **Open** daily.

The red rocks of the Potrero de la Aguada, Parque Nacional Sierra de las Quijadas

⓮ San Rafael

Road map B3. 143 miles (230 km) S of Mendoza. 🚍 110,000. 🚌 ℹ️ Ave Hipólito Yrigoyen 741, (0260) 442-4217. 🔳 sanrafaelturismo.gov.ar

A tidy mid-size city, San Rafael is known for the many sights that surround it. Located where Río Diamante and Río Atuel emerge from the Andean foothills, San Rafael has gradually enveloped many of the sprawling vineyards and prosperous wineries that once grew around it. It may lack the provincial capital's fashionable boutique operations, but growers such as **Bodega Valentín Bianchi** and Suter, both highly respected names in the wine industry, are located here. In addition to irrigating the vineyards, Río Atuel is a starter river for rafters while the wilder Río Diamante offers some of the most exciting white-water rafting in the country.

A fine wine from Bodega Valentín Bianchi

🏷️ Bodega Valentín Bianchi
Ruta Nacional 143, Las Paredes, San Rafael. **Tel** (0260) 444-9600. **Open** 9:30am–noon, 2:30–6pm Mon–Sat; 10:30am–noon, 2:30–5pm Sun. 🚗 📷 🔳 vbianchi.com

⓯ Malargüe

Road map B3. 115 miles (186 km) S of San Rafael. 🚍 17,710 🚌 ℹ️ Ruta Nacional 40 and Pasaje La Orteguina, (0260) 447-1659. 🎉 Fiesta Nacional del Chivo (Jan), Día de Malargüe (Nov). 🔳 malargue.gov.ar

A laid-back town, Malargüe has one of the most spectacular landscapes in Argentina. The town is perhaps best known for its lively week-long Fiesta Nacional del Chivo (National Goat Festival). One of the sights that the city offers is **Museo Regional Malargüe**. Housed in a colonial building, the museum has a varied collection that includes clay pipes required for religious ceremonies, jewelry, a mummified corpse, and even dinosaur remains. The small city is also the base for

exploring provincial preserves with caves, bird-rich wetlands, and volcanic cones.

Environs
A wealth of little-visited nature preserves surround Malargüe, the most popular of them being **Reserva Natural Laguna de Llancanelo**. Located 13 miles (20 km) south of the city, this is a sprawling 155-sq mile (400-sq km) wetland with flocks of migratory birds. **Reserva Natural La Payunia** is a 1,700-sq mile (4,400-sq km) volcanic preserve with at least 10,000 guanacos and other species of wildlife. **Reserva Natural Caverna de las Brujas** is a series of stunning limestone underground caves that are open to the public.

🏛️ Museo Regional Malargüe
Ruta Nacional 40, Km 327. **Tel** (0260) 447-1060. **Open** 9am–1pm, 5–9pm Tue–Sun. ♿ 📷

⓰ Las Leñas

Road map B3. 43 miles (70 km) NW of Malargüe. **Tel** (0260) 447-1281. 🚍 🏂 🖥️ 📷 🔳 laslenas.com

Located in the Andes, northwest of Malargüe, Las Leñas has abundant snow and the best infrastructure of any Argentinian ski resort north of Bariloche (see p242). Some consider it the best in the country. Open from mid-June to early October, it enjoys a longer season than Los Penitentes, the province's other popular ski center.

The resort has the capacity to house almost 3,000 skiers in hotels and apartments, and the base clientele at Las Leñas are mainly porteños and foreigners on week-long packages. Still, Las Leñas offers half-price lift tickets to day-trippers who lodge in nearby Malargüe.

Winter is high season here, but Las Leñas remains open over summer for mountain bikers, hikers, and other recreationists.

View of a snowcapped mountain at Las Leñas ski resort in summer

PATAGONIA

A vast wilderness of glistening lakes, vertiginous peaks, sweeping glaciers, empty, barren plains, and rugged coastline, Patagonia was first roamed by dinosaurs, and later was long the preserve of indigenous groups. The region is perhaps best known, though, for its pioneer era, when visionaries and adventurers came ashore in search of a better life at the bottom of the world.

Two main indigenous groups originally inhabited Patagonia – the Mapuche and Tehuelche. Portuguese explorer Ferdinand Magellan was the first European to discover the region, in 1520. Adventurers, merchants, and pirates followed in his wake, although no permanent colony was established until the late 18th century.

After gaining its independence, Argentina made concerted efforts to settle Patagonia. In 1865, Welsh pioneers landed at Puerto Madryn. In the same decade, the Argentinian government launched military campaigns against the Mapuche and Tehuelche, putting an end to all indigenous resistance in the region. Towns such as Junín de los Andes and Bariloche were founded in the Mapuche heartland and populated by European immigrants. Railroads, ports, and new settlements were built to serve the burgeoning wool industry. Today, oil, gas, and fishing have usurped wool as Patagonia's major source of income and a blossoming tourist industry has brought further prosperity to the region.

Visitors can enjoy a wide range of outdoor activities, including horse riding, trekking, fly-fishing, boating and rafting, and wildlife watching, all the while admiring Patagonia's spectacular scenery. Its cities and towns remain busy centers of culture and entertainment, offering excellent museums and restaurants. Some, like Trelew and Gaiman, are still quintessentially Welsh, complete with chapels, tea shops, and Welsh-style houses. In essence, the region has changed little since its pioneer past and remains a beautiful, remote, and sparsely populated wilderness.

A colony of sea lions basking on a gravel beach in Península Valdés

◀ The Llao Llao mountainside resort hotel in Bariloche

Exploring Patagonia

Dotted with lakes and overlooked by the Andes, the Lake District is Patagonia's most popular destination. Its biggest town, Bariloche, receives many visitors but there are quieter alternatives such as San Martín de los Andes, El Bolsón, and Villa La Angostura. In the deep south of Patagonia is Glaciar Perito Moreno, which is in the same national park as Argentina's trekking capital, El Chaltén, and Mount Fitz Roy. The Atlantic coast has great opportunities for spotting marine fauna, especially at the Península Valdés nature preserve. Inland is the remote Patagonian steppe with Cueva de las Manos and century-old estancias.

Key

≡ Highway
— Main road
⋯ Minor road
▬ International border
— Provincial border
△ Peak

Guanacos grazing on a mountain slope

Getting Around

The best way to get around Patagonia is by air or long-distance bus. Bariloche and El Calafate have international airports and many smaller destinations are served by domestic flights. Bus services linking towns and cities in the region are reliable, though some remote sights can be reached only by car or via organized excursion. Motorists should note that many roads are unpaved and gas stations scarce. This is especially the case on Ruta Nacional 40.

Sights at a Glance

Towns and Cities

1 Carmen de Patagones
2 Viedma
3 Puerto Madryn
5 Trelew
6 Gaiman
8 Camarones
9 Comodoro Rivadavia
11 Puerto Deseado
13 Puerto San Julián
15 Río Gallegos
18 Neuquén
20 Villa El Chocón
22 Aluminé
23 Junín de los Andes
24 San Martín de los Andes
26 Bariloche
28 El Bolsón
29 El Maitén
31 Esquel
32 Trevelin
34 Perito Moreno

35 Los Antiguos
38 Bajo Caracoles
40 Hipólito Yrigoyen
41 Gobernador Gregores
43 Tres Lagos
46 El Chaltén
48 El Calafate
49 Río Turbio

National and Provincial Parks

4 *Reserva Provincial Península Valdés pp230–31*
7 Reserva Provincial Punta Tombo
10 Bosque Petrificado José Ormachea
12 Monumento Natural Bosques Petrificados
14 Parque Nacional Monte León
17 Reserva Provincial Cabo Vírgenes
21 Parque Nacional Laguna Blanca

25 *Parque Nacional Lanín p241*
27 *Parque Nacional Nahuel Huapi pp242–3*
33 Parque Nacional Los Alerces
39 Parque Nacional Perito Moreno
45 *Parque Nacional Los Glaciares pp254–9*

Estancias

16 Estancia Monte Dinero
36 Estancia Nibepo Aike

Sites of Interest

19 Centro Paleontológico Lago Barreales
30 Museo Leleque
37 Cueva de las Manos
42 Lago Cardiel
44 Lago San Martín
47 Lago del Desierto

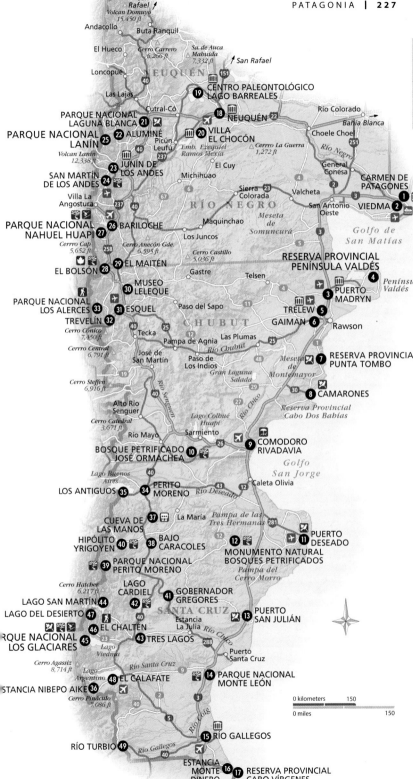

A view from Viedma across Río Negro to Iglesia Parroquial Nuestra Señora del Carmen

❶ Carmen de Patagones

Road map C4. 597 miles (960 km) S of Buenos Aires. 🏠 20,000. 🚌 🚆 ℹ️ Mitre 84, (02920) 464-819. 📅 Fiesta de 7 de Marzo (Mar).

Both the northern gateway to Patagonia and a historical jewel, the small town of Carmen de Patagones was founded as a fort settlement in 1779. The first settlers arrived from Spain a year later and were forced to dig caves into the banks of Río Negro for shelter, the remains of which can still be seen.

To explore the town's history, visitors should head to the jumble of streets between Plaza 7 de Marzo and the port area. On the waterfront, housed in a building dating from 1799, is **Museo Histórico Regional Emma Nozzi**. It has displays on 19th-century Carmen de Patagones; one of the old settlers' caves can be accessed via the museum's patio.

On the plaza is **Iglesia Parroquial Nuestra Señora del Carmen**. Two Brazilian flags hang on either side of its altar, captured in 1827 after the defeat of a Brazilian invasion force. On the same block, although slightly obscured, is the **Torre del Fuerte** watchtower, the single surviving remnant of the town's original military fort. Several mud-brick abodes from the early 1800s, located south of the tower, are open to visits, including **Rancho Rial**, while **Casa de la Cultura** is one block

east of the tower. Most famous, though, is **La Carlota**, an 1820s house accessed via guided tour from the Museo Histórico.

🏛 **Museo Histórico Regional Emma Nozzi**
Ave J. J. Biedma 64. **Tel** (02920) 462-729. **Open** varies (call in advance).

❷ Viedma

Road map C4. 1 mile (2 km) S of Carmen de Patagones. 🏠 60,000. 🚍 🚌 🚆 ℹ️ Ave Francisco de Viedma 51, (02920) 427-171. 📅 Fiesta de 7 de Marzo (Mar). 🌐 **viedma.gov.ar**

Located across Río Negro from Carmen de Patagones, Viedma is a small town but with good traveler services. It also boasts what is considered to be Patagonia's most aesthetically inspired museum, **Museo**

Salesiano Cardenal Cagliero. It is housed within the **Manzana Histórica**, which was once the headquarters of a Salesian mission established in 1880. The museum preserves some splendid architectural details and displays various religious artifacts. Also housed within the Manzana Historica is the **Museo Gardeliano**. Displaying vintage artifacts and showing films related to the singer-songwriter, filmmaker, and tango legend Carlos Gardel, it is also used as a multicultural, multimedia space for the arts.

🏛 **Museo Salesiano Cardenal Cagliero**
Manzana Histórica, Ave Rivadavia. **Tel** (02920) 1561-3355. **Open** varies.

🏛 **Museo Gardeliano**
As above. **Open** as above.

The Welsh in Patagonia

The Welsh presence in Patagonia dates from 1865, when 153 pioneers set sail for a land they saw as free of English domination. They made landfall two months later, founding Puerto Madryn on the Argentinian coast, before settling 60 miles (100 km) to the south in the more fertile Chubut Valley. It is this region that constitutes the heart of Welsh Patagonia. Here, Welsh chapels dot the landscape,

teahouses are run by the pioneers' descendants, and, in Gaiman especially, the Welsh language is widely spoken. The year's biggest celebration is the Eisteddfod *(see p44)*, a Welsh music and poetry festival that dates from medieval times.

A Welsh farmhouse in Gaiman

❸ Puerto Madryn

Road map B4. 227 miles (365 km) SW of Viedma. 🚶 80,000. ✈ 🚌 ℹ Ave Roca 223, (0280) 445-3504.
Ⓦ **madryn.gov.ar/turismo**

On the shores of Golfo Nuevo, Puerto Madryn has a historical background that dates from 1865, when the first group of Welsh pioneers landed on its shores. It is the gateway to one of the world's greatest marine spectacles, at Reserva Provincial Península Valdés, and is known for its sandy beaches, relaxed pace, and good seafood restaurants.

The town's excellent **Museo de Ciencias Naturales y Oceanografía** provides information on the thriving ocean life nearby, while the outstanding **EcoCentro** aims to promote an understanding of threatened marine species.

Located close by, Playa El Doradillo is a protected beach and breeding area for the Southern Right whale, while Punta Loma is home to a year-round sea lion colony.

🏛 **Museo de Ciencias Naturales y Oceanografía**
Domecq García & José Menéndez. **Tel** (0280) 445-1139. **Open** 9am–7pm Mon–Fri, 3–7pm Sat. 🚶

🏛 **EcoCentro**
Julio Verne 3784. **Tel** (0280) 445-7470. **Open** varies (call in advance).
Ⓦ **ecocentro.org.ar**

❹ Reserva Provincial Península Valdés

See pp230–31.

A summer day at the beach in Puerto Madryn

Prehistoric plants at Museo Paleontológico Egidio Feruglio

❺ Trelew

Road map B4. 40 miles (65 km) S of Puerto Madryn. 🚶 100,000. 🚌 ℹ Mitre 387, (0280) 442-0139.
Ⓦ **trelewpatagonia.gov.ar**

A small, attractive town, Trelew is an ideal base from which to explore the Welsh villages of the Chubut Valley. Its name in Welsh means "village of Lewis." Much of its original Welsh character has changed, and most visitors stop by instead for the town's **Museo Paleontológico Egidio Feruglio**, Argentina's premier paleontological museum. The museum has extensive fossil collections that date back 540 million years. The star exhibits, however, are the life-sized dinosaur skeletons and the dinosaur eggs. For an echo of Trelew's pioneer past, visit the historically themed **Museo Regional Pueblo de Luis**,

Sign outside a Welsh teahouse in Gaiman

housed within the city's old railroad station, and the settlers' graves at **Capilla Moriah** cemetery, which include that of Lewis Jones, the town's founder.

🏛 **Museo Paleontológico Egidio Feruglio**
Ave Fontana 140. **Tel** (0280) 443-2100. **Open** 9am–7pm daily. 🚶 🎫
Ⓦ **mef.org.ar**

🏛 **Museo Regional Pueblo de Luis**
Ave 9 de Julio & Fontana. **Tel** (0280) 442-4062. **Open** 8am–8pm Mon–Fri, 2–8pm Sat & Sun. 🚶

❻ Gaiman

Road map B4. 12 miles (20 km) W of Trelew. 🚶 11,000. 🚌 ℹ Belgrano, between Rivadavia & 28 de Julio, (0280) 449-1571. Ⓦ **gaiman.gov.ar**

Founded in 1874, Gaiman is the most quintessentially Welsh of all the villages of the Chubut Valley. Best known for its teahouses, Gaiman is also rich in history. The small **Museo Histórico Regional**, housed in the old railroad station, has excellent exhibits on Gaiman's pioneer past. Situated within a few blocks of the town's flower-filled Plaza Roca are **Primera Casa**, Gaiman's first-built house, and **Capilla Vieja**, its oldest chapel, both of which date from the pioneer era. The most authentic of Gaiman's teahouses, **Ty Gwyn**, **Ty Nain**, and **Plas y Coed**, are also located close to Plaza Roca.

Also near the plaza is **Parque El Desafío**, an interesting site filled with Joaquín Alonso's works. The "Dalí of recycling," Alonso has molded thousands of cans, bottles, and household appliances into works of art that include re-creations of the Taj Mahal and Picasso's paintings.

🏛 **Museo Histórico Regional**
28 de Julio 705. **Tel** (0280) 449-1007. **Open** 3–7pm Tue–Sun. 🚶

4 Reserva Provincial Península Valdés

A UNESCO World Heritage Site, Península Valdés is one of the world's great nature preserves. Its rugged 310-mile (500-km) coastline is a haven for an astonishing, and easily observable, array of marine fauna that includes Southern Right whales, killer whales, elephant seals, sea lions, Magellanic penguins, and millions of marine birds. Its interior is an arid wilderness, the eastern extension of the Patagonian steppe, populated by dry-land fauna including guanacos and the ostrich-like rhea. It is marked at its center by two large salt lakes. Day-long safaris depart from Puerto Madryn, though many visitors seek longer stays at one of the peninsula's estancias.

Visitors' Center
This is where visits to the peninsula begin. The center houses a small museum that provides a useful introduction to the reserve's stunning array of flora and fauna.

Puerto Pirámides
The peninsula's only village, Puerto Pirámides has a smattering of hotels and restaurants. It is one of the best places in the world to watch whales.

Golfo San Jo

Isla de los
Pájaros

Viedma

Istmo   Ameghino

Pue
Pirá

Golfo
Nuevo

Key

═══ Main road
═══ Minor road

Puerto
Madryn

0 km   10
0 miles   10

KEY

① **Sea lions and elephant seals** inhabit the peninsula's coast through the year.

② **Salina Grande** is one of two inland salt lakes that lie in a basin, which, at 138 ft (42 m) below sea level, is the fourth deepest depression on the planet.

★ **Golfo Nuevo**
The Southern Right whales visit the Golfo Nuevo between June and December each year to breed and bear young. Whale-watching excursions start from Puerto Pirámides and visitors can get extremely close to the whales.

Feeding Frenzy

Península Valdés is believed to be the only place in the world where orca (killer whales) engage in the spectacle of intentional beach stranding. The orca uses the tide and storms the beach head on, deliberately running itself aground to catch its prey, usually a sea lion pup or an adult penguin. When subsequent waves lift the orca back into the ocean it shares its prey with the rest of its pod. This phenomenon takes place at Caleta Valdés and, more often, at Punta Norte.

Orca attacking a sea lion pup in shallow surf

VISITORS' CHECKLIST

Practical Information
Road map C4. 35 miles (56 km) NE of Puerto Madryn. 🛈 Puerto Madryn: Administración Area Natural Protegida Península Valdés, Fournier 54, (0280) 445-0489; Istmo Ameghino: Centro de Interpretación; Puerto Pirámides: (02965) 495-048. 📱 📷 🐋 Faro Punta Delgada, (02965) 458-444. 🌐 **aanppv_nueva. peninsulavaldes.org.ar**

Transport
✈ Puerto Madryn. 🚌 from Puerto Madryn. 🚐 from Puerto Pirámides (Sep–Nov).

★ **Punta Norte**
This is a breeding spot for elephant seals and sea lions and the favorite hunting ground of killer whales. The place also has a marine museum.

Caleta Valdés
Magellanic penguins and elephant seals share the beach at this sheltered lagoon. It is also visited by killer whales that storm the beach and prey on these animals.

★ **Punta Delgada**
An easily observed colony of elephant seals inhabits the beach at the base of this blustery cliff. At the cliff top is luxury estancia Faro Punta Delgada, site of a century-old lighthouse.

For keys to symbols *see back flap*

❼ Reserva Provincial Punta Tombo

Road map B4. 68 miles (110 km) S of Trelew. **Open** Sep–Apr: 8am–8pm daily. ℹ Ruta Provincial 1, S of Trelew, (02965) 1520-9900. 🖥 💻
🔲 **puntatombo.com**

A narrow, stony peninsula that juts out abruptly into the Atlantic Ocean, Punta Tombo harbors South America's largest colony of Magellanic penguins. From September to April, over 650,000 of these black and white birds use the peninsula to incubate their eggs and prepare their offspring for migration. They nest in scrapes underneath the bushes and both male and female penguins take turns to guard their nests, protecting eggs from avian predators. These predators include the giant petrel as well as various species of gull, skua, and cormorant.

These humble penguins are not as glamorous as their larger cousins, the king and emperor penguins. While they can be observed from extremely close quarters, visitors need to be careful not to touch them. An ideal time to visit is between November and January when there are plenty of chicks. Apart from these penguins, several marine bird species can also be spotted.

The nearby countryside is a great place to see land fauna, including Patagonian hares, guanacos, and greater rheas.

A Magellanic penguin

Easy day trips run daily from Trelew and Puerto Madryn to the preserve.

❽ Camarones

Road map B5. 156 miles (252 km) S of Trelew. 🗺 2,200. 🚌 ℹ Estrada 467, (0297) 496-3013. 🎉 Fiesta Nacional del Salmón (Feb).

Literally translating into "shrimps," Camarones is a small, picturesque fishing village of one-story buildings and dusty streets. Located on the shores of an eponymous bay, this village is the main point of access to **Reserva Provincial Cabo dos Bahías**. Inaugurated as a tribute to Juan Perón, the **Museo de la Familia Perón** exhibits Perón family memorabilia from Juan and his brother Avelino's early youth in Patagonia. The family first lived in Río Gallegos, less than 60 miles (100 km) north of the Strait of Magellan, then further north near Camarones.

Environs
About 19 miles (30 km) southeast of the town is Reserva Provincial Cabo dos Bahías, which protects a 12,000-strong colony of Magellanic penguins. Visitors can also observe the sea lion colony on Isla Moreno.

🏛 **Museo de la Familia Perón**
Estrada 467. **Tel** (0297) 496-3014. **Open** 9am–7pm Mon–Fri, 2–7pm Sat, Sun, & hols.

Comodoro Rivadavia along the majestic Golfo San Jorge

❾ Comodoro Rivadavia

Road map B5. 229 miles (370 km) S of Trelew. 🗺 180,000. ✈ 🚌 ℹ Yrigoyen & Moreno, (0297) 444-0664.
🔲 **comodoroturismo.gob.ar**

Argentina's oil capital and one of the biggest cities on its Atlantic coast, Comodoro Rivadavia is located on the shores of the majestic **Golfo San Jorge** and is overlooked by **Cerro Chenque**. Also the leader in renewable energy, the city is home to Latin America's biggest wind farm.

Drilling rigs and storage tanks can still be seen in the city, where oil was first struck in 1907. The site can be visited at **Museo Nacional del Petróleo**, where exhibits trace the evolution of Argentina's oil industry. The city's railroad history is traced at **Museo Ferroportuario**. The short taxi ride to Cerro Chenque ends with breathtaking vistas of Golfo San Jorge, the city, and the beaches at the upscale resort of **Rada Tilly**.

Environs
The eerily silent wind farm, **El Parque Eólico Antonio Morán**, is 7 miles (12 km) outside Rada Tilly.

🏛 **Museo Nacional del Petróleo**
Carlos Calvo & San Lorenzo, Barrio General Moscón, Km 3. **Tel** (0297) 455-9558. **Open** 9am–5pm Tue–Fri, 3–6pm Sat, Sun, & hols. 🖥 🔲 Spanish only.

🏛 **Museo Ferroportuario**
Ave Rivadavia & 9 de Julio. **Tel** (0297) 444-4874. **Open** 9am–5pm daily.

Guanacos in the Reserva Provincial Punta Tombo

❿ Bosque Petrificado José Ormachea

Road map B5. 103 miles (165 km) W of Comodoro Rivadavia. **Open** Oct–Mar: 8am–8pm daily; Apr–Sep: 9am–6:30pm daily. 🚌 to Sarmiento, then taxi. 🏞 ℹ Ave San Martín, Sarmiento, (0297) 489-8282.

An otherworldly spectacle, this petrified forest has its origins in the Cretaceous period, 65 million years ago. Although far smaller and more recently formed than the Monumento Natural Bosques Petrificados, it is more easily accessible. Many tour operators in Comodoro Rivadavia run daily excursions to the forest.

Southern elephant seals on Isla Pingüino near Puerto Deseado

⓫ Puerto Deseado

Road map B5. 177 miles (286 km) S of Comodoro Rivadavia. 🏠 15,000. 🚌 ℹ San Martín 1525, (0297) 487-0220. 🎉 Fiesta del Marinero (Jan). 🌐 puertodeseado.tur.ar

Located on the sheltered estuary of Río Deseado, the little port town of Puerto Deseado is one of Patagonia's best-kept secrets. It owes its name to English privateer Thomas Cavendish, who sailed into the estuary in 1586, naming its natural harbor after his flagship, the *Desire*.
Reserva Natural Ría del Deseado protects the estuary's marine fauna. Boat excursions head into the preserve, which is a breeding ground for the graceful Commerson's dolphin and haven to many marine bird species. Trips include visits to the cliffside nesting sites of red-legged and rock cormorants, and to **Isla de los Pájaros**, home to a colony of Magellanic penguins. On the way to the

preserve, boats pass the spot where the British warship HMS *Swift* was shipwrecked in 1770. The wreck was only discovered in 1982. Rescued items, including bells and Wedgwood china, are displayed at **Museo Municipal Mario Brozoski**.
The town, Patagonia's busiest fishing port today, once depended on the shipping of wool and meat transported via rail from the interior. The former railroad station now houses **Museo de la Estación Ferro-carril**. At the center of the town stands a passenger wagon built in 1898, which was used to transport federal police during the Santa Cruz rebellion in 1921.

Environs
Around 16 miles (25 km) south of town, **Isla Pingüino** protects a small breeding colony of southern elephant seals and Patagonia's only nesting colony of the rockhopper penguin.

🏛 **Museo Municipal Mario Brozoski**
Belgrano & Colón. **Tel** (0297) 487-0673. **Open** 8am–8pm Mon–Fri, 3–7pm Sat & Sun.

Fossilized remains at the Monumento Natural Bosques Petrificados

⓬ Monumento Natural Bosques Petrificados

Road map B5. 159 miles (256 km) W of Puerto Deseado. 🚌 to Puerto Deseado, then taxi. **Open** 8am–6pm daily. 🚗 from Puerto Deseado.

Covering an area of 58 sq miles (150 sq km), the haunting Monumento Natural Bosques Petrificados is Patagonia's largest petrified forest. The park has its origins in the Jurassic period, 150 million years ago, when the Andes did not exist and humid winds blew in nonstop from the Pacific Ocean, causing incessant rain and encouraging the growth of tropical forests. When the Andes formed, volcanic activity buried these forests under volcanic ash. Fossilized trees are scattered across the landscape, rooted to the spot where they were petrified. Colossal in size, the biggest measure up to 115 ft (35 m) in height and 10 ft (3 m) in diameter. Tour operators run excursions from Puerto Deseado.

The fishing fleet on the Río Deseado in Puerto Deseado

Commerson's dolphins can be spotted easily in the bay of San Julián

⓭ Puerto San Julián

Road map B5. 238 miles (383 km) S of Puerto Deseado. 🚐 12,000. 🚌 ⓘ Ave San Martín, between Rivadavia & Moreno, (02962) 454-396.
W sanjulian.gov.ar

Claiming to be the birthplace of Patagonia, Puerto San Julián was the site of the first European settlement in Argentina, founded by Portuguese explorer Ferdinand Magellan in 1520. Francis Drake soon followed suit, dropping anchor in its shingle-banked bay in 1578. Despite numerous attempts at colonization, a permanent settlement was not established until the early 1880s, with the arrival of British sheep farmers from the Falkland Islands (Islas Malvinas).

City highlights include **Museo Rosa Novak**, which has displays on early sheep-farming pioneers, and **Monumento Primera Misa**, where the country's first mass was held the day after Magellan's landfall. Located nearby, **Muestra Arqueológica Florida Blanca** has exhibits on the region's indigenous cultures. However, the star attractions are the lively pods of Commerson's dolphins in San Julián's bay. Also in the bay are **Isla Cormorán** and **Isla Justicia**, whose shores are home to large colonies of Magellanic penguins.

Environs
Unspoiled beaches and some historical sites dot the beautiful coastal Avenida Hernán de Magallanes, which stretches north from San Julián. The stretch is a 34-mile (55-km) drive on the coastal circuit along the San Julián bay offering spectacular views.

🏛 Muestra Arqueológica Florida Blanca
Ave Costanera 900. **Tel** (02962) 414-396. **Open** varies. **Closed** mid-Mar–mid-Dec: Sat & Sun.

⓮ Parque Nacional Monte León

Road map B6. 28 miles (45 km) SE of Puerto Santa Cruz. 🚌 to Luis Piedra Buena, then taxi. ⓘ 9 de Julio and Belgrano, Puerto Santa Cruz, (02962) 498-184. **Open** Nov–Apr: daily. 🚗
🅿 **W** pnmonteleon.com.ar

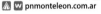

Cormorants on Monte León cliffs

Apart from being the newest national park in Argentina, this is also the only one situated along the country's Atlantic coast. Parque Nacional Monte León was created in 2004 to protect 25 miles (40 km) of coastline and 183 sq miles (474 sq km) of Patagonian steppe. Its virgin coastline, dotted with islands,

La Olla in Parque Nacional Monte León

reefs, coves, cliffs, and caverns, is its biggest attraction. The park provides refuge to marine fauna that includes sea lion and penguin colonies, pods of the graceful black and white Commerson's dolphin, and over 130 species of birds. The park's coast is also a station for cetaceans such as the Austral Frank whale. Highlights within the park include **Monte León Island**, a marine bird nesting site, and **La Olla**, a natural rock formation consisting of a circular cavity supported by a 98-ft (30-m) high natural arch.

A short way inside the park entrance, Hostería Monte León, part of the estancia of the same name, offers upscale lodging.

Hostería Monte León
Ruta Nacional 3, Km 2399. **Tel** (011) 4621-4780. **W** monteleon-patagonia.com

⓯ Río Gallegos

Road map B6. 215 miles (347 km) S of Puerto San Julián. 🚐 86,000. ✈ 🚌 ⓘ Ave Beccar 126, (02966) 436-920.
W turismo.riogallegos.gov.ar

An important port city, Río Gallegos is also the capital of Santa Cruz province. The first people to settle here were British sheep farmers from the Falkland Islands (Islas Malvinas) in the 1880s.

In 1885, Río Gallegos became the port from which local wool produce was exported. Nicknamed "white gold," wool sustained the local economy until the 20th century, when the shipping of coal from Río Turbio (see p251) brought about new prosperity. Today, it is this "black gold" and gas that provide Río Gallegos with most of its income.

Much of the city's architecture dates from the 1930s, especially along its main street, Avenida San Martín. However, some outstanding examples of pioneer-era construction can still be seen. Built by Salesian missionaries in 1899, the corrugated-tin and wood structure of **Catedral Nuestra Señora de Luján** is characteristic

Pioneer-era building from the 1890s, now housing Museo de los Pioneros, Río Gallegos

of that period, as is the 1890s building that houses **Museo de los Pioneros**. This museum narrates the story of the early sheep settlers. The nearby **Museo Ferroviario Roberto Gailán** is housed in an old railroad depot and run by workers laid off after the closure of the old Río Turbio–Río Gallegos train line. Restored 50-year-old steam engines that once worked the line are on display in the forecourt.

Catedral Nuestra Señora de Luján
Ave San Martín 739. **Open** 9am–6pm Mon–Fri. W catedralrg.com.ar

Museo de los Pioneros
Elcano & Juan Bautista Alberdi. **Tel** (02966) 437-763. **Open** 10am–7pm daily. Spanish only.

Museo Ferroviario Roberto Galián
Mendoza 75. **Tel** (02966) 426-766. **Open** 2–5pm Mon–Fri. Spanish only.

⓰ Estancia Monte Dinero

Road map B6. 75 miles (120 km) S of Río Gallegos. **Tel** (02966) 428-922. **Open** Oct–Apr.
W montedinero.com.ar

Founded in 1880 by a pioneering Patagonian family, the Fentons, this ranch is a working sheep farm. Guests stay in the main house, while activities include

sheep-shearing and herding demonstrations as well as trekking, and horse riding.

One trail leads to Monte Dinero, a hill with breathtaking vistas of the Magellan Strait and Tierra del Fuego. Excursions from the estancia run into Reserva Provincial Cabo Vírgenes, which is only 9 miles (15 km) away.

⓱ Reserva Provincial Cabo Vírgenes

Road map B6. 90 miles (145 km) S of Río Gallegos. Ave Kirchner 863, (02966) 438-725. Reserva: **Open** Sep–Apr: 8am–8pm daily.

Located at the far southern tip of the Argentinian mainland, at the entrance to the Strait of Magellan, Reserva Provincial Cabo Vírgenes protects the

second biggest colony of Magellanic penguins in South America after Reserva Provincial Punta Tombo (see p232). Over 100,000 penguins use the cape as a nesting ground from September to April. Visitors can observe these charismatic birds along a 1-mile- (2-km-) long nature trail.

In the northeastern corner of the preserve is the **Faro de Cabo Vírgenes** lighthouse, built by the Argentinian Navy in 1904. Its 400-watt bulb throws a beam at least 25 miles (40 km) over the sea. Visitors can climb the 91 steps to the top for splendid vistas of the strait. A short stroll away is the lovely **Al Fin y al Cabo** teahouse, owned by the Estancia Monte Dinero. Daily excursions to the preserve are arranged by tour operators from Río Gallegos.

The lighthouse built by the Argentinian Navy at Cabo Vírgenes

The Paleontology of Patagonia

Spectacular fossil finds in Patagonia since the 1980s have led scientists to hail the region as the paleontological promised land. Discoveries include some of the biggest dinosaurs to have roamed the planet, and other prehistoric beasts such as huge terror birds and ocean-dwelling crocodiles. These finds, viewed alongside Patagonia's petrified forests, have enabled experts to depict what prehistoric Patagonia looked like: a tropical jungle roamed by gargantuan beasts. The finds also provide an exciting dimension to traveling in Patagonia. With paleontological tourism taking off, most fossil parks, fossilized forest areas, and dig sites now welcome visitors.

One of the many fossilized trees in Patagonia's petrified forests

Argentinosaurus huinculensis is the biggest dinosaur discovered to date. This colossal herbivore lived 90 million years ago, measured 125 ft (38 m) in length, and weighed a massive 112 tons (102 tonnes).

Rodolfo Coria led the field study of both the Argentinosaurus and Giganotosaurus.

The Big Finds

Big fossil finds in Patagonia in the last two decades have included the discovery of several new prehistoric species and the world's biggest dinosaur nesting ground. These great finds have forced scientists to rewrite theory on the size, behavior, and evolution of prehistoric life.

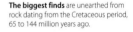

The biggest finds are unearthed from rock dating from the Cretaceous period, 65 to 144 million years ago.

Giganotosaurus carolinii was one of the world's biggest carnivores, 45 ft (14 m) long and weighing 10 tons (9 tonnes). Its skull was a frightening 6 ft (1.8 m) long, easily the size of a bathtub. The creature hunted Argentinosaurus in packs.

Dakosaurus andiniensis was nicknamed Godzilla for its dinosaur-like snout. This marine crocodile ruled the oceans 140 million years ago. Its discovery site in Patagonia was once a deep bay in the Pacific Ocean.

The Fossil Finders

Patagonia's biggest finds were first spotted by laymen. Rancher Guillermo Heredia found Argentinosaurus on his farm in northwest Patagonia; car mechanic Ruben Carolini unearthed Giganotosaurus; and the bones of Dakosaurus were found by visitors to northwest Patagonia in 2005.

The first dinosaur eggs were excavated from the world's largest dinosaur nesting ground in 1997 by scientists in Patagonia. Another discovery was by a family in Lamarque in Patagonia.

Raúl Vacca of Museo Paleontólogico Egidio Feruglio (MEF) in Trelew is a world expert in the preparing and mounting of fossilized skeletons.

Digging tools and excavation brushes are used to separate the fossil from its entombing sediments, and then to clean it.

Patagonia's Fossil Sites

1 Auca Mahuevo
2 Bosque Petrificado José Ormachea (see p233)
3 Bryn Gwyn
4 Lago Barreales (see p238)
5 Monumento Natural Bosques Petrificados (see p233)
6 Plaza Huincul
7 Villa El Chocón (see p239)

Important Events

1989: Argentinosaurus discovered near Plaza Huincul.

1995: The huge carnivore Giganotosaurus unearthed in Villa El Chocón.

1997: Dinosaur embryos with skin tissue intact discovered at Auca Mahuevo.

1999: MEF museum opens in Trelew, showcasing major fossil finds (see p229).

2000: Field work begins at Lago Barreales, Argentina's largest fossil site.

2005: Discovery of Dakosaurus, giant marine crocodile.

2006: World's largest-known terror bird, Phorusrhacid, uncovered in Patagonia.

2009: Discovery of a 65 million-year-old Plesiosaurus in El Calafate.

A Titanosaurus embryo seen within the surrounding rock

How They Looked

Argentinosaurus had massive limbs and a very long neck and tail. Giganotosaurus was an agile predator with short arms and powerful legs. *Dakosaurus andiniensis* had fins and a fish-like tail.

The ocean-dwelling *Dakosaurus andiniensis*

The herbivore *Argentinosaurus huinculensis*

The carnivore *Giganotosaurus carolinii*

Contemporary Argentinian paintings at Museo Nacional de Bellas Artes

⓲ Neuquén

Road map B4. 345 miles (557 km) NW of Viedma. 🚗 300,000. ✈ 🚌 from Viedma. ℹ Félix San Martín 182, (0299) 442-4089. 🏪 Sat & Sun. 🎉 Aniversario de la Ciudad Neuquén (Sep), Feria Artesanos (Nov).
w neuquentur.gob.ar

Patagonia's commercial hub, Neuquén is the capital of the province of the same name. It was a center for the region's wool and leather industry, and its location at the confluence of Río Limay and Río Neuquén made it an important agricultural center in the otherwise arid province. The arrival of the railroad in the early 1900s further benefited the town and the discovery of oil in the region in the 1960s and the development of a hydroelectric industry in the 1990s led to rapid growth.

A popular stopover for those visiting the dinosaur destinations Villa El Chocón and Plaza Huincul, Neuquén is a conurbation of low-rise buildings that can be divided into two distinct sectors: *el alto* (uptown) and *el bajo* (downtown). The tree-shaded Parque Central divides these two areas and is where most of Neuquén's cultural sights are found.

Lying north of the park is **Museo Nacional de Bellas Artes (MNBA)**, housed in a minimalist-style building and inaugurated in 2004. Its permanent collection features European art from the Renaissance to the 19th century, along with works from all over Argentina. Running along

the length of the park, but now largely in disuse, is the city's railroad line. Housed in the line's old accommodation building is **Museo Paraje Confluencia**, with displays on the history of Neuquén. In the renovated cargo warehouse nearby is the Sala de Arte Emilio Saraco, with temporary exhibitions by Argentinian artists.

Sculpture by Alfredo Bigatti, MNBA

Environs
About 31 miles (50 km) north of the town, in **San Patricio del Chañar**, are several vineyards that have raised the profile of Patagonian wine-making. Bodega del Fin del Mundo runs guided tours daily.

🏛 **Museo Nacional de Bellas Artes (MNBA)**
Mitre & Santa Cruz, Parque Central. **Tel** (0299) 443-6268. **Open** 10am–9pm Tue–Fri, 10am–2pm, 6–10pm Sat, 6–10pm Sun & hols. 🎫 6pm Tue–Sun (Spanish only). 🅿 ♿

🏛 **Museo Paraje Confluencia**
Independencia & Córdoba. **Tel** (0299) 442-5430. **Open** 9am–6pm Mon–Fri, 6–10pm Sat, Sun, & hols.

⓳ Centro Paleontológico Lago Barreales

Road map B3. 40 miles (65 km) N of Neuquén. 🚌 to Añelo, then taxi. ℹ (0299) 154-182295 . **Open** daily. 🎫 prior arrangement only.
w proyectodino.com.ar

Situated on the northern shore of Lago Barreales, Centro Paleontológico Lago Barreales is the largest paleontological excavation site in Argentina. It is also the only one of its kind in South America open to visitors all year round. Born out of an initial excavation in 2001, the site has a remote location which makes it difficult to get to, but those that make the effort are well rewarded.

The activities at the site range from a short yet informative guided tour to a two-day stay at the center during which visitors work alongside helpful site technicians and paleontologists in the extraction, preparation, and restoration of dinosaur fossils. The accommodation offered is rustic, but personalized service is emphasized with only four visitors permitted to stay at any one time.

Archaeological discoveries at the site, which so far number over a staggering 1,000 vertebral fossils and more than 300 plant fossils, have been the subject of worldwide attention since the dig began in 2001. Previously undiscovered dinosaurs include *Futalognkosaurus dukei*, a colossal 118-ft (36-m) long herbivore, and *Unenlagia*

Replica dinosaur skeletons on display at Museo Municipal Cármen Funes

For hotels and restaurants see pp278–83 and pp288–99

paynemili, thought to be an important link in the evolution of dinosaurs to birds. The fossilized remains of these and other finds are on display at the center.

Environs

Around 62 miles (100 km) southwest of Centro Paleontológico is Plaza Huincul, excavation site of *Argentinosaurus huinculensis* (*see pp236–7*), the largest dinosaur to have ever been discovered in the world. Visitors can see its huge fossilized skeleton at the town's **Museo Municipal Cármen Funes**.

🏛 **Museo Municipal Cármen Funes**
Ave Córdoba 55. **Tel** (0299) 496-5486. **Open** 9am–7pm Mon–Fri, 10:30am–8:30pm Sat, Sun, & hols.

A dramatic roadside sign outside the small town of Villa El Chocón

⑳ Villa El Chocón

Road map B4. 50 miles (80 km) SW of Neuquén. 🚍 1,500. 🚌 from Neuquén. 🛈 (0299) 155-413002. 🌐 chocon.gov.ar

The small settlement of Villa El Chocón was purpose-built in 1967 to provide housing for the workers of the nearby hydroelectric dam. It remained entirely anonymous until 1993 when local car mechanic and amateur paleontologist Ruben Carolini unearthed the virtually complete skeleton of the largest carnivorous dinosaur ever known to have walked the planet. The 100-million-year-old fossilized skeleton of the enormous 10.5 ton (9.5 tonne), 46-ft (14m) long *Giganotosaurus carolinii* (*see pp236–7*) is the star display at the town's **Museo Municipal Ernesto Bachmann**, along with myriad other fossils

A dinosaur skeleton at Museo Municipal Ernesto Bachmann

unearthed in the area. **Museo de Sitio** is situated 2 miles (3 km) south of the town's center, where on the shore of an artificial lake the large footprints of the herbivorous dinosaur Iguanodon lay preserved. More such footprints can be observed 4 miles (7 km) north of Villa El Chocón at Cañadon Escondido.

🏛 **Museo Municipal Ernesto Bachmann**
Accesso Centro Commercial. **Tel** (0299) 490-1230. **Open** Jan–Mar: 7am–9pm daily; Apr–Dec: 8am–7pm daily. 🛈 under 6 free. 🏛 Spanish only. ♿

🏛 **Museo de Sitio**
Ruta Nacional 237. **Open** 9am–6:30pm daily. 🏛

㉑ Parque Nacional Laguna Blanca

Road map B4. 93 miles (150 km) W of Neuquén. 🚌 🛈 Ejército Argentino 217, Zapala, Neuquén, (02942) 431-982. 🚍 🌐 pnlagunablanca.com.ar

Covering 44 sq miles (113 sq km), this national park is a haven for keen ornithologists.

It was created in 1940 to provide a protective habitat for the area's large population of black-necked swans, which today number over 2,000. Located in the western reaches of Neuquén province and surrounded by volcanic desert, this scenically stunning park also provides refuge to over 200 other bird species, including large colonies of wading and aquatic birds such as grebes, sandpipers, coots, ducks, and flamingos. These can be sighted in their thousands along the nature trail that hugs the western shore of the park's largest body of water, the **Laguna Blanca**. They can be observed at close quarters particularly during the southern hemisphere's spring season, when the elaborate courtship rituals take place. The best time to visit the lagoon is in the morning when it is far less windy.

Linked by the same trail, **Laguna Verde**, another large lake within the national park, is also populated by large colonies of colorful flamingos and is an important stopover site for migrating shorebirds. Swans are present all year round but birdlife is best observed between November and March.

Activities within the park include trout fishing but only by permit, which can be bought at the visitors' center. Camping is possible on the western shore of Laguna Blanca, although daily buses run to and from the park from the nearby town of Zapala.

A flock of flamingos at Parque Nacional Laguna Blanca

Sculpture of Jesus and his Disciples along Via Christi, Junín de los Andes

❷ Aluminé

Road map B4. 176 miles (284 km) W of Neuquén. ⛰ 1,300. 🚌 from Neuquén. *ℹ* Centro de Informes, Cristian Joubert 321, (02942) 496-661. 🌐 alumine.gov.ar

Situated within the Mapuche heartland, the pleasant settlement of Aluminé was founded as a military fortification in 1884. This was during the Conquista del Desierto *(see p54)*, the bloody campaign against the indigenous tribes. The fort no longer exists and Aluminé is today a sleepy Andean town, a rafting and fishing destination ringed by rugged hills. Rafting enthusiasts are drawn by the rapids of Río Aluminé; anglers by the trout- and perch-rich waters of Río Quillén and Río Pulmarí. The town is an ideal base for trips into the northern section of Parque Nacional Lanín.

❸ Junín de los Andes

Road map B4. 242 miles (390 km) SW of Neuquén. ⛰ 10,000. 🚌 from Neuquén. *ℹ* Padre Milanesio 590, (02972) 491-160. 🌐 Semana de la Artesanía (Jul); National Trout Festival (Dec). 🌐 junindelosandesturismo.wordpress.com

The region's oldest settlement, Junín de los Andes was founded in 1883 as an army outpost during the offensive against the Mapuche. Several expressions of this tribal culture are still found on the streets around the *araucaria*-shaded Plaza San Martín. **Museo Mapuche** is a good starting point, with Mapuche artifacts dating as far back as 12,000 years. The nearby **Iglesia Nuestra Señora de las Nieves** is an aesthetic blend of indigenous and Roman Catholic symbolism. Its stained-glass windows and main crucifix, portraying a resurrected Christ in Mapuche dress, are standout features. On a hillside overlooking the town there is the **Via Christi**, a 1-mile (2-km) walk comprising statues depicting the life of Christ, each handcrafted in the image of the Mapuche. The town is one of the gateways to Parque Nacional Lanín and visitors heading there should go first to **Delegación Parque Nacional Lanín**. Junín de los Andes is also Patagonia's fishing mecca, skirted by rivers rich in trout.

Fly-fishing sign near Junín

🏛 Museo Mapuche
Ginés Ponte & Joaquín Nogueira. **Open** 9am–noon, 3–8pm Mon–Fri.

Delegación Parque Nacional Lanín
Padre Milanesio 550. **Tel** (02972) 492-748. **Open** varies (call in advance).

❹ San Martín de los Andes

Road map B4. 118 miles (190 km) S of Aluminé. ⛰ 30,000. ✈ 🚌 from Neuquén. *ℹ* Ave San Martín and Juan Manuel de Rosas, (02972) 427-695. 🌐 Fiesta Nacional de Montañés (Aug). 🌐 sanmartin delosandes.gov.ar

Idyllically situated on the eastern lip of Lago Lácar, San Martín de los Andes is arguably Patagonia's loveliest town. Despite increased tourist interest and a construction boom, strict planning laws have ensured that it retains much of its original charm. At the center of town, **Museo Primeros Pobladores** has ethnographic exhibits on the region's colonization by Europeans. Several short treks lead into Parque Nacional Lanín nearby. Visitors wanting longer excursions into the park should head first to the **Intendencia Parque Nacional Lanín** for information.

Environs
Just 12 miles (19 km) from town is the Chapelco Ski Resort *(see p309)*, with 20 slopes of varying difficulty and a world-class snowboarding park. The maximum drop is 2,394 ft (730 m).

🏛 Museo Primeros Pobladores
Juan Manuel de Rosas 700. **Tel** (02972) 428-676. **Open** 10am–7pm Mon–Fri, 2–7pm Sat & Sun.

Intendencia Parque Nacional Lanín
Perito Moreno & Elordi. **Tel** (02972) 427-233. **Open** 8am–3pm Mon–Fri.

Boats for hire along the shore of Lago Lácar, San Martín de los Andes

㉕ Parque Nacional Lanín

Covering an area of 1,465 sq miles (3,795 sq km), this jewel of a national park was formed in 1937 and protects glacial lakes, volcanic summits, and lush forests. It is divided into north, central, and southern sections, each with its own gateway town, and each accessible by gravel road. Both roads and hiking trails traverse the park, skirting beautiful lakes and crossing various species of native forest. Over 200 animal species find refuge here, from the introduced wild boar to the native *pudú*, the world's smallest deer. Excellent campsites abound in the area as well.

VISITORS' CHECKLIST

Practical Information
Road map B4. 14 miles (22 km) SW of Aluminé. 🛈 E. Frey 749, San Martín de los Andes, (02972) 420-884. 🚲 🎒 ⛺
🌐 laninparquenacional.blogspot.com.ar

Transport
🚌 from Junín and San Martín de los Andes.

Lago Tromen is fringed with beaches of volcanic sand and *araucaria* forests. It has fabulous views of the volcano's north face.

Araucaria forests flourish here. The tree is sacred to the Mapuche, who eat its fruit and use its resin for medicine.

★ Volcán Lanín
A star attraction, Volcán Lanín is the park's highest peak at 12,385 ft (3,776 m). The 3-day trek that leads to its crater is physically extremely demanding.

Fly-fishing
The fly-fishing season runs from November to April. Angling hot spots include Lagos Huechulafquen and Tromen and Ríos Malleo, Quillén, and Chimehuin.

Lago Lácar is the most accessible of Lanín's lakes. It is worth exploring its southern shore, especially the beaches Quila Quina and Catritre, and the trek to Lago Escondido.

Key

— Main road
— Minor road
- - Park boundary
-■- International boundary

0 km   15
0 miles   15

Lago Huechulafquen
The park's biggest lake offers boat trips across its sparkling waters with spectacular views of Volcán Lanín's southern face.

㉖ Bariloche

Road map B4. 124 miles (200 km) S of San Martín de los Andes. ✈ 120,000. ✈ ➡ **ℹ** Centro Cívico, (0294) 442-9896. ⛷ La Fiesta de la Nieve (end Aug). **W** barilochepatagonia.info

Situated on the southeastern shore of Lago Nahuel Huapi, Bariloche attracts visitors all year due to its location within Parque Nacional Nahuel Huapi and its proximity to Villa Cerro Catedral. Founded in 1902, Bariloche was first populated by colonies of Swiss, Italians, and Germans. These communities left their imprint on the city's cultural landscape, not least by giving rise to Bariloche's reputation as Argentina's chocolate capital.

At the heart of the city, facing the lake, is the Centro Cívico, housing **Museo de la Patagonia Francisco P. Moreno**. This museum features exhibits on the region's flora, fauna, and indigenous cultures. Also located in the Centro Cívico is the tourist information office, which offers advice on traveling within the national park. The easiest hiking route from town is the Circuito Chico which skirts the beaches Playa Bonita and Serena. Those planning longer trips into the park should begin their trip at the park's Intendencia, a block away.

🏛 Museo de la Patagonia Francisco P. Moreno

Centro Cívico. **Tel** (0294) 442-2309. **Open** 2–7pm Tue–Fri, 10am–5pm Sat. 📷 under 10 free. 📷 **W** museodela patagonia.nahuelhuapi.gov.ar

Municipal building and clock tower in Centro Cívico, Bariloche

㉗ Parque Nacional Nahuel Huapi

Created in 1934 from land donated by naturalist and explorer Francisco P. Moreno, Parque Nacional Nahuel Huapi is Argentina's oldest national park. It is also its most visited, with over half a million people per year drawn by pristine landscapes and a range of outdoor activities th trekking, skiing, fly-fishing, and rafting. At the the park lies the huge and beautiful Lago Nah Bariloche, on its southeastern shore, is Patagonia's largest tourist center; Villa La Angostura and Villa Traful, farther north, are quieter, less-visited alternatives.

258

★ **Villa La Angostura**
Gateway to Parque Nacional Los Arrayanes within Parque Nacional Nahuel Huapi, Villa La Angostura is known for its boutique hotels and fine restaurants.

Parque Nacional Los Arrayanes
Covering the Quetrihué peninsula, this park protects ancient myrtle woods. Hiking trails cross to the forests at the peninsula's southern tip. Boat trips also run from Villa La Angostura.

Río Manso boasts class II–IV rapids and is a favorite with white-water rafting enthusiasts.

Villa La Angost
Osorno

Parque Na
Los Arra

Puerto
Blest

Cerro Tronador
11,400 ft

CHILE

Lago
Roca

La
Mar

0 kilometers   10
0 miles   10

Key

- ▬▬▬ Highway
- ══ Minor road
- – – Park boundary
- ▬∙ International border
- ▬∙∙ Provincial boundary

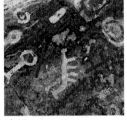

Isla Victoria
This is a forested island famous for its 2,000-year-old rock paintings.

VISITORS' CHECKLIST

Practical Information
Road map B4.
95 miles (153 km) SW of
Bariloche. 🛈 San Martín 24,
Bariloche, (0294) 442-3111.
🎿 🚣 ⛷ 🛶 🏔 Note: the
best time to go is from Dec to
Mar; skiing is late Jun to Aug;
trekking is from Dec to Mar;
and fishing is from Nov to Apr.
Snow is common between
May and Sep.
w parquesnacionales.gov.ar

Transport
✈ Bariloche.
🚌 from Bariloche.

★ Llao Llao Hotel and Resort
Open since 1938, this hotel *(see p282)* features a golf
course, private beach, and fantastic views of three lakes.
Its restaurant is open to non-guests.

Villa Cerro Catedral
Patagonia's premier
ski destination, this
resort owes its name
to the peak of Cerro
Catedral. Other
activities are hiking
and paragliding.

Cruce Andino

Of all the routes that cross the Andes between Patagonian Argentina and
Chile, the Cruce Andino is the most spectacular. The crossing, by land and boat,

begins in Bariloche and finishes in Puerto
Varas in Chile, traversing two national
parks along the way. Passengers travel
through forests thick with *alerce, lenga,*
and cypress trees, and cross four
separate lakes, including the emerald-
green Lago Todos los Santos in Chile.
Four volcanoes, including Chile's Volcán
Osorno and the mighty 11,400-ft
(3,478-m) Cerro Tronador in Argentina,
can be seen at close range. Both one-
and two-day tickets are available for the
crossings; the latter allows time to soak
up the scenery.

Picturesque cruise between Patagonian
Argentina and Chile

Map labels:
Lago Falkner
Caleufú
Neuquén
Lago Traful
Villa Traful
Valle Encantado
237
N E U Q U É N
231
Nahuel Huapi
kia
o Nahuel Huapi
ao
ao
Lopez ft
Villa Cerro Catedral
San Carlos de Bariloche
Bariloche
▲ Cerro Catedral 7,835 ft
258
R I O   N E G R O
Lago Mascardi
Villa Mascardi
Lago Steffen
El Bolsón

Landscape just south of the sleepy town of El Bolsón

❷❽ El Bolsón

Road map B4. 75 miles (120 km) S of Bariloche. 🔼 20,000. 🚌 **i** Ave San Martín y Roca, (0294) 449-2604. 🛒 Tue, Thu, & Sat. 🎉 La Fiesta Nacional del Lúpulo (Mar). **W** turismoelbolson.gob.ar

Gaining its reputation as a hippy retreat in the 1970s, El Bolsón is a laid-back town, where a relaxed atmosphere lingers to this day. Buskers, backpackers, and street vendors all converge in this town during summer, joined by an increasing number of families seeking a quieter alternative to Bariloche in the north.

Although tourism is growing in El Bolsón, the local economy has traditionally relied on forestry and hops grown on small farms called *chacras*. These *chacras* also produce excellent organic honey, jams, and soft fruits, and can be visited through the year. Good beers made from local harvests can be sampled at the well-known brewery nearby, **Cervecería El Bolsón**. The town's popular market place, **Feria Artesanal**, sells an assortment of woolen and leather products, jewelry, and ceramics, all made by local craftspeople.

Offering great walks and views is the nearby **Cerro Piltriquitrón**. Towering over El Bolsón, this summit, at 7,415 ft (2,260 m), is the highest in the

Spinning tops at Feria Artesanal

area. It offers great opportunities for adventure sport. **Mirador Plataforma** is a lookout point offering vistas of the Andean mountains and Lago Puelo. A further 40-minute walk away is the **Bosque Tallado**, a carved forest comprising sculptures worked from the trunks of trees burned by a forest fire in the early 1980s. A 3-hour trek leads hikers to the mountain's summit.

Environs
Around 10 miles (16 km) from El Bolsón, **Parque Nacional Lago Puelo** was created to protect trees such as the hazel and the *ulmo* native to Chile. The short **Bosque de las Sombras** nature trail is popular, and rafting, horse riding, and fly-fishing are also possible in the park.

🏕 **Parque Nacional Lago Puelo**
i Oficina de Informes, (02944) 499-232. 🏕 🏔 **W** parquesnacionales.gob.ar

❷❾ El Maitén

Road map B4. 43 miles (70 km) N of El Bolson. 🔼 5,000. 🚌 **i** Ave San Martín y Guido, (02945) 495-016. 🎉 Fiesta Nacional del Tren a Vapor (Feb). **W** turismoelmaiten.com.ar

An old railroad town, El Maitén is where the workshops for the **La Trochita** (Little Gauge) steam trains are located. First built in the early 1940s and still in use

today, these workshops can be visited on the old station grounds, where a small, efficient workforce hand-manufactures locomotive parts from old machinery to rebuild coaches. La Trochita is believed to be the world's oldest functioning steam train. It was built in 1922 to transport local wool and timber. Also on the station grounds is **Museo Ferroviario**, a small museum dedicated to the town's railroad heritage. La Trochita departs from El Maitén six times a week in summer.

🚂 **Museo Ferroviario**
Estación El Maitén. **Tel** (02945) 495-190. **Open** Dec–Mar: 8am–8pm daily; Apr–Nov: 9am–5pm daily. 🚉 📷 on request.

La Trochita steam train halted at El Maitén station

㉚ Museo Leleque

Road map B4. 25 miles (40 km) S of El Maitén. **Tel** (02945) 492-600. **Open** Thu–Tue. **Closed** May & Jun

A rustic estancia converted into a museum, Museo Leleque holds a 14,000-strong collection of artifacts narrating Patagonia's history. Displays are divided between four rooms and follow a historical itinerary, beginning with the arrival of the first indigenous populations in Patagonia 13,000 years ago and continuing up to the present day. Among the fascinating exhibits is a contract for the acquisition of horses signed by Santiago Ryan, a pseudonym used by outlaw Butch Cassidy.

A partially woven Tehuelche rug exhibit at Museo Leleque

㉛ Esquel

Road map B4. 112 miles (180 km) S of El Bolsón. 🚶 35,000. 🚗 🚌 **i** Ave Alvear & Sarmiento, (02945) 451-927. 🎿 La Fiesta del Esquí (Sep). **W** esquel.gov.ar

With its beautiful valley setting and snowcapped Andean backdrop, Esquel is a welcome change from the surrounding arid steppe. A laid-back town with a handful of tourist sites, it is the ideal base from which to visit nearby attractions such as Parque Nacional Los Alerces and the popular **La Hoya** ski resort. With 24 pistes of varying difficulty, this family-oriented ski resort keeps Esquel open to tourism in the winter months. The town's biggest draw, La Trochita, departs from Esquel's well-preserved railroad station.

Butch Cassidy and the Sundance Kid

In 1901 the SS *Soldier Prince* set sail from New York for Argentina. On board were James Ryan and Harry Place – better known as

The cabin built by Butch Cassidy and the Sundance Kid

Butch Cassidy and the Sundance Kid – America's most notorious bank robbers and members of the feared Wild Bunch. Fleeing the law, the two Americans, together with Sundance's girlfriend, Etta Place, had decided to head to remote Patagonia. In the village of Cholila, near Esquel, where Butch and Sundance eventually settled, locals still talk of the gringo gunslingers, while the house they built and lived in for six years can be visited on the edge of town.

㉜ Trevelin

Road map B4. 14 miles (24 km) S of Esquel. 🚶 10,000. 🚌 **i** Plaza Coronel Fontana, (02945) 480-120. **W** trevelin.gob.ar

A short drive from Esquel is the Welsh village of Trevelin. Though officially founded in 1918, it had been a settlement since the 1880s, when pioneers made the journey from their settlements near the Atlantic Coast. Here, they built the mills that gave the town its name. Housed within one of the flour mills is **Museo Regional Trevelin**, displaying Welsh artifacts. Capilla Bethel is the town's small Welsh chapel. A short trip from Trevelin are the **Nant y Fall** waterfalls – seven separate falls that drop majestically from heights of up to 197 ft (60 m).

🏛 Museo Regional Trevelin

Calle Viejo Molino. **Tel** (02945) 480-545 **Open** varies. 🚶 📷 on request.

㉝ Parque Nacional Los Alerces

Road map B4. 28 miles (45 km) W of Esquel. **i** Villa Futalaufquen, Ruta Provincial 71, (02945) 471-015. **Open** daily. 🚶 🚗 🏔 🚶 📷 **W** parquesnacionales.gob.ar

Covering 1,015 sq miles (2,630 sq km) and considered to be the most pristine of northern Patagonia's parks, Parque Nacional Los Alerces was created to protect the *alerce* tree, a beautiful, towering species that can exceed 197 ft (60 m) in height and live for 4,000 years.

Though numerous hiking trails crisscross the park, the only way to access its *alerce* woods is via the **Circuito Lacustre**, a boat and trekking excursion that traverses majestic lake and glacier scenery. The excursion's highlight is its end point, the striking Millennium tree, a 2,600-year-old *alerce*.

A beautiful lake located in Parque Nacional Los Alerces

One of the quiet streets running through Perito Moreno

➌➍ Perito Moreno

Road map B5. 334 miles (538km) S of Esquel. 🏠 4,500. 🚌 ℹ️ Ave San Martín & Gendarmería Nacional, (02963) 432-732. 🎭 Festival Cueva de las Manos (Feb).

Named for the Argentinian naturalist and explorer, Francisco Moreno, and not to be confused with Glaciar Perito Moreno (see p258) or Parque Nacional Perito Moreno (see p248), this town is a popular stopover for those traveling along Ruta Nacional 40. The most populous town in this area of the Santa Cruz province, it is an ideal base from which to explore the World Heritage Site of **Cueva de las Manos** as well as Parque Nacional Perito Moreno to the south. Most will find this town a sprawling and somewhat nondescript settlement, where little goes on. Life revolves around the main avenue, Avenida San Martín,

which is ideal for evening walks. The avenue is given dashes of color by the politically motivated graffiti.

➌➎ Los Antiguos

Road map B5. 35 miles (56km) W of Perito Moreno. 🏠 4,000. 🚌 ℹ️ Lago Buenos Aires 59, (02963) 491-261. 🎭 Fiesta Nacional de la Cereza (Jan). 🌐 **losantiguos.tur.ar**

With its benign microclimate and idyllic location on the shore of **Lago Buenos Aires**, this little town derives its name from the Tehuelche *I Keu Kenk*, meaning "place of my ancestors."

Los Antiguos was built on a site used millennia ago by the Tehuelche as a place of retirement. The archaeological richness of the area is such that ancient burial mounds are still being discovered. The town is now known as Argentina's cherry capital, although its

chacras also produce other high-quality jams and liqueurs. Family-run **Chacra Don Neno**, at the center of town, is among the best of these farms. The town's other highlight is Lago Buenos Aires, the second biggest freshwater lake in South America, on the border between Argentina and Chile. Its pristine trout- and salmon-rich waters attract anglers.

➌➏ Estancia Nibepo Aike

Road map B6. 35 miles (56 km) S of El Calafate. **Tel** (02902) 492-797, (011) 5272-0341. **Open** Oct–mid-Apr. 🌐 **nibepoaike.com.ar**

Set up by Santiago Peso, a Croatian immigrant, at the start of the 20th century, Nibepo Aike is a working farm, which primarily produces beef but also rears sheep. The farm is located within Parque Nacional Los Glaciares (see p254–5), an area of great natural beauty.

Visitors can watch several activities – some seasonal and others daily – such as milking the cows, cattle branding, breaking in horses, sheep shearing by hand, and rounding up cattle. The ranch also arranges horseback rides and hikes to various places including the southern part of Lago Argentino and the Tres de Abril lake.

A view of the majestic Andes across a sparkling river and a shelter belt of poplar trees, Los Antiguos

The ancient stenciled handprints at Cueva de las Manos

☞ Cueva de las Manos

Road map B5. Ruta Provincial 97, 100 miles (161 km) S of Perito Moreno. **Open** 9am–7pm daily. 🈀 🗓 🏠 Ⓦ cuevadelasmanos.org

Hidden deep within the Río Pinturas Canyon, inside the borders of breathtaking Parque Nacional Perito Moreno, Cueva de las Manos (Cave of Hands) is Argentina's finest example of prehistoric cave art. Declared a UNESCO World Heritage Site in 1999, it has dumbfounded experts since its discovery in 1881 and still hosts ongoing archaeological work.

The main cave measures 79 ft (24 m) in depth, with an entrance 49 ft (15 m) wide and an initial height of 33 ft (10 m). The ground inside the cave, however, has an upward slope and soon the height is reduced to no more than 7 ft (2 m).

A visit to the cave, where the rock paintings date from as far back as 9,500 years ago, is a moving experience. Vivid, kaleidoscopic, stenciled hand negatives, left by children and adults, are spread throughout the 1,968-ft (600-m) long trail. Numbering more than 2,000, they are thought to be evidence of the artists' belief in the permanent contact between man and mother earth. The paint used in the negatives would have been mixed orally, using mineral pigments found at the site combined with anything from water to saliva and even urine. Once in liquid form the paint would be spat out over the hand on the wall.

The hunters' intimate relationship with nature is depicted in the early paintings; the hunting scenes are of great anecdotal value, showing guanacos being chased across the canyon, surrounded, and then killed with long spears and stones. The sense of movement is striking, with both energetic hunter and prey depicted in dynamic form. Other paintings illustrate the link between the hunters' earthly world and its spirit equivalent. Paintings from 7,000 years ago show hundreds of heavily pregnant guanacos standing still. These are thought to be some kind of painted prayer, beseeching the return of the animals during a period of drought that had seen them migrate to better pastures.

Stylized forms mark the cave's most recent art, dating from 1,500 to 4,000 years ago. Biomorphic motifs of frogs, lizards, hawks, and pumas, and geometrical shapes such as concentric circles, zigzag lines, and combined triangles adorn the cave walls. These abstract forms continue to confound experts.

Archaeological work at Cueva de las Manos is ongoing, so visitors get a chance to marvel at the rock art on guided tours only. Tour groups leave the visitor center several times daily. Tour agencies in Perito Moreno run excursions to the cave; visitors can also seek lodging with Estancia Telken or Estancia Cueva de las Manos (see pp310–11), both of which are conveniently located nearby.

Argentina's Loneliest Road

No road in Argentina inspires solitude and introspection quite like Ruta Nacional 40. Never winding and seemingly never ending, Ruta Nacional 40 runs the entire length of Argentina, but finds its true heart in the wilderness of Patagonia; and nowhere more so than in the 390-mile (628-km) stretch of nothingness that lies between Perito Moreno and El Calafate. Here, Ruta Nacional 40 becomes a rocky, gravel artery, surrounded by a featureless landscape of scrub grass and broad horizons. A howling wind is the traveler's only accompaniment; encounters are few and far between, this being a region of isolated, century-old sheep estancias and forgotten villages. Left behind by time, they evoke the spirit of a Patagonia of old.

An empty, lonely stretch along Ruta Nacional 40

The only hotel in the village, Hotel Bajo Caracoles

❸ Bajo Caracoles

Road map B5. 80 miles (130 km) S of
Perito Moreno. 🚠 100. 🚌

For motorists driving south
on Ruta Nacional 40 from Perito
Moreno, Bajo Caracoles is the
first stopover point. Surrounded
by the vast Patagonian steppe,
it is a remote settlement of
about 15 families. The town
has the only gas station on the
national highway between
Perito Moreno and Tres Lagos,
a stretch of over 310 miles (500
km). The village is home to a
small hotel that contains its sole
restaurant and phone booth.

❸ Parque Nacional Perito Moreno

Road map B5. 102 miles (165 km) SW
of Bajo Caracoles. 🛈 Ave San Martín
882, Gobernador Gregores, (02962)
491-477. 🚠 🌐 **parquesnacionales.
gob.ar**

Due to its remote location
and extreme climatic conditions, Parque Nacional Perito
Moreno remains Patagonia's
wildest and best-preserved
national park. Visitors able to
traverse its borders will find
landscapes of pristine beauty
abundant in wildlife.
    Covering 490 sq miles (1,268
sq km), the park encompasses
two separate ecological regions.
The Patagonian steppe covers
its eastern section, forming an
elevated plain of scrub and
grassland at 2,950 ft (900 m)
above sea level. In the park's
western section this scrub is
replaced by thick swathes of
lenga forest, which rise to an
altitude of 3,936 ft (1,200 m),

and have as their backdrop the
snowy peaks of the beautiful
Andean cordillera. Opportunities
for nature-spotting are varied
and many. Well-marked trails
cross breathtaking scenery that
features eight beautiful lakes.
Elegant fine-boned guanaco
abound along their shores, and
some 160 bird species are found
in the park.
    Visitors should expect
extreme weather conditions.
In winter temperatures drop to
a chilling -25° C (-13° F), and it
can snow even in summer.
The best times to visit are in
the southern hemisphere's
late spring and early fall. Luxury
accommodations in and around

the park are offered
by Estancia La Oriental and
Estancia Menelik *(see pp310–11)*.

❹ Hipólito Yrigoyen

Road map B5. 122 miles (197 km) S of
Perito Moreno. 🚠 250. 🚌

Off Patagonia's more beaten
track but beautifully situated,
Hipólito Yrigoyen is a small
settlement on the shore of
Lago Posadas, at the foot of
the southern Andes. It is still
usually known by its old name,
Posadas, taken from the lake.
People who visit the town do
so for three main reasons –
fishing, hiking, and mountain
climbing. The lake is a popular
spot among anglers and the
catch includes smelt, perch,
and salmon.

Environs
Around 2 miles (3 km) south
of Hipólito Yrigoyen is the
Cerro de Los Indios archaeological site with 3,000-year-old
rock paintings. The area's star
attraction is **Cerro San Lorenzo**.
At 12,155 ft (3,702 m), it is
one of the highest peaks in
southern Patagonia.

Breathtaking view of Lago Posadas with the Andes in the distance

A herd of guanaco wandering on the vast Patagonian steppe near Tres Lagos

❹ Gobernador Gregores

Road map B5. 218 miles (352km) S of Perito Moreno. 🚏 3,500. 🚌 ❶ Ave San Martín & Ruperto Barrenchea, (02962) 491-228.

Situated in the middle of the windy Patagonian steppe, deep in sheep territory, Gobernador Gregores is characteristic of the many isolated settlements that dot the southern stretch of Ruta Nacional 40. A farming town that was once an important stopover for landowners transporting wool from the Andes to the ports on the Atlantic coast, its chief attractions today are the working estancias that dot the surrounding landscape.

As well as farming sheep, these beautiful ranches provide visitors isolation and relaxation, together with activities such as horse riding, bird-watching, and fishing. Estancia La Angostura, in the same family since 1878, and Estancia Río Capitán *(see pp310–11)* are two of the most recommended. Motorists driving along Ruta Nacional 40 should note that the town, situated 45 miles (72 km) off the national highway, provides basic accommodations and also has the only gas station between Bajo Caracoles to the north and Tres Lagos to the south, a stretch of over 248 miles (400 km).

❹ Lago Cardiel

Road map B5. 43 miles (70 km) W of Gobernador Gregores. 🚌 ❶ Ave San Martín & Ruperto Barrenchea, Gobernador Gregores; (02962) 491-192.

The clear turquoise waters of Lago Cardiel are easy to spot for those traveling along Ruta Nacional 40. The lake is overlooked by the dramatic peak of **Mount El Puntudo**, and stands out from the surrounding steppe, providing welcome relief for eyes grown accustomed to scrub grass and flat plains. The colorful colonies of black-necked swans and pink flamingos that inhabit the lake's shores can also be seen from the roadside.

Brimming with rainbow trout and salmon, the lake is a prime spot for angling. The nearby estancias can make arrangements for excursions.

❹ Tres Lagos

Road map B6. 108 miles (174km) S of Gobernador Gregores. 🚏 200. 🚌 🚕

The tiny settlement of Tres Lagos owes its name to its proximity to the lakes **Viedma**, **San Martín**, and **Tar**. The town was originally founded to serve the sheep ranches that could be found around the three lakes. Wool from the estancias would be brought to Tres Lagos where it was loaded onto wagons for the two-month long journey to the port at Puerto Santa Cruz on the Atlantic coast. More prosaically, this remote settlement today serves mainly the motorists traveling along Ruta Nacional 40, its gas station being the only one on the long, empty stretch of highway between Bajo Caracoles and El Calafate *(see p251)*. It also has a free municipal campsite.

Flamingos over the turquoise waters of Lago Cardiel

❹ Lago San Martín

Road map B5. 138 miles (222 km) N of Tres Lagos. 🏔 500. 🚌 from El Chaltén. 🛈 Ave Güemes 21, El Chaltén, (02962) 493-370. 🌐 elchalten.com

Straddling the border between Argentina and Chile, where it is known as Lago O'Higgins, this lake derives its two names from the popular Independence heroes of the two countries, who united forces in the early 19th century to defeat Spain. Lago San Martín marks the starting point of the Austral, Argentina's Deep South, and its surrounding landscape is one of dramatic Andean peaks and glacial lakes.

Though remote, the lake has two lovely estancias located on its shores, Estancia La Maipú and Estancia El Cóndor (see pp310–11). Both offer treks, horse rides, and bird-watching tours into the surrounding forests. Trails, along which Andean condors are seen, lead to a number of lookout points that offer breathtaking views of the lake and the Andes. Excursions to the lake are run by tour agencies in El Chaltén. However, the lake is rendered inaccessible at times due to unpredictable weather that makes navigation difficult.

Hikers on their way to Mount Fitz Roy, El Chaltén

❺ Parque Nacional Los Glaciares

See pp 254–9.

❻ El Chaltén

Road map A5. 81 miles (130 km) W of Tres Lagos. 🏔 500. 🚌 🛈 Ave Güemes 21, (02962) 493-370. 🎏 Fiesta Nacional del Trekking. 🌐 elchalten.com

With its wind-pummeled gravel streets and rugged Andean setting, El Chaltén gives every impression of being an old frontier settlement rather than the country's newest town. It was created in 1985 as a geopolitical maneuver in a long-running border dispute between Argentina and Chile. First populated by border guards and government employees, El Chaltén has since blossomed into Argentina's foremost trekking destination. Situated within Parque Nacional Los Glaciares, it is an ideal base from which to explore the northern section of the park. In summer, its 500 permanent residents are joined by almost 60,000 hikers and climbers drawn by the trails that lead to the base of the highest summit, Mount Fitz Roy, in the Fitz Roy massif. The base offers an opportunity to go ice-trekking on the Viedma and Torre glaciers.

The best time to visit is fall as well as October and November when the town is less crowded.

❼ Lago del Desierto

Road map A5. 23 miles (37 km) N of El Chaltén. 🚌 Dec–Mar daily. 🚌 🛈 (02962) 493-370.

A long-hidden jewel, Lago del Desierto (Lake of the Desert) was unveiled to tourists in 1995, when Argentina's border dispute with Chile came to an end and sovereignty over the lake's shores was finally ruled in its favor.

Tours lasting a full day pass through the forests of the Río de las Vueltas valley before arriving at the lake's southern shore. From there a number of treks are possible, the low-difficulty hike to **Glaciar Huemul** being highly

Río de las Vueltas making its way through forests

recommended. The trail passes through dense forests of *lenga* and *ñire* before reaching the glacier and the emerald-green lagoon that sits at its base. From the lake's southern bank, visitors can also go to **Punta Norte** on its northern bank, which offers fabulous views of the lake and the north face of awe-inspiring Mount Fitz Roy.

From Punta Norte, tourists can trek to the Chilean border post on the coast of Lago San Martín. Boats depart from the border post, crossing the lake to the Chilean town of Villa O'Higgins.

⊕ El Calafate

Road map B6. 137 miles (220 km) S of El Chaltén. 🌄 17,000. ✈ 🚌 from El Chaltén. 🛈 Terminal de Omnibus, Ave Julio A Roca 1004, (02902) 491-090. 🎣 Fiesta de Bautismo del Lago Argentino. 🅦 turismo.elcalafate.gov.ar

Located on the shore of Lago Argentino, El Calafate is the area's biggest tourist center. The town is the perfect base from which to explore the southern section of Parque Nacional Los Glaciares, including the magnificent Glaciar Perito Moreno.

With shops, restaurants, and a mostly benign microclimate, El Calafate comes as a welcome relief to visitors arriving from the barren Patagonian steppe to the north. The city's main cultural point of reference is the **Museo Regional Municipal El Calafate**, which recounts the area's history from the point of arrival of its first indigenous groups. **Centro de Interpretación Histórica Calafate** also traces local history. Its photographic and pictorial displays explain the region's human and environmental past. Another fascinating place is the **Glaciarium**, a rare glacier museum. A short walk away is **Reserva Municipal Laguna Nimez**, a nature preserve on the shore of Lago Argentino that protects about 100 species of birds.

Environs

Several ranches near town offer comfortable accommodations. Guests can take part in ranch activities at the estancia El Galpón del Glaciar *(see pp310–11)*. Hostería Alta Vista, a ranch built in the late 19th century, is in the grounds of Estancia La Anita. Excursions across the estancia include views of Glaciar Perito Moreno.

🏛 **Museo Regional Municipal El Calafate**
Ave del Libertador 575. **Tel** (02902) 491-924. **Open** 8am–7pm Mon–Fri. ♿

🏛 **Centro de Interpretación Histórica Calafate**
Almirante G. Brown & Guido Bonarelli. **Tel** (02902) 492-799. **Open** Dec–Mar: 10am–8pm daily; Apr–Nov: 11am–6pm daily. 🎣 🖥 📷
🅦 museocalafate.com.ar

🏛 **Glaciarium**
Camino al Glaciar Perito Moreno. **Tel** (02902) 497-912. **Open** 9am–8pm daily (May–Aug: 11am–8pm daily). 🎣 📷 🅦 glaciarium.com

El Galpón del Glaciar, a working sheep ranch, near the town of El Calafate

Brightly colored shops at the main shopping center, El Calafate

⊕ Río Turbio

Road map B6. 160 miles (257km) S of El Calafate. 🚌 from El Calafate, Río Gallegos. 🛈 Plazoleta Augustín del Castillo, (02902) 422-850.

Situated in a remote corner of Patagonia, 4 miles (6 km) from the border with Chile, the gritty mining town of Río Turbio was known mainly for one thing – coal. Due to Argentina's ongoing mining industry depression, the coal mines lie abandoned at the edge of town, a short distance from the Villa Dorotea border patrol. A small section, where miners give demonstrations of their work, can be visited by guided tour, arranged at the tourist information office in town. The town's other highlight is its narrow-gauge railroad line, laid in the early 1950s to transport Río Turbio's coal to Río Gallegos on the Atlantic coast. The ageing locomotives that work the line are a throwback in time. Once the most southerly line in the world, the railroad ceded this distinction after the construction of the new railroad line in Ushuaia in 1994. Turbio's other draw is its attractive wooded hillsides 2.5 miles (4 km) south of the town. This is where the **Valdelén** winter-sports complex is located. This ski center has gentle slopes which are ideal for beginners.

View of the walkway that runs close to the astonishing Glaciar Perito Moreno ▶

㊺ Parque Nacional Los Glaciares

A UNESCO World Heritage Site, Parque Nacional Los Glaciares derives its name from the 47 major glaciers and numerous smaller ones that lie within its boundaries. In its northern sector is Argentina's trekking capital, El Chaltén, gateway to the magnificent Mount Fitz Roy; in its southern zone lies the awe-inspiring Glaciar Perito Moreno. Trips combining both sections of the park are increasingly popular, although the southern zone remains more accessible; its dazzling glaciers and lakes are just a day trip away from the town of El Calafate.

Locator Map

▪ Area illustrated

▦ International border

★ Mount Fitz Roy
The towering granite needles of Mount Fitz Roy dominate the park's northern region. Trails run from El Chaltén to the foot of Mount Fitz Roy and Cerro Torre, the two highest peaks in the massif.

★ Glaciar Upsala
The giant Upsala descends into the northern arm of Lago Argentino. Boat excursions cruise past its front wall after winding their way across the iceberg-studded lake, all the while under the gaze of snowy mountains.

0 kilometers 15

0 miles 15

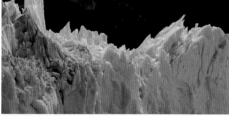

Glaciar Spegazzini
Visited on excursions to Glaciar Upsala, Glaciar Spegazzini boasts the biggest snout in the national park, rising to a height of 443 ft (135 m) in parts.

KEY

① **Glaciar Agassiz**, with few tourists and no walkways, is the antithesis of Glaciar Perito Moreno.

② **Glacier Onelli** is one of three glaciers that converge on iceberg-choked Laguna Onelli.

For hotels and restaurants see pp278–83 and pp288–99

Ice Calving

The periodic rupture and collapse of Glaciar Perito Moreno's 197-ft (60-m) front wall provides a great spectacle. This extraordinary

phenomenon is caused when the glacier advances close to Península Magellanes, damming the Brazo Rico (Rico Arm) of Lago Argentino. With no outflow, the lake's water rises until the pressure of its weight forces the dam to burst and, in a cataclysmic explosion of ice and water, causes the glacier's front wall to come crashing down. Visitors in 2008 were the last lucky witnesses of this event.

The spectacular ice calving on Glaciar Perito Moreno

Key

═══ Main road
═══ Minor road
- - - Trail
- - - Park boundary

Exploring the Park

Once inside the park, Puerto Punta Bandera in the southern sector is the departure point for lake excursions on Lago Argentino and to see Glaciar Perito Moreno. In the park's northern section, several trails of varying levels of difficulty begin at the national park office at El Chaltén, and organized excursions go to remote sections of the park.

Lago Argentino
Fed by the glacial meltwater of several rivers, Lago Argentino is the country's biggest lake. Cruises take visitors around its drifting icebergs before approaching the front walls of glaciers.

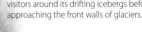

★ Glaciar Perito Moreno
The park's single greatest attraction, Glaciar Perito Moreno is visited every year by thousands hoping to witness the astonishing spectacle of the collapse of the glacier's front wall.

Map labels: Lago Viedma, Manso, Río Guannaco, Lago Argentino, Estancia Union, El Calafate, Puerto Punta Bandera, Canal de los Tempanos, Península Magellanes, Muelle Perito Moreno, Muelle Bajo de las Sombras, Glaciar Perito Moreno, Brazo Rico, Lago Roca, Cerro Cristal 4,220 ft, Estancia Nibepo Aike, 40

Exploring the Northern Sector

The northern sector of Parque Nacional Los Glaciares is dominated by the awe-inspiring peaks of Mount Fitz Roy. Since the 1930s, climbers have attempted to conquer the 11,168-ft (3,402-m) Mount Fitz Roy and the 10,280-ft (3,133-m) Cerro Torre. They are considered two of the world's most technically challenging mountains as their summits are formed by "mushrooms" of snow and ice that are in constant danger of collapse. More recently, avid hikers have also flocked to the area, converting the tiny settlement of El Chaltén into Argentina's trekking mecca.

Campsite on a sunny hillside

Centro de Visitantes Guardaparque Pedro Fonzo

Ruta 23, before entering El Chaltén.
Tel (02962) 493-004.
Open 10am–5pm daily.

Visitors planning to go for treks in the national park should first register at this office. It is conveniently located at the entrance to El Chaltén. The staff are friendly, helpful, and able to give advice on difficult trails and expected weather conditions. Climbing permits can also be purchased here.

🏕 Sendero Laguna Torre

This low-difficulty, 6-mile (10-km) hike can be done in one day from El Chaltén. Hikers should note that the return journey takes about 7 hours. The trail follows the Río Fitz Roy valley and climbs through lush *lenga* and *ñire* forests, finally ending at Laguna Torre, a hidden emerald lake that sits at the foot of the magnificent Cerro Torre. Breathtaking views from the lake encompass the mountain, its sister peaks, Egger at 9,514 ft (2,897 m) and Standhart at 9,186 ft (2,798 m), and the sweeping **Glaciar Torre**.

Ice-trekking excursions on Glaciar Torre can be arranged in El Chaltén. Hikers can choose between the single- and two-day options; the latter involves a night's stay at the basic yet comfortable Thorwood base camp, with simple facilities, close to the beautiful Laguna Torre.

🏕 Sendero Laguna de los Tres

Laguna de los Tres is a glacial tarn that sits at the base of Mount Fitz Roy. The trail to its shores is arguably the most scenic in the park. The outward trek from El Chaltén takes around 5 hours, making a return hike just about possible in a day. Otherwise, it is best to plan for two days and set up camp.

The trail's first section, an easy 3.5-hour hike to **Río Blanco**, traverses a landscape of ancient woodland, marshy wetlands, and crystal-clear lagoons. Visitors must note that camping here is permitted only for climbers who have made arrangements at the park office. Midway to Río Blanco, and a 10-minute detour from the main trail, is **Laguna Capri**, a secluded lake with fantastic vistas of the Fitz Roy range. Basic campsites for visitors are located here and at **Campo Poincenot**, 2 miles (3 km) away.

Río Blanco marks the trail's final section to Laguna de los Tres, named in honor of the trio of French climbers, René Ferlet, Guido Magnone, and Lionel Terray, who became the first to scale Mount Fitz Roy in 1952. A medium-level trek, it ascends an incline that gets progressively steeper, rising 1,312 ft (400 m) in a mile (2 km). Views from the lake are magnificent, with towering Mount Fitz Roy rising above the lake and the **Glaciar de los Tres** spilling downwards towards its far shore.

The spectacular Laguna de los Tres at the foot of Mount Fitz Roy

⛏ Sendero Piedra del Fraile

Hikers wishing to further explore the national park should make the trek to Piedra del Fraile, a base camp located at the northern edge of the massif. A 4-hour trail to the camp starts at Campo Poincenot and follows the Río Blanco and Río Eléctrico valleys. The trail skirts **Glaciar Piedras Blancas** and passes through quiet *lenga* forests. The latter half of the trail offers great views of Mount Fitz Roy's north face.

On reaching Piedra del Fraile there is a private camping ground with hot water and cabins. Trails from Piedra del Fraile lead up to the **Southern Patagonian Ice Field**. Week-long expeditions to the ice fields, suitable only for experienced snow- and ice-trekkers, can be organized with tour operators in El Chaltén.

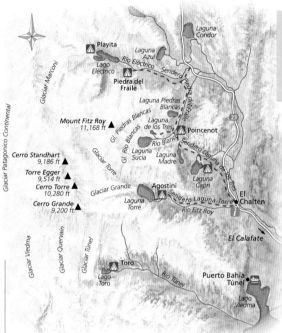

View of Glaciar Viedma rising from the waters of Lago Viedma

⛏ Glaciar Viedma

Covering an immense area of 378 sq miles (978 sq km), this vast river of ice is the biggest glacier in South America. Boat excursions to its 131-ft (40-m) high face leave from **Puerto Bahía Túnel** on Lago Viedma's northern shore. Most trips range from 2 to 6 hours in length. The longer excursions are the most spectacular, allowing visitors to disembark and see the magnificent glacier close-up. There are also undemanding hikes that can be arranged to the beautiful glacial caves or a 1.5-hour trek across the glacier's icy surface. Professional guides provide equipment, including crampons. The guides are all knowledgeable and speak both Spanish and English. Many tour operators run excursions to the glacier from El Chaltén.

Key

═══ Minor road

– – Trail

The Cerro Torre Controversy

It was hailed as the greatest mountaineering feat of all time but many doubt that it actually happened. On January 28, 1959, Italian climber Cesare Maestri, together with Austrian Toni Egger, set out to scale the unconquered Cerro Torre, then considered the world's toughest peak. Six days later, Maestri alone reached the base. He said that both Egger and he had made it to the summit but the Austrian had been killed by an avalanche on their descent. The pair's camera was also lost in the accident. One of the greatest climbers of his day, Maestri demanded to be taken on his word. Investigations found no trace of the pair's equipment beyond the lower reaches. Embittered, Maestri's response to his critics was to make two more attempts to climb the summit, but in vain. Now in his seventies, he still holds that he and Egger were the first to conquer Cerro Torre.

The Italian mountaineer Cesare Maestri

Exploring the Southern Sector

The southern sector of Parque Nacional Los Glaciares is characterized by the magnificent glaciers that spill downward from the Southern Patagonian Ice Field, the great frozen plateau of ice that sits atop the southern Andes. These glaciers are remnants of the Ice Age, when they stretched far beyond their current boundaries, reaching the Patagonian steppe and gouging deep U-shaped valleys as they advanced. On the glaciers' retreat at the end of the Pleistocene era, 10,000 years ago, these huge troughs were filled with meltwater, forming the region's great lakes.

Glaciar Perito Moreno

53 miles (85 km) W of El Calafate. from El Calafate. from Península Magellanes. Ave Libertador 1302, (02902) 491-005. parquenacionales.gob.ar

Glaciar Perito Moreno is a spectacular sight at 19 miles (31 km) in length and 2.5 miles (4 km) in width. Its ice flows down from the cordillera into the milky, mineral-rich waters of **Lago Argentino**.

The most popular way to observe the glacier is from the catwalks on **Península Magellanes**, 492 ft (150 m) across Lago Argentino from the glacier's face. Descending the catwalks is an auditory and visual experience heightened each time a huge chunk of ice breaks off the glacier's face and tumbles into the **Canal de los Témpanos** (Iceberg Channel) in a process known as calving.

Boat excursions start from docks **Muelle Bajo de las Sombras** and **Muelle Perito Moreno**, ferrying visitors to the glacier's front wall.

Glaciar Upsala

75 miles (120 km) NW of El Calafate. from Puerto Punta Bandera. Fernandez Campbell, Ave Libertador 867, (02902) 491-155. patagonia-argentina.com

Although less accessible than Glaciar Perito Moreno, this glacier is far bigger, stretching to a mammoth 31 miles (50 km) in length and covering a surface area of 230 sq miles (595 sq km). Once the biggest glacier in South America, it is now fast disappearing at a rate of 656 ft (200 m) per year and has lost its title to Glaciar Viedma. Scientists attribute this to global warming.

Full-day catamaran excursions to Glaciar Upsala depart daily from **Puerto Punta Bandera**. The outward journey sails the **Brazo Upsala** (Upsala Arm) of Lago Argentino, threading its way through a mass of huge blue icebergs towards the glacier's face. Tour operators also take visitors to Glaciars **Onelli**, **Agassiz**, and **Spegazzini** before returning to dock.

Lago Roca

34 miles (55 km) SW of El Calafate. **Tel** (02902) 492-797. from El Calafate. Camping Lago Roca, (02902) 499-500 losglaciares. com/campinglagoroca/indexe.html

A hidden gem, Lago Roca is a turquoise lake fringed with forests and overlooked by snowy peaks. It offers excellent camping and trekking opportunities. For hikers, the highlight is the 3-hour, medium-level trail to the 4,220-ft (1,286-m) summit of **Cerro Cristal**; from the top there are tremendous views of Glaciar Perito Moreno, Lago Argentino, and the Torres del Paine mountain range in Chile.

At the foot of Cerro Cristal and by the lake is **Camping Lago Roca**, which offers plenty of outdoor activities including bicycle hire.

Hostería Helsingfors

112 miles (180 km) N of El Calafate. **Tel** (02966) 1567-5753. **Open** Nov–Mar. helsingfors.com.ar

Located on the beautiful southwestern shore of Lago Viedma is Hostería Helsingfors. Founded in 1917 by Finnish pioneer Alfred Ranstrom, the ranch was named for his country's capital Helsingfors (Helsinki in Swedish).

At the estancia, guests can choose from eight beautifully fitted rooms and enjoy a range of excursions that include boat trips across the lake to Glaciar Viedma and treks into the spectacular surrounding mountains.

The turquoise Lago Roca overlooked by forests and snowy peaks

Flora of Parque Nacional Los Glaciares

Although over half of its surface area is cloaked in ice, Parque Nacional Los Glaciares, with three distinct habitats within its borders, also shelters a rich diversity of flora. In its eastern section, the Patagonian steppe is given dashes of color by the flowers of *calafate* and *mata guanaco* shrubs. Heading west the steppe gives way to a transition forest of *ñire* trees and colorful species such as the *Zapatito de la Virgen* flower. In the park's far west this transition zone meets the great Magellanic forest, a humid area that is home to the region's greatest concentration of plant life. Receiving an annual rainfall of 30–80 inches (80–200 cm), this forest is thick with *lenga* trees and, during the southern hemisphere's spring season, dappled with flowers, including five species of orchid. Different species of flora can be sighted along trails that flank glaciers and Mount Fitz Roy.

The Magellanic Forest

This forest of southern beech grows upwards from the edges of glaciers and lakes, ascending the slopes of surrounding mountains to an altitude of 3,280 ft (1,000 m). Dominant *lenga* and smaller *coihue* trees are its signature species.

Lengas grow in a variety of shapes according to altitude and sun exposure.

Zapatito de la Virgens are bell-shaped flowers that decorate trails around Mount Fitz Roy and Cerro Torre.

Calafates dot the steppe, with yellow flowers and sweet blue berries. According to myth, whoever eats a *calafate* berry will return to Patagonia.

Chilcos are delicate, intensely colored flowers that flourish in the shady, damp undergrowth of the Magellanic forest.

Notro shrubs thrive in the humid Magellanic forest, blooming with red flowers in spring. They are easily sighted on trails.

White dog orchids are one of the five species of orchid that adorn the forest floor during springtime.

TIERRA DEL FUEGO AND ANTARCTICA

The remote archipelago of Tierra del Fuego really does feel like *el fin del mundo* – the end of the world – where the great Andean mountain range finally meets the sea. Only the continent of Antarctica lies beyond, and the area serves as the main jumping-off point for intrepid travelers eager to glimpse this sparkling, shifting mass of blue and white ice, the world's last great wilderness.

Tierra del Fuego is separated from the rest of South America by the Strait of Magellan. The archipelago consists of a main island, Isla Grande, and a group of smaller islands. Its land mass is divided equally between Argentina and Chile, the border between the two countries running from the Strait in the north to Canal Beagle in the south.

The Strait is named for Portuguese explorer Ferdinand Magellan, who became the first European to discover the archipelago, in 1520. He called it Tierra del Fuego (Land of Fire) for the numerous fires he witnessed along its coastline, warning signals from one indigenous tribe to another that something unusual had arrived.

The Selknam, Kaweskar, Manekenk, and Yámana tribes would later draw the attention of English naturalist Charles

Darwin, before Anglican missionaries became the first outsiders to settle the region in 1871, near the present-day city of Ushuaia. Sheep farmers followed, together with further missionaries in the form of the Salesians of Don Bosco, who established their mission near what is now Río Grande, the region's biggest city.

Antarctica, the world's coldest and driest continent, sits 620 miles (1,000 km) across the Drake Passage from Ushuaia. For centuries a source of mystery – the ancient Greeks thought it a populated and fertile land, only blocked by monsters – the continent was not discovered until the 1820s. Today, Antarctica is experiencing a tourist boom, with up to 30,000 visitors drawn each year to its silent world of icebergs and glaciers, a haven for an astonishing array of marine fauna.

Cormorants crowding the rocks on an island in Canal Beagle, near Ushuaia

◀ Ice cave formed by collapse of a glacial wall

Exploring Tierra del Fuego and Antarctica

Ushuaia is the region's biggest tourist draw, home to some outstanding museums and a gateway to the natural spectacles of Canal Beagle and Parque Nacional Tierra del Fuego, and the ski resort of Cerro Castor. North of Ushuaia, Río Grande is a popular angling destination and site of an historic Salesian mission. In the summer, Ushuaia is the departure point for 10- to 21-day Antarctic cruises to the South Shetland Islands and the Antarctic Peninsula. Longer routes take in the Falkland Islands and South Georgia.

CHILE
ARGENTINA
Ushuaia
Falkland Islands (UK) (Islas Malvinas)
South Georgia
ATLANTIC OCEAN
South Shetland Islands
South Orkney Islands
PACIFIC OCEAN
Ross Sea

CRUISING ANTARCTICA

7

ANTARCTICA

Key

— Area of main map

---- Possible cruise route

Tourists in a Zodiac landing craft view an iceberg in waters off Antarctica

Cabo Espíritu Santo
Estancia Culler
Campamento
Cerro Páramo 400 ft
Pto. Boñas
Península El Páramo
Punta de Arenas
3
Bahía San Sebastián
Punta Arenas
San Sebastián
Campamento Los Chorrillos
Cerro Ora 728 ft
Estancia Sara
Lagos de la Pascua
Cabo Domingo
Estancia Salvador
Estancia San Julio
Estancia María Behety
Estancia Violeta
Misión Salesiana de la Candelaria
3
CHILE
Río Moneta
Río Grande
6
RÍO GRANDE Cabo Peñas
Estancia Aurelia
Estancia José Menéndez
TIERRA DEL FUEGO
Estancia Viamonte
Estancia La Rosita
Estancia El Rodeo
Estancia La Porteña
Cabo Santa Inés
Estancia Inés
Estancia Marina
Pto. Río Apen
Estancia Los Cerros
Estancia La Criolla
Estancia Rolito
Pto. La Cumbre
Lago Chepelmuth
Estancia María Cristina
Estancia Carmen
Lago Yehuín
Estancia Ushuaia
Tolhuin
Lago Fagnano
3 CERRO CASTOR
Estancia La Porfiada
Cerro Quintana 3,772 ft
PARQUE NACIONAL TIERRA DEL FUEGO
5
Cerro Martial 3,182 ft
Cerro Cornú 4,888 ft
Sierra Lucas Bridge
USHUAIA
1
Monte Olivia 4,356 ft
ESTANCIA HARBERTON
4
Faro Les Éclaireurs
Las Islas de los Lobos
Puerto Almanza
Isla Martillo
Estancia Moat
2
CANAL BEAGLE
Mar Argentina
Punta Arenas

For keys to symbols *see back flap*

Modern residences fringing the shoreline of the sheltered bay of Ushuaia

Sights at a Glance

Towns and Cities

1 Ushuaia
6 Río Grande

National Parks and Areas of Natural Beauty

2 Canal Beagle
5 Parque Nacional Tierra del Fuego
7 *Cruising Antarctica pp268–71*

Historic Site

4 Estancia Harberton

Ski Resort

3 Cerro Castor

Getting Around

The best way to get around Tierra del Fuego is by air or long-distance bus. Both Ushuaia and Río Grande have international airports; regular bus services run between the two cities (journey time 8 hours) and link both cities to the Argentinian mainland. Journeys to the mainland from the archipelago cross the Argentina-Chile border and foreign passports will be stamped at the border control. Medium-sized icebreakers and ice-proof cruise ships depart from Ushuaia for Antarctica, each with Zodiac landing craft for onshore excursions. Icebreakers also carry on-board helicopters.

Key

▬▬ Highway
▭▭▭ Minor road
‑ ‑ Track
▬▬▬ International border
△ Peak

0 kilometers 30
0 miles 30

❶ Ushuaia

Road map B6. 🚠 60,000. ✈️ 🚌 from Río Grande or El Calafate. ℹ️ Ave San Martín 674, (02901) 432-000. 🎭 Festival Música Clásica de Ushuaia (Apr). 🇼 turismoushuaia.com

Situated at the bottom tip of Isla Grande, Ushuaia is best reached by air. Coming in to land over the icy peaks of Cerro Martial and Monte Olivia, and the frigid waters of Canal Beagle, only heightens one's sense of arrival at the end of the world.

The city began as a penal colony in 1884, part of an Argentinian government plan to populate their half of the archipelago as a means of reaffirming sovereignty. The colony foundered but the convicts remained, transferred to the infamous Ushuaia prison, which, from 1902 to 1947, housed the country's most notorious criminals.

Visitors can explore the old prison at the fascinating **Museo Marítimo de Ushuaia**. Guided tours take in the prison's cramped cells and recount the crimes of its most notorious convicts. A separate section is devoted to Ushuaia's maritime history, with displays covering 500 years of navigation. Also of interest are **Museo del Fin del Mundo** and **Museo Yámana**:

the former houses historical and zoological displays, its star exhibit the rescued figurehead of the *Duchess of Albany*, an English vessel shipwrecked off the coast in 1883; the latter traces the history of the region's indigenous people.

High above Ushuaia, the beautiful **Glaciar Martial** offers panoramic views of the city and Canal Beagle. To reach it, take the chairlift from **Centro Recreativo Glaciar Martial** before trekking the final stretch to its base.

🏛 Museo Marítimo de Ushuaia
Yaganes & Gobernador Paz. **Tel** (02901) 437-481. **Open** mid-Dec–mid-Mar: 9am–8pm daily; mid-Mar–mid-Dec: 10am–8pm daily. 🅿️ 📷 mid-Dec–mid-Mar: 10am daily. ♿ 🖥 📷 🇼 museomaritimo.com

🏛 Museo del Fin del Mundo
Ave Maipú 175. **Tel** (02901) 421-863. **Open** mid-Dec–mid-Mar: 9am–8pm daily; mid-Mar–mid-Dec: noon–7pm Mon–Sat. 🅿️ 📷 in Spanish only. ♿ 📷

🏛 Museo Yámana
Rivadavia 56. **Tel** (02901) 422-874. **Open** mid-Dec–mid-Mar: 10am–8pm daily; mid-Mar–mid-Dec: noon–7pm daily. 🅿️ 📷 🇼 museoyamana.com.ar

Centro Recreativo Glaciar Martial
Ave Luis Fernando Martial. **Open** 10:30am–5:30pm daily. 🅿️ 🖥 Note: no buses to the chairlift, best to hire a taxi and walk back down.

Jagged peaks near Ushuaia, seen from across Canal Beagle

❷ Canal Beagle

Road map B6. 🚤 Muelle Turístico, Ushuaia, (02901) 437-666.

Several agencies run tours by catamaran along the icy waters of Canal Beagle (Beagle Channel). Tickets can be bought at Ushuaia's Tourist Pier from where excursions depart. The shortest of these head for the **Faro Les Eclaireurs** lighthouse, before returning via Las Islas de los Lobos, home to a sea lion colony, and Las Islas de los Pájaros with its bird colony. Longer excursions head out to the 19th-century **Estancia Harberton**, still managed by the descendants of an Anglican missionary who named the estancia for his wife's birthplace in England.

❸ Cerro Castor

Road map B6. Ruta Nacional 3, Km 26.5, 16 miles (26 km) E of Ushuaia. **Tel** (02901) 499-302. 🚌 from Ushuaia. **Open** mid-June–mid-Oct. 🅿️ 🚠 🖥 📷 🚠 🇼 cerrocastor.com

The world's southernmost ski resort, Cerro Castor boasts 19 slopes with a maximum drop of 2,532 ft (772 m), the majority appropriate for beginner and intermediate skiers. There is good off-piste skiing, plus a snowboarding park and, at the resort's base, a cross-country skiing circuit that has a good claim to being the most scenic in Argentina, passing through forests thick with *lenga* beech trees.

The former Government House, Ushuaia

❹ Estancia Harberton

Road map B6. 53 miles (85 km) E of Ushuaia. **Tel** (02901) 422-742.
Open mid-Oct–mid-Apr: 10am–7pm daily. 🦌 📷 🖼 💻 🛶 ⛰
W estanciaharberton.com

The oldest estancia in Tierra del Fuego, Estancia Harberton was built in 1886 for Anglican missionary Thomas Bridges in return for his pioneering work among the region's native people, which included compiling the first English-Yámana dictionary. His son Lucas continued the literary tradition, writing *The Uttermost Part of the Earth*, an account of a young boy growing up among the Yámana.

The family estancia is now run by their descendants and can be reached by road or boat excursion along Canal Beagle. Guided tours take in its extensive gardens, wool shed, boathouse, carpenter shops, and family cemetery. Visitors can also make the boat trip to **Isla Martillo** (or Yecapasela), a nature preserve with colonies of Magellanic and gentoo penguins.

❺ Parque Nacional Tierra del Fuego

Road map B6. 🚌 from Ushuaia.
🛈 Ruta Nacional 3, Km 3047; Ave San Martín 1395, Ushuaia, (02901) 421-315.
Open 24hrs daily. 🦌 ⛰
W parquesnacionales.gob.ar
Tren del Fin del Mundo: station off Ruta Nacional 3, 5 miles (8 km) W of Ushuaia. **Tel** (02901) 431-600.
W trendelfindelmundo.com.ar

Stretching north from Canal Beagle and across Lago Fagnano, this beautiful park was founded to protect 266 sq miles (689 sq km) of *lenga*, *ñire*, and *coihue* woods. The park encompasses lakes, mountains, glaciated valleys, and a pristine sea coast, which form a protective haven for more than 100 bird and mammal species. Numerous trails run through the park; short treks include forest and shoreline walks. Of the more demanding hikes, the trek to **Pampa Alta** offers

A view along the Río Oyando, Parque Nacional Tierra del Fuego

outstanding vistas of the channel. Access to the national park is via road or the **Tren del Fin del Mundo**, a narrow-gauge tourist train that follows the line of the old "Convict Train," which used to ferry prisoners into the forest for hard labor.

❻ Río Grande

Road map B6. 137 miles (220 km) NE of Ushuaia. 🚹 80,000. ✈ 🚌 from Ushuaia or Río Gallegos. 🛈 Rosales 350, (02964) 431-324.
W interpatagonia.com/riogrande

The largest settlement on Tierra del Fuego, Río Grande is known mainly as a fishing destination due to its proximity to the trout-rich waters of Río Menéndez. Its history dates back to 1893 when the first Salesian missionaries, led by a Monseñor Fagnano, arrived to evangelize the Selknam. Now an agricultural college, the Misión Salesiana can still be visited, where the excellent **Museo Regional Monseñor Fagnano** traces its history and that of the people it aimed to convert. In town,

Museo de la Ciudad Virginia Choquintel has displays on the city's past.

Environs
Along the coast from Río Grande is **Estancia Viamonte**, a jewel of a sheep estancia founded in 1902 by the sons of Thomas Bridges, and today run by their descendants. Visitors are sometimes even allowed to stay in Lucas Bridges' bedroom. Named for the founder of the Misión Salesiana, **Lago Fagnano** is the largest lake on Tierra del Fuego, excellent for trout fishing. The tiny village of Tolhuin sits on the lakeshore and is a tranquil base for exploring the area.

🏛 Museo Regional Monseñor Fagnano
Misión Salesiana, Ruta Nacional 3, Km 2800. **Tel** (02964) 421-642. **Open** mid-Dec–mid-Mar: 10am–7pm Tue–Sun; mid-Mar–mid-Dec: 9am–12:30pm, 3–7pm Mon–Fri (8pm Sat & Sun). 🦌 📷 on request.

🏛 Museo de la Ciudad Virginia Choquintel
Alberdi 555. **Tel** (02964) 430-647.
Open 9am–5pm Mon–Fri, 3–7pm Sat. 📷 on request. ♿

The southerly city of Ushuaia, seen from the Canal Beagle ▶

❼ Cruising Antarctica
The Subantarctic Islands

Ice-strengthened cruise ships depart from Ushuaia for the vast, white expanse of the Antarctic continent. There are myriad routes to choose from but popular ports of call include the Antarctic Peninsula and the South Shetland Islands and, on longer cruises, the rugged island chains of Subantarctica. Trips explore a breathtaking, silent world of gigantic icebergs, tumbling glaciers, dazzling ice shelves, and marine wildlife that includes numerous species of whales and dolphins, seals and penguins, and millions of marine birds. A human history is palpable too, in the haunting form of abandoned whaling stations and gravesites bearing the names of Heroic Age explorers.

Planning a cruise

Cruises: (11–13 days) to the Antarctic Peninsula always include the South Shetland Islands. Longer trips (18–20 days) include South Georgia and the Falkland Islands.

Ship types: vary, but all are ice-strengthened. Remote Weddell Sea and Ross Sea areas are accessed by icebreaker ships.

Best time: to travel is in summer from November to March: days are longer and warmer, and the wildlife more abundant.

See also pp308–9.

Brightly painted houses around Christ Church cathedral, Stanley

The Falkland Islands (Islas Malvinas)

310 miles (500 km) NE of Ushuaia. 🚶 3,140. ✈ weekly flights via Punta Arenas, Chile, and monthly via Río Gallegos. 🚢 from Ushuaia. ℹ Jetty Visitor Center, (00500) 22215. 🌐 falklandislands.com

Surrounded by the cold South Atlantic Ocean and shrouded in controversy throughout their modern history, the Falkland Islands (Islas Malvinas) are a popular stop-off on longer Antarctic cruises. An archipelago consisting of two main islands, East and West Falkland, and several hundred smaller ones, the Falklands attract thousands of visitors each year. Their marine wildlife is as prolific as it is spectacular, with over 60 breeding bird species and numerous marine mammals. Easily approached, this fauna is observed in its greatest numbers on small offshore islands such as **West Point Island**, **New Island**, and **Carcass Island**, all essential stops on Subantarctic itineraries. Star attractions include five kinds of penguin, the rare rockhopper penguin included, and the world's largest breeding populations of black-browed albatross. Offshore, elephant seals, sea lions, fur seals, dolphins, and killer whales roam the waters.

All cruises to the Falklands include a stop at the capital, **Stanley**. Built on a north-facing slope to catch the sun throughout the year and lined with rows of colorful cottages and well-kept gardens, Stanley, with a population of some 2,000, is more reminiscent of an English village than a capital city. Tours should start at the Jetty Visitor Center by the passenger dock before taking in the main sights, which include the **Falkland Islands Museum**, with displays on the islands' natural and human history; the cathedral and 1982 War Memorial; and Government House, which dates from 1845. The Maritime History Trail tours Stanley Harbor, once an important port of call for vessels crossing Cape Horn and today dotted with hulking shipwrecks. At low tide visitors can explore a number of ships and dive to see others.

Outside Stanley, short excursions include visits to **Gypsy Cove** and **Volunteer Point**, home to large penguin colonies, and to Goose Green, site of fierce fighting in the 1982 Falklands War.

🏛 **Falkland Islands Museum**
Holdfast Rd, Stanley. **Tel** (00500) 27428. 🚢 from jetty. **Open** 9am–4pm daily. 🐾 📷 ♿ 🏛
🌐 falklands-museum.com

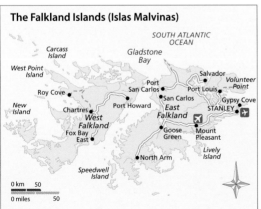

The Falkland Islands (Islas Malvinas)

SOUTH ATLANTIC OCEAN

Carcass Island
Gladstone Bay
West Point Island
Roy Cove
New Island
Chartres
Fox Bay East
West Falkland
Port Howard
Salvador
Volunteer Point
Port San Carlos
Port Louis
San Carlos
East Falkland
Gypsy Cove
STANLEY
Goose Green
Mount Pleasant
Lively Island
North Arm
Speedwell Island

0 km 50
0 miles 50

Key
═══ Main road   – – Track

A blue-colored pinnacle iceberg near Coronation Island, South Orkneys

South Georgia

860 miles (1,385 km) E of the Falkland Islands. 🆆 sgisland.org South Georgia Museum: 🆆 sgmuseum.gs

A dramatic island of soaring, ice-clad mountains and huge glaciers, South Georgia is a haven for an astonishing concentration of marine fauna. The best and most visited wildlife sites are on its more hospitable northern coast, where **Salisbury Plain** and the **Bay of Isles** are home to large rookeries of king penguins, and **Albatross Islet**, a nesting colony of the rare, semimythical wandering albatross. Cruise stops also explore the human history of South Georgia, which was a magnet to thousands of seal hunters and whalers in the late 19th and early 20th centuries, though today the island has no permanent population. At **Grytviken** visitors can explore the eerie remnants of an abandoned whaling station, complete with the rusting hulks of several ships slowly sinking into the harbor. Within its grounds are the **South Georgia Museum**, which houses displays on the island's human and natural history, a small restored church, and an old whalers' cemetery. The cemetery includes the grave-site of British explorer Ernest Shackleton, who made the first crossing of South Georgia on the final leg of his rescue of the crew of the stricken *Endurance (see p271)*.

South Orkney Islands

574 miles (924 km) SW of South Georgia.

En route from South Georgia to the Antarctic, but much less visited than the other Subantarctic islands, are the remote South Orkney Islands. Linked to the Antarctic Peninsula by a massive range of submarine mountains, the South Orkneys comprise two large and several smaller islands, each covered in snow and ice and punctuated by barren mountains. Zodiac landings take place on the biggest island in the chain, **Coronation Island**, where Shingle Cove is refuge to a rookery of Adelie penguins and a breeding colony of Weddell seals. Conditions permitting, visits also explore **Laurie Island**, site of an Argentinian meteorological station that has been in operation since 1904.

Antarctic Wildlife

The wildlife of the Subantarctic islands and Antarctica is every bit as breathtaking as the region's stunning landscapes. Biggest of all is the blue whale, the world's largest animal, which visits Antarctica during the summer to feed on abundant krill. Humpback, minke, sei, fin, and orca whales can also be sighted, together with several species of dolphin. Onshore, penguins are the greatest attraction: eight different species form breeding colonies, from smaller chinstrap and punk-like macaroni penguins to colorful king and emperor penguins. Seals, including huge elephant seals, crabeater, Weddell, leopard, and fur seals, slumber on ice floes and beaches. On cliff sides, an incredible array of marine birds, from petrels, shags, terns, and skuas to rare species of albatross, gather in nesting colonies. Like most Antarctic fauna, they are best observed in summer, February especially.

Macaroni penguins congregating on the shoreline, South Georgia

Cruising Antarctica
The Antarctic Peninsula

The biggest thrill of any Antarctic cruise is setting foot on the frozen continent itself. The simplest and most popular way of doing so is on routes that explore the Antarctic Peninsula, the northern tip of the Antarctic continent, and the South Shetland Islands, an archipelago of over twenty islands that lies to its north. Onshore excursions to both peninsula and islands enter a magical, blue-white world of hypnotic scale and beauty, in which glaciers, peaks, and abundant marine wildlife vie for attention with gigantic icebergs and haunting historical sites.

Locator Map
— Area of main map

Paradise Bay is one of the peninsula's most magical spots, with a backdrop of ice-blue water, glacier-covered islands, and huge floating icebergs. Its waters are visited by humpback and minke whales. Elephant, crabeater, and Weddell seals doze on ice floes.

Port Lockroy is home to an historic research station and the world's most southerly post office, complete with souvenir shop and museum.

The Lemaire Channel is Antarctica's most picturesque channel, earning it the nickname "Kodak Gap." Its immense scenery includes sheer-sided, precipitous peaks that rise over 3,000 ft (1,000 m) from the water's edge, hanging glaciers, and deep-blue icebergs of all shapes and sizes.

The Ross Sea region can be accessed on extended icebreaker cruises. Helicopter excursions fly over Mount Erebus volcano and the Dry Valleys, one of the world's most extreme deserts.

To Ross Sea

Neko Harbor faces a magnificent glacier that calves regularly: the loud crack and boom of tumbling ice can be heard from the beach.

Whale-spotting is best in the Antarctic summer, February especially. Easily observed species include humpback and minke whales. Endangered sei and fin whales can also be sighted.

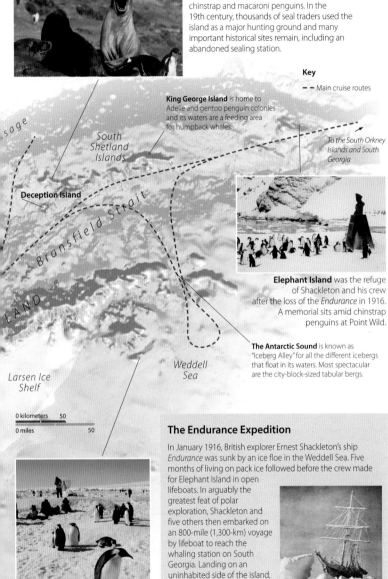

Livingston Island is rich in wildlife. Elephant, Weddell, and leopard seals abound as well as chinstrap and macaroni penguins. In the 19th century, thousands of seal traders used the island as a major hunting ground and many important historical sites remain, including an abandoned sealing station.

Key

– – Main cruise routes

King George Island is home to Adélie and gentoo penguin colonies and its waters are a feeding area for humpback whales.

South Shetland Islands

…sage

To the South Orkney Islands and South Georgia

Deception Island

Bransfield Strait

…LAND

Larsen Ice Shelf

Elephant Island was the refuge of Shackleton and his crew after the loss of the *Endurance* in 1916. A memorial sits amid chinstrap penguins at Point Wild.

The Antarctic Sound is known as "Iceberg Alley" for all the different icebergs that float in its waters. Most spectacular are the city-block-sized tabular bergs.

Weddell Sea

0 kilometers   50
0 miles   50

Snow Hill Island is off-the-beaten-track Antarctica. Refuge to a nesting colony of emperor penguins, it is accessed on icebreaker cruise ships that scythe through the pack ice of the Weddell Sea.

The Endurance Expedition

In January 1916, British explorer Ernest Shackleton's ship *Endurance* was sunk by an ice floe in the Weddell Sea. Five months of living on pack ice followed before the crew made for Elephant Island in open lifeboats. In arguably the greatest feat of polar exploration, Shackleton and five others then embarked on an 800-mile (1,300-km) voyage by lifeboat to reach the whaling station on South Georgia. Landing on an uninhabited side of the island, they hiked 36 hours over mountains, glaciers, and cliffs before reaching their goal. Three failed rescue attempts followed before Shackleton finally reached his near-starving men on Elephant Island in August 1916.

The *Endurance* trapped in ice before sinking

TRAVELERS' NEEDS

WHERE TO STAY

Accommodations in Argentina are varied enough to satisfy every taste and budget. At the top end of the range are five-star deluxe hotels, which provide exclusive service and first-class amenities. A quintessentially Argentinian experience, luxury estancias in the country's rural interiors combine bucolic relaxation and breathtaking vistas. International and domestic chain hotels are well represented in urban and tourist destinations, together with a vibrant boutique hotel scene that offers a more personable and aesthetically driven alternative. Visitors traveling to national parks can stay at well-equipped campsites, while economical hotel options include modern hostels, cabin complexes, and budget hotels.

Gradings

Hotels are graded from one to five stars, although Argentina's classification system differs from the international star system and is often not the best guide to quality, with the exception of five-star hotels. A common anomaly involves a hotel receiving a lower rating than it deserves, often because the local tourist office has not yet upgraded it, or because hotels themselves have opted to stay in a lower category in order to avoid higher taxes. Cabin complexes and *hosterías* (small hotels) are awarded a separate grading of between one and three stars.

The Ave María at Tandil in the Pampas region (*see p280*)

Pricing and Booking

Pricing depends greatly on location – hotel rates in Buenos Aires and popular tourist destinations such as Patagonia's Lake District are higher than those in other parts of the country. At the top end are five-star deluxe hotels, which typically charge US$300 or more per night. These are followed in order of cost by five-star and boutique hotels, four- and three-star hotels, and cabin complexes. At the low end of the price range, hostels and campsites are often better-value alternatives to budget hotels.

Exclusive fishing and hunting lodges charge up to US$750 per night. Services provided include access to the best game areas and helicopter or light airplane transport. Outside of this category, most estancias, including working ones in Patagonia and guest ranches in the Buenos Aires province, charge between US$150 and US$250 per night.

Rates vary greatly between low (April to November) and peak season (December to March), when prices rise considerably, especially at Atlantic beach resorts and in Patagonia's Lake District. Conversely, they tend to drop in Buenos Aires as business travel slows and porteños leave the city for their summer vacations.

Taxes

Hotels in Argentina charge 21 percent in *Impuesto de Valor Agregado* or IVA (value-added tax or VAT). This tax should be included in the quoted rate, but it is worth checking when booking in order to avoid any unwelcome surprises when checking out. While calculating price ranges listed on pages 278–83, IVA is taken into account.

The stylish tango-themed Mansión Dandi Royal, San Telmo (*see p278*)

◄ Vibrantly colored store exterior in the La Boca barrio, Buenos Aires

The lobby of the luxurious Alvear Palace Hotel, Recoleta (see p279)

Luxury Hotels

Ranging from the palatial to the chic and Post-Modern, Argentina's luxury hotels are comparable to the best and the most exclusive anywhere in the world. Besides prime locations, they offer spacious, beautifully furnished suites and rooms, first-rate services, and a wealth of amenities. These usually include state-of-the-art conference facilities, spas, swimming pools, modern fitness centers, well-maintained gardens, boutique shops, and excellent multicuisine restaurants. Depending on location, luxury hotels may also provide access to a marina, a golf course, or a private beach. It is advisable to make reservations well in advance, especially during Argentina's peak season.

Chain Hotels

There are various Argentinian chain hotels at the mid- and upper ranges of the market, as well as the usual big international names. Local operator **Dazzler Hoteles** has several hotels in the capital and one in Bariloche. **Design Suites**, emphasizing stylish and contemporary design, has hotels in El Calafate, Salta, and Bariloche, as well as Buenos Aires. International chains such as **Hilton**, **Sofitel**, and **Hyatt** are also well represented in the country.

Boutique Hotels

Boutique hotels are an increasingly common option in design-conscious Argentina. Buenos Aires leads this trend, especially its fashionable Palermo Viejo district, where numerous boutique establishments have opened, mostly in converted *belle époque* houses. Historic San Telmo, in the city's south, and Recoleta, an upscale district in the city's north, have quickly followed suit. Boutique hotels can now also be found in several destinations across Argentina, including major tourist centers such as Salta, Mendoza, and Patagonia's Lake District. The **Best Boutique Hotels** website covers most of Argentina, with helpful profiles. "Chain" boutique hotels have also entered the market. The **Esplendor** chain, run by Argentina's Fen Group, has boutique hotels in Buenos Aires, Mendoza, and El Calafate.

Hosterías

Sometimes known as *posadas*, *hosterías* usually house between three and 15 rooms. The room rates vary, depending on the degree of comfort and style provided. At the top end, deluxe *hosterías* offer exclusive luxury and charge accordingly; lower down the scale, one- to three-star *hosterías* often provide

Elegant town house exterior of the A Hotel, Recoleta (see p279)

much more welcoming and comfortable alternatives to equivalently priced hotels.

Budget Accommodation

One- and two-star hotels are mostly centrally located within towns and cities. Most of them include breakfast in their rate and access either to a *baño compartido* (shared bathroom) or *baño privado* (private bathroom). Many have rooms with ceiling fans and cable TV. Bed linen is provided, but in some cases, guests may have to bring their own towels.

Other alternatives for cheap accommodation include *hospedajes* and *pensiones*. The former is a large family home with bedrooms to spare, while the latter is also a family house offering short-term stays for visitors and permanent lodgers.

Clean contemporary design at the boutique Home Hotel in Buenos Aires (see p279)

Estancias

Estancias can be found all across the Argentinian interior and visitors have the luxury of choosing from a wide and varied range of options. The architectural styles of these estancias are varied, from Italianate mansions to adobe haciendas and century-old prefabricated buildings.

There are primarily two types of accommodations available – working and guest estancias. Working estancias remain primarily dedicated to cattle or sheep farming and offer a more authentic ranch experience. Guests take part in farm activities and evening meals are enjoyed together with the owners. Patagonia and Tierra del Fuego have the largest numbers of such ranches. Guest estancias, on the other hand, are dedicated solely to tourism. There are many of these in the Buenos Aires province as well as in the Andean Northwest and Argentinian Litoral. At both types of ranches, visitors can enjoy a host of activities that range from horse-riding and fishing to bird-watching, trekking, and biking (see pp306–11).

Many estancias have offices in Buenos Aires, where English-speaking staff take bookings and answer queries. The NGO **Estancias de Santa Cruz** handles reservations and enquiries on behalf of many ranches in the Patagonia and Tierra del Fuego regions. **Red Argentina de Turismo Rural** and **Estancias Argentinas** both represent estancias in the

The spa at Cavas Wine Lodge, Mendoza (see p281)

Buenos Aires province as well as across Argentina. Specialist travel agencies can also organize estancia stays; **Lan & Kramer Travel Services** is one of the most reputable. Alternatively, visitors can also contact the ranches directly.

Bodegas

Catering to the luxury travel market, several bodegas (wineries) in Argentina's wine-growing regions offer exclusive lodging. Most are located in Mendoza, although some bodegas in Salta also feature wine lodges. All boast extraordinary settings and stunning mountain views, and offer insights into the world of viticulture (see pp212–15).

Guests can take part in many activities from wine tastings and vineyard visits to the annual harvest. A growing trend is the incorporation of a wine spa, where treatments are based on grapes and other wine products.

Self-Catering and Cabin Complexes

There are several self-catering options. Most cities have apart-hotels, which have standard hotel features, but also larger rooms with a kitchenette and small eating area. In the south of Argentina, cabañas (cabin complexes) are extremely common, especially in the Patagonian Lake District. The cabins typically consist of a master bedroom, kitchen, lounge, and spare bedrooms. Most are designed in the style of Alpine log cabins, situated within shaded woods or on riverbanks, and are well-equipped with phone and cable television. The cabin complexes are ideal for families and anyone wishing to avoid more nondescript, but equivalently priced, three-star hotels.

Rented Apartments

For longer stays in Buenos Aires, several agencies specialize in short- and long-term rented apartments for foreign visitors, fully furnished with modern appliances. **Buenos Aires Travel Rent** and **Buenos Aires Stay** are two well-established rental agencies with over 500 apartments to offer, while **Oasis Collections** offers a more sophisticated range of properties.

Youth Hostels

Argentina is served by an extensive network of youth hostels and most cities have at least one establishment recognized by Hostelling

Communal living space on a sunny balcony, Ostinatto Buenos Aires Hostel (see p278)

International (HI), where both rooms and single-sex dorm accommodations are available. Student travel agency **Asatej** is the representative of HI in Argentina and makes hostel reservations throughout the country. Enquiries can be made at tourist information offices.

National Parks and Campsites

There are three types of campsites within Argentina's national parks. The best-equipped are *camping organizados*, usually located near park entrances. These have hot showers, cooking facilities, laundry services, and supply stores. Located deeper within the parks, *camping agrestes* are limited to cooking facilities, water supplies, and toilets. The basic *acampe libre* are for hikers exploring remote areas. All three are marked on park maps and on hiking trails. Basic wooden cabins situated on mountain trails within national parks are known as *refugios*. They are used by trekkers or climbers on overnight ascents.

Disabled Travelers

Few hotels in Argentina have special facilities for disabled travelers. Those that do are

Spacious rooms and beautiful wooden furnishings at Mio Buenos Aires *(see p279)*

mostly in the five-star category in larger towns and cities; check websites for details. In many cases, however, staff in hotels without special facilities will do all they can to accommodate people in wheelchairs by giving them easily accessible, ground-floor rooms (when available), and help with stairs and entering and leaving lifts.

Tipping

Tipping in Argentina is in proportion with most other parts of the world. Hotel porters who help with bags on arrival are usually given a *propina* (tip) of between US$1 and US$2. For waiting staff in hotels it is customary to leave about 10 to 15 percent of the total value of the bill. On checking out it is a good idea to leave a small tip for the cleaning help.

Recommended Hotels

The hotels listed on the following pages have been put into one of several categories that are indicative of that hotel's most prominent feature, from luxury retreats and boutique hotels to mid-range B&Bs, guesthouses, and hostels. These themes provide a good idea of the kind of accommodation options visitors are likely to find in Argentina.

Many of the most interesting and remarkable places in the country are not necessarily the most expensive ones, so look out for the hotels marked as DK Choice. These establishments have been highlighted in recognition of an exceptional feature – a stunning location, notable history, inviting atmosphere or, quite often, outstanding value. The majority of these are exceptionally popular, so reserve well ahead.

Where to Stay

Buenos Aires

Plaza de Mayo and Microcentro

Gran Hotel Hispano $
Boutique   Map 3 E5
Ave de Mayo 861, Monserrat
Tel *(011) 4345-2020*
🆆 hhispano.com.ar
Great budget hotel built in the
Spanish colonial style. Charming
rooms face a sunlit interior patio.

Milhouse $
Hostel   Map 3 D5
Hipólito Yrigoyen 959, Monserrat
Tel *(011) 4345-9604*
🆆 milhousehostel.com
Lively hostel and party hub for
budget travelers to Buenos Aires.

Moreno Hotel $
Boutique   Map 3 E5
Moreno 376, Monserrat
Tel *(011) 6091-2000*
🆆 morenobuenosaires.com
The Moreno offers chic suites
within a stunningly refurbished
Art Deco building.

725 Continental Hotel $$
Modern   Map 3 E5
*Ave Roque Sáenz Peña 725,
Microcentro*
Tel *(011) 4131-8000*
🆆 725continental.com
High-end hotel with gourmet
dining, modern suites, and a
rooftop spa.

Castelar Hotel & Spa $$
Historic   Map 3 D5
Ave de Mayo 1152, Monserrat
Tel *(011) 4383-5000*
🆆 castelarhotel.com.ar
Dating from the 1920s, this
marbled spa hotel evokes
Argentina's golden age.

La Cayetana Historic House $$
Boutique   Map 3 D5
México 1330, Monserrat
Tel *(011) 4383-2230*
🆆 lacayetanahotel.com.ar
Quiet retreat in a beautifully
restored 1820s house. The
contemporary suites face
two verdant patios.

NH City & Tower $$
Modern   Map 3 E5
Bolívar 160, Monserrat
Tel *(011) 4121-6464*
🆆 nh-hoteles.com
Pleasant business hotel set in
an Art Deco tower. Facilities
include meeting rooms and
a rooftop pool.

DK Choice

Faena Hotel + Universe $$$
Luxury   Map 1 F1
*Martha Salotti 445, Puerto
Madero*
Tel *(011) 4010-9070*
🆆 faenahotelanduniverse.com
The spectacular Faena is set
within an iconic port building
dating from 1902. Its Philippe
Starck design conserves the
cavernous building's original
redbrick shell and transforms
its interior into a lavish space
with crystal and cut-glass
furnishings. Its all-red-velvet
cabaret salon hosts avant-garde
tango shows.

Hilton Buenos Aires $$$
Luxury   Map 3 F5
*Macacha Guemes 351, Puerto
Madero*
Tel *(011) 4891-0000*
🆆 3.hilton.com
This waterfront Hilton has a
rooftop pool, executive floors,
and rooms with views of the
docklands and river.

San Telmo and La Boca

Ostinatto Buenos Aires Hostel $
Hostel   Map 1 D1
Chile 680, San Telmo
Tel *(011) 4362-9639*
🆆 ostinatto.com
Set in a 1920s building, this
hostel has five floors of dorms
plus a micro-cinema, a pool,
and a terrace.

Clean, modern styling at the Home Hotel in
old Palermo

Bonito B&B $$
B&B   Map 1 E2
Juan de Garay 458, San Telmo
Tel *(011) 4362-8451*
🆆 bonitobuenosaires.com
A lovely B&B in an Art Nouveau
house where each room is
decorated by a different artist.
Lush outside spaces.

Mansión Dandi Royal $$
Boutique   Map 1 D1
Piedras 922/936, San Telmo
Tel *(011) 4307-7623*
🆆 mansiondandiroyal.com
Tango-themed hotel in an
Art Nouveau mansion, with
dance lessons, a pool, and a
sun terrace.

Mansión Vitraux $$
Boutique   Map 1 E1
Carlos Calvo 369, San Telmo
Tel *(011) 4300-6886*
🆆 mansionvitraux.com
A designer hotel set amid
colonial surrounds. Lovely
views of Spanish cupolas from
its rooftop pool.

Plaza San Martín and Retiro

V&S Hostel $
Hostel   Map 3 E4
Viamonte 887
Tel *(011) 4322-0994*
🆆 hostelclub.com
A relaxed hostel set within
a 1920s building. Has smart
dorms, big breakfasts, and
excellent amenities.

Dazzler Tower San Martín $$
Modern   Map 3 E4
San Martín 920, Retiro
Tel *(011) 5256-7700*
🆆 dazzlertower.com
A glossy tower in the financial
district, the Dazzler has
minimalist suites, business
facilities, and a wellness spa.

Esplendor de Buenos Aires $$
Modern   Map 3 E4
San Martín 780, Retiro
Tel *(011) 5256-8800*
🆆 esplendorbuenosaires.com
Set in a restored 19th-century
building, this hotel has smart
interiors and original artwork.

Hotel Bel Air $$
Modern   **Map** 2 C3
Arenales 1462
Tel *(011) 4021-4000*
W hahoteles.com
Chain hotel in a grand *belle
époque* building, offering elegant
rooms and business facilities.

Four Seasons Hotel $$$
Luxury   **Map** 3 D3
Posadas 1086/88
Tel *(011) 4321-1200*
W fourseasons.com
This stately hotel has luxury suites,
five-star amenities, and a *fin-de-
siècle* mansion for an annex.

Marriott Plaza Hotel $$$
Luxury   **Map** 3 E4
Florida 1005, Retiro
Tel *(011) 4318-3000*
W marriott.com
Housed in a *belle époque*
mansion, the Marriott has a regal
interior and superb facilities.

Recoleta

A Hotel $$
Boutique   **Map** 2 B3
Azcuenaga 1268
Tel *(011) 4821-4744*
W arthotel.com.ar
Colorful works by local artists
decorate this family-friendly hotel.

Algodón Mansion $$$
Boutique   **Map** 2 C3
Montevideo 1647
Tel *(011) 3530-7777*
W algodonmansion.com
This *belle époque* mansion has
sumptuous suites, butler service,
and a spa.

Alvear Palace Hotel $$$
Luxury   **Map** 2 C2
Ave Alvear 1891
Tel *(011) 4808-2100*
W alvearpalace.com
At the palatial Alvear, butlers
attend to guests amid marble, gilt,
and almost every luxury. Has
hosted several world leaders.

Mio Buenos Aires $$$
Boutique   **Map** 2 C3
Ave Quintana 465
Tel *(011) 5295-8500*
W miobuenosaires.com
Bathtubs hewn from hardwoods
are one of many luxuries at this
stylish yet intimate hotel.

Park Hyatt Buenos Aires $$$
Luxury   **Map** 3 D3
Ave Alvear 1661
Tel *(011) 5171-1234*
W buenosaires.park.hyatt.com
Set in a beautiful mansion with
columns and marbled passage-
ways. Excellent amenities.

Elegant decor and furnishings at the Alvear Palace Hotel

Palermo and Belgrano

Eco Pampa Palermo $
Hostel   **Map** 5 D4
Guatemala 4778, Palermo Viejo
Tel *(011) 4831-2435*
W hostelpampa.com.ar
Eco-hostel with solar power and
recycled furnishings. The doubles
have private bathrooms.

Bo Bo Hotel $$
Boutique   **Map** 5 D4
Guatemala 4882, Palermo Viejo
Tel *(011) 4774-0505*
W bobohotel.com
The ultra hip Bo Bo has themed,
individually designed rooms and
a variety of stylish eating areas.

Cypress In $$
B&B   **Map** 5 D4
Costa Rica 4828, Palermo Viejo
Tel *(011) 4833-5834*
W cypressin.com
Doubles at this modern B&B are
well equipped, if a little
small. Has a sunny terrace.

Fierro Hotel $$
Boutique   **Map** 4 C3
Soler 5862, Palermo Viejo
Tel *(011) 3220-6800*
W fierrohotel.com
Modern suites, gourmet dining,
and a rooftop pool at this hotel.

Krista Hotel Boutique $$
Boutique   **Map** 4 C4
Bonpland 1665, Palermo Viejo
Tel *(011) 4771-4697*
W kristahotel.com.ar
A lovingly restored period
building with both antique
and contemporary touches.

Querido B&B $$
B&B   **Map** 4 B5
*Juan Ramírez de Velasco 934,
Villa Crespo*
Tel *(011) 4854-6297*
W queridobuenosaires.com
Run by its Anglo-Brazilian
owners, this B&B has bright
rooms with private balconies.

DK Choice

Home Hotel $$$
Boutique   **Map** 4 C3
Honduras 5860, Palermo Viejo
Tel *(011) 4778-1008*
W homebuenosaires.com
The Home Hotel's airy ground
floor features a lounge with
retro Scandinavian furnishings,
a spa, and a swish cocktail bar.
The ultracool rooms have 1920s
wallpapers, while suites feature
private terraces with Jacuzzis.
There is a heated pool in the
jasmine-scented garden.

Jardin Escondido $$$
Boutique   **Map** 5 D5
Gorriti 4746, Palermo Viejo
W coppolajardinescondido.com
Filmmaker Francis Ford Coppola
converted his Buenos Aires home
into this hotel. Beautiful suites.

Legado Mítico $$$
Boutique   **Map** 5 D4
Gurruchaga 1848, Palermo Viejo
Tel *(011) 4833-1300*
W legadomitico.com
Upscale retreat with a historical
theme – each suite depicts a
famous Argentine personage.

Farther Afield

Casona La Ruchi $
Budget   **Map** C3
Lavalle 557, Tigre
Tel *(011) 4749-2499*
W casonalaruchi.com.ar
An 1892 house with a garden,
pool, and waterfront views.

Posada Plaza Mayor $$
Guesthouse   **Map** C3
*Calle de Comercio 111, Colonia de
Sacramento, Uruguay*
Tel *(0598) 4552-3193*
W posadaplazamayor.com
This 1860s waterside inn has
shuttered rooms surrounding
an ornamented courtyard.

The Pampas

BAHÍA BLANCA: Hotel Austral $
Modern   **Map** C3
Ave Colón 159, 8000
Tel *(0291) 456-1700*
W hotelesaustral.com
Modern hotel with comfortable,
airy rooms, helpful staff, and a
great Sunday brunch.

LA PLATA: San Marco Hotel $
Budget   **Map** C3
Calle 54 no. 523, 1900
Tel *(0221) 422-9322*
W sanmarcohotel.com.ar
Basic, cheerful interiors and
rooms with en-suite bathrooms.
Ask for a room with a view.

MAR DEL PLATA: Sheraton $$$
Modern   **Map** C3
Alem 4221, 7600
Tel *(0223) 414-0000*
W sheratonmardelplata.com.ar
Modern, mid-rise tower with
great views of the beach and
golf course. Pleasant rooms.

MIRAMAR: Refugio de Mar $
Cabins   **Map** C3
Ave 9 no. 749, 7607
Tel *(02291) 434-115*
W refugiodemarmiramar.com.ar
Clean, well-maintained cabins
with maid service and fridges.
Can accommodate up to six.

**NECOCHEA: Hostería del
Bosque** $
Boutique   **Map** C3
Calle 89 no. 350, 7630
Tel *(02262) 420-002*
W hosteria-delbosque.com.ar
Dignified French-Basque mansion
offering romantic, old-fashioned
rooms and 24-hour room service.

Ayelen Hotel de Montaña, a long-
established hiker's favorite

Key to Price Guide *see page 278*

PINAMAR: Hotel Las Calas $$
Boutique   **Map** D3
Bunge 560, 7630
Tel *(02254) 405-999*
W lascalashotel.com.ar
Hotel Las Calas offers lots of
amenities and delicious breakfasts.
Has a pleasant interior courtyard.

DK Choice

TANDIL: Ave María $$$
Boutique   **Map** C3
*Circuito Turístico Paraje la
Porteña s/n, 7000*
Tel *(0249) 442-2843*
W avemariatandil.com.ar
A charming hotel in a bucolic
setting. Personable staff can
help arrange bike rides, horse-
back riding, and more. The
superlative cuisine on offer
includes an ample breakfast.

VILLA GESELL: Palazzo Ariete $$
Modern   **Map** D3
Ave 1 no. 472, 7165
Tel *(02255) 454-800*
W palazzoarietehotel.com
Welcoming rooms await at this
centrally located hotel that
directly faces the Atlantic.

Argentinian Litoral

DK Choice

COLÓN: Hotel Costarenas $$
Modern   **Map** C2
Ave Quirós, cnr 12 de Abril, 3280
Tel *(03447) 425-050*
W hotelcostarenas.com.ar
A contemporary hotel with crisp,
clean interiors and understated
decor, the Costarenas offers a
state-of-the-art spa, reading
room, restaurant, and terrace bar.
Alcove rooms have river views.

**CORRIENTES: Turismo Hotel
Casino** $$
Luxury   **Map** C1
Entre Ríos 650, 3400
Tel *(0379) 446-2244*
W ghturismo.com.ar
This hacienda-style retreat offers
casino passes, a mini-cinema, and
complimentary tea in the rooms.

**ESTEROS DEL IBERÁ:
Irupé Lodge** $$
Lodge   **Map** D2
Calle Yacaré & Ysipó s/n, 3471
Tel *(0376) 443-8312*
W ibera-argentina.com
Lovely lodge situated in natural
surroundings. The superior rooms
offer more privacy.

**GUALEGUAYCHÚ:
Hotel Aguay** $$
Modern   **Map** C2
Costanera Morrogh Bernard 130, 2820
Tel *(03446) 422-099*
W hotelaguay.com.ar
This hotel is designed to provide
as many views of the river as
possible from rooms, the rooftop
pool, and other vantage points.

PARANÁ: Gran Hotel Paraná $
Modern   **Map** C2
Urquiza 976, 3100
Tel *(0343) 422-3900*
W hotelesparana.com.ar
Ideally located facing the plaza.
Room categories range from
budget to business. Excellent staff.

**PUERTO IGUAZÚ: Hotel Saint
George** $$
Modern   **Map** D1
Ave Córdoba 148, 3370
Tel *(03757) 420-633*
W hotelsaintgeorge.com
Bright, comfortable rooms and
plenty of amenities including a
lush garden and a pool.

**PUERTO IGUAZÚ: Raíces
Esturión Iguazú** $$
Scenic   **Map** D1
Ave Tres Fronteras 650, 3370
Tel *(03757) 420-100*
W hotelesturion.com
Designed for relaxation, this hotel
offers many room options, includ-
ing lodges, suites, and apartments.

ROSARIO: Hotel Majestic $
Historic   **Map** C2
San Lorenzo 980, 2000
Tel *(0341) 440-5872*
W hotelmajestic.com.ar
Housed in a grand French-style
1908 building with a modern
interior. Spacious common areas.

**SAN IGNACIO MINÍ:
Hotel Portal del Sol** $
Budget   **Map** D1
Rivadavia 1105, 3322
Tel *(0376) 447-0096*
W portaldelsolhotel.com
The decor is sparse, but rooms
boast powerful showers and
firm mattresses. Helpful staff.

Córdoba and the
Andean Northwest

**CAFAYATE: Viila Vicuña
Hotel Boutique** $
Boutique   **Map** B1
Belgrano 76, 4427
Tel *(03868) 422-145*
W villavicuna.com.ar/cafayate
A small, rustic inn built around a
central courtyard. Rooms have
cozy blankets and cowhide rugs.

Sunset views over the veranda dining area, Irupé Lodge

CÓRDOBA: Tango Hostel International $
Hostel **Map** C2
Fructuoso Rivera 70, 5000
Tel *(0351) 425-6023*
w tangohostelcordoba.com
Colorful hostel with enthusiastic staff and lots of common areas.

DK Choice

CÓRDOBA: Dos Lunas Horse Riding Lodge $$$
Boutique **Map** C2
Ruta Provincial 17 s/n, Alta Ongamira, 5148
Tel *(011) 5032-3410*
w doslunas.com.ar
A remote country estate high in the hills, Dos Lunas is full of exquisite antiques and has ponchos hanging on the walls. The all-inclusive rates include excursions and culinary activities.

HUMAHUACA: Hostel Azul $
Budget **Map** B1
Barrio Medalla Milagrosa s/n, 4630
Tel *(03887) 421-596*
w hostalazulhumahuaca.com.ar
Eco-friendly hotel decorated with artisanal crafts and wooden furniture. Accepts cash only.

MOLINOS: Hacienda de Molinos $
Historic **Map** B1
Abraham Cornejo s/n, 4419
Tel *(03868) 494-094*
w haciendademolinos.com.ar
This lovely 18th-century adobe hacienda has cobblestone courtyards and a good restaurant.

PURMAMARCA: El Manantial del Silencio $$
Boutique **Map** B1
Ruta Nacional 52, Km 3.5, 4618
Tel *(0388) 490-8080*
w hotelmanantialdelsilencio.com
Neo-colonial architecture and minimalist, tasteful decor in a stunning natural setting. Excellent Andean cuisine.

SALTA: Legado Mítico $$$
Boutique **Map** B1
Bartolomé Mitre 647, 4400
Tel *(0387) 422-8786*
w legadomitico.com
A converted historic home with book-lined walls and individually themed rooms. Ideal for couples.

TAFÍ DEL VALLE: Hostería Lunahuana $$
Boutique **Map** B1
Ave Gobernador Critto 540, 4137
Tel *(03867) 421-330*
w lunahuana.com.ar
Offers neat, rustic-style rooms with regional textiles adorning the whitewashed walls. Serves Andean fare.

TILCARA: Rincón de Fuego $$
Boutique **Map** B1
Ambrosetti 445, 4624
Tel *(0388) 495-5130*
w rincondefuego.com
Stunning hotel with adobe and stone walls, and a warm central hearth. The restaurant uses home-grown organic vegetables.

Cuyo and the Wine Country

LOS PENITENTES: Ayelen Hotel de Montaña $$
Resort **Map** B2
Ruta 7, Km 165, 5553
Tel *(0261) 425-3443*
Long-established mountain hotel run by two very helpful expats. Offers spacious, though plain, rooms. Closed mid-Mar–mid-Jun.

MALARGÜE: Eco Hostel Malargüe $
Hostel **Map** B3
Finca 65, Colonia Pehuenche, 5613
Tel *(0260) 423-2312*
w hostelmalargue.net
A small eco-hostel offering basic rooms with small heated floors, home-style meals, kitchen access, and bike rental.

MENDOZA: Hostel Independencia $
Hostel **Map** B2
Mitre 1237, 5500
Tel *(0261) 423-1806*
w hostelindependencia.com.ar
Offers crowded dorm quarters as well as spacious private rooms.

MENDOZA: Hostel Lao $
Hostel **Map** B2
Rioja 771, 5500
Tel *(0261) 438-0454*
w laohostel.com
A friendly place with kitchen access, free wine in the evenings, several common areas, and a pool.

MENDOZA: Diplomatic Hotel $$
Luxury **Map** B2
Belgrano 1041, 5500
Tel *(0261) 405-1900*
w diplomatichotel.com.ar
This sleek hotel, with full services, makes guests feel pampered without the high prices.

MENDOZA: Huentala Boutique Hotel $$
Boutique **Map** B2
Primitivo de la Reta 1007, 5500
Tel *(0261) 420-0766*
w huentala.com
Offers luxurious rooms with Francophile decor, plus a cellar wine bar and an outdoor pool.

MENDOZA: Cavas Wine Lodge $$$
Luxury **Map** B2
Costaflores s/n, Alto Agrelo, 5507
Tel *(0261) 410-6927*
w cavaswinelodge.com
Beautiful private adobe suites, each with its own deck, plunge pool, and outdoor fireplace. Superlative restaurant.

MENDOZA: Club Tapiz $$$
Lodge **Map** B2
Pedro Molina s/n, Ruta 60, Km 2.5, Maipú, 5517
Tel *(0261) 496-3433*
w club-tapiz.com.ar
A full-service wine lodge and spa. Guests can participate in the wine-making process. Nightly tastings.

DK Choice

MENDOZA: Entre Cielos $$$
Boutique **Map** B2
Guardia Vieja 1998, Vistalba, 5509
Tel *(0261) 498-3377*
w entrecielos.com
A boutique winery estate with superlative service and ultramodern interiors heavy on poured concrete and soft pastels. There is also a sybaritic *hammam* and spa, gourmet dining, and an Olympic-sized pool.

The peaceful lakeside location of Aguas Arribas Lodge

MENDOZA: Hotel Termas Cacheuta $$$
Resort   Map B2
Ruta Provincial 82, Km 38, 5549
Tel *(02624) 490-152*
W termascacheuta.com
A sprawling, traditional spa resort with natural hot springs and pools on landscaped grounds.

SAN AGUSTÍN DEL VALLE FÉRTIL: Hostería Valle Fértil $
Hostel   Map B2
Rivadavia s/n, 5449
Tel *(02646) 420-015*
W hosteriavallefertil.com
Hilltop hostel with comfortable rooms. Kitchen and grill facilities.

SAN LUIS: Hotel Aiello $
Budget   Map B2
Ave Presidente Illia 431, 5700
Tel *(0266) 442-5609*
W hotelaiello.com.ar
Good option in a busy, yet quiet, location. Close to restaurants.

SAN RAFAEL: Tower Inn & Suites $$
Modern   Map B3
Ave Hipólito Yrigoyen 774, 5600
Tel *(0260) 442-7190*
W towersanrafael.com
Amenity-packed hotel with a casino and a spa. Good for groups.

TUNUYÁN: Posada Salentein $$
Luxury   Map B3
Ruta 89 s/n, 5560
Tel *(02622) 429-090*
W bodegassalentein.com
Secluded guesthouse offering gourmet dining and great views.

USPALLATA: Gran Hotel Uspallata $$
Resort   Map B2
Ruta Nacional 7, Km 1149, 5545
Tel *(02624) 420-003*
W granhoteluspallata.com.ar
Pleasant rooms amid sprawling grounds with towering poplars.

Patagonia

ALUMINÉ: Hotel de la Aldea $
Lodge   Map B4
Ruta Provincial 23, Km 82, 8345
Tel *(02942) 496-340*
W hoteldelaldea.com.ar
Traditional, Swiss-style lodge with a cozy fireplace in the lounge.

BARILOCHE: Hostería Costas del Nahuel $
Inn   Map B4
Ave Bustillo 937, 8400
Tel *(0294) 443-9919*
W costasdelnahuel.com.ar
Offers en-suite rooms, good views, a pool, and helpful service.

BARILOCHE: Hotel Quillén $
Budget   Map B4
Ave San Martín 415, 8400
Tel *(0294) 442-2669*
W hotelquillen.com
Rooms at this budget hotel are decorated with Mapuche Indian-inspired textiles. Has a small spa.

BARILOCHE: Design Suites Bariloche $$
Boutique   Map B4
Ave Bustillo, Km 2.5, 8402
Tel *(0294) 445-7000*
W designsuites.com
Amenities here include a spa, pools, and free shuttle service.

DK Choice

BARILOCHE: Llao Llao Hotel & Resort $$$
Lodge   Map B4
Ave Bustillo, Km 25, 8409
Tel *(0294) 444-5700*
W llaollao.com
The grand Llao Llao is a classic mountain lodge with timber-heavy architecture, huge lobbies, and antler chandelier-style decor. Epic views, 18-hole golf course, spa, restaurants, and more.

COMODORO RIVADAVIA: Comodoro Hotel $$
Historic   Map B5
9 de Julio 770, 9000
Tel *(0297) 447-2300*
W comodorohotel.com.ar
Good mid-range choice, with simply furnished, clean, spacious rooms.

EL BOLSÓN: La Posada de Hamelín $
Inn   Map B4
Int. Granollers 2179, 8430
Tel *(02944) 492-030*
W posadadehamelin.com.ar
A cottage-style *posada* with ivy-clad walls, wooden furniture, and charming rooms. Warm service.

EL CALAFATE: Hostería Los Ñires $
Guesthouse   Map B6
9 de Julio 281, 9405
Tel *(02902) 493-642*
W hosterialosnires.com.ar
Spacious inn with a fireplace in the lobby and cable internet.

EL CALAFATE: Los Canelos $$
Resort   Map B6
Pto. San Julián 149, 9405
Tel *(02902) 493-890*
W loscanelos.com.ar
Alpine-style place with snug rooms and a flower-filled garden. Closed Jun–late Aug.

EL CHALTÉN: Hotel Lunajuim $$
Lodge   Map B6
Trevisán 45, 9301
Tel *(02962) 493-047*
W lunajuim.com.ar
Tasteful mountain lodge with nice views. The lounge has a library.

EL CHALTÉN: Aguas Arriba Lodge $$$
Lodge   Map B6
Ruta Provincial 23, Km 130, 9301
Tel *(05411) 4152-5697*
W aguasarribalodge.com
A nature lodge nestled by a lake in a forest. Offers trekking excursions. Closed May–Sep.

ESQUEL: Cumbres Blancas $$
Inn   Map B4
Ave Ameghino 1683, 9200
Tel *(02945) 455-100*
W cumbresblancas.com.ar
This lovely inn has warm, elegant rooms, and extensive gardens. Rates include use of the sauna.

GAIMAN: Hostería Ty Gwyn $
B&B   Map B4
9 de Julio 111, 9105
Tel *(0280) 449-1009*
W tygwyn.com.ar
Cozy B&B in a traditional teahouse. Rooms open onto balconies with views. Delicious breakfasts.

JUNÍN DE LOS ANDES: Hostería Chimehuin $
Inn   Map B4
Coronel Suarez 750, 8371
Tel *(02972) 491-132*
W hosteriachimehuin.com.ar
Located in four buildings over-looking a stream and a private islet, accessible only to guests.

LOS ANTIGUOS: Hostería Antigua Patagonia $$
Budget   Map B5
Ruta Provincial 43, Acceso Este, 9041
Tel *(02963) 491-038*
W antiguapatagonia.com.ar
Offers rooms with views on the shore of Lake Buenos Aires. Closed May–Sep.

NEUQUÉN: Hotel del Comahue $$
Modern   Map B4
Ave Argentina 377, 8300
Tel *(0299) 443-2040*
W hoteldelcomahue.com
Neuquén's premier hotel has elegant rooms and good service.

PENÍNSULA VALDÉS: Hostería The Paradise $$
Inn   Map C4
2° bajada al mar, Puerto Pirámides, 9121
Tel *(02804) 495-030*
W hosteriatheparadise.com.ar
Romantic hideaway close to the beach. Staff can arrange marine safaris and trekking excursions.

PERITO MORENO: Hotel Belgrano $
Budget   Map B5
Ave San Martín 1001, 9040
Tel *(02963) 432-019*
W hotelbelgrano.guiapatagonia.net
This long-established hotel is a popular pit stop on Route 40. Offers very basic amenities.

PUERTO DESEADO: Hotel Los Acantilados $
Budget   Map B5
España 1611, 9050
Tel *(0297) 487-2167*
W hotellosacantilados.com
Perched on a cliff above the port, offering the best lodging in town. Ask for a room in the new wing.

PUERTO MADRYN: Hostería Hipocampo $
Budget   Map B4
Vesta 33, cnr Blvd Almirante Brown, 9120
Tel *(0280) 447-3605*
Expect basic, clean rooms with mini-fridges and microwaves.

PUERTO MADRYN: Hotel Territorio $$
Luxury   Map B4
Blvd Alte. Guillermo Brown 3251, 9120
Tel *(0280) 447--0050*
W hotelterritorio.com.ar
Stylishly modern hotel with a luxurious spa and all amenities.

RÍO GALLEGOS: Hotel Comercio $
Budget   Map B6
Ave Nestor Kirchner 1302, 9400
Tel *(02966) 420-209*
W hotelcomerciorgl.com
Small but clean and comfortable rooms. Colorful, eclectic decor.

SAN MARTÍN DE LOS ANDES: Cabañas Arco Iris $$
Resort   Map B4
Los Cipreses 1850, 8370
Tel *(02972) 428-450*
W arcoirisar.com
Located on the banks of a stream, these woodland cabins provide an escape into nature. All have kitchens. Exceptional service.

SAN MARTÍN DE LOS ANDES: Le Village $$
Boutique   Map B4
General Roca 816, 8370
Tel *(02972) 427-698*
W hotellevillage.com.ar
Swiss-inspired hotel with rustic decor and business facilities.

TRELEW: Hotel Touring Club $
Budget   Map B4
Ave Fontana 240, 9100
Tel *(02965) 425-790*
A little faded, but a good-value choice. Past guests include Butch Cassidy and the Sundance Kid.

VILLA EL CHOCÓN: La Posada del Dinosaurio $
Modern   Map B4
Costa del Lago, Barrio 1, 8311
Tel *(0299) 490-1201*
W posadadinosaurio.com.ar
In a stunning location, with lakeview rooms. The restaurant serves delicious trout and pasta dishes.

VILLA LA ANGOSTURA: Hostería La Escondida $$$
Boutique   Map B4
Ave Arrayanes 7014, 8407
Tel *(02944) 475-313*
W hosterialaescondida.com.ar
Beautiful rooms with lake views. Excellent restaurant and a pool.

Tierra del Fuego and Antarctica

RÍO GRANDE: Hostería Posada de los Sauces $
Modern   Map B6
Elcano 839, 9420
Tel *(02964) 430-868*
W laposadadelossauces.com.ar
A charming place with homey rooms and a great restaurant. The cozy bar has an open fireplace.

TOLHUIN: Hostería Kaikén $
Modern   Map B6
Ruta Nacional 3, Km 2958, 9412
Tel *(02901) 492-372*
W hosteriakaiken.com
Rooms as well as cabins face the lake. Staff can arrange transfers and excursions.

USHUAIA: Hotel Cap Polonio $$
Modern   Map B6
Ave San Martín 746, 9410
Tel *(02901) 422-140*
W hotelcappolonio.com.ar
A functional, no-frills hotel with an on-site playroom for kids. Helpful staff.

USHUAIA: Hotel Los Naranjos $$
Modern   Map B6
Ave San Martín 1446, 9410
Tel *(02901) 435-862*
W losnaranjosushuaia.com
Warm, spacious, and inviting hotel on Ushuaia's main avenue, offering efficient service.

USHUAIA: Hotel Tierra del Fuego $$
Modern   Map B6
Gobernador Deloqui 198, 9410
Tel *(02901) 424-901*
W tierradelfuegohotel.com
Hospitable hotel with clean, large rooms, and rustic stone and wood interiors.

USHUAIA: Los Acebos $$$
Luxury   Map B6
Luis F. Martial 1911, 9410
Tel *(02901) 430-710*
W losacebos.com.ar
Family-friendly hotel with a golf course, casino, and kids' activities.

DK Choice

USHUAIA: Tierra Las Leyendas $$
Luxury   Map B6
Tierra de Vientos 2448, 9410
Tel *(02901) 446-565*
W tierradeleyendas.com.ar
A cheery little owner-operated hotel with cozy common areas and well-lit, spacious rooms, most with views. The restaurant, for guests only, is very good.

Timber-roofed, chalet-style accommodations at Cabañas Arco Iris

For more information on types of hotels *see pp274–7*

WHERE TO EAT AND DRINK

The people of Argentina are as passionate about good food and drink as they are about life, music, and tango. Their culinary tastes have evolved over the years and now incorporate a variety of world cuisines. The definitive dining experience, however, is still to be found at a neighborhood *parrilla* (steakhouse). Roadside *parrillas* are located all across Argentina, offering a country-style family barbecue experience. Here, meat is propped up on stakes, roasted around a fire, and served alfresco. In this diverse country, it is also possible to grab a quick bite at a chain pizza outlet, enjoy ethnic cuisines of the Old World, and discover new, creative cooking.

A bustling local restaurant, Buenos Aires

Parrillas

Sprinkled throughout the country, *parrillas* (steakhouses) are the most popular eating places in Argentina. Typically, a visit starts off with a plate of bites, often tasty mini-empanadas (stuffed pastries) and a glass of red wine, before moving on to *chorizo* (flavorful sausage), provolone cheese, and assorted offal. The main meal that follows is almost always a grilled steak, accompanied by a side salad.

Grilled salmon is often served at *parrillas*, and some offer vegetarian alternatives as well. The dessert menu usually consists of fruit, ice cream, or perhaps a crème caramel. The main point of eating at a *parrilla* is to stretch out the eating experience and chat between courses. If a *parrilla* is packed, it probably means it is really good, and the bustle and the banter is all part of the general bonhomie that makes this Argentinian institution so special.

Bars and Confiterías

After the *parrilla*, the other institution that every *barrio* must have is a bar. In Argentina, this implies a "café-bar" and it is a good place for meeting friends and family members. Besides coffee and juices, most café-bars serve toasted sandwiches, *medialunas* (sweet croissants), and liquor.

For a more substantial salad or steak sandwich, head to a *confitería* – a larger café with more tables, longer menus, and sadly, often less atmosphere. During the last decade, these classic ancient bars and *confiterías* have been joined by a wave of dimly lit cocktail and wine bars which, although ideal for a night out, tend to attract a younger crowd of drinkers.

Chain Restaurants

Global franchises are well represented in Argentina, and chain burger outlets and pizzerias are common. Their local competitors include *tenedor libres* (free forks) – "all-you-can-eat" restaurants that offer a fixed-price menu. Dishes at *tenedor libres* are spread out in a self-service buffet and include grilled meat, pastas, and even Chinese food.

Going up in price, most middle- and higher-bracket restaurants focus on the 3Ps – *parrilla*, pasta, and pizzas. Excitingly, the last decade has witnessed the emergence of Modern Argentinian restaurants, where creative chefs prepare inventive contemporary cuisine using indigenous ingredients. Modern Argentinian cuisine, or *Cocina de Autor*, is served at fashionable restaurants in big cities and tourist destinations.

Eating Hours

In Argentina, eating between 9 and 10pm is normal and between 10pm and midnight is completely acceptable. Most restaurants close very late while *confiterías* and cafés are open dawn to dusk and often round the clock. Lunch and breakfast are served at the usual times.

Prices and Paying

Due to price inflation, the cost of eating out in Argentina is now nearly on a par with Europe or

An established and popular *parrilla* serving grilled meats

Softly lit outdoor dining terrace at Anna Bistro, Mendoza

North America. Lunchtime dining is cheaper, as most restaurants offer a midday fixed-price menu encompassing three courses plus a beverage. By comparison, à la carte dining in the evening is more expensive.

Prices on menus do not usually show the obligatory 21 percent *Impuesto de Valor Agregado* or IVA (value-added tax or VAT). In addition, some of the more upscale restaurants in Buenos Aires and other tourist areas charge a *cubierto* (cover charge) of AR$10–25 per person. Service charge is almost never included in the bill, and a typical tip would be 10 percent of the bill, left on the table or handed to the waiter.

Credit cards are accepted in most restaurants, with Visa and MasterCard being the most popular, but in far-flung provinces or villages off the beaten track, it is important to carry cash. Travelers' checks may be accepted in big hotels or restaurants.

Wheelchair Access

In big cities, upmarket restaurants will have ramps or designed access. Elsewhere, however, few eateries make special provision for wheelchair users. That said, Argentinian waiting staff are generally helpful and will do everything short of knocking down a wall to open a door and make a diner feel welcome.

Children

Argentinians, as a rule, adore children and, much to the chagrin of couples and peace-loving singles, restaurants will happily accommodate families with noisy infants. Big *parrillas* and upscale restaurants will have high chairs, but there is rarely room for maneuvering strollers. Child portions are usually available, or visitors can ask for a spare plate and dish out a portion from their meal.

Food Hygiene

In well-visited areas of Argentina, food hygiene and health standards are generally good. Visitors should drink purified water, bottled carbonated water, or *gaseosas* (soft drinks) if they are wary of the water. Bottled water is available in *kioskos*, hotels, bars, and service stations. Avoid salads and uncooked vegetables in the smaller towns and villages in the subtropical regions and in villages that are less visited. Shellfish and seafood on the coast are generally fresh and properly washed, but treat open-air markets and roadside vendors with caution.

Vegetarians

Vegetarian restaurants are not common in Argentina and it is important to insist *"No como carne"* (I do not eat meat). Vegetables are grown across the country, so most restaurants will have fresh squash, salad, potatoes, and other roots. Fruit is abundant and cheap.

Smoking

Following a nationwide ban in 2011, smoking is prohibited in any enclosed public space.

Recommended Restaurants

The restaurants listed in this guide have been selected with budget, variety and quality of cuisine, and setting in mind, and aim to provide the visitor with the best possible choice of restaurants in an area. Listings have been arranged by region, starting with Buenos Aires. Within each particular region, the entries are defined by separate themes, including Traditional Argentinian (embracing indigenous cuisines) and *parilla*, Modern Argentinian, Italian, International, and Vegetarian. Taken together, these themes form an accurate reflection of the food choices available today in Argentina.

A DK Choice entry is considered to be an outstanding restaurant. It might be a romantic place, have great views or fantastic design, be excellent value, have a significant dish, or fabulous outside eating. Most of these are very popular, so make a reservation where possible.

The Flavors of Argentina

Argentinians really do eat the best and biggest steaks on the planet, and the *asado* (open-air barbecue) is an important community ritual as well as a delicious feast. Other meats, especially lamb and pork, are also integral to the national diet, sometimes described as *cocina criolla* (Creole cuisine). Fish is less popular, despite the extensive coastline and large hake and squid reserves of the South Atlantic. A few vestiges of the pre-Columbian kitchen have survived, and corn (maize) remains an important ingredient in the kitchens of the Andean Northwest.

Freshly picked corn

Rounding up a herd of cattle on an estancia

Central Argentina and the Pampas

The cattle-grazing heartland is around Buenos Aires, and some of the best beef is sold to smart *parrillas* in the capital. As well as prime cuts of beef, most *parrillas* offer spicy pork and blood sausages and a range of *achuras* (offal) such as sweetbreads, kidneys, and tripe. An *asado* has the same fare, cooked outdoors over a wood fire and often served on a *brasero* (coal-heated platter). *Provoleta* (grilled provolone cheese) is also served, and accompaniments include a *criolla* salad of lettuce, onions, tomato, and piquant *chimichurri* (sauce of red peppers, herbs, and garlic). In winter, the favorite traditional dish is a warming stew called *locro*.

The Northwest

The cuisine of the Andean Northwest often features grilled goat's meat and, in specialty restaurants, the meat of the

Beefsteaks
Provoleta cheese
Chimichurri sauce
Morcilla (blood sausage)
Sausages
Salami, cheese, and olives
Criolla salad

Some of the elements of a typical Argentinian *asado*

Everyday Eating in Argentina

Street food and finger food are very popular in Argentina although there are really only a few options – Argentinians remain largely loyal to their local cuisine. Two iconic snacks are *choripán* (pork sausage sandwich) and empanadas, savory pastries which can be baked or fried and stuffed with anything from ground beef to corn to plums and Roquefort. Café society is important in the cities, with coffee accompanied by delicate sandwiches *de miga* (slices of ham and cheese on crustless ultrathin bread), and sweet pastries. All towns have cooks of Italian descent, and pizzas (often served with a slice of *fainá*) are excellent. Almost everywhere visitors will see locals tucking in to basic pasta dishes, *milanesas* (veal and chicken cutlet), grilled hake, *criolla* salads, empanadas, and barbecued meat. These are the staples of everyday Argentinian eating, and they are usually delicious.

Pizza con fainá is a cheese-laden pizza accompanied by slices of *garbanzo* (chickpea) pancake called *fainá*.

Preparing an *asado* for hardworking and hungry gauchos

llama. There is superb trout in the rivers of the Córdoba sierras, and the German colonists brought a taste for cured meats with them – often washed down with beer from a local microbrewery. Traveling farther north, visitors are more likely to be offered pre-Columbian staples such as *tamales* (corn wraps, stuffed with ground meat and onion) and *humitas* (steamed corn wraps sometimes containing cheese). Quinoa is starting to appear on menus promoting regional cuisine. Desserts often feature local conserves, made from *cayote* (sweet pumpkin) and *tuna* (prickly pear), perhaps served with goat's cheese or a mild cow's milk cheese.

The Northeast

This is the region for grilled fish such as *pejerrey*, dorado, and *surubí*. The meat of the caiman and capybara, the latter considered an acquired taste, is served in some rural eateries. The subtropical climate promotes an abundance of fruits, and fruit-based sauces accompany meat and fish dishes. *Mandioca* (cassava) is used instead of wheat for empanadas, and rice, grown across the wetlands, is often served in place of potatoes.

Fresh trout caught in the clear waters of the Córdoba sierras

Patagonia and Tierra del Fuego

Many specialties of the south, such as fine lamb, were introduced by colonists. Cured meats are popular and, in most Andean regions, platters of venison and wild boar are typical appetizers. The huge coast is the source of culinary riches such as *centolla* (spider crab), hake and shrimp dishes, and paellas. In Chubut, the Welsh community serves scones and *torta galesa* (fruit cake) in colorful teahouses.

ON THE MENU

Alfajor Cookie sandwich filled with *dulce de leche* (caramel) or chocolate.

Empanadas Semicircular savory stuffed pastries.

Matambre Pork flank or skirt steak, usually grilled.

Medialuna Sweet croissant served in cafés.

Milanesa con papas fritas Veal or chicken schnitzel with French fried potatoes.

Ñoquis Potato dumplings traditionally eaten on the 29th of the month.

Pulpo a la Gallega Octopus in oil with hot red pepper and coarse salt, usually served with potatoes in the Galician style.

Ubre Cow's udder – only to be found on the most gaucho-friendly menus.

Cazuela de Mariscos, a dish of Spanish origin, is made with mussels and clams, baked in herb tomato sauce.

Locro, a stew of beans, pork, potato, corn, and squash, is traditionally eaten on May 25 – Independence Day.

Flan is a light crème caramel dessert to which Argentinians often add whipped cream or *dulce de leche*.

Where to Eat and Drink

Buenos Aires

Plaza de Mayo and Microcentro

Bi Won $
International   Map 2 B4
Junín 548, Once
Tel *(011) 4372-1146*
Authentic Korean restaurant, where meats are cooked at the tables. Enjoy the seafood, aromatic rice, hot sauces, and seaweed.

Brasserie Petanque $
International   Map 1 E1
Defensa 596, Monserrat
Tel *(011) 4342-7930*   **Closed** *Mon*
This French-owned eatery serves traditional Gallic dishes, like steak tartare with fries, in a bright, busy setting.

Cantina Pierino $
Italian   Map 2 A4
Lavalle 3499, Abasto
Tel *(011) 4864-5715*   **Closed** *Mon*
Opened in 1909 and still run by the same Italian-Argentinian family, this one-time haunt of tango legends has fabulous pastas.

Chiquilín $
Traditional Argentinian   Map 2 C5
Sarmiento 1599, Congreso
Tel *(011) 4371-1652*
Tango memorabilia covers this atmospheric eatery, which has been running since 1927. Excellent *parrillas*, pastas, and pizzas served here.

D'Oro $
Italian   Map 3 E5
Perú 159, Monserrat
Tel *(011) 4342-6959*   **Closed** *Sat & Sun*
Office workers crowd this modern dining spot at lunch. Pastas, pizzas, and risottos are a part of its fixed menu.

El Cuartito $
Italian   Map 2 B4
Talcahuano 937, Tribunales
Tel *(011) 4816-1758*   **Closed** *Mon*
Whirling fans and walls adorned with soccer memorabilia give this raucous pizzeria plenty of character. The superb pizzas are justly popular.

i Central Market $
Modern Argentinian   Map 1 F1
Pierina Dealessi & Macacha Guemes, Puerto Madero
Tel *(011) 5775-0330*
A truly vibrant food spot, this integrated space comprises a waterfront restaurant serving seasonal dishes, plus a deli and fresh food market.

Moreneta de Montserrat $
Modern Argentinian   Map 3 E5
Moreno 477, Monserrat
Tel *(011) 4331-1428*   **Closed** *Sat & Sun*
Take advantage of bargain breakfast, brunch, and lunchtime dishes with Mediterranean flair from Michelin-starred chefs, caterers, and co-owners Luciana Conte and Sebastián Raggiante.

Status $
International   Map 2 C5
Virrey Cevallos 178, Congreso
Tel *(011) 4382-8531*
Much loved by the city's Peruvian community, Status serves fresh *ceviche* dishes and other Peruvian specialties. There are vegetarian options as well. The pisco sour is superb.

Aldo's Vinoteca & Restorán $$
Modern Argentinian   Map 3 E5
Moreno 372, Monserrat
Tel *(011) 4334-2380*
Attached to the Moreno hotel, this Art Deco-esque wine store with a delectable eatery is a favorite haunt of politicians and businessmen.

M Buenos Aires $$
Fusion   Map 3 E5
Balcarce 433, Monserrat
Tel *(011) 4331-3879*   **Closed** *Sun*
A glamorous spot set beneath bare-brick archways, M Buenos Aires offers Peruvian-Japanese

Part of the seven-course taster menu at El Baqueano

fusion cuisine, and a great cocktail bar. Fashionable clientele.

El Baqueano $$$
Modern Argentinian   Map 1 E1
Chile 495, Monserrat
Tel *(011) 4342-0802*   **Closed** *Sun & Mon*
Favored by adventurous gastronomes, the seven-course menu at El Baqueano offers Argentina's most exotic meats including llama, caiman, and rhea.

Tomo I $$$
Traditional Argentinian Map 3 E5
Hotel Panamericano, Carlos Pelligrini 521, Microcentro
Tel *(011) 4326-6695*   **Closed** *Sun*
Visit award-winning Tomo I for a superb fine-dining experience, with swanky surroundings and gourmet Argentinian cuisine that includes rare game meats and fine wines.

San Telmo and La Boca

Amici Miei $
Italian   Map 1 E1
Defensa 1072, San Telmo
Tel *(011) 4362-5562*   **Closed** *Mon*
Popular Italian eatery with balcony tables overlooking a colonial square. The menu has pastas, pizzas, and Italian desserts.

Caseros $
Modern Argentinian   Map 1 E2
Ave Caseros 486, San Telmo
Tel *(011) 4307-4729*   **Closed** *Sun*
Small, romantic spot with pavement tables. The menu has delicious salads, seafood, and meat dishes, made with local and seasonal ingredients.

Comedor Nikkai $
International   Map 1 D1
Ave Independencia 732, San Telmo
Tel *(011) 4300-5848*   **Closed** *Sun*
Popular with the city's Japanese community, offering authentic Japanese food at great prices.

El Desnivel $
Parrilla   Map 1 E1
Defensa 855, San Telmo
Tel *(011) 4300-9081*
The open grill at this famous *parrilla* sizzles with beefsteaks,

chorizos, and blood sausages. A huge favorite with families and local bohemians alike.

Fine dining to the strains of live piano music, La Bourgogne *(see p290)*

DK Choice

El Obrero   **$**
Traditional
Argentinian   **Map**1 F3
Agustín Caffarena 64, La Boca
Tel *(011) 4362-9912* **Closed** *Sun*
The lively El Obrero with its old-fashioned ambience, is frequented by locals plus the occasional celebrity. In fact, U2's Bono and actor Susan Sarandon have dined at this portside restaurant. Waiters recommend the day's specials, but the chorizos, beefsteaks, and sea bass are always great choices.

Gran Parrilla del Plata   **$**
Parrilla   **Map** 3 E5
Chile 594, San Telmo
Tel *(011) 4300-8858*
Dine with local families at this old-fashioned *parrilla*. The menu offers beefsteak, offal, and chorizo dishes, plus wines and salads.

Naturaleza Sabia   **$**
Vegetarian   **Map** 1 E1
Balcarce 958, San Telmo
Tel *(011) 4300-6454*   **Closed** *Mon*
Set in a town house, this place prepares tasty vegan and veggie dishes such as lentil burgers and spinach-stuffed pastas.

La Brigada   **$$**
Parrilla   **Map** 1 E1
Estados Unidos 465, San Telmo
Tel *(011) 4361-4685*
Enjoy the beefsteaks and buzz at this lively, upscale *parrilla*, which is famed for its red-meat delicacies. Argentinian soccer memorabilia festoons its interior.

Patagonia Sur   **$$$**
Traditional Argentinian   **Map** 1 F4
Rocha 801, La Boca
Tel *(011) 4303-5917*   **Closed** *Sun & Mon*
Famous Argentinian chef Francis Mallmann owns this portside restaurant. Dishes using recipes from across Argentina are traditional food at its best.

Plaza San Martín and Retiro

El Establo   **$**
Traditional Argentinian   **Map** 3 E4
Paraguay 489, Retiro
Tel *(011) 4311-1639*
With large, well-priced beefsteaks on the menu, this downtown

institution is a popular spot. Salads and pastas are good too.

Filo   **$**
Italian   **Map** 3 E4
San Martín 975, Retiro
Tel *(011) 4311-0312*
Office workers flock to this downtown spot in the evenings for some fun and the modern Italian cuisine. DJs play sets.

Gran Bar Danzón   **$**
Modern Argentinian   **Map** 3 D3
Libertad 1161, Tribunales
Tel *(011) 4811-1108*
This hip dining spot attracts a stylish crowd. The smart wine bar is well stocked with an impressive collection. Go to dine or for drinks only.

Milión   **$**
Modern Argentinian   **Map** 3 D3
Paraná 1048, Tribunales
Tel *(011) 4815-9925*
The ideal spot for moonlit dining and cocktails, Milión operates out of a *belle époque* mansion. Diners can opt to sit in the romantic private garden.

Sabot   **$**
Traditional Argentinian   **Map** 3 E4
25 de Mayo 756, Retiro
Tel *(011) 4313-6587*   **Closed** *Sat & Sun*
A classic eatery, Sabot has old-fashioned tables, stellar service, and seafood specialties. Red and white meats, salads, and pastas are also served.

Irifune   **$$**
International   **Map** 3 E4
Paraguay 436, Retiro
Tel *(011) 4312-8787*   **Closed** *Sun*
Simplicity reigns at Irifune, which blends Japanese cuisine with

minimalist design. The open kitchen allows you to see the raw fish being expertly prepared.

Mullu   **$$**
Fusion   **Map** 3 E3
Ricardo Rojas 451, Retiro
Tel *(011) 4311-2812*   **Closed** *Sun*
An intimate high-end Peruvian fusion restaurant. Fresh fish and sushi rub shoulders with traditional Argentinian dishes that have had a distinctive makeover.

Recoleta

Cumaná   **$**
Traditional Argentinian **Map** 2 C3
Rodriguez Peña 1149
Tel *(011) 4813-9207*
Cumaná serves the indigenous foods of northern Argentina, including *locro* (stew), empanadas (meat-stuffed corn wraps), and delicious desserts made from sweet pumpkin and native fruits.

Duhau Restaurante   **$$**
Traditional Argentinian **Map** 3 D3
Park Hyatt Buenos Aires, Ave Alvear 1661
Tel *(011) 5171-1340*
Argentinian cuisine served in chic surroundings. There's a garden terrace for alfresco dining, plus world-class wines and Cuban cigars.

Tandoor   **$$**
International   **Map** 2 B3
Laprida 1293, Barrio Norte
Tel *(011) 4821-3676*
Tandoor makes few concessions to the spice-averse Argentinian palate, whipping up flavor-infused dishes from across India.

For more information on types of restaurants *see pp284–5*

La Bourgogne $$$
International **Map** 2 C2
*Alvear Palace Hotel, Ave
Alvear 1891*
Tel *(011) 4808-2100* **Closed** *Sun*
This city's only Relais Gourmand restaurant offers luxury dining at its finest, combining a chic ambience, live piano, and gourmet French cuisine.

Oviedo $$$
International **Map** 2 B3
Beruti 2602
Tel *(011) 4822-5415* **Closed** *Sun*
Specializing in seafood, this Spanish restaurant serves raw oyster starters, plus delicious salmon and trout entrées.

Sottovoce $$$
Italian **Map** 3 D2
Libertador 1098
Tel *(011) 4807-6691*
Beautifully executed Italian cuisine served in a refined setting. Stuffed, home-made pastas with regional sauces precede bountiful desserts.

Palermo and Belgrano

BIO $
Vegetarian **Map** 4 C3
Humboldt 2192, Palermo Viejo
Tel *(011) 4774-3880*
A pioneer of local vegetarian cooking, BIO uses only organic, seasonal produce. The decor is charming yet simple.

El Preferido de Palermo $
Traditional Argentinian **Map** 5 D4
Guatemala 4801, Palermo Viejo
Tel *(011) 4774-6585* **Closed** *Sun*
A bright, rustic interior renders this economical steak house a delight. Good beef cuts and red wines. Pavement tables add to its charm.

Airy Scandinavian decor, ambience, and cuisine at Olsen

Las Cabras $
Traditional Argentinian **Map** 4 C4
Fitz Roy 1795, Palermo Viejo
Tel *(011) 5197-5301*
A hit with the younger crowd, Las Cabras offers beefsteaks as well as northwestern Argentinian cuisine such as *locro* and sweet pumpkin desserts.

Olsen $
International **Map** 4 C3
Gorriti 5870, Palermo Viejo
Tel *(011) 4776-7677* **Closed** *Mon*
Excellent Scandinavian cooking, fashionable cocktails, and minimalist design. Enjoy the Nordic cuisine while lounging in the lush dining garden.

Oui Oui $
Modern Argentinian **Map** 4 C3
Nicaragua 6068, Palermo Viejo
Tel *(011) 4778-9614* **Closed** *Mon*
This charming French-style café is a great lunch spot. Brightly painted walls, wooden furniture, pavement tables, and a chalk-board menu of healthy items.

Sarkis $
International **Map** 4 C4
Thames 1101, Villa Crespo
Tel *(011) 4772-4911*
Shish kebabs, hummus, falafel, Arabian-style empanadas – this lovely, low-key Middle-Eastern restaurant serves them all. Go with friends and share dishes.

Xalapa $
Mexican **Map** 5 D4
El Salvador 4800, Palermo Viejo
Tel *(011) 4833-6102*
Xalapa brings the vibrant flavours of Mexican cooking to Buenos Aires with beef-filled tacos, chicken-stuffed peppers, mole dishes, and more.

Azema Exotic Bistró $$
International **Map** 4 C3
Carranza 1875, Palermo Viejo
Tel *(011) 4774-4191* **Closed** *Sun*
The eclectic menu at this atmospheric bistro is inspired by the cuisines of France, Southeast Asia, and North Africa.

Cabaña Las Lilas $$
Parrilla **Map** 5 D2
*Alicia Moreau de Justo 516,
Puerto Madero*
Tel *(011) 4313-1336*
Upscale *parrilla* with a waterfront dining terrace and a lush interior of leather and wood. World-class beefsteaks, wines, and cigars.

Don Julio $$
Parrilla **Map** 5 D4
Guatemala 4691, Palermo Viejo
Tel *(011) 4831-9564*

Romantic *parrilla* set on a cobbled street, with a rustic interior and pavement tables. Succulent beefsteaks and great wines on offer.

Green Bamboo $$
International **Map** 4 C3
Costa Rica 5802, Palermo Viejo
Tel *(011) 4775-7050*
Hip Southeast Asian restaurant serving Vietnamese flavors. The deliberately kitsch decor includes portraits of Ho Chi Minh.

La Cabrera $$
Traditional Argentinian **Map** 4 C4
Cabrera 5127/5099, Palermo Viejo
Tel *(011) 4832-5754*
A small, popular steakhouse with a rustic ambience. Fantastic beefsteaks, delicious Argentinian delicacies, and top wines.

Lupita $$
Mexican **Map** 4 C3
Fitz Roy 1834, Palermo Viejo
Tel *(011) 5197-5149*
Kitsch portraits of Mexican icons cover the walls at this fun eatery. Specialties here include honey-glazed pork tacos and extra-spicy enchiladas.

Osaka $$
Fusion **Map** 4 C3
Soler 5608, Palermo Viejo
Tel *(011) 4775-6964* **Closed** *Sun*
One of this city's star restaurants, Osaka serves Peruvian-Japanese fusion food, merging varied ingredients and preparations of both cuisines.

Siamo nel Forno $$
Italian **Map** 4 C3
Costa Rica 5886, Palermo Viejo
Tel *(011) 4775-0337* **Closed** *Mon*
Family-owned pizzeria making thin-crust Neapolitan pizzas with simple, delicious toppings, including imported cheeses. The ambience is friendly and warm.

Tô $$
Fusion **Map** 4 C3
Costa Rica 6000, Palermo Viejo
Tel *(011) 4772-8569* **Closed** *Sun*
Innovations at the trendy Tô include a sushi belt, joining the menu of specialty Japanese-French fusion cuisine.

Sucre $$$
Modern Argentinian **Map** 4 C1
Sucre 676, Belgrano
Tel *(011) 4782-9082*
With a lavish interior, a creative, contemporary menu, and an ultraglamorous clientele to boast of, Sucre is loved by many as the very latest in sophisticated dining.

Tegui $$$
Modern Argentinian   Map 4 C3
Costa Rica 5852, Palermo Viejo
Tel *(011) 5291-3333*   **Closed** *Sun & Mon*
Exclusive restaurant deliberately hidden behind a graffitied wall. Choose from a four-course or eight-course tasting menu of seasonal Argentinian dishes.

DK Choice

Unik $$$
Modern Argentinian Map 5 D4
Soler 5132, Palermo Viejo
Tel *(011) 4772-2230*   **Closed** *Sun*
Eye-catching design and exciting cuisine combine at Unik, the floor space of which dazzles with Modernist seating and lighting produced in 1960s and 70s Europe. In its marbled open kitchen, chefs turn out seasonal specialties like sole carpaccio and slow-roasted lamb. A guest menu by Argentina's only two-Michelin-starred chef rounds out this superb culinary experience.

Farther Afield

Il Novo María del Luján $$
Traditional Argentinian   **Map** C3
Paseo Victoria 611, Tigre
Tel *(011) 4731-9613*
This family restaurant has a waterfront deck. The menu features meat and seafood dishes, including shellfish stews and king-crab-stuffed pastas with shrimp sauce.

Retro styling complements an inventive menu at Unik

The Pampas

BAHÍA BLANCA: Gambrinus $
German/Argentinian   **Map** C3
Arribeños 174, 8000
Tel *(0291) 456-2750*
Steeped in history and decorated with bric-a-brac, this casual institution serves German-influenced fare such as *knackwurst* along with hearty meat and fish dishes, and cold beer on tap.

BAHÍA BLANCA: Oliva $
Italian/Argentinian   **Map** C3
Dorrego 27, 8000
Tel *(0291) 451-8060*
Located near the Municipal Theater, Oliva offers a good range of entrées including pastas, risottos, seafood, and desserts such as New York cheesecake and tiramisu.

LA PLATA: Casa Enna $
Seafood   **Map** C3
Ruta 45 no. 940, 1900
Tel *(0221) 483-0485*   **Closed** *Sun*
Expect excellent high-concept gourmet cuisine with an emphasis on seafood that might include octopus and grouper in a regional herb glacé. A daily changing menu takes advantage of whatever is fresh and seasonal.

LA PLATA: Don Quijote $
Surf'n'Turf   **Map** C3
Plaza Paso 146, 1900
Tel *(0221) 483-3653*   **Closed** *Sun dinner*
Delicious cuisine and a welcoming staff is what makes this classic neighborhood restaurant such a favorite. Superb pastas and grilled meats as well as seafood offered at reasonable prices.

MAR DEL PLATA: Chichilo $
Seafood   **Map** C3
Comercial de Pul Puerto Local 17
Tel *(0223) 489-6317*
Casual seafood restaurant in the old port. Popular dishes include fried squid and hake, with most fish caught from the restaurant's own boat. Choose between cafeteria-style and sit-down service.

MAR DEL PLATA: Viento en Popa $
Seafood   **Map** C3
Ave Martínez de Hoz 257, 7600
Tel *(0223) 489-0220*   **Closed** *Mon–Wed*
This popular restaurant offers simple yet excellent seafood prepared to allow the natural flavors to come through. The delicious paella or cazuelas (seafood casserole) are popular choices.

NECOCHEA: Parrilla Chimichurri $
Parrilla   **Map** C3
Calle 83, 7630
Tel *(02262) 420-624*
Make a pit stop at this steakhouse, which serves up tasty cuts from an authentic *asador* grill, *brochettes*, offal delicacies, and sausage. It's a favorite with locals.

NECOCHEA: Terra Refugio Gastronomico $$
Fusion   **Map** C3
Calle 4 no. 4352, 7630
Tel *(02262) 523-335*
Terra Refugio Gastronomico offers inventive, well-prepared cuisine with thoughtful presentation, and an excellent selection of daily specials according to season. Vegtarians will rejoice at the variety of meat-free dishes.

Alfresco dining on the waterside terrace at Il Novo María del Luján

For more information on types of restaurants *see pp284–5*

PINAMAR: El Viejo Lobo $$
Seafood   **Map** D3
Ave del Mar, cnr Bunge, 7630
Tel *(02254) 483-218*
Acclaimed for its seafood dishes, this spacious restaurant combines a stylish dining experience with sea views. Not to be missed are the *gambas al ajillo* (prawns in garlic sauce) and the cod with butter and capers.

PINAMAR: Jalisco $$
Mexican   **Map** D3
Bunge 456, 7630
Tel *(02254) 493-166*   **Closed** *Mon & Thu*
Jalisco may be a little dearer than the *parrillos* serving local cuisine, but the food here is more authentic than most Mexican food in Argentina, and guests can ask the chef to make the meals as spicy as they want. The ambience is festive, and there are large fajita platters to share.

SAN ANTONIO DE ARECO: Almacen de Ramos Generales $
Parrilla   **Map** C3
Zapiola 143, 2760
Tel *(02326) 456-376*
The *asado* (barbecue) is popular here and diners can order premium cuts such as *bife de chorizo* (sirloin). Alternatives include a tasty *conejo al verdeo* (rabbit with spring onions) or a Basque seafood stew.

SAN ANTONIO DE ARECO: El Rancho $
Parrilla   **Map** C3
Zerboni and Belgrano, 2760
Tel *(02326) 1543-4934*
With a refreshing location in front of the Areco river, open-air grilled meats and fresh-caught river fish are the name of the game at this picture-postcard steakhouse.

SANTA ROSA: Los Pinos $
Parrilla   **Map** C3
Ave Spinetto 815, 6300
Tel *(02954) 437-242*   **Closed** *Sun*
Located in downtown Santa Rosa, Los Pinos is a traditional steakhouse that is always crowded. Dig into enormous sides of beef brought straight from the local cattle-rearing countryside, and relax in the friendly atmosphere.

SANTA ROSA: Siete 10 $
Italian/Argentinian   **Map** C3
Ave San Martín, cnr Urquiza, 6300
Tel *(02954) 243-030*
Go for the pizza and beer, stay for the lively music, young, upbeat vibe, and warm service. Reasonably priced set menus

on offer at lunchtime on the weekdays, and live DJ sets on the weekends.

DK Choice

TANDIL: Época de Quesos $
Cheese & Charcuterie   **Map** C3
14 de Julio 604, 7000
Tel *(0249) 444-8750*
The historic 1860 monument that Época de Quesos is housed in is itself worth a visit, but the irresistible platters of local cheeses and sausages make the experience all the more enjoyable. The food can be sampled on site as well as taken away. Ask for a *picada* (pre-meal platter served in small portions) if you want to try a morsel of everything.

VILLA GESELL: El Estribo $
Parrilla   **Map** D3
Ave 3, cnr Paseo 109, 7165
Tel *(02255) 460-234*
A much-loved *parrilla*, this Argentinian-style barbecue restaurant offers every possible cut of meat, including offal – salted and grilled until crunchy. Try the *bondiola* (pork shoulder) in a brown ale sauce. Do not miss the excellent "Don Pedro" dessert.

VILLA GESELL: El Viejo Hobbit $
Cheese & Charcuterie   **Map** D3
Ave 8 no. 1165, 7165
Tel *(02255) 465-851*   **Closed** *Sun–Thu*
Built to resemble a rustic hobbit house with a grass roof and wagon-wheel chandeliers, this casual pub-style restaurant specializes in home-brewed ale, cheese and sausage platters, and fondue.

Small but stylish in its decor and cuisine, Restaurant del Puerto, Colón

Argentinian Litoral

COLÓN: La Estancia $
Surf 'n' Turf   **Map** C2
Urquiza 158, 3280
Tel *(03447) 423-312*
Warm and atmospheric with creaky wooden floorboards, and walls decorated with ranch tools and wild boar and deer heads, La Estancia is a traditional, meat-dominated restaurant with friendly service.

COLÓN: Restaurant del Puerto $
Surf 'n' Turf   **Map** C2
Alejo Peyret 158, 3280
Tel *(03447) 422-698*   **Closed** *Wed*
A folksy little restaurant housed in a century-old antique home that is one of Colón's prettiest buildings. Expect creative takes on pasta, meats, and seafood. The *pacú* and *boga* fish are especially recommended.

CORRIENTES: La Morocha $
Surf 'n' Turf   **Map** C1
Salta 498, 3400
Tel *(0379) 443-8699*   **Closed** *Sun; Sat dinner*
Located in the heart of the city's historic neighborhood, this restaurant is housed in an atmospheric colonial building. The bistro-style menu has pastas, seafood, and meat dishes.

ESQUINA: El Aljibe $
Surf 'n' Turf   **Map** C2
Ave Costanera 628, 3450
Tel *(03777) 460-788*
Diners can watch cooks bake home-made empanadas and make fresh pastas at this local favorite. Other specialties include river fish such as *surubí* and *pacú*. There is occasional live music.

GUALEGUAYCHÚ: La Cascada $
Parrilla   **Map** C2
Ave Costanera 370, 2820
Tel *(03446) 432-451*
This family-oriented *parrilla* has a convenient location and a convivial atmosphere. Beef sizzles on a fixed spit, and there are crisp pizzas. Adults can visit the on-site wine-tasting salon.

MERCEDES: Sabor Único Restobar $
Italian/Argentinian   **Map** C2
Ave San Martín 518, 3470
Tel *(03773) 441-557*   **Closed** *Mon*
Located in a beautiful historic home, this eatery serves standard Argentinian fare such as *milanesas* (breaded veal cutlets), steaks, and pastas. There is a garden and a play area for kids.

Glass-walled dining area at La Rueda 1975, Puerto Iguazú

PARANÁ: Bilú $
Fusion   Map C2
*Gregoria Matorras de San Martín
898, 3100*
Tel *(0343) 431-2324*   **Closed** *Mon*
Bilú offers a fun, relaxed
ambience, outdoor seating, and
a lovely view of the river – the
source of most of the fresh fish
on the menu. There are pasta and
meat dishes too. Good wine list.

PARANÁ: Giovani $
Surf 'n' Turf   Map C2
Urquiza 1047, 3100
Tel *(0343) 423-0527*
Giovani serves decent food in a
prime location. While river fish
dishes feature prominently on this
menu, steak and pastas are also
available, and diners rave about
the lasagne. Laid-back service.

**PUERTO IGUAZÚ:
La Rueda 1975** $
Traditional Argentinian   Map D1
Ave Córdoba 28, 3370
Tel *(03757) 422-531*   **Closed** *Mon &
Tue: lunch*
A favorite with Iguazú's well-
to-do residents, La Rueda 1975
has a bustling atmosphere, and a
subtropics-inspired menu
and decor. Mouthwatering
river fish as well as standard
parrilla options are available.

PUERTO IGUAZÚ: La Vitrina $
Traditional Argentinian   Map D1
Ave Victoria Aguirre 773, 3370
Tel *(03757) 422-465*
La Vitrina is a great spot
for a long, leisurely lunch,
especially on the garden
terrace with its tables dressed
in crisp white tablecloths and
formally arranged tableware.
Mains are fairly standard but
the desserts are divine.

PUERTO IGUAZÚ: Aqva $$
Surf 'n' Turf   Map D1
Ave Córdoba, cnr Carlos Thays, 3370
Tel *(03757) 422-064*
Softly lit and romantic, Aqva's
decor features native wood
and stone. The menu includes
caviar starters and exquisite
pasta, as well as decadent
fish dishes accented with
passion fruit and coconut.
Top-notch service.

**PUERTO IGUAZÚ: La Vaca
Enamorada** $$
Parrilla   Map D1
Ave Republica Argentina 79, 3370
Tel *(03757) 421-179*   **Closed** *Mon*
The immensely popular La Vaca
has an ever-changing bistro-style
menu featuring fresh, seasonal
products. There is ample seating
should you want to eat outdoors.

ROSARIO: Deck del Náutico $
Surf 'n' Turf   Map C2
*Club Náutico de Rosario, Comunidad
Foral de Navarra & 104, 2000*
Tel *(0341) 426-3352*   **Closed** *Sun;
Mon dinner*
Housed within Rosario's yacht
club, Deck del Náutico is a
romantic dining spot with
stylish decor and a candlelit
terrace overlooking Rio Parana.
The menu features river fish, like
surubí, and barbecued meats.

ROSARIO: Puerto Gaboto $
Seafood   Map C2
Pellegrini 584, 2000
Tel *(0341) 447-1024*
This recently renovated
restaurant is highly
recommended for its catch of
the day and seafood menu.
Great ambience and located
close to the river. Other cuisines
also available.

DK Choice

**ROSARIO: Verde Que te
Quiero Verde** $
Vegetarian   Map C2
Córdoba 1358, 2000
Tel *(0341) 530-4419*   **Closed** *Sun*
Occupying an attractive, light-
filled space, Verde Que te
Quiero Verde is a mecca for
vegetarians, health nuts, and
design lovers alike. Serving
breakfast, lunch, and dinner as
well as Saturday brunch, Verde
uses organic ingredients and
prepares everything in-house.

SANTA FE: La Vuelta del Pirata $
Seafood   Map C2
*Calle Mandubé s/n, Pje. Los Zapallos
(Sta. Rosa de Calchines), 2000*
Tel *(0342) 499-7024*
A Santa Fe classic set on the
river, with a family-friendly
ambience. All diners pay the
same price (drinks not included)
and are offered a list of mains
heavy on river fish preparations
such as *suburí* fish croquettes.
Milanesa also available.

SANTA FE: Resto España $$
Spanish/Argentinian   Map C2
Calle San Martín 2644, 2000
Tel *(0342) 400-0472*
Traditional eatery housed in a
century-old building with
colonnades and stained-glass
windows, and owned by the
same Spanish family for more
than 30 years. The menu
features Spanish specialties
such as paella.

Córdoba and the
Andean Northwest

**ALTA GRACIA: El Bistro del
Alquimista** $
International   Map B2
Arzobispo Castellanos 351, 5186
Tel *(0351) 615-4312*   **Closed** *Sun*
Experimental bistro with a menu
that changes daily to explore
different themes and national
cuisines. The 14-course tasting
menu is an outstanding culinary
experience, with Chef Max
introducing each dish.

CACHI: Comedor El Aujero $
Parrilla   Map B1
Ruis de los Llanos s/n, 4417
Tel *(03868) 1545-5711*
No-frills *parrilla* with only outdoor
seating, known for grilling up
llama and goat meat and for
their stuffed green peppers.
The portions are big enough
to share.

Pared-down interior design at Brindillas in Luján de Cuyo

CACHI: Sala de Payogasta $$
Andean   **Map** B1
Ruta Nacional 40, Km 4509, 4417
Tel *(03868) 496-052*
Excellent place to savor regional specialties such as *humitas* (corn tamale), *locro*, and variations on goat's cheese and honey for dessert.

CAFAYATE: El Rancho $
Andean   **Map** B1
Toscano 4, 4427
Tel *(03868) 421-256*
El Rancho serves consistently good local corn-based dishes such as *humitas*, along with their wonderful grilled goat and baked empanadas. Desserts include white cheese with fruit preserves.

CAFAYATE: Finca Las Nubes $$
Cheese & Charcuterie   **Map** B1
El Divisidero, 4427
Tel *(03868) 422-129*   **Closed** *Sun, except Jan & Feb*
This restaurant is a part of wine tours and requires reservations be made two days in advance. Sample top wines paired with delicious cheese, cured meats, and empanadas, with a set menu centered on grilled meats. Lunch only.

CÓRDOBA: Belgrano 1340 $
Italian/Argentinian   **Map** B2
Belgrano 1340, 5889
Tel *(03544) 471-110*
Refreshingly simple restaurant serving well-prepared, fresh pastas using local trout, goat's cheese, superb bruschetta, and other regional products. Attentive service.

CÓRDOBA: Doc Vinos & Cocina $$
Fine Dining   **Map** C2
Ave Concepción Arenal 718, 5000
Tel *(0351) 460-8012*   **Closed** *Sun & Mon*
Detail-oriented staff at this intimate place. Upmarket takes on seafood and meat courses, and a seasonal menu that promises freshness. Tasting menu available with wine pairings selected by the chef.

LA CUMBRE: El Buho $
Pub   **Map** B2
Belgrano 437, 5194
Tel *(03548) 452-314*   **Closed** *Mon–Wed during low season*
A warm, inviting pub, El Buho serves four kinds of the name-sake artisanal beer along with sandwiches, wraps, pizza, tacos, and other brewpub-style food. Reserve in advance or arrive early to beat the crowds.

LA CUMBRE: La Casona del Toboso $
Surf 'n' Turf   **Map** B2
Belgrano 349, 5194
Tel *(03548) 451-436*
Housed in a little cottage, La Casona del Toboso is La Cumbre's best-known restaurant, popular for its fresh local trout, succulent goat, grilled meats, and pasta. There is a charming outdoor patio.

MOLINOS: Estancia Colomé $
Cheese & Charcuterie   **Map** B1
Ruta Provincial 53, Km 20, 4419
Tel *(03868) 494-200*
Elegant dining at Argentina's oldest winery. Open for lunch only, Estancia Colomé offers refined cheese and meat platters, empanadas, and salads. Most of the ingredients are grown organically on site. Reservations required.

SALTA: El Solar del Convento $
Parrilla   **Map** B1
Caseros 444, 4400
Tel *(0387) 421-5124*
This is the best place in Salta town to come for a huge steak. There is a complimentary glass of fizz to start off the meal. The decor is rustic, with handwoven saddle blankets and animal masks.

SALTA: José Balcarce $
Surf 'n' Turf   **Map** B1
Necochea 594, 4400
Tel *(0387) 421-1628*
José Balcarce is a must-visit for anyone coming to Salta, for innovative cuisine using the best ingredients from the Andean larder. Standout dishes include llama carpaccio and trout with ginger.

SALTA: La Casona de Molino $
Andean   **Map** B1
Luis Burela 1, 4400
Tel *(0387) 434-2835*   **Closed** *Mon*
An authentic *peña*, or gathering place, with food, drink, and traditional folk music. Each spacious dining room has a different set of singers who perform around the tables. The cuisine consists of traditional Andean fare.

DK Choice

SALTA: La Table de House of Jasmines $$
Fine Dining   **Map** B1
Ruta Nacional 51, Km 6, 4427
Tel *(0387) 497-2002*
Impeccable taste and stunning natural beauty meld perfectly at this wine lodge restaurant. The menu offers the best of Andean and Argentinian cuisine – and the dishes are made with herbs and vegetables from their own garden.

SAN MIGUEL DE TUCUMÁN: El Fondo $
Parrilla   **Map** B1
San Martín 848, 4000
Tel *(0381) 422-2161*   **Closed** *Sun dinner*
One of the best *parrillas* in town, El Fondo is famous for its sweet and slightly spicy empanadas, and steaming bowls of *locro*. There is a salad bar and an excellent wine list as well. Live music on the weekends.

SAN SALVADOR DE JUJUY: Manos Jujeñas $
Traditional Argentinian   **Map** B1
Senador Pérez 379, 4600
Tel *(0388) 424-3270*
This place was started by a group of women more than two decades ago with the aim of preserving traditional recipes. Affordable regional specialties on offer here include empanadas, *humitas*, and *locro*.

VILLA GENERAL BELGRANO: Viejo Munich $
German/Argentinian   **Map** B2
Ave San Martín 362, 5194
Tel *(03546) 463-122*
A local favorite, Viejo Munich has a German-influenced menu serving venison and trout platters, sauerkraut, and traditional smoked meats. Wash them down with an artisanal beer brewed on site.

Cuyo and the Wine Country

GODOY CRUZ: 1884 $$$
Fine Dining   Map B2
Belgrano 1188, 5501
Tel *(0261) 424-3336*
This prestigious restaurant by famous Argentinian chef Francis Mallmann is located in the beautiful surroundings of Bodegas Escorihuela Gascón. Fresh, regional ingredients, and a superb Patagonian-style menu.

LUJÁN DE CUYO: Casa de Contratista $$
Traditional Argentinian   Map B2
Almirante Brown 1761, 5505
Tel *(0261) 496-5967*   **Closed** *Mon–Thu; Sun dinner*
Food, wine, and art come together at this country estate turned cultural center. The hearty, simple menu offers fish, meats, casseroles, and snacks. Outdoor tables overlook Malbec vineyards.

LUJÁN DE CUYO: Brindillas $$$
Fine Dining   Map B2
Guardia Vieja 2898, 5509
Tel *(0261) 496-3650*   **Closed** *Sun & Mon*
An enjoyable restaurant with a sleek design and superlative food. Try their five- to seven-course tasting menu for inventive and flavorful gourmet takes on local products.

LUJÁN DE CUYO: Cavas Wine Lodge $$$
Fine Dining   Map B2
Costaflores s/n, Alto Agrelo, 5507
Tel *(0261) 410-6927*
Romantic candlelit ambience at a luxury hotel, with panoramic views of the Andes. Meats such as slow-roasted lamb and beef are served with organic vegetables. Reservations required. No children under 12.

LUJÁN DE CUYO: Ruca Malén $$$
Fine Dining   Map B2
Ruta Nacional 7, Km 1059, 5507
Tel *(0261) 413-8909*
A winery restaurant known for fine five-course meals of beef, trout, or chicken, paired with generous samples of premium red and white vintages. Indoor and terrace dining are available.

MAIPÚ: Cavé Gourmet $
Gourmet   Map B2
Zanichilli 709, 5515
Tel *(0261) 410-6597*   **Closed** *Apr–Sep*
This delicatessen is known for signature items grown, dried, pickled, and packed in-house,

most of which the restaurant features in its five-course tasting menu. A guided tour is included with lunch.

MALARGÜE: El Bodegón de María $
Italian/Argentinian   Map B3
Ave Gral Ortega 502, 5613
Tel *(02627) 471-655*
Quality home-style cooking in an unpretentious, rural environment with pleasant service. The pasta, pizza, and beef are worthwhile, but the *caprese* empanadas and trout are amazing.

MENDOZA: Décimo $
International   Map B2
Garibaldi 7, 10th Floor, 5500
Tel *(0261) 434-0135*   **Closed** *Sun*
Located on the 10th floor of a nondescript building, Décimo is the place for sweeping views of the glittering lights of Mendoza. Well-prepared cocktails and standard fare. Laid-back service.

MENDOZA: Facundo $
Parrilla   Map B3
Sarmiento 641, 5500
Tel *(0261) 420-2866*
Well-established, bright, and cheerful grill, popular with tourists. There are *parrilla* meat classics, international dishes, a salad bar, and great appetizers on offer.

MENDOZA: La Florencia $
Parrilla   Map B3
Sarmiento 698, 5500
Tel *(0261) 429-1564*
This casual *parrilla* caters more to Mendoza locals than tourists, with Argentinian favorites like *milanesa* cutlets and grilled beef. Rustic-chic decor as well as relaxed outdoor seating.

MENDOZA: Mar y Monte $
Chilean/Argentinian   Map B3
Perú 765, 5500
Tel *(0261) 200-4929*
Mar y Monte merges Chilean seafood with Argentinian standards that include wild game. A distinctive menu offers enjoyable meals.

MENDOZA: Tasca de La Plaza España $
Spanish/Argentinian   Map B3
Montevideo 117, 5500
Tel *(0261) 423-1403*   **Closed** *Sun*
A casual spot with eclectic decor. Come here for wonderfully executed tapas and superb seafood dishes.

MENDOZA: Anna Bistro $$
Fine Dining   Map B3
Ave Juan B. Justo 161, 5500
Tel *(0261) 425-1818*
Elegant, acclaimed bistro founded by two French brothers. Choose from several set menus and over 200 wines. Attentive service and charming garden seating.

MENDOZA: Azafrán $$
Fine Dining   Map B3
Sarmiento 765, 5500
Tel *(0261) 429-4200*
This casual yet refined place is a pleasant place to dine. Good salad selection and beautifully presented mains. Try the kid and mushroom raviolis.

MENDOZA: Bistro M $$
Italian/Argentinian   Map B3
Chile 1124, 5500
Tel *(0261) 441-1200*
Located off the lobby of the Park Hyatt, with delightful terrace seating. Authentic dishes made from fresh, local ingredients prepared in an open kitchen.

Palatial architecture at hotel and restaurant Cavas Wine Lodge

For more information on types of restaurants *see pp284–5*

Enjoy charming garden seating at the acclaimed Anna Bistro (see p295)

MENDOZA: Francesco $$
Italian/Argentinian **Map** B3
Chile 1268, 5500
Tel (0261) 425-3912 **Closed** Sun
One of the most well-respected Italian restaurants in Mendoza, and the sister-restaurant of La Marchigiana (below), Francesco's specialties include pastas and risotto, as well as fish and red meat dishes. Formal ambience and an extensive wine list.

MENDOZA: La Marchigiana $$
Italian/Argentinian **Map** B3
Patricias Mendocinas 1550, 5500
Tel (0261) 423-0751
Flagship location of a traditional Italian eatery that is well loved by locals. Tempting home-made pastas, especially the lasagne, gracious service, and good wines.

MENDOZA:
María Antonieta $$
Gourmet **Map** B3
Belgrano 1069, 5500
Tel (0261) 420-4322 **Closed** Sun dinner
This delightful restaurant serves basic dishes with a gourmet tilt, using seasonal produce, including pastas, casseroles, and grilled meats. Home-baked pastries and freshly squeezed juice make for a first-rate brunch.

MENDOZA: Praga $$
Seafood **Map** B3
Julio Leonidas Aguirre 413, 5500
Tel (0261) 425-9585 **Closed** Sun
Praga has attractive dining rooms with open-air seating that faces a small park. Quality seafood includes octopus, salmon, and trout, along with meats and pasta, and a good selection of white wines.

SAN AGUSTÍN DEL VALLE FÉRTIL: La Gran Picada $
Traditional Argentinian **Map** B2
Rivadavia s/n, 5449
Tel (0264) 154-991970
Excellent restaurant but with limited menu options. The simple yet cozy ambience is enhanced by the personalized attention bestowed by the on-site owner. Try the goat-meat empanadas.

SAN JUAN: De Sánchez $
Fusion **Map** B2
Rivadavia 61 Oeste, 5400
Tel (0264) 420-3670 **Closed** Sun
San Juan's only high-end restaurant has a French-inspired menu and light dishes with visual flair incorporating quail eggs and other delicacies. Music and books for sale line the walls.

SAN JUAN: Club Sirio Libanés - Palito $$
Fusion **Map** B2
Entre Rios 33 Sur, 5402
Tel (0264) 422-3841 **Closed** Sun
Unique mix of Middle Eastern and Argentinian cuisine set against a grand backdrop of Moorish architecture. Offerings include falafel, stuffed grape leaves, and lamb empanadas. Efficient, formal service.

SAN LUIS: Floating Tearoom at Potrero de los Funes $
Modern Argentinian **Map** B2
Ruta 18, Km 16, 5701
Tel (0266) 444-0038
This sleek, sophisticated hotel restaurant floats atop the lake and offers splendid views of the Andes. Modern cuisine with a good variety of seafood, meat, and pasta dishes, along with an extensive wine list.

Simple fare in cozy surroundings at Patagonicus, El Chaltén

SAN LUIS: Los Robles $
Parrilla **Map** B2
9 de Julio 754, 5701
Tel (0266) 443-6767
Locally considered the best *parrilla* in town for its hearty steaks, especially the *bife de chorizo* (sirloin). Good wine list, pleasant service, and an airy ambience with brick walls and lofty wood-beam ceilings.

SAN RAFAEL: Naranja-Blue $
German/Argentinian **Map** B3
Las Vírgenes 7200, 5600
Tel (0267) 1534-3931 **Closed** Sun–Wed
Authentic German cuisine served in a rustic cabin in a country setting. Expect pork with *spaetzle* (dumplings), vegetarian strudel (layered pastry), *gulasch* (meat stew), and home-baked bread paired with excellent artisanal and imported beers.

DK Choice

SAN RAFAEL: L'Obrador $$
Argentinian **Map** B3
Camino Bentos 50, 5600
Tel (0260) 443-2723
A truly unparalleled experience. Chef and owner Daniel welcomes guests to this ranch house with a spread of home-cooked, regional favorites, and takes suggestions for the main course. Come with a GPS, cash, and lots of time. Call ahead to make reservations since they do not have a fixed day for closing.

TUNUYÁN: La Posada del Jamón $
Cheese & Charcuterie **Map** B3
Ruta 92, Km 14, 5502
Tel (02622) 492-053
Pork done every which way, even dried ham cured in the region's famous Malbec wine. Large portions are great for sharing. Extensive wine list and great staff eager to share advice about the area. Lunch daily, dinner on Thursday and Friday only.

TUNUYÁN: Killka $$
Fine Dining **Map** B3
Ruta 89 s/n, Los Árboles, 5502
Tel (02622) 429-570
Part of the ultramodern cultural center at winery Bodegas Salentein. Fixed-price lunches with trout and lamb as specialties can be combined with wine tastings. Fine views of the vineyards and the Andes.

Patagonia

BARILOCHE: Jauja $
Traditional Argentinian   Map B4
Elflein 148, 8400
Tel *(0294) 442-2952*
A delightful, popular eatery
that excels in Argentinian
specialties, from trout to
salmon and lamb to venison.
The ambience is lively; request
a table on the main level as the
upstairs can get noisy.

BARILOCHE: Mundo de la Pizza $
Italian/Argentinian   Map B4
Mitre 759, 8400
Tel *(0294) 442-3461*
This upbeat pizzeria, set in
the house of former pro-skier
Hugo Francioni, has more
than 100 varieties of pizza
on its menu, some including
exotic toppings such as salmon
and wild boar.

**BARILOCHE: El Boliche
de Alberto** $$
Parrilla   Map B4
Villegas 347, 8400
Tel *(0294) 443-1433*
Cowhide menus set the tone for
the sizzling, juicy steaks to come
at this classic, family-owned
parrilla. Alberto's relatives man a
huge flame grill and wait tables,
serving authentic, reasonably
priced food.

BARILOCHE: Kandahar $$
Surf 'n' Turf   Map B4
20 de Febrero 698, 8400
Tel *(0294) 442-4702*
This elegant restaurant serves
traditional fare that focuses on
local meats such as venison,
lamb, and wild hare, and pastas
made with superbly fresh
mushrooms and herbs from
their own garden.

**COMODORO RIVADAVIA:
Puerto Cangrejo** $$
Seafood   Map B5
Ave Costanera 1051, 9000
Tel *(0297) 444-4590*
Located in the port area,
Puerto Cangrejo is the city's
most traditional restaurant,
serving decent seafood and
offering spectacular sea views.
Very popular, so plan to arrive
early or reserve ahead of time.

EL BOLSÓN: Patio Venzano $
Traditional Argentinian   Map B4
Sarmiento and Hube, 8430
Housed in a cypress-wood
cabin, this family-run eatery
dishes up delicious house
specialties such as fresh trout,
lamb stew, pastas, and tasty

Elegant dining with an attentive host at L'Obrador, San Rafael

sweet and savory pancakes.
Romantic ambience.

EL CALAFATE: Mi Rancho $
Traditional Argentinian   Map B6
Gobernador Moyano 1089, 9405
Tel *(02902) 490-540*
Tucked away on a quiet side
street, this cosy and traditional
spot specializes in lamb and
steak. Intimate ambience and
good service. Tables fill up fast, so
come early or reserve a table to
avoid disappointment.

DK Choice

EL CALAFATE: Pura Vida $
Italian/Argentinian   Map B6
*Ave Libertador Gral San Martín
1876, 9405*
Tel *(02902) 493-356* **Closed** *Wed*
Pura Vida is all about relaxed
dining, with lakeside views and
a homey, eclectic decor. The
menu offers mouthwatering
home-made pastas, pot pies,
and stews made of pumpkin
and rabbit, as well as many
vegetarian dishes.

**EL CALAFATE: Casimiro
Biguá** $$
Fine Dining   Map B6
*Ave del Libertador Gral San
Martín 963, 9405*
Tel *(02902) 492-590*
An upmarket *parrilla* and wine
bar on the main street that hums
with the chatter of diners. Expect
king crab, wild boar, and other
regional specialties, served in a
cozy, fireside ambience.

EL CALAFATE: Don Pichón $$
Parrilla   Map B6
Puerto Deseado 242, 9405
Tel *(02902) 492-577* **Closed** *Mon*
Perched on a hill, this restaurant
offers beautiful views of the
Andes peaks and Lake Argentino.
Wagon-wheel chandeliers light
the spacious dining room.

Lamb and beef barbecue is
the speciality here. Shuttle
service available.

EL CALAFATE: La Tablita $$
Parrilla   Map B6
Coronel Rosales 28, 9405
Tel *(02902) 491-065*
An iconic if no-frills *parrilla* open
since 1968, La Tablita is popular
among travelers and locals for its
tender spit-roasted Patagonian
lamb, and ice cream made from
the local Calafate berry.

EL CHALTÉN: Patagonicus $
Italian/Argentinian   Map A5
Güemes 140, 9301
Tel *(02962) 493-025* **Closed** *May–
Sep; Wed*
Perhaps the best pizza in
El Chaltén, made thin-crust-
style and with no skimping
on excellent toppings
that include local lamb. Start
with a hot, fresh soup, and
then wash everything down
with an artisanal ale.

EL CHALTÉN: Estepa $$
Surf 'n' Turf   Map A5
Cerro Solo, cnr Antonio Rojo, 9301
Tel *(02962) 493-069*
A snug spot, Estepa has a
cabin-like atmosphere and live
jazz upon occasion. The service
is charming. The restaurant is
known for its Patagonian lamb
but also serves freshwater
fish, pastas, and other
vegetarian options.

EL CHALTÉN: Ruca Mahuida $$
Traditional Argentinian   Map A5
Lionel Terray 55, 9301
Tel *(02962) 493-018* **Closed** *Apr–
late Oct*
Standout menu based on
regional ingredients with
irresistible combinations such as
tenderloin in Malbec with
quinoa, mushroom ragout and
yams, and lavender-roasted pork.
Cozy, rustic ambience.

For more information on types of restaurants *see pp284–5*

ESQUEL: Don Chiquino $
Italian/Argentinian Map B4
Ameghino 1641, 9200
Tel *(02945) 450-035*
This Esquel establishment is known for its pastas, the country clutter-chic decor, and the animated owner Tito, who moves from table to table performing magic tricks and regaling guests with stories of his family's history.

ESQUEL: La Luna $
Pub Map B4
Ave Fontana 656, 9200
Tel *(02945) 453-800*
Good food and drink in a pub-style ambience with beer posters and a long bar ideal for solo diners. Standard fare including pizzas, burgers, and sandwiches. Pleasant outdoor seating.

GAIMAN: Gwalia Lan $$
Traditional Argentinian Map B4
Ave Eugenio Tello, cnr Jones, 9105
Tel *(02965) 1568-2352* **Closed** *Mon; Sun dinner*
Homey and inviting, this is the perfect place to recoup after battling Patagonia's elements. It has a dimly lit, cavern-like interior, and excels at home-made pastas and sweet confections served as dessert or during tea hour.

PUERTO MADRYN: Mariscos del Atlántico $$
Seafood Map B4
Fennen 43, 9120
Tel *(02965) 1555-2500* **Closed** *Sun*
The ideal fisherman's restaurant with ocean views, clapboard walls, and nets hung from rafters. Serves up first-rate seafood including fresh clams hand-picked on dawn dives by family members. Friendly service.

PUERTO MADRYN: Plácido $$
Surf'n'Turf Map B4
Ave Roca 506, 9120
Tel *(0280) 445-5991*
The restaurant for travelers who like to dine in style, Plácido has romantic ocean views, smooth service, and an above-par wine list. The menu has everything from Patagonian lamb to pastas to seafood. Jazz music plays.

PUERTO MADRYN: Unamesa $$
Fine Dining Map B4
Belgrano 346, 9120
Tel *(02965) 474-479* **Closed** *Mon*
Excellent little owner-operated restaurant decorated with local art, in a cozy, cheery environment. The seasonally changing menu uses produce grown onsite, fresh fish, and meats cooked to perfection.

PUERTO MADRYN: Vernardino Club del Mar $$
Surf'n'Turf Map B4
Blvd Brown 860, 9120
Tel *(0280) 547-4289*
On the beach or close to the sea on the terrace, Vernardino boasts panoramic ocean views. Surprisingly, the meat dishes are usually better than the seafood. Friendly service and a kid's play area makes this good for families.

SAN MARTÍN DE LOS ANDES: Doña Quela $$
Surf'n'Turf Map B4
Ave San Martín 1017, 8370
Tel *(02972) 420-670*
Housed in a former hotel – the oldest building in town – this restaurant retains an authentic historic feel. Hearty meals include lake trout, wild boar, and venison smoked in a 100-year-old fire pit.

SAN MARTÍN DE LOS ANDES: Ku $$
Parrilla Map B4
Ave San Martín 1053, 8370
Tel *(02972) 427-039*
Snug and rustic, Ku is a mainstay of the San Martín culinary scene, offering the most delicious desserts in town and hearty meals mainly consisting of wild meats such as venison or boar.

SAN MARTÍN DE LOS ANDES: La Tasca $$
Traditional Argentinian Map B4
Mariano Moreno 866, 8370
Tel *(02972) 428-663*
Part restaurant, part treasure trove, La Tasca is an Alpine-style restaurant with antique wine caskets and machinery and other knick-knacks as decor. Hearty meals include venison ravioli and wild mushroom soup.

Robust, warming fare at Ku, in San Martín de los Andes

SAN MARTÍN DE LOS ANDES: Reserva Merlot $$
Fusion Map B4
Belgrano 940, 8370
Tel *(02972) 428-734*
Elegant and romantic interiors with pleasant outdoor dining. Elaborate dishes range from sushi to pastas to grilled trout, all prepared with the "slow food" philosophy, sourcing produce locally.

VIEDMA: El Barco $
Fusion Map C4
Ave Villarino 850, 8500
Tel *(02920) 426-353* **Closed** *Sun*
A decent restaurant in a town with few options, El Barco offers standard Argentinian fare with nightly themes such as Sushi Wednesdays and Mexican Thursdays. Good deck seating with river views.

VILLA LA ANGOSTURA: Tinto Bistro $$
Fusion Map B4
Nahuel Huapi 34, 8407
Tel *(02944) 494-924* **Closed** *Sun*
Tinto is considered a top dining spot for its creative, international-style menu serving gourmet quesadillas, stir-fries, *ceviches*, declicious salads, rib-eye steak, and fresh trout, all subtly flavored. Excellent wine selection.

Tierra del Fuego and Antarctica

RÍO GRANDE: Don Peppone $
Italian/Argentinian Map B6
Perito Moreno 247, 9420
Tel *(02964) 432-066*
Friendly service and comfortable surroundings can be found in this recently revamped pizzeria. Expect classic Italian fodder and a lively atmosphere.

RÍO GRANDE: El Roca $
Confitería Map B6
Espora 643, 9420
Tel *(02964) 4230-693*
This longstanding classic Argentinian café is considered part of local history. Admire the photograph-adorned walls as you warm up with a cup of coffee or tuck into a hearty sandwich or hamburger.

RÍO GRANDE: Posada de los Sauces $
Traditional Argentinian Map B6
Elcano 839, 9420
Tel *(02964) 430-868*
This is Río Grande's best dining option, located within an inn of the same name and

Ushuaia's cosmopolitan dining option and wine bar, Gustino

offering meat, fish, and pasta mains. Head upstairs for post-prandial drinks and chatter.

USHUAIA: Christopher Grill & Cerveza $
Parrilla   Map B6
Maipu 828, 9410
Tel *(02901) 425-079*
Located on the waterfront, Christopher's serves up mouthwatering barbecue ribs and pork loin, king crab raviolis, and brick-oven pizza. It can get quite lively during busy hours.

USHUAIA: Dublin Pub $
Pub   Map B6
9 de Julio 168, 9410
Tel *(02901) 430-744*
A convivial atmosphere makes the Dublin Pub popular with locals and tourists alike who come to kick back with a cold beer. Casual fare such as pizza and burgers is served. Come early to beat the crowds.

USHUAIA: La Casa de los Mariscos $
Seafood   Map B6
San Martín 232, 9410
Tel *(02901) 430-100*
A more inexpensive alternative to other Ushuaia restaurants. Savor king crab in various guises – with Parmesan, in casseroles, cold and fresh with mayonnaise, or as chowder. Old-fashioned decor and helpful wait staff.

USHUAIA: Moustacchio $
Parrilla   Map B6
Ave San Martín 298, 9410
Tel *(02901) 423-308*
For nearly 40 years, this family-run barbecue restaurant has served traditional Argentinian meat cuts, which diners can watch sizzle over a fire. Good wine list.

USHUAIA: Tierra Mayor $
Parrilla   Map B6
Ruta 3, Km 3018, 9410
Tel *(02901) 423-240*
Though located out of town, the all-you-can-eat spit-roasted lamb at this winter activity hub is worth the drive. Husky-sled rides and snowshoe hikes are also available. Closed from mid-May through mid-Jun.

USHUAIA: Chez Manu $$
Fine Dining   Map B6
Luis Martial 2135, 9410
Tel *(02901) 432-253*
Featuring wraparound windows and panoramic views, Chez Manu is a taxi ride or 10-minute walk from the center. The French chef employs French techniques with regional products such as hake, rabbit, lamb, and scallops.

USHUAIA: Kaupé $$
Seafood   Map B6
Roca 470, 9410
Tel *(02901) 422-704*   **Closed** *Sun*
Located a short walk up an incline from the city center, Kaupé is a small yet sophisticated restaurant and wine bar specializing in king crab, including a rich crab crêpe in saffron sauce. A tasting menu is also available.

USHUAIA: Le Martial $$
Fine Dining   Map B6
Las Hayas Resort Hotel, Luis Martial 1650, 9410
Tel *(02901) 430-710*
Part of the luxurious Las Hayas hotel, Le Martial is Ushuaia's most elegant eatery. Exquisitely furnished, it is known for its beautifully executed and seafood-focused cuisine. Stunning views of the Canal Beagle.

USHUAIA: María Lola $$
Seafood   Map B6
Deloqui 1048, 9410
Tel *(02901) 421-185*   **Closed** *Sun*
Clean architectural lines and a hip, refreshing interior. House specialties include seafood risotto and salmon ravioli. Super desserts as well, and a great view of the Canal Beagle.

USHUAIA: Tante Nina $$
Seafood   Map B6
Godoy 15, 9410
Tel *(02901) 432-444*
What this family-run seafood establishment lacks in personality it makes up for in quality dishes. Try the black hake in leek sauce and king crab stew.

USHUAIA: Tía Elvira $$
Seafood   Map B6
Maipú 349, 9410
Tel *(02901) 424-725*   **Closed** *Jul; Sun*
Housed in a pretty oceanfront building and run by a German-Argentinian family, Tía Elvira serves uncomplicated seafood specialties and tasty German-inspired desserts such as home-made apple strudel.

USHUAIA: Volver $$
Seafood   Map B6
Maipú 37, 9410
Tel *(02901) 423-977*   **Closed** *Mon lunch*
The popular and atmospheric Volver is a throwback to the region's pioneer past, with a jumble of antiques hanging throughout the interiors. The seafood dishes are simply presented but packed full of flavor.

USHUAIA: Gustino $$$
Surf'n'Turf   Map B6
Maipú 505, 9410
Tel *(02901) 430-003*
A light-filled café, restaurant, and wine bar with a seasonally changing menu that offers regional specialties such as black sea bass, king crab, and lamb. The wine bar has extensive offerings.

For more information on types of restaurants *see pp284–5*

SHOPPING IN ARGENTINA

Shopping is tremendous fun in Argentina and reason enough in itself to visit the country. Foreign visitors will find that prices for locally produced goods, including luxury buys such as leather items and jewelry, are very reasonable. Added to this is a great variety of shopping centers: in the major cities there are swanky, modern malls, department stores, and exclusive high-fashion boutiques that stock imported goods and brand names. In the country's interior, several small towns are renowned for their colorful and atmospheric artisans' markets that usually take place over the weekends. They sell locally made products that include crafted gaucho paraphernalia and high-quality weavings and ceramics.

The glittering interiors of Galerías Pacífico, Buenos Aires *(see p95)*

Bargaining

Bargaining is much less common in Argentina than in other Latin American countries. Try the question *Cuanto vale?* (How much is it worth?) in place of the usual *Cuanto cuesta?* (What is the price?) Only at crafts' markets and antiques shops do vendors sometimes start at a higher price than the one they accept. Visitors may feel confident enough to make a lower offer here, particularly when purchasing a combination of items.

Opening Hours

In cities, malls usually open from 10am to 10pm daily. Food courts and cinemas within malls stay open later. Street shops usually open from 9am to 8pm on weekdays; some close at 1pm on Saturdays, and remain shut on Sundays. In the small towns of Argentina, store owners usually close for a siesta between 1 and 4:30pm.

How to Pay

Cash is universally accepted, preferably the Argentinian peso. Many places also accept US dollars. Credit cards are widely accepted in cities, unlike small towns in Argentina's interior. Preferred cards are MasterCard and Visa, and to a lesser extent American Express.

Taxes and Refunds

Argentina's local sales tax is called *Impuesto al Valor Agregado* (IVA). The current rate is 21 percent and is included in the advertised price for goods.

Visitors are able to reclaim IVA on their purchase when buying products made in Argentina worth AR$70 or more from shops displaying a **Global Refund** logo. Ask for a *factura* (receipt) and a Global Refund cheque when making a purchase. These should be stamped at customs prior to departure; you will then be sent to a *puesto de pago* for the refund. These desks are located at several Argentinian airports.

Handicrafts shop in Quilmes, Tucumán *(see p193)*

Shopping Malls and Boutiques

Shopping malls, ranging from modest buildings to plush, air-conditioned establishments, are ubiquitous in Argentinian towns and cities. Some, such as the Galerías Pacífico *(see p95)* mall in Buenos Aires and **El Palacio** in Salta, are housed in lovely, old landmark buildings. Many of these malls have multiplex cinemas, food courts, and also play areas for kids. High-end international brands of clothing, perfume, and jewelry can be found in boutiques on the main avenues in big cities. In Buenos Aires, the trendy neighborhood of Palermo Viejo is known for its chic boutiques run by independent Argentinian designers. Some designer names such as **Ricky Sarkany**, **Prune**, and **Bensimon** have shops in Buenos Aires and branches across the other major cities of Argentina.

Specialist Stores

Specialist stores that sell high-quality merchandise produced or manufactured in Argentina's interiors can be found in most cities. *Vinotecas* sell wines from Cuyo and other wine-growing regions, as well as imported spirits and cigars. *Talabarterías* stock products of the Pampas, including gaucho gear, leather-wear, polo shirts, *mate* gourds, and *bombillas* (metal straws). One of the best-known chains is **Cardon**, which has outlets in most cities. For leather specifically, there are *casas de cuero*. Similarly, *casas de lana* sell luxury woolen products, made from both sheep and guanaco wool. In the theater district of Buenos Aires, there are *casas de tango*, which specialize in showy outfits worn by tango performers.

Argentinian antiques are increasingly popular with collectors and dealers from abroad. The major concentrations of antiques shops are in Buenos Aires (see pp122–5).

Artisans' Markets

On weekends, main squares in almost every town in Argentina are taken over by *ferias artesanales* (artisans' markets). These fairs sell good souvenirs and gifts, such as ceramics, *mate* gourds, native weavings, and gaucho ware. The most authentic markets are held in the interior, particularly El Bolsón in Patagonia (see p244) and the villages of Quebrada de Humahuaca in the high Andean Northwest (see pp200–4).

The wine cellar of Bodegas Salentein in Mendoza (see pp214–15)

Bodegas and Chacras

Argentinian wines have a deservedly burgeoning reputation. The best vintages can be acquired at *bodegas*, most of which are concentrated in the Cuyo region. In Mendoza, **Bodega La Rural**, **Bodega y Cavas de Weinert**, **Bodegas Salentein**, and **O. Fournier** are some of the best-stocked *bodegas* (see pp214–15). In San Juan, **Graffigna Wines** have the best merchandizing facilities, while some of the best Torrontés white wines in Argentina come from the *bodegas* of Salta. Larger wineries in Mendoza will help prepare wines for shipping.

Chacras (small farms) cluster on the outskirts of several towns in the interior, particularly in Patagonia. Here, visitors can buy organic foods including fruits, honey, cheeses, and beers, all at low prices. In Patagonia, the *chacras* of El Bolsón, Viedma, and Los Antiguos are well-known for their produce.

Purmamarca's crafts market, Quebrada de Humahuaca (see p202)

DIRECTORY

Taxes and Refunds

Global Refund
City office: Buquebus Ferry Lines,
Ave Antartida Argentina 821,
Buenos Aires. **City Map** 3 E3.
🔳 globalblue.com

Shopping Malls and Boutiques

Bensimon
🔳 bensimon.com.ar

El Palacio
Mitre 37/ Caseros 660, Salta.
Tel (0387) 422-8008.
🔳 galeriaelpalacio.com.ar

Prune
Patio Olmos, Local 249, Ave Velez
Sarsfield, Córdoba.
Tel (0351) 5704-215.
🔳 prune.com.ar

Ricky Sarkany
🔳 rickysarkany.com

Specialist Stores

Cardon
🔳 cardon.com.ar

Bodegas and Chacras

Bodega La Rural
Monte Caseros 2625,
Coquimbito, Maipú, Mendoza.
Tel (0261) 497-2013.
🔳 bodegalarural.com.ar

Bodegas Salentein
Ruta 89 s/n, Los Arboles,
Tunuyán, Mendoza.
Tel (02622) 429-500.
🔳 bodegassalentein.com

Bodega y Cavas de Weinert
Ave San Martín 5923 (M5505),
Luján de Cuyo, Mendoza.
Tel (0261) 4960-409.
🔳 bodegaweinert.com

Graffigna Wines
Colon 1342 norte,
Desamparados, San Juan.
Tel (0264) 421-4227.
🔳 graffignawines.com

O. Fournier
Calle de los Indios s/n, La
Consulta, Mendoza.
Tel (02622) 451-579.
🔳 ofournier.com

What to Buy in Argentina

Shopping is tremendous fun in Argentina given the wide range of beautiful and unique items available. Major cities have modern shopping malls and high-fashion boutiques, while in provincial towns artisans' markets sell everything from beautifully crafted gaucho gear to high-quality weavings. Prices, including the cost of luxury items, are low compared to those in Europe and the US. Some of the bigger stores will ship purchases home and, if requested, shop attendants will gift wrap the item.

Indigenous Handicrafts

Visitors will find artisans selling regional handicrafts across the country – woolens made of guanaco and llama wool in Patagonia, the Andean Northwest, and Cuyo, and excellent ceramics in the Andean North-west. Jewelry is another quality Argentinian product and is available in a variety of designs and metals.

Warm woolen gloves

Poncho woven with traditional patterns

Indigenous pattern woven on woolen polo bands

Woven carpet from Purmamarca, Jujuy

Woolens and Weavings

Bright handwoven rugs, ponchos, and shawls are on offer, made from a variety of wools, including the rare alpaca and vicuña wools. Indigenous symbolism pervades many of the designs.

Jewelry

Artisanal fairs across Argentina offer exquisite jewelry that is handmade from nickel, silver, or gold with semiprecious stones and indigenous motifs.

Inexpensive silver pendants found all across Argentina

Gold earrings with semiprecious stones

Necklace with gold beads

Metal straw and scoop for herbal tea

Two *mate* gourds

Ceramic item made by indigenous people

Handmade earthen pot

Mate

Mate drinking is an age-old Argentinian ritual and *mate* gourds range from highly wrought silver to those crafted from calabash (pumpkin). The *bombilla* (drinking straw) is the main accessory.

Earthenware

Sold at crafts markets across the Andean Northwest and the Northeast of Argentina, ceramics are often embellished with indigenous motifs and patterns dating back millennia.

Traditional Products

Many shops in Buenos Aires sell authentic gaucho ware and items decorated with brightly colored *fileteado*. Quality and prices can vary from shop to shop, so it is best to look around before buying anything. Traditional gaucho ware may also be found at estancias all across the country, especially in Patagonia.

Fileteado Art

Filete is a flamboyant folk art that has adorned shop fronts, buses, and tango halls in Buenos Aires since the 19th century. It typically sets elaborately designed calligraphy within a stylized border of climbing plants, flowers, or even dragons.

Wall-hanging embellished with elaborate *fileteado* design

Gaucho Ware

Coltskin boots, sombreros, and *bombachas* (cotton trousers) are typically worn by the cowboys. *Facones* (knives) and *espuelas* (spurs) are their accessories.

Traditional belt worn by cowboys

Well-carved gaucho knife

A typical gaucho hat

Traditional spurs

A pair of leather boots

Souvenirs

Fine wines and authentic leather goods make interesting souvenirs. Wines are available at any shopping mall in Buenos Aires. However, the best option is to visit a vineyard in the Cuyo region or less well-known vineyards in Salta to buy directly from the *bodegas*. Exotic leather goods are available, mainly in the Northeast, but visitors have to be careful about fakes.

Wines

White wine from José L. Mounier

Red wine made with Malbec grapes

Wines are labeled according to region and grape. The signature red grape is Malbec from Mendoza and the Cuyo region. The pick of Argentina's white varieties is Torrontés, particularly from the vineyards of Salta.

Leather Accessories

Most leather goods are handmade from cowhide. Exotic leathers from the Northeast, used to make luxury gifts, include caiman and lizard leathers.

Belt with pampa pattern

Leather dog collars commonly sold in street stores in Buenos Aires

Leather handbag made from cow and capybara leathers

ENTERTAINMENT IN ARGENTINA

The variety of entertainment in Argentina is a reflection both of its rich cultural heritage and the passion of the Argentinians. Tango, the dance that grew out of the immigrant slums of Buenos Aires, is undergoing a vigorous revival, and folkloric music, inextricably linked to the Pampas and native Northwest, is enjoyed across the country. Towns and cities stage classical music recitals, avant-garde plays, and dance productions at festivals or grand, century-old theater venues. Cinema is also extremely popular, and ranges from Argentinian and foreign art house films to the latest Hollywood blockbusters. Nightlife buzzes beyond sunrise in cities and beach resorts. Popular sports are followed fanatically and the atmosphere within stadiums can be electric. For annual events throughout Argentina, see *pages 44–7*.

Practical Information

Local newspapers and magazines carry regular listings and advertisements of events. Often, hotels have in-house publications highlighting programs in the city. Tourist information offices also publish annual calendars of events. **Ticketek** offices in Buenos Aires, Rosario, and Mar del Plata list upcoming events for those cities.

Spectator Sports

Argentina's sports stadiums are not to be missed. Apart from the famous ones in Buenos Aires, there are several outside the capital that are worth visiting, especially when a *clásico* match of *fútbol* (soccer) is being played between two First Division rivals. The popular matches worth watching are ones between **Newell's Old Boys** and **Rosario Central**. Tickets for games can be bought from ticket agencies or directly from stadiums. Standard ticket prices start at AR$40, but can cost as much as AR$200 especially when it is a clash between top soccer teams. Argentinians are very passionate about equestrian sports, especially *el turf* (horse racing) and polo. Car racing is also popular and the Argentinian round of the World Rally Championship takes place in Córdoba province every May. The Dakar Rally has also made Argentina its new home, with the race taking place in the Northwest each January.

Bars and Nightclubs

Argentinian cities are famous for their nightlife and visitors can revel until sunrise. In most cities there are happy hours from 5 to 9pm though bars and pubs get busy after 10pm, while clubs fill up from around 2am onwards. Buenos Aires has the liveliest nightlife *(see p127)*,

Club Del Vino, a popular bar in Microcentro, Buenos Aires

closely followed by Rosario. In the summer, bars and clubs in coastal resorts such as Mar del Plata and Pinamar are filled with young vacationers.

Classical Music and Dance

Lovers of classical music enjoy an extensive calendar with Buenos Aires boasting the most concert venues, including Teatro Colón *(see pp76–7)*. There are venues in other cities as well including **Teatro El Círculo** and **Teatro Lavarden** in Rosario, and **Teatro Municipal Colón** in Mar del Plata. Music festivals take place through the year, led by the Festival Música Clásica in Ushuaia. Other recommended festivals are the Conciertos en el Bosque in Buenos Aires province and Música Clásica por los Caminos del Vino in Mendoza, where recitals are given in the atmospheric *bodegas* and churches of Mendoza's wine regions. Another major

A polo match at the Argentina Polo Open Championship, Buenos Aires

Poster advertising bands at a music festival, Buenos Aires

attraction is Argentina's most practiced classical dance form, ballet. Julio Bocca, a star performer, has popularized Argentinian ballet through his company, Ballet Argentino. The company tours the country frequently, staging stunning performances.

Folkloric Music

Mainly found in Argentina's interiors, folkloric music is most popular in the province of Salta. In its namesake capital city, there are several restaurants that offer dinner-and-show packages. A more authentic experience is offered in *peñas*, small clubs that host informal folk-music gatherings where visitors can bring their own instruments. These clubs can be found in towns across the country, especially in Salta. The Festival Nacional de Folklore in Cosquín, the biggest folkloric festival in Argentina, is held in Córdoba province and attracts the cream of performers.

Theater and Film

The biggest concentration of theaters in the country is found in Buenos Aires, but other cities such as Rosario, Mendoza, and Córdoba also have important venues with regular performances. During summer, large companies in Buenos Aires switch location to Mar del Plata, where the **Teatro Auditorium** stages grand productions.

Argentina has its own thriving film industry *(see pp36–7)*. There are cinema halls in most towns and multiplexes in cities, the biggest chain being **Cinemark**. Art house cinemas such as **Cosmos** survive in Buenos Aires, and Rosario's screenings include Hollywood and Argentinian movies, with a smattering of world cinema. Mar del Plata's Festival Internacional de Cine de Mar del Plata and BACIFI, the Festival Internacional de Cine Independiente in the capital, are two of the most important film festivals in Argentina.

Contemporary Music

Argentina's rock music scene is vibrant and soloists such as Charly García and various local bands enjoy large followings. International groups stage their concerts mainly in football stadiums. Festivals, including Cosquín Rock in Córdoba, and Epecuén Rock and Gesell Rock in Buenos Aires, attract big names. Festival Jazz en Miramar takes place in Buenos Aires province. Smaller concert venues in provincial cities host Argentinian and international jazz and blues musicians.

DIRECTORY

Practical Information

Ticketek
Abasto, Ave Corrientes 3247 1°, Capital Federal, Buenos Aires.
City Map 2 A4.
Tel (011) 5237-7200.
W ticketek.com.ar
San Lorenzo 1319, Mar del Plata.
Tel (011) 5237-7200.
Shopping Paseo del Siglo, Córdoba 1643, Rosario.
Tel (011) 5237-7200.

Spectator Sports

Newell's Old Boys
Estadio Parque Independencia, Ave Las Palmeras s/n, Rosario.
Tel (0341) 425-4422.
W newellsoldboys.com.ar

Rosario Central
Estadio Club Atlético Rosario Central, Blvd Avellaneda & Ave Génova, Rosario.
Tel (0341) 421-000.
W rosariocentral.com

Classical Music and Dance

Teatro El Círculo
Laprida 1223, Rosario.
Tel (0341) 424-5349.
W teatro-elcirculo.com.ar

Teatro Lavarden
Mendoza & Sarmiento, Rosario.
Tel (0341) 472-1462.
W plataformalavarden.com.ar

Teatro Municipal Colón
Yrigoyen 1665, Mar del Plata.
Tel (0223) 499-6555.
W mardelplata.gov.ar

Theater and Film

Cinemark
Beruti 3399, Palermo, Buenos Aires. **City Map** 5 D3.
Tel (0800) 222-2463.
W cinemark.com.ar

Cosmos
Ave Corrientes 2048, Buenos Aires. **City Map** 2 C5.
Tel (011) 4953 5405.

Teatro Auditorium
Blvd Maritimo 2280, Mar del Plata.
Tel (0223) 493-7786.
W mardelplatafilmfest.com

Musicians performing at Casa Blanca, Buenos Aires

OUTDOOR ACTIVITIES AND SPECIALIZED HOLIDAYS

Argentina's dazzling range of landscapes and good tourist facilities make the country ideal for almost every kind of adventure holiday, from mountaineering and trekking to polo and paragliding. Thanks to the extensive coastline, beautiful lakes, and complex network of rivers and wetlands, visitors have many water-based outdoor options. Come winter, skiing, snowboarding, and ice climbing are offered by tour companies along the Andes from Mendoza to Ushuaia. The country's open landscapes across its interior are ideal for sprawling golf courses. Driving, whether down the lonely roads or through well-developed resorts, can also be fun. For a relaxed holiday, spas, wine tours, and estancias are extremely inviting. The best organizers are local operators who offer subsidized deals.

Cycling along a trail through Parque Nacional Los Arrayanes

Cycling and Mountain Biking

Argentina's terrain in the Andean regions, ranging from gravel tracks and rocky inclines to undulating foothills and shady copses, has made mountain biking popular. However, only cyclists who can handle gusty winds should cross the Patagonian steppe by bike. Popular with road and mountain bikers are the Lake District and sierras of Córdoba, de la Ventana, and Tandil. Northwest hubs such as Tucumán and Salta have tour agencies that hire out bikes. Local firms such as adventure specialist **Andestrack** in San Martín de los Andes and **Montañas Tucumanas** in San Miguel de Tucumán offer guided and self-guided mountain biking tours. Not many opt to bike down Buenos Aires avenues, but there are highways and long-distance roads for those using racing bicycles.

Golf

There are more than 240 golf courses in Argentina recognized by **Asociación Argentina de Golf**, ranging from **Lagos de Palermo Municipal Club** in Buenos Aires to the most southerly golf course in the world, the 9-hole **Ushuaia Golf Club** close to Parque Nacional Tierra del Fuego.

The provinces of Neuquén and Río Negro, with their well-forested lakelands at the foot of the Andes, have proved popular with golfers. Just south of Bariloche, the **Llao Llao Hotel and Resort** boasts undulating fairways and challenging holes, while the **Arelauquen Lodge**, also near Bariloche at Lago Gutierrez, organizes golf and polo excursions. The hotel has its own 18-hole course. The Jack Nicklaus-designed **Chapelco Golf and Resort** is a first-class par-72 course near San Martín de los Andes. Argentinian tour companies **Covitour** and

Secontur create golfing itineraries across the country. In the southern provinces, **Patagonia Golf** can add on fly-fishing trips.

Driving Holidays

Ruta Nacional 40 is legendary *(see p247)* but there are many paved highways and other trunk roads that are also fun to explore.

Off-road driving experiences can be exciting, from bumpy excursions in the Andean high plains to rough drives across salt lakes and down gravel and mud roads. **Movitrak** in Salta offers adventurous off-road driving experiences. Patagonia has also boomed as a driving destination. The Seven Lakes drive between Villa La Angostura and San Martín de los Andes is a great excursion on excellent roads. **Argentina Vision**, in Puerto Madryn, can arrange vehicles for tours. In Córdoba, the **Caravana Club**

A lonely road heading westwards across Patagonia to Perito Moreno

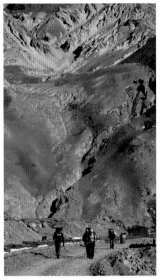

Hikers at Parque Provincial Aconcagua

offers a wide range of 4WD tours across the roads of Traslasierra, while fans of quad biking can also try **Kumbre** in Tandil. Another Argentina-based specialist to contact is **Canal Fun and Nature** in Ushuaia.

Walking and Climbing

With several beautiful sierras and challenging summits, Argentina is a walkers' and climbers' heaven. The Chaltén and Fitz Roy area, Córdoba province, and the sierras of Tandil and de la Ventana offer all levels of challenges. **Huilén Viajes y Turismo** in Villa La Angostura offers a wide range of services for walkers, riders, climbers, and rafters in the lake region. Mendoza has long attracted serious rock climbers and experienced walkers and **Andes Vertical**, offering hiking expeditions and guided climbing in the Andes and Patagonia, offers a package tour for climbers who want to ascend Aconcagua. **Centro Andino Buenos Aires**, a team that plans mountaineering trips, has branches in the capital and in major climbing centers such as Mendoza, Bariloche, and El Chaltén.

Spas and Luxury Holidays

Famous for its spa, the Park Hyatt in Mendoza uses wine-based oils for massages. Llao Llao Hotel and Resort near Bariloche also offers health treatments. In Buenos Aires, many hotels such as Faena Hotel & Universe *(see p278)* have spas offering a range of treatments. The revamped **Cielo Spa** at the downtown Four Seasons is a favorite with porteños. Argentina's largest spa town is Termas de Río Hondo *(see p192)*, which is said to have "healing" waters.

Skiing and Winter Sports

The winter sports season starts in early July and lasts until early October. Luxury ski resorts include Las Leñas *(see p223)* in Mendoza province, **Villa Cerro Catedral** near Bariloche, and **Chapelco Ski Resort** near San Martín de los Andes. Managed by local Mapuches is Batea Mahuida near **Villa Pehuenia** in Neuquén. An operator that can arrange ski trips is **Ripio** in the capital. Glacier tours are available through local operators such as **Calafate Mountain Park** in Calafate and **Camino Abierto** in Patagonia. For ice climbing, **Compañia de Guias de la Patagonia** in Ushuaia is recommended.

Paraglider at Cerro Otto in Bariloche, Patagonia

In the Air

The wide blue skies in Argentina can be explored by balloon, helicopter, glider, or paraglider. These activities are ideal even for beginners. Bariloche and Córdoba are established centers for all airborne activities, and it is possible to arrange gentle balloon flights across the rolling Pampas. Operators such as Lan & Kramer *(see p277)* in Buenos Aires plan all kinds of flights for learners and more experienced pilots.

Tango

The tourist industry has attracted dozens of tango operators, from cowboys to expert historians, who can enrich a trip through the lesser known barrios in the capital, where tango was born and evolved. Tango-themed hotels such as **Lina's Tango Guest House** and Mansión Dandi Royal *(see p278)*, as well as major service providers such as **Kallpatour**, can organize tango shows and lessons to be combined with sightseeing trips in Buenos Aires.

Wine and Food

Many vineyards now have organized tours and tasting sessions *(see pp214–15)*. Those in the Mendoza region with an international reputation include Salentein *(see p282)*, **Club Tapiz**, and Cavas Wine Lodge *(see p281)*. **The Grapevine** in Mendoza is good for tours led by knowledgeable, locally based experts. Other regions are less developed, but **Terra Riojana** is opening doors to fascinating cellars in San Juan and La Rioja. **Arblaster & Clarke**, based in the UK, are highly respected. They plan detailed tours to explore *bodegas* and their exclusive vintages, and can combine tours with trips to Chile and Uruguay. Food trails have just started to become popular. Buenos Aires-based **Alejandro Frango** organizes meals out for individuals and small groups, during which local food delicacies are explained.

Whale-Watching

Península Valdés is one of the world's most famous whale-watching locations. Operators such as **Jorge Schmid**, **Whales Argentina**, and **Tito Bottazzi** arrange transport and expert guides to help visitors spot dolphins, killer whales, and porpoises. Southern Right whales, however, are the star attraction. All major international tour operators that feature Argentina in their itineraries offer packages for whale-watching. Puerto Deseado *(see p233)* is an excellent location for observing porpoises and many other marine species, and almost all tours include the rockhopper penguin colony on Isla Pingüino *(see p233)*. **Darwin Expediciones** is the main operator in the town.

Fishing and Hunting

Fly-fishing for trout and salmon is growing in popularity, especially in Patagonia and the Lake District. **Tiempo de Pesca** in San Martín de los Andes arranges river trips. Patagonia Golf offers a variety of fly-fishing tours. **Fly Fishing Patagonia** specializes in trout, golden dorado, and sea-run brown trout fishing trips in Mendoza, Corrientes, and Patagonia. Argentinian river fishing is also popular and **Pira Lodge** and **Estancia San Alonso**, both in Esteros del Iberá, can arrange boats and guides. Hunting expeditions to exclusive hunting estates and estancias can be organized by **Argentina Adventure**.

Fly-fishing in Río Chimehuin, which flows out of Lago Huechulafquen

Windsurfing off Playa El Doradillo beach in Puerto Madryn

Sailing and Windsurfing

In Bariloche, **Inter Patagonia** offers luxury sailing trips to Victoria Island in Lago Nahuel Huapi. Canal Beagle is popular with sailors and **Rumbo Sur** in Ushuaia can organize boats and combine itineraries with land-based excursions. Windsurfing is gaining in popularity in Argentina, and Lago Traful on the Seven Lakes road is a good choice; **Dormis Costa Traful** can arrange windsurf gear as well as kayaking and horse-riding excursions. Waterskiing or speedboating across Río Plata, as well as fishing trips combined with visits to Uruguay, can be arranged by luxury tour agent, **Fueguito**.

Rafting

There are many grades of white-water rafting in the Andean valleys, with the busy rafting centers located in Bariloche and Mendoza. In the former, **Extremo Sur** and **Aguas Blancas** can organize full-day rafting adventures down Río Manso (which has grades II to IV white-water sections) as well as gentle kayaking trips through the chain of lakes that connects Bariloche with Puerto Montt in Chile. In Mendoza, **Rios Andinos** – based in the main rafting center, Potrerillos – offers a range of river tours, from moonlit rafting and kayaking to hydrospeed trips.

Cruises

Buenos Aires and Ushuaia are favorite stopovers for the long-haul luxury cruises that come down from Brazil and the US. For smaller cruises around Canal Beagle and around Cape Horn, try Rumbo Sur in Ushuaia and **Mare Australis**, which has offices in the US. International adventure tour operators, such as **Peregrine Adventures** and **Explore**, hire medium-sized icebreaker and ice-proof ships during the summer to explore the South Atlantic and Antarctica. There are no longer any regular passenger services up Río Paraná, but cruises and fishing voyages around a stretch of this river in Corrientes can also be organized. UK-based luxury operator **Exsus** arranges a range of tailor-made river and ocean cruises.

Diving and Snorkeling

There have been concerns raised by environmentalists over people swimming with whales, and it is important to check the credentials of anyone offering whale-watching off the Puerto Madryn coast.

However, there are many exciting diving opportunities off the Atlantic coast, in Lago Traful, famous for its submerged forest, Lago Nahuel Huapi, and in the Falkland Islands (Islas Malvinas). In Ushuaia, **Ushuaia Divers** arranges snorkeling and shipwreck dives.

Diver approaches a Southern Right whale off Península Valdés

DIRECTORY

Cycling and Mountain Biking

Andestrack
🅦 andestrack.com.ar

Montañas Tucumanas
🅦 montanas
tucumanas.com

Golf

Arelauquen Lodge
Opp Lake Gutiérrez,
Bariloche.
Tel (02944) 476-110.
🅦 arelauquen
lodge.com

Asociación Argentina de Golf
🅦 aag.org.ar

Chapelco Golf and Resort
🅦 chapelcogolf.com

Covitour
🅦 covitour.com

Lagos de Palermo Municipal Club
Ave Tornquist 6397,
Buenos Aires.
City Map 2 A3.
Tel (011) 4772-7261.

Llao Llao Hotel and Resort
Ave Bustillo, Bariloche.
Tel (0294) 444-8530.
🅦 llaollao.com

Patagonia Golf
🅦 patagoniagolf.
com.ar

Secontur
🅦 secontur.com

Ushuaia Golf Club
Tel (02901) 432-946.

Driving Holidays

Argentina Vision
Puerto Madryn.
Tel (02965) 445-5888.
🅦 argentinavision.com

Canal Fun and Nature
🅦 canalfun.com

Caravana Club
San Martín 1140,
Córdoba.
Tel (03544) 470-261.

Kumbre
🅦 kumbre.com

Movitrak
🅦 movitrack.com.ar

Walking and Climbing

Andes Vertical
Tel (0261) 664-7259.
🅦 andes-vertical.com

Centro Andino Buenos Aires
Rivadavia 1255, Buenos
Aires. **City Map** 5 D5.
Tel (011) 4381-1566.
🅦 www.caba.org.ar

Huilén Viajes y Turismo
Tel (0294) 449-5489.
🅦 huilenviajes.com.ar

Spas and Luxury Holidays

Cielo Spa
Four Seasons, Posadas
1088, Buenos Aires.
City Map 3 F3.
Tel (011) 4321-1200.

Skiing and Winter Sports

Calafate Mountain Park
Tel (02902) 491-034.
🅦 www.calafate
mountainpark.com

Camino Abierto
🅦 caminoabierto.com

Chapelco Ski Resort
🅦 cerrochapelco.com

Compañía de Guías de la Patagonia
Gobernador Campos 795,
Ushuia. **Tel** (02901) 437-
753. 🅦 compania
deguias.com.ar

Ripio
🅦 ripioturismo.com.ar

Villa Cerro Catedral
Ave Ant. Argentina Base,
near Bariloche.
Tel (0294) 446-0140.

Villa Pehuenia
🅦 villapehuenia.org

Tango

Kallpatour
🅦 kallpatour.com

Lina's Tango Guest House
🅦 tangoguesthouse.
com.ar

Wine and Food

Alejandro Frango
🅦 gastrosofia.com

Arblaster & Clarke
🅦 arblasterandclarke.
com

Club Tapiz
Pedro Molina, Ruta 60 s/n,
Maipú, Mendoza.
Tel (0261) 496-3433.

The Grapevine
🅦 latinadventures.
co.uk

Terra Riojana
🅦 terrariojana.com.ar

Whale-Watching

Darwin Expediciones
🅦 darwin-expeditions.
com

Jorge Schmid
🅦 puntaballena.
com.ar

Tito Bottazzi
Puerto Pirámides.
Tel (0280) 495-050.
🅦 titobottazzi.com

Whales Argentina
🅦 whalesargentina.
com.ar

Fishing and Hunting

Argentina Adventure
🅦 argadventure.com

Estancia San Alonso
Esteros del Iberá.
Tel (03782) 497-172.
🅦 sanalonso.com

Fly Fishing Patagonia
🅦 flyfishingpatagonia.
com

Pira Lodge
🅦 piralodge.com

Tiempo de Pesca
Ragussi 26, San Martín de
los Andes.
🅦 tiempodepesca.com

Sailing and Windsurfing

Dormis Costa Traful
Ruta 65, Lago Traful.
Tel (0294) 447-9005.
🅦 hosteriavillatraful.
com

Fueguito
🅦 fueguito.com

Inter Patagonia
🅦 interpatagonia.com

Rumbo Sur
San Martín 350, Ushuaia.
Tel (02901) 422-275.
🅦 rumbosur.com.ar

Rafting

Aguas Blancas
🅦 aguas blancas.
com.ar

Extremo Sur
Morales 765, Bariloche.
Tel (0294) 442-7301.
🅦 extremosur.com

Rios Andinos
Ruta Internacional 7, Km
55, Potrerillos.
Tel (0261) 517-4184.
🅦 riosandinos.com

Cruises

Explore
55 Victoria Rd,
Farnborough, UK.
Tel (0044) 843 643-6478.
🅦 explore.co.uk

Exsus
118–119 Fenchurch St,
London EC3M 5BA, UK.
Tel (0044) 20 7337 9010.
🅦 exsus.com

Mare Australis
🅦 australis.com

Peregrine Adventures
Tel (001) 416 355-5174.
🅦 peregrine
adventures.com

Diving and Snorkeling

Ushuaia Divers
LN Alem 4509, Ushuaia.
🅦 tierradelfuego.
org.ar

On the Open Range

Many estancias once served as the second homes of rich urbanites and today, some of them offer the most luxurious rural accommodation in the country for tourists. Many activities such as bird-watching, trekking, and polo keep visitors occupied. Aspiring gauchos can gallop across the plains or go on horseback treks while skilled riders can try horse-breaking. During walks in the area, it is possible to see abundant birdlife and spot hares, rheas, skunks, and foxes. On some working estancias, visitors can also help with sheep-shearing, watching over the cattle, and preparing a barbecue. In the evenings, local dance performances as well as engaging storytelling sessions around the campfire can be arranged for visitors.

Visitors going on a horse-riding tour with the help of a guide

Gaucho for a day

Argentinian gauchos have always been proud of their legacy and are more than pleased to show visitors how to become a gaucho for a day. In the Pampas, Estancia La Bamba and Estancia El Ombú, both located in San Antonio de Areco *(see p149)*, are well-known for their traditional rustic accommodation. Here, visitors can participate in sheep-shearing activities or just watch the gauchos in action.

Working sheep estancias include **El Galpón del Glaciar** near El Calafate, and the isolated **Estancia La Angostura** in Patagonia. The 130-year-old Estancia Monte Dinero *(see p235)*, near Río Gallegos in Patagonia, also offers trekking apart from gaucho activities. **Estancia Río Capitán**, located in southern Patagonia, also organizes wildlife tours.

Bird-Watching, Treks, and Horse Riding

Life on an estancia entails being close to nature. Most ranches offer bird-watching as part of their package. Estancia Telken *(see p247)*, near Perito Moreno in Patagonia, is known for bird-watching, as is **Estancia Rincón del Socorro** in Esteros del Iberá *(see pp170–71)*. The latter also organizes trekking trips and is

a good base to explore the World Heritage Site of Cueva de las Manos.

An excellent option for horse riding is **Estancia Huechahue** in Neuquén, from where there are expeditions into Parque Nacional Lanín *(see p241)*. In Patagonia, visitors who opt for leisurely horse rides are also treated to views of the region's glaciers and awesome peaks. Some of the well-known estancias that offer bird-watching, trekking, and horse riding are **Estancias La Maipú** and **El Cóndor**, both located on Lago San Martín.

Luxury Estancias

Some estancias provide the perfect laid-back getaway. These include **Estancia Cerro de la Cruz** near Tandil, in the Pampas, and **Estancias La Oriental**, **Menelik**, and **Cueva de las Manos** in Patagonia. They have in common fine dining, specta-cular locations, and personalized service. **Estancia Peuma Hue** is a luxurious stopover for trips into Parque Nacional Huapi *(see pp242–3)*. Hostería Helsingfors *(see p258)* in Los Glaciares and **Hostería Alta Vista** in El Calafate are other excellent options. There are two beautiful estancias in Córdoba – **Estancia El Colibrí**, famous for their wines and haute cuisine, and Estancia La Paz, once the residence of President Roca. Near Esteros del Iberá is **Estancia Rincón del Socorro**, which is an ideal place to relax before heading into the preserve.

The well-furnished living room of Estancia Cerro de la Cruz

The vast Estancia El Galpón del Glaciar, near Los Glaciares, Patagonia

Other Activities

Many estancias boast excellent in-house libraries. They usually have a good collection of books on the country's culture and include classy coffee-table books as well as classics on rural life, such as Hernández's *Martín Fierro*. Some estancias arrange for evening dance performances where visitors can watch or participate in lively country dances such as the foot-stamping *chacarera*, the playful *gato*, and the sensous *zamba*. Some estancia owners recount anecdotes around the communal dining table, while others organize formal story-telling sessions. More adventurous visitors can opt for hot air balloon rides that provide magnificent views of the Argentinian countryside.

Tours and Reservations

Many firms help visitors plan tours to Argentina's estancias. International tailor-made tour operator **Last Frontiers** has expert knowledge of horse ranches and arranges stays at exclusive polo estancias. **MacDermott's Argentina** in Buenos Aires organizes tours and **Trekking Travel** in Mendoza provides trekking information and arranges wine tours in the region. **Aves Patagonia** is a good option for trips to ranches across Patagonia where rare bird species can be found. **Sol Iguazú** and **Yacutinga Lodge** are useful for trips to the Misiones area. A major Argentinian tour operator for activities related to wildlife is **Lihue Expediciones**. UK-based **Naturetrek** offers guidance to estancias and their activities. Some of the grandest ranches can be found in a comprehensive list on the Estancias de Santa Cruz and Estancias Argentinas websites *(see p277)*.

DIRECTORY

Gaucho for a Day

El Galpón del Glaciar
Ruta Provincial 11, near
El Calafate.
Tel (02902) 497-503
w elgalpondelglaciar.
com.ar

Estancia La Angostura
Ruta Nacional 40, near
Tres Lagos.
Tel (02962) 491-501.
w estancia
laangostura.com.ar

Estancia Río Capitán
Ruta Provincial 35, Province
of Santa Cruz, Patagonia.
Tel (02286) 490-938.

Bird-Watching, Horse Riding, and Treks

Estancia El Cóndor
Ruta Nacional 40, Lago
San Martín.
Tel (011) 4765-8085.
w cielospatagonicos.
com

Estancia Huechahue
A.E 12 –Junín de los
Andes, (8371) Neuquén.
Tel (02972) 491-303.
w huechahue.com

Estancia La Maipú
Maipú 864, Buenos Aires.
City Map 3 E4. **Tel** (011)
4901-5591. w estancia-
lamaipu.com.ar

Estancia Rincón del Socorro
Casilla 45, 3470 Mercedes,
Corrientes. **Tel** (03773)
1547-5114. w rincon
delsocorro.com

Luxury Estancias

Estancia Cerro de la Cruz
Ruta Provincial 72, near
Sierra de la Ventana.
Tel (011) 155-805-9710.
w estanciacerro
delacruz.com

Estancia Cueva de las Manos
Ruta 40, 60 Km S of Perito
Moreno, Province of Santa
Cruz. **Tel** (02963) 432-319

Estancia El Colibrí
Camino a Santa Catalina,
Km 7, Santa Catalina,
Córdoba.
Tel (03525) 465-888.
w estanciaelcolibri.com

Estancia La Oriental
Junín, Province of Buenos
Aires.
Tel (02362) 1564--0866.
w estancia-laoriental.
com

Estancia Menelik
Tel (011) 4311-5550.
w cielospatagonicos.
com/english/menelik.
html

Estancia Peuma Hue
Tel (0294) 450-1030.
w peuma-hue.com

Hostería Alta Vista
Ruta Provincial 15, Km 35,
(9405) El Calafate, Santa
Cruz. **Tel** (02902) 491-247.
w hosteriaaltavista.
com.ar

Tours and Reservations

Aves Patagonia
w avespatagonia.com.ar

Last Frontiers
w lastfrontiers.com/
argentina

Lihue Expediciones
Ave Córdoba 827, Buenos
Aires. **City Map** 2 A3.
Tel (011) 5031-0070.
w lihue-expediciones.
com.ar

MacDermott's Argentina
w macdermotts
argentina.com

Naturetrek
Cheriton Mill, Hants, UK.
Tel (0044) 1962 733-051.

Sol Iguazú
w soliguazu.com.ar

Trekking Travel
w trekking-travel.com.ar

Yacutinga Lodge
w yacutinga.com

SURVIVAL GUIDE

PRACTICAL INFORMATION

Mass tourism is a relatively new phenomenon in Argentina, and the quality of the country's tourist infrastructure and services is gradually improving. It is a relatively easy country to travel around, although tourist facilities may still be limited in its remote rural interiors. All major cities, towns, and resorts have visitor information centers that provide maps and brochures detailing activities, hotels, restaurants, and attractions. Hotel desk staff are usually very helpful and almost everyone on the street will gladly stop to give directions and advice. Contrary to conventional wisdom, visitors are not dogged by bureaucracy and red tape at every step, although it is advisable to carry relevant documentation at all times.

A bustling summer day at Plaza de Mayo, the capital's major tourist hub

When to Go

Argentina can be visited all year round, except for skiing (Jun–Sep) and whale-watching (Jun–Dec). Most Argentinians holiday in summer (Jan–Feb), a period when Buenos Aires can be humid and popular resorts often crowded. The capital is at its best during spring and fall. Climatic conditions vary from region to region: the north is hotter than the south; the west is drier than the east; and the wind rarely stops blowing in Patagonia.

Visas and Passports

Citizens of North America, Australasia, South Africa, the UK, and all other Western European countries require no visa to enter Argentina for a stay of up to 90 days. However, Canadian, US, and Australian citizens must pay a reciprocal entry fee of US$160, which is valid for 10 years. Citizens of other countries should check their requirements at their Argentinian embassy or consulate. Visits can be extended by showing your passport at the immigration center or by leaving and re-entering the country. This is usually done by taking the short trip to Uruguay from Buenos Aires. Information on long-term stays for business travelers can be obtained at their local Argentinian embassy. US citizens cannot enter Brazil without a visa, an important consideration when traveling to Iguazú Falls. In case of loss of passport, visitors should inform their embassy.

Customs Information

Visitors may enter Argentina from overseas with up to 2 liters of alcoholic beverages, 400 cigarettes, 50 cigars, and 11 lb (5 kg) of food. For travelers entering from a neighboring country, half these quantities can be brought in. Declaration forms must be completed, and vegetables, plants, fruits, and other perishable foods are prohibited. Pets must be certified in advance and have all their vaccinations up-to-date. If traveling from tropical countries where diseases such as cholera or yellow fever are prevalent, obtain a vaccination certificate.

Tourist Information

The state tourist board in Argentina is the **Secretaría de Turismo de la Nación**. Although it may be difficult to find one in the interior, all major cities have tourist offices that provide maps and brochures, plus information on where to stay and what to see in their area.

Well-equipped tourist information center providing brochures and maps

◀ El Tren del Fin del Mundo – the train at the end of the world – in Tierra del Fuego

Visitors on the foredeck of a tour boat, Parque Nacional Los Glaciares

What to Wear

For visits to Buenos Aires and central Argentina, visitors should bring light summer clothes and a raincoat for trips taken between November and March. The rest of the year, cold winds, morning frosts, and even snow can bring the temperature down.

During the summer in Patagonia, travelers must take sunblock and clothes that cut out UV rays. Visitors will also need to carry warm winter clothing and harsh weather gear, especially if visiting the mountain areas. The northeast and northwest are in the subtropical region and have hot, humid days and sudden rainstorms. Nights in the Andean high plains are intensely cold all through the year and sweaters or llama wool ponchos are required.

Social Customs and Etiquette

Argentinians are generally courteous but friendly and informal, and have a relaxed attitude towards protocol and etiquette. Depending on age and degree of acquaintance, they greet one another with either a kiss on one cheek or a handshake. Men practice the former as well as a pat on the back, but it is by no means universal. If in doubt, proffer a hand.

Dress is typically casual though it is better to attend a business meeting in a smart shirt than in a rumpled suit or tie. Everything moves at a slower pace outside the major cities in Argentina, and in hotter regions the afternoon siesta still remains a popular custom.

Language

The official language of Argentina is Spanish, spoken by everyone in the main cities, towns, and interior. Outside the university-educated middle classes and those who work full-time in the tourism sector, English is not spoken widely. For anyone who is traveling off the beaten track, a smattering of Spanish is a great advantage. Small pockets of native people speak Aimará or Quechua in the Northwest, and Guaraní is still strong in Misiones and along the Paraguayan border.

In Buenos Aires, many people still use elements of *lunfardo*, an argot that arose in prisons in the late 19th century that is a mix of Spanish, Italian, and Genovese.

Admission Prices

Many of the major museums in Argentina's bigger cities are subsidized by the federal or state government and are therefore cheap, and often free, to enter. The admission charge is likely to be in the order of US$1. In the free museums, visitors are encouraged to give a voluntary contribution, essential to the survival of these underfunded institutions. To enter private museums, visitors should expect to pay around US$4 to US$5. Note, however, that most such museums have days (often Wednesday) when admissions are either half-price or free. Entrance to MALBA in Buenos Aires *(see pp114–15)*, for example, is cheaper on Wednesdays.

Cinemas are less expensive Monday through Wednesday. The door charge at nightclubs varies substantially, but is not less than US$5 and can go up to US$15 in the most modern and fashionable venues.

Opening Hours

Banks are generally open from 10am to 3pm on weekdays and closed over the weekends. Museums, art galleries, and other cultural venues usually open at 10am and close at 7 or 8pm.

Most supermarkets and shops, including big shopping malls, don't close until 9 or 10pm. Bars, pubs, and restaurants stay open very late, making nightlife vibrant and lively. In the provinces, many shops and services close in the afternoon for siesta.

Art exhibition space in Museo de Arte Latinoamericano, Buenos Aires

Travelers with Special Needs

Although Argentina is yet to develop an efficient tourist infrastructure for disabled travelers, there has been an improvement in recent years. Modern museums, art galleries, and upscale hotels now have access facilities, although it is advisable for visitors to check in advance. An increasing number of buses in the major Argentinian cities have sidewalk-level doors for accompanied wheelchair users.

The organizations **Disabled Travelers** and the **Society for Accessible Travel and Hospitality (SATH)** both promote awareness and accessibility for travelers with special needs. The website www.justargentina. org provides some useful advice on the best places to visit and when for disabled travelers visiting the country.

Traveling with Children

Argentina is an extremely child-friendly country and youngsters are welcomed everywhere. However, navigating a buggy over the potholed sidewalks of Buenos Aires can be stressful. Some cultural differences should be noted – Argentinian children do not, as a rule, have separate meal times and rarely go to bed before their parents do. Most restaurants and hotels are more child-friendly than their first-world counterparts and

Backpackers trekking through Parque Nacional Los Glaciares, Patagonia

will happily bring out a high chair and a child-sized food portion. Many restaurants also have supervised play areas.

Senior Travelers

Senior travelers will find no particular problems getting around in Argentina, though the usual common sense precautions regarding safety and medical care apply here as everywhere else. While concession prices are less common here than in first-world countries, it never harms to enquire at museums and other tourist sites.

Go Ahead Tours is a tourist agency that organizes special tours mainly for groups of senior travelers around Argentina. They also arrange Antarctic cruises. **ElderTreks** is an adventure travel company that deals exclusively with travelers above the age of 50. They organize a wide variety of tours around Argentina that focus on wildlife, tango, gaucho experiences, wine tasting, and national parks.

Gay and Lesbian Travelers

Argentina was the first Latin American country to pass a Gay Marriage Bill, in 2010. Buenos Aires has a vibrant and eclectic scene including bars, restaurants, and lodgings. Other big cities also have plenty to offer the gay traveler, and the majority of hotels around the country have no qualms about accommodating gay or lesbian couples. This is still a macho society, however, meaning that gay men have greater visibility than lesbians. The **International Gay and Lesbian Travel Association (IGLTA)** offers a wealth of information on tour agencies and accommodation options.

Backpackers

Argentina has recently become firmly entrenched on the backpacker trail. The number of youth hostels in Buenos Aires has increased and other top destinations such as Salta, Bariloche, and El Calafate are also well served by hostels and budget accommodations. Students who belong to youth hosteling associations may get a discount for lodging, but concessions are not available for transport and other services. Hitchhiking is still a good way to get around the country, though all the usual precautions should be taken.

Senior travelers on a winery tour at Bodega Nieto Senetiner

Women Travelers

It is rare that women travelers, whether in groups or pairs, face problems in Argentina. However, it is advisable to take the usual precautions, including not walking alone late in the evening. If there is a need to take a taxi, call for radio taxis *(see p331)*. Note that they charge a small fee to come to the doorstep. **Radio Taxi Porteño** and **Radio Taxi del Plata** in Buenos Aires are some popular ones.

Women traveling alone may attract attention, although it is usually of the harmless kind. Argentinian men sometimes pass a stream of *piropos* (unsolicited comments or sexual advances), which range from *Que linda que sos!* (You're lovely!) to *De qué juguetería te escapaste?, ¡muñeca!* (Which toyshop did you escape from? You doll!). It is best to ignore them. On beaches, keep to minimum exposure to avoid attention. The **Young Women's Christian Association (YWCA)** has a branch in Buenos Aires that offers basic and comfortable accommodations.

Time

There is only one time zone in Argentina, though certain provinces, particularly those with large agricultural sectors, occasionally put the clocks back or forward an hour during summer. Argentina is

Plugs used across Argentina

3 hours behind GMT during its summer, and 4 hours behind during its winter.

Electricity

Electricity in Argentina runs on 220 volts and sockets take either two- or three-pronged plugs and these plugs are flat-shaped. Adapters for foreign appliances can be purchased at *ferreterías* (hardware stores) and major supermarkets. Power outages are usually short-lived.

Conversions

US to Metric
1 inch = 2.54 centimeters
1 foot = 30 centimeters
1 mile = 1.6 kilometers
1 ounce = 28 grams
1 pound = 454 grams
1 pint = 0.6 liters
1 gallon = 3.79 liters

Metric to US
1 millimeter = 0.04 inch
1 centimeter = 0.4 inch
1 meter = 3 feet 3 inches
1 kilometer = 0.6 mile
1 gram = 0.04 ounces
1 kilogram = 2.2 pounds
1 liter = 2.1 pints

Visitors seated at tables outside a restaurant, Bariloche

DIRECTORY

Visas and Passports

Australia
Tel (011) 4779-3500.
🖳 argentina.embassy.gov.au

Canada
Tel (011) 4808-1000.
🖳 cic.gc.ca

UK
Tel (011) 4808-2200.
🖳 ukinargentina.fco.gov.uk

US
Tel (011) 5777-4533.
🖳 argentina.usembassy.gov

Tourist Information

Secretaría de Turismo de la Nación
🖳 turismo.gov.ar

Travelers with Special Needs

Disabled Travelers
🖳 disabledtravelers.com

Society for Accessible Travel and Hospitality (SATH)
Tel (001) 212 447-7284.
🖳 sath.org

Senior Travelers

ElderTreks
Tel (0416) 588-5000.
🖳 eldertreks.com

Go Ahead Tours
Tel (1-800) 590-1170.
🖳 goaheadtours.com

Gay and Lesbian Travelers

International Gay And Lesbian Travel Association (IGLTA)
🖳 iglta.org

Women Travelers

Radio Taxi del Plata
Tel (011) 4505-1111.
🖳 delplataradiotaxi.com

Radio Taxi Porteño
Tel (011) 4566-5777.

Young Women's Christian Association (YWCA)
Tel (011) 4941-3775.

Personal Security and Health

Argentina is relatively safe, though in popular tourist cities such as Mendoza, Córdoba, Buenos Aires, and other areas, petty theft and assaults are increasing. Take particular care in the La Boca area of Buenos Aires and keep valuables locked away in the hotel safe. It is advisable to bring prescribed drugs, as well as a first aid kit and water purification tablets when traveling anywhere off the beaten track. If you have a persistent medical condition it is a good idea to have a doctor's letter translated into Spanish, although most Argentinian doctors will have at least a basic grasp of English.

Traffic jam along a city road, a common sight in Argentina

A Federal policeman in his uniform, Buenos Aires

Police

The Federal Police has jurisdiction across Argentina but in reality is active mainly in the capital, alongside the Metropolitan Police Force. Most routine police work is under-taken by the provincial police forces. Visitors may find that local police are not always helpful and the problems afflicting police forces in most developing nations, such as corruption and low salaries, are evident here.

Those who find themselves a victim of, or witness to, a serious crime must report to their embassy and the relevant law enforcement authority. In Buenos Aires, this is the

Comisaría del Turista, which has English-speaking staff. Never hand over important documents, such as a passport, to a police officer without a witness being present and a receipt provided.

Lost and Stolen Property

There is little point in reporting lost or stolen property to the police unless there is a need to file a *levantar un acta* (official report) for insurance purposes. Visitors will need to do this at the nearest *comisaría* (police station), usually within 24 hours of the robbery. Lost passports and credit cards should be reported as soon as possible to the embassy *(see p317)* and to the card issuer respectively.

Petty theft is not a major problem in Argentinian cities but visitors must always be on guard, particularly in unsafe neighborhoods and when using ATMs outside banking hours. Hotel thefts are rare but it is wise to leave valuables in a safe.

Street Hazards

Not all Argentinian drivers follow road regulations and as a pedestrian it is best to be alert at all times and look carefully while crossing a busy junction. Be prepared for uneven road surfaces and pavements, and flying grit while driving on gravel roads.

Noisy street marches and protests are part of the daily routine in Buenos Aires, although their effect is mainly felt by commuters traveling from the province to the city. It is safer to always allow for a bit of spare time to reach a destination.

Natural Disasters

Argentina has had very few large-scale natural hazards that present a threat to human life. Heavy rainstorms result in flooding due to a poor drainage system in some parts of the capital. Earthquakes are a theoretical risk in provinces such as Mendoza and San Juan, which border the Andean range. The last tremor of serious note occurred in Santiago del Estero in 2011. In the unlikely event of an earthquake, it is advisable to move away from electricity poles and high structures.

In an Emergency

It is best to call an ambulance in case of an emergency and to go to a state hospital *emergencia* (emergency room) if not covered by medical insurance. Visitors are advised to carry along their medical papers in case the doctor wants to take a look at the prescription.

A black and white police car in Buenos Aires

Hospitals and Pharmacies

Argentina has two types of hospitals: public and private. The former are usually underequipped and under-funded, although the doctors and nurses are highly qualified as many also work in the private sector. Some well-maintained goverment hospitals are **Hospital Zonal General de Agudos San Roque Manuel B. Gonnet** in La Plata and **Hospital de Urgencias** in Córdoba. Private hospitals are generally of a high standard, offering first-class health services and spotless rooms. These include Buenos Aires's **Hospital Alemán** and **Hospital Británico**. There is also a medical institute exclusively for children called **Hospital de Niños Dr. Ricardo Gutiérrez**.

Some "prescription only" drugs available in more developed countries, such as anti-biotics and birth-control pills, can be bought over the counter in Argentina. Most *farmacias* (pharmacies) are open from 9am to 8pm and major cities have 24-hour outlets such as **Farmacity Malabia** and **Farmacity Santa Fe** in the capital and **Farmacia 2001** in Tucumán.

One of the many pharmacies found in Argentina's cities

Serious Diseases

Malaria or cholera may be found in some rural regions. A more common disease is dengue, a viral illness spread by mosquitos. *Chagas* is a chronic condition transmitted through a blood parasite carried by the cone nose or "kissing bug." It is prevalent in rural parts but the risk of contracting it is minor.

Minor Hazards

The most common minor ailments to afflict visitors to Argentina are dehydration and sunstroke. Both of these can easily be avoided by carrying a strong sunscreen, a hat, and bottled water on any excursion or trip to the beach. Tap water is also potable all across the country.

Some serious diseases are carried by insect bites but a nasty rash is by far the most likely irritant a visitor can get. It is wise to keep a good brand of repellent always at hand. Altitude sickness can, in extreme cases, be dangerous but is only an issue for visitors traveling to the Andean highlands.

Food poisoning is rarer here than in most Latin American countries, although the usual commonsense precautions apply.

Public Toilets

Good public bathrooms are scarce in Argentina and the well-maintained ones are mainly in cities. It is best to use the services of public toilets in the nearest fast food chain, shopping mall, or department store.

Travel and Health Insurance

Visitors traveling to Argentina are advised to purchase private travel insurance that includes full medical coverage. This is useful in case of emergencies which require treatment at private clinics where medical care can be very expensive. Argentina shares no reciprocal health insurance scheme with any other country.

Vaccinations

Visitors traveling to remote areas of the country should ensure that their regular immu-nizations, such as tetanus, are up-to-date. They should also consider having a Hepatitis B vaccination. Except for a few rural areas bordering Bolivia and Paraguay, Argentina is mainly malaria-free.

DIRECTORY

Emergency Numbers

Ambulance
Tel 107.

Comisaría del Turista
Ave Corrientes 436, Buenos Aires.
City Map 3 E4.
Tel (0800) 999-5000.

Fire Service
Tel 100.

Police
Tel 911.

Hospitals and Pharmacies

Farmacia 2001
Monteagudo 501, Tucumán.
Tel (0800) 555-2001.

Farmacity Malabia
Corrientes 5288, Buenos Aires.
City Map 4 B5.
Tel (011) 4857-2978.
W farmacity.com

Farmacity Santa Fe
Santa Fe 2822, Buenos Aires.
City Map 2 B3.
Tel (011) 4821-3000.
W farmacity.com

Hospital Alemán
Ave Pueyrredón 1640, Buenos Aires. **City Map** 2 B3.
Tel (011) 4827-7000.
W hospitalaleman.com.ar

Hospital Británico
Pedriel 74, Barracas, Buenos Aires.
Tel (011) 4309-6400.
W hospitalbritanico.org.ar

Hospital de Niños Dr. Ricardo Gutiérrez
Gallo 1330, Buenos Aires.
City Map 2 A3.
Tel (011) 4962-9247.

Hospital de Urgencias
Calle Catamarca 441, Córdoba.
Tel (0351) 427-6200.

Hospital Zonal General de Agudos San Roque Manuel B. Gonnet
Calle 508 btwn 18 & 19, La Plata.
Tel (0221) 484-0290.

Banking and Currency

The unit of currency in Argentina is the peso, but US dollars are widely accepted in tourist areas and most supermarket chains. The majority of tourist-oriented hotels, shops, and restaurants accept all major credit cards. Bring cash or travelers' checks in either US dollars or euros; other foreign currencies are not readily exchanged in all banks and will not be accepted as cash. The Argentinian peso slumped in 2002 and again in 2014, resulting in an eightfold devaluation against the dollar. One consequence of this is that a dual exchange system has evolved: the official rate, and a more favorable "dollar blue" rate, widely offered through unofficial channels. As always in such circumstances: buyer beware.

Visitors changing money at a *casa de cambio* in Córdoba

Banks and Casas de Cambio

Argentina's banks range from the state-run **Banco de la Nación Argentina** to local independent banks, as well as international banks such as **Citibank**. Opening hours are normally from 10am to 3pm on weekdays. Avoid lunch hours, to escape long queues. Ask hotel staff for opening hours of the nearest branches.

Casas de cambio (bureaux de change) are generally open longer hours than banks and tend to offer quicker service and better exchange rates in comparison to shops and hotels. It is advisable not to exchange money in a hotel unless there is absolutely no other alternative. Ministro Pistarini International Airport in the capital also has several *casas de cambio*, including **Banco Piano**, but rates at the airport are not competitive.

Automatic Teller Machines (ATMs)

Most banks have ATMs – look out for the Banelco and Link machines that display the symbol of the card issuer. Visitors will be charged between US$1 and US$5, depending on the bank and the card issuer.

Getting change in Argentina can be difficult and many vendors blanch at the sight of a 100 peso note, so it is better not to withdraw cash in multiples of 100. Instead, put in a request for 190 pesos rather than 200. For safety reasons, always withdraw money only during business hours, preferably in well-populated areas such as bank lobbies or shopping malls.

Standard ATM, found across Argentina

Travelers' Checks and Credit Cards

Travelers' checks still remain the safest way of carrying money. However, not all banks exchange them, so it is better to check beforehand instead of joining the long queue. A better option for exchanging money is at a *casa de cambio*. Their opening hours vary from region to region, though they are usually open until at least 6pm. In Buenos Aires, most are situated in the Microcentro, close to where Reconquista and Calles Sarmiento intersect. The commission is around 2 percent, with a minimum service charge of about US$5. **American Express** travelers' checks can be changed without commission at their office in Retiro.

Credit cards are accepted in most major outlets, but it is wise to ask first, especially in restaurants. The most widely accepted cards are **MasterCard** and **Visa**, followed by American Express. Visitors will have to show a photo ID, if the need arises.

Wiring Money

It is advisable to use the facility of wiring money as a last resort. Instead, it is better to go to either **Forex Cambio**, who, like Banco Piano, can also cash foreign checks, or **Western Union**. Charges fluctuate and a minimum fee would be about US$50. It is advisable to call ahead to check for the best rates.

Currency

The Argentinian peso is divided into 100 centavos. In the 2002 economic crisis a number of provinces issued their own paper money bonds. These are no longer legal tender. Do not accept any note that is not marked "pesos" and check the watermark and ink carefully.

The peso's symbol, ARS, is easily confused with that of the US dollar (US$). Assume that a product is priced in pesos unless it is stated otherwise. Always carry small amounts of cash in coins and small-denomination bills for tips and minor purchases. Buses only accept coins (as well as the electronic SUBE card) and taxi drivers may be unable or unwilling to give change for larger-denomination notes.

Coins

Centavo coins come in denominations of 5¢, 10¢, 15¢, 25¢, and 50¢. The centavo coins were introduced in 1994, followed by 1 peso. 1¢ was also available but it has been withdrawn from circulation.

5 centavos   10 centavos   25 centavos

50 centavos   1 peso   2 pesos

Bank Notes

In 1992, banknotes were introduced in denominations of AR$2, AR$5, AR$10, AR$20, AR$50, and AR$100. The $1 was replaced by a coin in 1994. The notes usually have images of the country's heroes on one side and, on the other, some of the major events in Argentinian history.

5 pesos

2 pesos

20 pesos

10 pesos

100 pesos

50 pesos

Communications and Media

Public telephones are the cheapest way to make calls in Argentina although cellular phones are now affordable and coverage is excellent. Booths in Internet cafés (*locutorios*) are far more efficient than pay phones on the street. Most major cities and even remote villages have at least one Internet café. The mail service may not be very reliable but it is still cheap and efficient by Latin American standards. Mailboxes are usually the British-style red letterboxes found around street corners. For entertainment, Argentina has five free television channels transmitting numerous programs ranging from documentaries and talk shows to soap operas. The radio is quite popular with Argentinians, featuring breakfast shows and pop music programs.

Dialing Codes

- For operator services, dial 000.
- To make a collect call inside Argentina, dial 0800-222-1919.
- For a long-distance call to the capital from within Argentina, dial 011 followed by the 8-digit number.
- For a long-distance call from the capital to other places in Argentina, add the code of the region before the number.

Telephone Numbers

The country code for calling Argentina is 54, followed by an area code, which can be one, two, three, or four digits; for example Buenos Aires's area code is 11 followed by the telephone number. All landline numbers in Buenos Aires have eight digits. Public telephones are found everywhere, but more rarely in remote areas. Public call centers are assigned a cabin with a meter which displays the charged amount. It is better to check at the counter for discounts on international or domestic calls. Prepaid phonecards can be bought at these call centers to call abroad.

Cell Phones

Visitors should ask their phone provider at home about international roaming before going abroad. All Argentinian cell numbers begin with 15 and

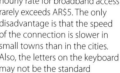
Telephone sign at El Cuyo

are followed by eight digits. To call cell phones in Buenos Aires from overseas, dial +54 9 11 and the number, leaving out the 15. Some hotels offer a cell phone renting service, but this can be expensive. SIM cards for unblocked phones are available for AR$15.

Internet and Fax

Most Argentinian hotels, hostels, and guesthouses have Internet facilities. Even small villages in the interior have an Internet café since many homes do not have personal computers. The hourly rate for broadband access rarely exceeds AR$5. The only disadvantage is that the speed of the connection is slower in small towns than in the cities. Also, the letters on the keyboard may not be the standard

Western letters. Printing pages is also quite cheap at less than US$1 per page. Fax machines are available in most hotels with basic facilities and all *locutorios*. Faxes are normally charged at AR$3 to AR$6 per sheet.

Mail Services

Sending and receiving parcels through the regular mail service in Argentina is not recommended. Registering both letters and parcels improves the odds against pilfering. However, the safest way to send anything other than a letter or postcard abroad is through one of the international courier companies such as **FedEx**, **DHL**, and **UPS**.

The main *oficinas de correos* (post offices) in large towns and cities are open from 8am to 6pm on weekdays and from 8am to 1pm on Saturdays. **Correo Central** (see p71) is inexpensive for domestic mail. A *poste restante* (mail holding service) is available at main post offices in the major cities; letters should be addressed to the recipient's name, followed by the words "*Lista de Correos*," and then by the name and address of the post office. Collecting the mail will cost the recipient around AR$6, and they will need to show ID.

Argentinian Addresses

Argentinian addresses list the house number after the name of the street. Other useful

A *locutorio* in the town of El Bolsón, Patagonia

Popular talk show with Argentinian presenter Susana Giménez on Telefe

words to recognize are *departamento* (apartment), *piso* (floor), and *local* (unit). Always include the *código postal* (zip or postal code).

Radio and Television

The majority of Argentinian households have cable television, giving them access to over 70 channels. Some of these are Argentinian channels such as Crónica, a news channel, and others are foreign channels such as Sony. Most hotels in the country also have cable television in the rooms.

There are five free *canales abiertos* (open channels). The state-run Canal 7 specializes in documentaries, live folk music, and panel shows. There is also América, which airs soap operas and panel shows, and Canal 13, with news programs and sitcoms based on US teleserials. Telefe features one of the most famous talk shows in the country with the popular host Susana Giménez.

Radio is quite popular in Argentina. The most listened to radio station is La 100 on 99.9 FM, which plays Latin pop. Some well-known names in radio are Mario Pergolini and Roberto Pettinato, who host breakfast shows that blend conversation and English-language pop and rock. Almost every city in the country has a local radio station. These small-time stations help visitors in the case of lost possessions by putting out an appeal to recover the property.

Newspapers and Magazines

The daily *Buenos Aires Herald (see p123)* is popular for English-language news and listings in the capital. It dates back to 1876 and is an iconic newspaper whose finest hour was during the 1970s military dictatorship, when it was one of the few press organs to openly criticize the government's rule. The *International New York Times*, *Time*, and *Newsweek* are usually available at larger newsstands and airports.

The two biggest local papers are the broadsheet *La Nación* and the tabloid *Clarín (see p126)*. Though they once had differing political voices, they are now united in their displeasure with the Fernández de Kirchner government's Media Bill curbing media monopolies. Although both are in Spanish, they are worth picking up on a Friday for the listings supplements.

Magazines in Argentina are a mix of home-grown titles and Spanish-language versions of international magazines. Popular gossip magazines are *Gente*, *Caras*, and *Noticias*, which specialize in celebrity news. Fashion magazines include *OHLÁLA*, while *Remix* is a good guide to clubs and restaurants.

DIRECTORY

Cell Phones

Phonerental
w phonerental.com.ar

Mail Services

Correo Central
Sarmiento 189, Buenos Aires.
City Map 3 E4.
Tel (011) 4891-9191.
w correoargentino.com.ar

DHL
Ave Córdoba 783, Buenos Aires.
City Map 3 D4.
Tel (011) 4630-1100.
w dhl.com.ar

FedEx
Maipú 753, Buenos Aires.
City Map 3 E4.
Tel (011) 4630-0300.
w fedex.com/ar

UPS
Pres. Luis Sáenz Peña 1351,
Buenos Aires. **Tel** (0800) 222-2877. w ups.com/ar

A news *kiosko* at the pedestrianized Calle Florida in Buenos Aires

TRAVEL INFORMATION

Transport infrastructure in Argentina, although still not highly efficient, is much improved. Politicians and bureaucrats have finally woken up to the numerous problems faced by the country's transport network. Now, tourists can arrive at the sleek and modern terminal at Ministro Pistarini International Airport or travel the length and breadth of Patagonia in a comfortable, air-conditioned *micro* (coach). Visitors can opt to arrive in Argentina via the other five countries it shares its borders with or even choose to come across by sea from Uruguay. With a couple of exceptions, cross-country train journeys are, unfortunately, a thing of the past, so visitors should expect to get around the country mainly by air or by road. Major cities and important tourist destinations across Argentina usually have small airports, and almost all places are accessible by *micro*. The vast majority of Rutas Nacionales (major highways) are asphalted and operate as turnpikes; *rutas provinciales* (smaller roads) off the beaten track are often graveled.

Arriving by Air

All international flights arrive at Buenos Aires's Ministro Pistarini International Airport, usually known as Ezeiza after the area in which it is located, 22 miles (35 km) west of the city center. The only exceptions are flights between Buenos Aires and Chile, Uruguay, and Brazil, most of which use Aeroparque Jorge Newbery. Ezeiza has three inter-linked terminals, A, B, and C, with B used exclusively by Argentina's main airline, **Aerolíneas Argentinas**. Baggage collection and customs operate smoothly, although baggage handlers at Ezeiza airport are notoriously light-fingered, so ensure that suitcases are locked and preferably shrink-wrapped. Other airlines that fly to Buenos Aires are **Air France**, **American Airlines**, **Iberia**, **KLM**, **British Airways**, and **Gol**.

Airports

After Ezeiza, Argentina's most important airport is Aeroparque Jorge Newbery, more commonly known as Aeroparque, located a mile (2 km) from downtown Buenos Aires. This is a hub for domestic flights to provincial airports around the country and to Uruguay.

There are 33 airports in Argentina that receive commercial flights. Apart from these, there are smaller airfields for chartered services. Most airports are located some distance from the population centers they serve, but are generally well connected to them by bus, taxi, or *remis* (licensed cab).

Signboard at Ezeiza International Airport

Air Fares

Air fares to Argentina are generally expensive. Prices are high from mid-December through to March, when the demand for tickets out of and into the country is at its highest. Internal flight prices also peak at these times, at Easter, and in June and July.

Expect to pay around US$1600 for a round-trip flight from the United States, and a few hundred more for a flight from Europe. It is possible to find special deals on the Internet which are significantly cheaper, although the flights are unlikely to be direct.

Fixed date returns are always cheaper than open tickets, though there are often some good offers available on round-the-world tickets. For internal flights, Aerolíneas Argentinas has the largest and most reliable network in the country. Unfortunately, it operates a highly controversial "dual pricing" system, where tourists pay at least 25 percent more than locals for the same journeys.

The bustling check-in hall at Ministro Pistarini International Airport, Buenos Aires

Tourist coaches parked at the Cristo Redentor near the Chilean border

Package Deals and Organized Tours

Packages for resorts around Argentina can be competitive. There is a lively market for holidays in Argentina from neighboring countries Peru and Chile, and even from Spain, where many tour agencies offer weekend breaks or longer-stay deals. These include flight transfers and accommodations at three- or four-star hotels, with a tango show occasionally thrown in. The most popular destinations for package tour operators are Iguazú, Bariloche, Buenos Aires, the Andean Northwest, and the more obvious tourist towns of Patagonia. The all-inclusive package-holiday concept is, however, not yet very popular in Argentina.

Adventure tour firms offer everything from whale-watching and rafting trips to specialist bird and wildlife holidays (*see pp306–11*). It is best to contact recommended operators in Europe, North America, and Australasia. They have very high health and safety requirements that are certainly higher than those deemed acceptable by Argentinian law. It is also useful to visit a local travel agent for detailed and up-to-date information.

Arriving by Land

Argentina shares its borders with five countries: Paraguay, Bolivia, Brazil, Uruguay, and Chile. It is possible to arrive into Argentina via any of these countries, although it is important to check visa requirements beforehand. Travelers arriving by coach will usually be asked to show their passports at the border. Tourists arriving in their own vehicles may be waved through or subjected to a thorough search of their car, depending largely on the whim of the *gendarme* (border guard) on duty.

Arriving by Sea

Boats from Uruguay arrive at the port terminal Dársena Norte at Avenidas Córdoba and Alicia Moreau de Justo in Puerto

DIRECTORY

Arriving by Air

Aerolíneas Argentinas
Perú 2, Buenos Aires.
City Map 3 E5.
Tel (0810) 222-86527.
W **aerolineas.com.ar**

Air France
San Martín 344, Floor 23, Buenos Aires. **Tel** (011) 4317-4711.
W **airfrance.com**

American Airlines
Córdoba 1882, Floor 2, Buenos Aires. **Tel** (011) 4318-1111.
W **aa.com**

British Airways
Tel (0800) 222-0075.
W **britishairways.com**

Gol
Tel (0810) 266-3131.
W **voegol.com.br**

Iberia
Tel (011) 4131-1001.
W **iberia.com**

KLM
Tel (011) 4317-4711.
W **klm.com**

Arriving by Sea

Buquebus
Ave Ant. Argentina 821, Buenos Aires. **Tel** (011) 4316-6500.
W **buquebus.com**

Madero (*see p79*). There are regular services from Colonia del Sacramento (*see p121*) and other towns in Uruguay. **Buquebus** is a popular operator. Cruise ships berth at Terminal Benito Quinquela Martín at Ramon Castillo street, near Avenida de los Inmigrantes, Puerto Madero.

Docked passenger boats at Puerto Madero

Domestic Flights

While the idea of crossing Argentina by car holds great appeal, most visitors prefer to travel by air, enabling them to see many of the country's sights during a fortnight's holiday. Most tourist hot spots, such as the Glaciar Perito Moreno and Parque Nacional Iguazú, are well served by flights from and to Buenos Aires, and the Aerolíneas Argentinas commuter belt links major cities from Iguazú to Ushuaia. Travelers going around the country by air, therefore, will become familiar with Buenos Aires's main domestic airport, Aeroparque Jorge Newbery.

The control tower at Mendoza's international airport

Domestic Airlines

The number of domestic airlines is expected to grow in line with the Argentinian economy and the expansion of the tourist sector. Presently, Aerolíneas Argentinas (see p324) is the country's largest domestic carrier, handling about 80 percent of the total traffic.

Its sister airline, Austral Líneas Aéreas, is more commonly known as Austral. It provides a good flight network across Argentina, linking the capital with more than 30 destinations.

The main competitors of Aerolíneas Argentinas and Austral are **Lade** and **LAN Argentina**. The former is a state-owned airline operated by the Argentinian military that runs domestic flights to a number of key destinations. LAN Argentina operates services to major cities around South America, the US, and Europe. The LAN group merged with Brazilian airline TAM in 2012 to form the largest airline in the region.

Sol Línéas Aéreas was the first regional low-cost airline in Argentina. It serves destinations mainly in the center of the country, such as Rosario and Córdoba, as well as coastal resorts such as Mar del Plata, Villa Gesell, and Punta del Este in Uruguay. Another low-cost airline is **Andes Líneas Aéreas**, which has flights from Buenos Aires to Salta. **Baires Fly** planes can carry a maximum of 19 passengers, but it has a flight network for both international and national flights.

Reservations

Reservations can be made via the websites of various domestic airlines or at their branch offices. Electronic tickets are valid, though paper versions can only be collected by the credit card holder. It is advisable for travelers to carry a printout of the email sent to them confirming the booking. Visitors who are prepared to spend some time surfing online travel agencies, and are flexible about the days on which they travel, will usually be able to secure discounted fares. Aerolíneas Argentinas and Austral offer by far the greatest choice of flights and destinations, but those searching for a bargain should check with their competitors.

A view of the domestic airport in Buenos Aires, Aeroparque Jorge Newbery

Checking In

Checking in is usually very straightforward. Travelers must have their ticket or flight reference number at hand along with their passports. At Aeroparque Jorge Newbery it is advisable to arrive at least an hour before the departure time, and about 2 hours in advance at provincial airports. Online check-in is possible for travelers with electronic tickets from 36 hours prior to departure time up to two hours before the flight is scheduled to take off. Industrial action by pilots or ground crew is not unknown, so keep an eye on the news.

Baggage Restrictions

Visitors can carry up to 33 lb (15 kg) on domestic flights with Aerolíneas Argentinas, and up to 44 lb (20 kg) with LAN Argentina. However, both airlines only allow 11 lb (5 kg) as hand luggage. Travelers on hunting trips will have to get a special license to carry firearms.

Air Passes and Concessionary Fares

Domestic flights in Argentina can, unfortunately, be expensive. Aerolíneas Argentinas offers a discount called Visite Argentina. Those who book a flight from a foreign airport to Ezeiza International Airport and book an onward domestic flight at the same time can secure discounts of between 20 to 30 percent. For example, instead of paying US$272 for a flight from Buenos Aires to Bariloche, the same route will cost only US$170.

LAN's Sudamérica Airpass offers special rates for those who purchase three or more one-way LAN flights within Latin America. The pass must be bought 14 days before the first flight and it is better to check the discount percentage before booking. If arriving in Argentina from another Latin American country or from Spain, it is wise to check the package deals on offer. Up until the age of two, children travel free or with a 90 percent discount and between 2–11 years old, they are charged only 67 percent of the ticket price for adults. There are no special prices for senior citizens or students. Most airlines also offer concessionary fares to groups of more than nine people traveling together.

Passengers waiting by information screens at Jorge Newbery airport

Shuttle Services

There are regular shuttle services between Ezeiza and Aeroparque Jorge Newbery organized by the company **Manuel Tienda León**. These provide air-conditioned buses that seat at least 45 passengers. They organize pick-up and delivery, luggage deposit, special services such as guided tours, and even chauffeured limousines.

Flight Duration Chart

1:15 = Duration in hours: minutes
(This chart does not include layover time)

Buenos Aires								
1:10	Córdoba							
2:15	3:15	Salta						
3:40	4:50	5:55	Ushuaia					
0:55	2:10	3:10	4:35	Mar Del Plata				
2:20	3:30	4:35	6:00	3:15	Bariloche			
3:13	4:10	3:28	6:53	4:07	5:33	El Calafate		
1:50	3:00	4:05	4:30	2:45	4:10	5:03	Mendoza	
1:25	2:40	3:40	5:05	2:20	3:45	4:38	3:15	Corrientes

Traveling Around Argentina

As most airlines charge tourists in American dollars for domestic flights, flying around Argentina is expensive. There are, however, many other safe and convenient options. *Micros* travel virtually everywhere and are usually air-conditioned and comfortable. Traveling within Argentina's towns and cities is convenient, with plenty of taxis and *colectivos* (city buses). It is easy to journey by train from Buenos Aires to surrounding cities although there is no single national railroad network. Visitors can cross to Uruguay by ferry or opt for boat excursions in national parks and along major rivers.

One of Argentina's sleek modern *micros*

Micros

Long-distance coaches are a great way to get around the country: they are far cheaper than flights and go to more destinations, more frequently. Fares vary according to the season, but expect to pay AR$700–900 one way for a sleeper service to Bariloche or Mendoza from Buenos Aires. As well as the time of year, the price also depends on the type of seat reserved. Most companies offer three options in ascending price order: *semi-cama* (reclining seat), *cama* (seat with a greater reclining angle), and *super cama* (seat that reclines 120 degrees). Air conditioning is usually very efficient, so wear extra layers, even if it is hot outside.

Established companies such as **Via Bariloche** and **Andesmar** have efficient online booking services that accept all major credit cards. Tickets can be collected or purchased from Buenos Aires's Retiro bus terminal *(see p330)* where all the major companies are based, or from provincial stations. While top operators offer regular services between Argentina's major cities, to get from village to village in the interior, visitors have to take a minibus. Luggage limits can be checked with the operator, and bags are handled by *maleteros* (porters) who expect a tip of around AR$2.

Trains

Only a handful of private and provincial companies operate train services outside of greater Buenos Aires. Among them is the smart commuter service **Ferrovías**. However, other trains can be occasionally ill maintained and uncomfortable. Note too that coach class on some trains may not be heated in winter and can be very cold without a blanket.

There are around six main routes that depart from the capital for destinations such as Mar del Plata, Rosario, and Bahía Blanca. Train enthusiasts will enjoy a ride on one of the touristy routes traversed by **El Tren del Fin del Mundo**, La Trochita *(see p265)*, **Tren Patagónico**, which links the Atlantic coast with Bariloche, and Salta's amazing Tren a las Nubes *(see p199)*.

Ferries

Apart from the popular route connecting Buenos Aires with Colonia del Sacramento in Uruguay, there are very few sea-based transport services in Argentina. Buquebus *(see p325)* sells tickets for this trip. Boat excursions, however, are common, including ones along Canal Beagle in Tierra del Fuego, in the Patagonian lakes around Bariloche and San Martín de los Andes, and, most spectacular of all, cruises to Antarctica out of Ushuaia *(see pp268–71)*.

DIRECTORY

Micros

Andesmar
W andesmar.com

Via Bariloche
W viabariloche.com.ar

Trains

El Tren del Fin del Mundo
W trendelfindelmundo.com.ar

Ferrovías
W ferrovias.com.ar

Tren Patagónico
W trenpatagonico-sa.com.ar

People travelling by train from Buenos Aires to Tigre

Argentina by Road

For the adventurous of spirit looking for a different kind of holiday experience, there is the option of traveling across Argentina by road. An increasingly popular tourist activity, driving around the country has become much safer and more convenient. Argentina's road network is comprehensive – if a place is listed on a map, it can usually be reached by car or motorbike. Driving offers an intimate view of the country. Roads pass spectacular scenery along the Atlantic coast or run across barren Patagonia where wide open spaces encourage a sense of freedom and adventure.

General Safety

Though paved, most of the country's Rutas Nacionales can be narrow, making overtaking tiring and sometimes dangerous. Windscreen and headlamp guards are essential on the roughly graveled *rutas provinciales* as there is a danger of flying stones. By law, drivers must carry warning triangles, a first-aid kit, and an international driving license. Seat belts must be worn and spare tyres, a carjack, car pump, spare wiper blades, and oil must be carried, along with antifreeze if driving in the south.

It is also important to trust in local knowledge – if someone says that a road is impassable at a particular time of year, it is safer to assume that they know what they are talking about.

Renting Cars and Motorbikes

Most of the main international hire companies such as **Avis** and **Hertz** have offices in Argentina. Expect to pay between US$40 and US$60 per day depending on the required mileage. Some smaller, local companies offer the same level of service for a significant discount; visitors should ask for details at their hotel or travel agent. By law a person must be at least 23 to hire a car in Argentina. A driving license, passport and, often, a credit card are required. It is crucial that the renting agency hands over the ownership documents for the vehicle, which must be shown at police checkpoints.

Off-Road Driving

Conventional wisdom dictates that travelers need a 4WD (four-wheel drive) vehicle with truck-tyre tread to get around Argentina, but that is not always the case. Roads often look worse than they actually are. For off-road driving, however, a solid 4WD vehicle with strong suspension is a must. Maintenance gets more expensive farther away from towns and cities, so it is worth installing extra shock absorbers and taking on plenty of fuel before starting out on a long journey.

Distance marker along Ruta Nacional 40

Great Drives

The 3,100-mile (5,000-km) long trunk road Ruta Nacional 40 is easily the country's most famous highway *(see p247)*. However, there are plenty of other routes to satisfy those with a thirst for both adventure and awe-inspiring scenery. If visitors want to get a sense of how enormous, dry, and featureless most of Patagonia is, they can try the fully paved Ruta Nacional 3, which runs down the Atlantic coast. Ruta Nacional 23, on the other hand, running from Ruta Nacional 40 to El Chaltén, is a difficult, high drive with a spectacular backdrop. For the purist road-tripper, Ruta Nacional 25 from Trevelin to Trelew is perfect, with the requisite remote gas stations staffed by friendly local people. Ruta Provincial 9 runs from Buenos Aires to the Bolivian border, following the old Camino Real to the silver mines. It also passes through Quebrada de Humahuaca *(see pp200–4)*.

The journey across South America taken by Che Guevara and his friend, Alberto Granado, in 1952 is becoming an increasingly popular driving route. The famous 8,700-mile (14,000-km) drive was documented in the 2004 biopic *The Motorcycle Diaries*. It is, however, not advisable to try it on a battered Norton 500, as Che and Granado did.

DIRECTORY

Renting Cars and Motorbikes

Avis
Tel (011) 4378-9640, (0810) 9991-2847. W avis.com.ar

Hertz
Tel (011) 4816-0101.
W milletrentacar.com.ar

Lonely stretch of Ruta Nacional 40 going through Bajo Caracoles, Patagonia

Getting Around Buenos Aires

A delightful city for tourists to navigate, Buenos Aires has a good public transport system, one of the cheapest in Latin America, that features an expanding subway and extensive bus routes; taxis and minicabs are also numerous. The city is laid out in the rectangular grid pattern common to most big cities in Latin America, and most areas of interest are concentrated between La Boca in the south and Belgrano in the north, bounded to the east by the river. Porteños are usually very friendly and enjoy helping lost tourists to get back on track.

Passengers on the Subte, South America's oldest subway

The Subte and Overland Trains

The quickest and simplest way to get around the capital is by using the subway, known as the Subte. There are six subway lines (A to E, and H). A one-way ticket to any destination costs AR$4.50. A good tip is to buy a magnetic SUBE card, which is valid on buses and Subtes; they can be purchased and charged in shops where you see the SUBE logo. The downside of the Subte is that coverage is quite limited when compared with the area covered by the city's extensive bus network.

The overland train network is not the most useful form of public transport for tourists and is thus the least used. Commuter trains going to the mainly affluent northern suburbs are tolerably comfortable, while the ones going to the more impoverished southern suburbs are usually overcrowded and poorly maintained, and not suitable for visitors. Some of the major stations in Buenos Aires include **Retiro Mitre**, **Retiro San Martín**, and **Constitución**.

Colectivos

Colectivos (city buses) cover the entire city of Buenos Aires. There are around 180 lines with some subdivided into additional numbers according to the route they take. Lines 1 and 2 of the No. 39, for example, travel from La Boca along Avenida Santa Fe to their terminus in Chacarita; Line 3 has the same starting and finishing point but passes through Palermo Viejo. The colored plate at the bottom of the bus windscreen shows its sub-route, if any, and number. Other useful lines include the No. 60, which connects Constitución station with the delta town of Tigre; the No. 93, which travels along one of the city's major thoroughfares, Avenida del Libertador; and the No. 152, which connects La Boca in the south via Recoleta with Belgrano in the north.

The Guía "T" booklet, available at every kiosk, is a useful guide to the city's bus services. The main bus station is in **Retiro**. A single *colectivo* journey to anywhere in the federal capital, or to anywhere in the suburbs provided the journey begins inside the federal capital, costs a flat AR$2.50. Note that the ticket machines accept only coins.

Open-top tourist buses, run by Buenos Aires Bus, are a good way to see the sights of the city. Buses depart every 20 minutes from 9am to 5:30pm from the corner of Florida and Avenida Roque Sáenz Peña. Visit www.buenosairesbus.com for more information.

Stop sign in Buenos Aires

Driving

The legal age to drive a car in Buenos Aires is 17. It is compulsory to wear front seatbelts and children under 10 must sit at the back. The speed limit is 25 mph (40 kmph) and overtaking is done on the left, while right of way is given to cars crossing intersections from the right. Most of the laws are routinely flouted but the legal age is strictly followed. The blood alcohol content limit is 0.05 percent and penalties for drunken driving include the risk of trial and imprisonment if an accident takes place.

Walking

Buenos Aires is a huge city, but the main areas of tourist interest are fairly compact and easy to get around on foot. The condition of the pavements in most barrios is tolerable, although drivers rarely pay much attention to pedestrians. Also, it is advisable not to wander alone into uncharted territory after dark.

A brightly colored *colectivo*, Buenos Aires

Black and yellow taxis, a familar sight in Buenos Aires

Taxis and Remises

There are many cabs on the streets of Buenos Aires and it is usually easy to find one at any time. Taxis are painted black and yellow and run on meters; *remises*, which are licensed minicabs, look like any other private car. For safety reasons, it is recommended that visitors use either a radio taxi or a *remis*. If a tourist must hail a taxi, it is advisable to make sure that the vehicle is marked with a company name and serial number and that the red *libre* light in the front window is on. A fee must be agreed before setting off when using *remises*, and there may be an AR$5 fee for booking one by phone. On no account will a driver change anything over a AR$20 peso note, unless agreed upon in advance; always check the change. Some of the popular *remises* include **Amistax** and **Radio Taxi Premium**. Taxis are not the quickest option during rush hours.

DIRECTORY

The Subte and Overland Trains

Constitución Station
Gral Hornos 11.
Tel (011) 4304-0028.

Retiro Mitre
Ramos Mejía 1430.
City Map 3 E3.
Tel (0800) 333-3822.

Retiro San Martín
Ramos Mejía 1430.
City Map 3 E3.
Tel (0800) 122-8736.

Colectivos

Retiro
Ave Ant. Argentina & Calle 10.
Tel (011) 4310-0707.

Taxis and Remises

Amistax
Tel (011) 4582-7774.

Radio Taxi Premium
Tel (011) 5238-0000.

Buenos Aires Subte Map

Key
— Subte lines
○ Interchange
═ Planned

General Index

Acknowledgments

Dorling Kindersley would like to thank the many people whose help and assistance contributed to the preparation of this book.

Main Contributors
Wayne Bernhardson first visited Buenos Aires in 1981 during a military dictatorship. He has contributed to both magazines and newspapers including Trips, National Geographic Traveler, and San Francisco Chronicle.

Declan McGarvey visited Argentina in 1999 and decided to stay after falling in love with the country. He is co-author of Eyewitness Top 10 Buenos Aires, has collaborated on and edited several Time Out guides to Patagonia and Buenos Aires, and has contributed to DK's Where to Go When series.

Chris Moss lived in Argentina for 10 years and commutes there regularly from his home in London. He has written on Latin American topics for the Daily Telegraph, Independent, Guardian, New Internationalist, and Condé Nast Traveller, and is the author of Landscapes of the Imagination: Patagonia (Signal Books).

Fact Checkers
Ariel Waisman, Sofí Saul

Proofreader
Deepthi Talwar

Indexer
Jyoti Dhar

Editorial and Design
Publisher Douglas Amrine
List Manager Vivien Antwi
Managing Art Editor Jane Ewart
Publishing Manager Scarlett O'Hara
Project Editor Alastair Laing
Project Designers Sonal Bhatt, Paul Jackson
Senior Cartographic Editor Casper Morris
Managing Art Editor (jackets) Karen Constanti
Jacket Design Tessa Bindloss
DTP Designer Natasha Lu
Picture Researcher Ellen Root
Production Controller Louise Daly

Revisions Team
Louise Abbott, Damaris Allegrini, Shruti Bahl, Hilary Bird, Rajesh Chhibber, Samantha Cook, Caroline Beactrice D'Cruz, Karen D'Souza, Hannah Dolan, Mariel Donda, Caroline Elliker, Alexandra Farrell, Fay Franklin, Anna Freiberger, Allan Kelin, Sumita Khatwani, Jason Little, Bhavika Mathur, Margaret McHugh, Casper Morris, Sorrel Moseley-Williams, George Nimmo, Susie Peachey, Mariane Petrou, Susana Smith, Jaynan Spengler, Hollie Teague, Nikky Twyman, Catherine Waring, Ed Wright

DK Picture Library
Emma Shepherd, Romaine Werblow

Additional Photography
Philip Dowell, Mike Dunning, Frank Greenaway, Cyril Laubscher, Richard Leeney, Ian O'Leary, Neil Setchfield.

Special Assistance
DK would like to thank the following for their assistance: Analia Martino at Museo de la Plata, German Maschwitz at Fronterasur, Preeti Pant, Guadalupe Requena and Cintia Mezza at Museo de Arte Latinamericano de Buenos Aires.

Photography Permissions
DK would like to thank the following for their assistance and kind permission to photograph at their establishments:
Alvear Palace Hotel, Ateneo Grand Splendid, Banco de la Nación Argentina, Basílica Nuestra Señora de Luján, Cabildo de Buenos Aires, Café La Biela, Café Tortoni, Catedral de la Inmaculada Concepción, Catedral Metropolitana, Catedral Nuestra Señora del Valle, Cementerio de la Recoleta, Centro Cultural Recoleta, Che Lulu hotel, Congreso Nacional Argentino, Correo Central Argentino, Estancia Cerro de la Cruz, Estancia La Bamba, Estancia Rincón del Socorro, Estación Retiro, Galerías Pacífico, Iglesia de la Compañía, Iglesia de Nuestra Señora del Pilar, Iglesia Parroquial Nuestra Señora de la Merced, Iglesia San Francisco, Instituto Nacional de Estudios de Teatro, Mansión Dandi Royal, Museo Argentino de Ciencias Naturales Bernardino Rivadavia, Museo Casa de Ricardo Rojas, Museo de Arqueología de Alta Montaña de Salta, Museo de Arte Español Enrique Larreta, Museo de Arte Hispanoamericano Isaac Fernández Blanco, Museo de Arte Latinoamericano de Buenos Aires, Museo de Arte Popular José Hernández, Museo de Artes Plasticas Eduardo Sivori, Museo de la Pasion Boquense, Museo de La Plata, Museo de la Shoá, Museo del Mar, Museo del Puerto (Bahía Blanca), Museo Etnográfico (Buenos Aires), Museo Folklórico, Museo Gauchesco Ricardo Güiraldes, Museo Histórico Nacional, Museo Judío de Buenos Aires Dr. Salvador Kibrick, Museo Municipal Carmen Funes, Museo Municipal Ernesto Bachmann, Museo Nacional de Arte Decorativo, Museo Nacional de Bellas Artes, Museo Nacional del Hombre, Museo Paleontológico Egidio Feruglio, Museo Regional Malargüe, Museo Xul Solar, Palacio de las Aguas Corrientes, Palacio San José, Palacio San Martín, Palais de Glace, Parque Nacional Iguazú, Parque Provincial Ischigualasto, Restaurant Notorious, Taller y Museo de Platería Criolla y Civil, Teatro Catalinas Sur, Teatro Municipal General San Martín, Templo de la Congregación Israelita, Villa Gesell.

Picture Credits

(Public Demonstration) (Temple on Burlap) 180 x 249 cm by Antonio Berni © José Antonio Berni 114cla; Siete últimas canciones, 1986, de la serie homónima (Last Seven Songs, from the homonymous series) (Acrylic painting on canvas) 141,5 x 226 cm © Guillermo Kuitca 114br; Abaporu, 1928 (Oil on canvas) 85,3 x 73 cm by Tarsila do Amaral © Guillermo Augusto Do Amaral 115tc; Rompecabezas, 1968-1970 (Puzzle) (Acrylic on canvas, 17 panels to be assembled) 100 x 100 cm each panel by Jorge de la Vega © Ramón de la Vega 115crb; Sin título, 1979 (Untitled) (Stainless steel wire and silver weldings) 100 x 40 x 40 cm © León Ferrari 115bc.

4corners: Antonino Bartuccio 174-5.

A Hotel, Buenos Aires: 275tr. Aguas Arriba Lodge: Florian von der Fecht 282tl. **Akg-Images**: 57bl. **Alamy**: AA World Travel Library 11bl, 298bc; Arco Images 31tc, 51bc, 166c, 188bc, 190tr, 190br, 191tc, 221cr, /Therin-Weise 205t; Purvis Beau 287c; Blickwinkel 23br, 83br; Steve Bly 6-7, 44cl; Tibor Bognar 64, 67cr; Brianlatino 100tr; James Brunker 241br; Bryan & Cherry Alexander Photography 271bl; Cristina Cassinelli 302bl; Cephas Picture Library 138cl, 207b; Frederic Cholin 40cb; Classic Image 51c; Gary Cook 254cla; Javier Corripio 243crb; CuboImages srl 89br; Tim Cuff 255br; Danita Delimont 5clb, 30cl, 46b; David R. Frazier Photolibrary, Inc. 76tr, 176tr, 284br, 286cla, 305bl, 326b; Saturno Dona' 5crb; Emilio Ereza 302fbl; Javier Etcheverry 39cr, 39bc, 141b, 230br, 259clb; f1 online 24bl; Mark O'Flaherty 213cra; Folio 270clb; Robert Fried 39bl, 39br, 177ca, 243bc; Rodney Griffiths 8bl; Martin Harvey 262bl; Gavin Hellier 252-3; Jeremy Hoare 19tl, 26-7c, 42tr, 76bl, 127tl, 251bc; Peter Horree 331tl; Chris Howarth 92cl; Imagebroker 42ca, 48bl; Interfoto Pressebildagentur 9br; Jon Arnold Images Ltd 254clb; Norma Joseph 8tc, 21tr, 268cl, 303tc; Jupiter Images /Brand X 255tl; Christian Kapteyn 259crb, 259br, 307bc; Lemarco 63cr, 67br, 318tr; Yadid Levy 12bl; LightTouch Images/Colin Harris 269t; MAF 302br; Mary Evans Picture Library 59tl; MB-America 9tl; Network Photographers 63br; A. Parada 40tr; Peter Llewellyn (L) 40cl; Photos-12 31tr; Christopher Pillitz 35br; Popperfoto 42ca, 42-3c, 43cr, 43cb, 43crb, 43bl, 43bc, 57cra, 155c; Richard Wareham Fotografie 165tl, 177crb; Robert Harding Picture Library Ltd/Geoff Renner 258b, 271cr; Emiliano Rodríguez 4-5tc, 24tr, 202cl, 242ca, 242cb; Marcelo Rudini 24crb; Gordon Sinclair 303cb; Paul Springett 257clb, 310cl; Stephen Frink Collection 22clb; Stockbyte 67cra; James Sturcke 245tc, 311tl; Tbkmedia.de 139tr; Tom Till 206; Travel Excellence 22cr, 38cl; Travel Stock Collection/Homer Sykes 68clb; Genevieve Vallee 173c; Joan Vendrell 191tc; Simon Vine 259bc; Visual&Written SL 230tr, 234tl; Visions of America/LLC/Joe Sohm 261b; Westend 61 148tl; Wim Wiskerke 39crb, 124b, 284cl; WoodyStock/Elsen Reiner 127bc; WorldFoto 269br, 270br, 271tl; Anna Yu 303ca. Alvear Palace Hotel: 279tr, 289tr. Anna Bistro: 285t, 296bl. Archivo general de la naciÓn: 36br. Archivolatino: Diego Giudice 41tl. AWL Images: Demetrio Carrasco 80; Danita Delimont Stock 140; Nigel Pavitt 312-313; Ian Trower 160; Allan White 260. Ayelen Hotel de Montaña: 280bl.

El Baqueano: Pablo Baracat 288bc. **The Bridgeman Art Library**: Military encampment of the governor Jeronimo Matorras during the Gran Chaco campaign, Cabrera,

Tomas (18th century)/Museo Histórico Nacional, Buenos Aires, Argentina 50; The Congress of Tucumán – Declaration of the Independence of the United Provinces of Río and the Plata on 9th July 1816, Fortuny, Francisco (19th century) (after)/Private Collection 53tr; Shield of the Confederation of Argentina, Argentinian School, (19th Century) /Private Collection 53br; Battle of Tuyutí, from the paintings depicting the Triple Alliance War, 1866, López, Cándido (1840-1902) /Museo Histórico Nacional, Buenos Aires, Argentina 54t; The Arrival of General Juan Facundo Quiroga (1790-1835) in Madrid on the 24th June 1820, French School, (19th century) /Bibliotheque des Arts Decoratifs, Paris, France, Archives Charmet 189crb. The Granger Collection, New York: 7c, 52t, 54bc, 111b. Brindillas: Lorena D'Amico and Mariano Valdivieso 294tl.

Cabañas Arco iris: 283bl. Cavas Wine Lodge: 295br. Jadd Cheng: 116br. **Corbis**: Theo Allofs 231tl; Yann Arthus-Bertrand 176cl, 179tr; Bettmann 31cb, 56bc, 57tl, 57c, 57cb, 58tc, 58clb, 58bl, 117bl; Marcello Calandrini 139br; Corbis Sygma 37tr, /Diego Goldberg 59bl, 107c; Pablo Corral V 76cla, William Coupon 31br; Owen Franken 25br; Diego Giudice 41tr, 167ca; Jon Hicks 121br, 314cl; Dave G. Houser 57bc; Hulton-Deutsch Collection 56clb; Bob Krist 270cla; Yadid Levy / Robert Harding World Imagery 9cr; Michael Lewis 30crb; Eduardo Longoni 287tl; Craig Lovell 66cl, Francesc Muntada 231cra; Diego Lezama Orezzoli 121tr; Peter Langer - Associated Media / Design Pics 12tr; Radius Images 2-3; Hubert Stadler 1c; 304bl; Anthony John West 17b; Zefa/Hugh Sitton 26tr. Gerald Cubitt: 243cra.

DK Images: Philip Dowell 23bc. Dreamstime.com: Elxeneize 38tr; Alexandre Fagundes De Fagundes 212-213c; Glynspencer 13tr, 13bc; Hel080808 8br; Javarman 10tr, 218-219c; Jesse Kraft 266-267; Eduardo Mariath 224, 999cl; Patrick Poendl 8cla; Stef22 43br; Aníbal Trejo 60-61, 136-137; King Ho Yim 10bl.

Frank Lane Picture Agency: Minden Pictures/ Konrad Wothe 226cl. **Fronterasur.com**: 302ca, 302cr, 303bl, 303bc.

Getty Images: AFP Photo 31br, /Pedro Armestre 31crb, / Daniel Garcia 30tr, /Jeff Haynes 41br, /Juan Mabromata 47tc, /Mauricio Lima 41cr; AFP Photo/Staff/Roland Magunia 33br; AFP Photo/Stringer 56bl; AFP Photo/ Stringer/Mayela Lopez 20tr, /Juan Mabromata 33bl; Hulton Archive /Nobby Clark 35tr, /Stringer/Keystone 56br, 56-7c, 257bc; LatinContent 108; Science Faction /Louie Psihoyos 236-7c, 237tl; Minden Pictures, /Flip Nicklin 308br; Stocktrek Images 10bl; Stone /Andrea Booher 26br; Time & Life Pictures /Mansell 271br, /Hart Preston 55tc, /Frank Scherschel 36cra, /Stringer/Thomas D. McAvoy 56cl. **Gustino**: 299tl.

Ova Hamer: 318bl. Home Hotel, Buenos Aires: 275br, 278bc.

Il Novo Maria del Lujan: 291bl. Irupé Lodge: 281tr. Latin Photo: Rodrigo Buezas 40bl; Fernando Calzada 21b, 24br, 24-5c, 29tr, 32tr; Silvina Enrietti 46tr; German Falke 23cb, 24clb, 26bl, 78cr, 161b, 167cl, 173tc, 249br; Miguel Fleitas 22cl; Carlos Ortiz Fragala 46tl, 213clb; Christian Heit 25cr; Guillermo Jones 66tr, 169br; Norberto Lauria 44br, 302cl; Enrice Limbrunner 26cla; Patrick Lüthy 25tr, 105tl;

Maria Menegazzo 120tr; Mule 71tr; Patricio Murphy 39cla; Pepe Pride 41tl; Diego Ivo Piacenza 121cl, 167crb, 167bl; Nicolas Pousthomis 24cl; Pronatura 196tr; Pablo Rey 323tl; Aznarez Soledad 59crb; Sub.coop/ Juan Vera 19bc. Lebrecht Music & Arts. Patrick Liotta: 33cr. Alejandro Lipszyc: 32br. Lonely Planet Images: Chris Barton 234bc; Krzysztof Dydynski 12, 304cr; Andrew Peacock 316bl. L'Obrador: 297tr.

Mary Evans Picture Library: 55crb. Masterfile: T. Ozonas 45bc. Mio Buenos Aires: 277tr. Museo de La Plata: 146ca, 146cl. Museo del cine: 83cr.

National Geographic Image Collection: Damnfx 236br. Natural Visions: Richard Coomber 159tr. Nature Picture Library: Ross Couper-Johnston 170br; Luiz Claudio Marigo 171br; Pete Oxford 23cla.

Odyssey Productions, Inc.: Robert Frerck 25cra, 26c, 30bl, 62cl, 63tl, 67tl, 77ca, 77br, 98; Russell Gordon 27tl. Olsen, Buenos Aires: 290bl. Joshua Ong: 77cr. Ostinatto, Buenos Aires: 276bl. Ignacio Otheguy: 158br.

Patagonicus: 296bc. Photographers Direct: David Alayo 20bl; Andres Perez Moreno Photography 243tc; Archivolatino/Diego Giudice 36bl; CFW Images/Rachel Tisdale 199br; Fotoscopio /Gustavo Di Pace 32cl, 33tl, 77tl, 201bl; Javier Etcheverry Photography 236tr; Dale Mitchell 23cl; Lebrecht Music & Arts Photo Library /Elbie Lebrecht 54clb; Sylvia Cordaiy Photo Library Ltd /Sylvia Cordaiy 256b; Fotozonas.com /Tomeu Ozonas 49br.Photolibrary: Cephas Picture Library Ltd 181b, /Andy Christodolo 212br, /Kevin Judd 212cl; Foodanddrink Photos 213c; Iconotec /H.FougFre 18b; Index Stock Imagery,Inc. /Garry Adams 204tl; Jon Arnold Travel /Peter Adams 8c; Jtb Photo Communications Inc 139cr; Oxford Scientific Films /Colin Monteath 259c; Photodisc /Glen Allison 4br, 86-7; Photononstop /Yvan Travert 225b, /Marc Vérin 182bl, 272-3. Photoshot: Nhpa /Thomas Kitchin & Victoria Hurst 22fcrb; Kevin Schafer 23crb.Producciones Centauro: 27bl. The Picture Desk: The Art Archive /Museo Naciónal de Bellas Artes Buenos Aires /Gianni Dagli Orti 34br; The Kobal Collection /Historias/Progress 37tl, /MGM 35c, /Paramount 36cl, /La Pasionaria/ Maria Gowland 37cr. Tornasol Films 37cr, Justin Tyler: 113br.

Redferns Music Picture Library: Jon Lusk 33tr; Philip Ryalls 32clb. Restaurant del Puerto: 292bc. Robert Harding Picture Library: Jordi Cami 11tr, imageBROKER 150-151; Stengert Nico / age fotostock 180. Reuters: Marcos Brindicci 40-41c, 47br, 128tl, 316bl; Viktor Korotayev 37br; Enrique Marcarian 27cra, 42bl; Handout/ Rodolfo Coria 237br; STR New 164cl. La Rueda 1975: 293tl. Diego Manuel Rodriguez: 31cr.

South American Pictures: 30-1c; Frank Nowikowski 117tr. SuperStock: Max W. Hunn 152tc, Prisma 90. Hanne Therkildsen: 83tl.

Emma Werner de Oliver: 190bl, 191bl, 191br.

Unik, Buenos Aires: 291tr.

Wikipedia, The Free Encyclopedia: 33cl, 33clb, 37cl, 42cl, 53bl, 55bl, 56tr, 159bc. Wine Republic Argentina: Richard Gordon 213br.

Front Endpaper: Alamy: BKWine.com /Per Karlsson bc; Tibor Bognar cr; Tom Till tl; Corbis: ftr; Jon Arnold Images Ltd: Walter Bibikow cl; Odyssey Productions, Inc.: Robert Frerck br; Photographers Direct: Emiliano Rodríguez Photography /Emiliano Rodríguez Ruiz de Gauna fcr; Photolibrary: Mauritius /Michael Obert tr, Michael Runkel ftl, Nordic Photos /Chad Ehlers fbr, Oxford Scientific Films / Colin Monteath fcl.

Jacket images: Front: AWL Images: Aurora Photos; Dorling Kindersley: Linda Whitwam bl; Spine: AWL Images: Aurora Photos.

All other images © Dorling Kindersley
For further information see: www.dkimages.com

Special Editions of DK Travel Guides

DK Travel Guides can be purchased in bulk quantities at discounted prices for use in promotions or as premiums. We are also able to offer special editions and personalized jackets, corporate imprints, and excerpts from all of our books, tailored specifically to meet your own needs.

To find out more, please contact:
in the United States **SpecialSales@dk.com**
in the UK **travelspecialsales@uk.dk.com**
in Canada DK Special Sales at **general@ tourmaline.ca**
in Australia **business.development@pearson. com.au**

Phrase Book

In Argentina, waves of immigration at the end of the 19th century and at the beginning of the 20th century (especially from Italy, but also from France and Spain) influenced the way people spoke. The variant of Spanish spoken in Argentina is known as *rioplatense*. "Ll" and "y" are both pronounced like English "sh" as in "she," as opposed to the "y" sound in Castilian Spanish. The "s" sound can become like an "h" when it occurs before another consonant or at the end of a word as in "tres" – "treh"; it may be omitted altogether, as in "dos" – "do." As in other Latin American countries, "c" and "z" are pronounced as "s," as opposed to "th" in Castilian Spanish.

In an Emergency

Help!	¡Socorro!	sokorro
Stop!	¡Pare!	pareh
Call a doctor!	¡Llamen al médico!	shamen al medeeko
Call an ambulance	¡Llamen a una ambulancia!	shamen a oona amboolans-ya
Police!	¡Policía!	poleesee-a
I've been robbed	Me robaron	meh rrobaron
Where is the nearest hospital?	¿Dónde queda el hospital más cercano?	dondeh keda el ospeetal mas sairkano
Could you help me?	¿Me puede ayudar?	meh pwedeh a-shoodar

Communication Essentials

Yes	Sí	see
No	No	no
Please	Por favor	por fabor
Pardon me	Perdone	pairdoneh
Excuse me	Disculpe	deeskoolpeh
I'm sorry	Lo siento	lo s-yento
Thanks	Gracias	gras-yas
Hello!	Hola	ola
Good day	Buen día	bwen dee-a
Good afternoon	Buenas tardes	bwenas tardes
Good evening	Buenas noches	bwenas noches
Night	Noche	nocheh
Morning	Mañana	man-yana
Tomorrow	Mañana	man-yana
Yesterday	Ayer	a-shair
Here	Acá	aka
How?	¿Cómo?	komo
When?	¿Cuándo?	kwando
Where?	¿Dónde?	dondeh
Why?	¿Por qué?	por keh
How are you?	¿Qué tal?/¿Cómo va?	keh tal/komo ba
Very well, thank you	Muy bien, gracias	mwee byen gras-yas
Pleased to meet you	Encantado/mucho gusto	enkantado/ moocho goosto

Useful Phrases

Fine!	¡Qué bien!	keh b-yen
Do you speak a little English?	¿Habla un poco de inglés?	abla oon poko deh eengles
I don't understand	No entiendo	no ent-yendo
Could you speak more slowly?	¿Puede hablar más despacio?	pwedeh ablar mas despas-yo
I agree/OK	De acuerdo/bueno	deh akwairdo/ bweno
Let's go!	¡Vámonos!	bamonos
How do I get to/which way to..?	¿Cómo se llega a...?/¿Por dónde se va a...?	komo se shega a/por dondeh seh ba a
That's great!	¡Qué piola!	keh pyola

Useful Words

large	grande	grandeh
small	pequeño	peken-yo
hot	caliente	kal-yenteh
cold	frío	free-o
good	bueno	bweno
bad	malo	malo
sufficient	suficiente	soofees-yenteh
open	abierto	ab-yairto
closed	cerrado	serrado
entrance	entrada	entrada
exit	salida	saleeda
full	lleno	sheno
right	derecha	dairecha
left	izquierda	eesk-yairda
straight on	(todo) derecho	(todo) derecho

over	arriba	arreeba
quickly	pronto	pronto
early	temprano	temprano
late	tarde	tardeh
now	ahora	a-ora
soon	ahorita	a-oreeta
less	menos	menos
much	mucho	moocho
in front of	delante	delanteh
opposite	enfrente	enfrenteh
behind	detrás	detras
first floor	segundo piso	segoondo peeso
ground floor	primer piso	preemair peeso
lift	ascensor	asensor
bathroom	baño	ban-yo
women	mujeres	moohaires
men	hombres	ombres
toilet paper	papel higiénico	papel eeh-yeneeko
camera	cámara	kamara
batteries	pilas	peelas
passport	pasaporte	pasaporteh
visa	visa	beesa
tourist card	tarjeta turistica	tarheta tooreesteeka
thief	chorro	chorro
lazy	atorrante	atorranteh
nightclub	boliche	boleecheh
idiot	boludo	booloodo
cop	cana	kana
to tease	cargar	kargar
money	dinero	dee-nairo
to eat	comer	ko-mare
kid	pibe	peebeh
mess	quilombo	keelombo
driver's license	registro	reheestro
shanty town	villa miseria	beesha meesair-ya
to nick, to steal	afanar	afanar
to get frightened	achicarse	acheekarseh
No way	¡Ni en pedo!	nee en pedo
to put up with	bancar	bankar
girl/woman	muchacha	moochacha

Health

I don't feel well	Me siento mal	meh s-yento mal
I have a stomach ache	Me duele el estómago	meh dweleh el estomago
headache	la cabeza	la kabesa
He/she is ill	Está enfermo/a	esta enfairmo/a
I need to rest	Necesito descansar	neseseeto dekansar

Post Offices and Banks

I'm looking for a	Busco una	boosko oona
Bureau de change	casa de cambio	kasa deh kamb-yo
What is the dollar rate?	¿A cómo está el dolar?	a komo esta el dolar
I want to send a letter	Quiero mandar una carta	k-yairo mandar oona karta
postcard	postal	postal
stamp	estampilla	estampee-sha
to draw out money	sacar dinero	sakar deenairo

Shopping

I would like/want...	Me gustaría/quiero...	meh goostaree-a/k-yairo
Do you have any...?	¿Tiene...?	t-yeneh
expensive	caro	karo
How much is it?	¿Cuánto cuesta?	kwanto kwesta
What time do you open/close?	¿A qué hora abre/cierra?	a ke ora abreh/s-yairra
May I pay with a credit card?	¿Puedo pagar con tarjeta de crédito?	pwedo pagar kon tarheta deh kredeeto

Sightseeing

beach	playa	pla-sha
castle, fortress	castillo	kastee-sho
guide	guía	gee-a
motorway	autopista	owtopeesta
road	carretera	karretaira
street	calle, callejón	ka-sheh, ka-shehon
tourist bureau	oficina de turismo	ofeeseena deh tooreesmo
town hall	municipalidad	mooneeseepaleedad

Getting Around

When does it leave?	¿A qué hora sale?	a keh ora saleh
When does the next train/bus leave for...?	¿A qué hora sale el próximo tren/ autobús a...?	a keh ora saleh el prokseemo tren/ owtoboos a
customs	aduana	adwana
Could you call a taxi for me?	¿Me puede llamar un taxi?	meh pwedeh shamar oon taksee
port of embarkation	puerta de embarque	pwairta deh embarkeh
boarding pass	tarjeta de embarque	tarheta deh embarkeh
car hire	alquiler de autos	alkeelair deh owtos
bicycle	bicicleta	beeseekleta
rate	tarifa	tareefa
insurance	seguro	segooro
petrol station	estación de servicio	estas-yon deh sair-vee-see-oh
garage	garage	garaheh
I have a flat tyre	Se me pinchó una goma	seh meh peencho oona goma

Staying in a Hotel

I have a reservation	Tengo una reserva	Tengo oona rresairfa
Are there any rooms available?	¿Tiene habitaciones disponibles?	Tyones deesponeebles
single/double room	habitación sencilla/ doble	abeetas-yon sensee-sha/dobleh
twin room	habitación con camas gemelas	abeetas-yon kon kamas hemelas
shower	ducha	doocha
bath	bañadera	ban-yadaira
I want to be woken up at...	Necesito que me despierten a las...	neseseeto keh meh desp-yairten a las
warm/cold water	agua caliente/fría	agwa kal-yenteh/free-a
soap	jabón	habon
towel	toalla	to-a-sha
key	llave	shabeh

Eating Out

I am a vegetarian	Soy vegetariano	soy behetar-yano
fixed price	precio fijo	pres-yo feeho
glass	vaso	baso
cutlery	cubiertos	koob-yairtos
Can I see the menu, please?	¿Me deja ver el menú, por favor?	me deha ber el menoo por fabor
The bill, please	la cuenta, por favor	la kwenta por fabor
I would like	Quiero un poco	k-yairo oon poko
some water	de agua	deh agwa
breakfast	desayuno	desa-shoono
lunch	almuerzo	almwairso
dinner	comida	komeeda

Menu Decoder *See also pp286–7*

bife de chorizo a caballo	*beefeh deh choreeso a kabasho*	chargrilled sirloin steak with two fried eggs on top
bife de chorizo	*beefeh deh choreeso*	chargrilled sirloin steak
bife de lomo	*beefeh deh lomo*	chargrilled fillet steak
centolla	*sentosha*	spider crab
chimichurri	*cheemeechoorree*	hot sauce
choripán	*choreepan*	pork sausage sandwich
churrasco	*choorrasko*	chargrilled rump steak
churrasco a caballo	*choorrasko a kabasho*	chargrilled rump steak with two fried eggs on top
matambre	*matambreh*	pork flank or skirt steak
mollejas	*moshehas*	sweetbreads
torta de humita	*torta deh oomeeta*	yellow sweet pumpkin and sweet corn mixed with cheese, onion and red pepper
arroz	*arros*	rice
atún	*atoon*	tuna
azúcar	*asookar*	sugar
bacalao	*bakala-o*	cod
bizcochuelo	*beeskochwelo*	cake
camarones	*kamarones*	prawns

carne	*karneh*	meat
cebolleta	*se-boy-eta*	spring onion
chip	*cheep*	bread roll
huevo	*webo*	egg
jugo	*hoogo*	fruit juice
langosta	*langosta*	lobster
leche	*lecheh*	milk
mantequilla	*mantekee-sha*	butter
marisco	*mareesko*	seafood
pan	*pan*	bread
papas	*papas*	potatoes
pescado	*peskado*	fish
pollo	*po-sho*	chicken
postre	*postreh*	dessert
potaje	*potaheh*	soup
sal	*sal*	salt
salsa	*salsa*	sauce
sopa	*sopa*	soup
té	*teh*	tea
vinagre	*beenagreh*	vinegar
zapallito	*sapa-sheeto*	zucchini/courgette

Time

minute	**minuto**	*meenooto*
hour	**hora**	*ora*
half-hour	**media hora**	*med-ya ora*
quarter of an hour	**un cuarto**	*oon kwarto*
Monday	**lunes**	*loones*
Tuesday	**martes**	*martes*
Wednesday	**miércoles**	*m-yairkoles*
Thursday	**jueves**	*hwebes*
Friday	**viernes**	*b-yairnes*
Saturday	**sábado**	*sabado*
Sunday	**domingo**	*domeengo*
January	**enero**	*enairo*
February	**febrero**	*febrairo*
March	**marzo**	*marso*
April	**abril**	*abreel*
May	**mayo**	*ma-sho*
June	**junio**	*hoon-yo*
July	**julio**	*hool-yo*
August	**agosto**	*agosto*
September	**septiembre**	*sept-yembreh*
October	**octubre**	*oktoobreh*
November	**noviembre**	*nob-yembreh*
December	**diciembre**	*dees-yembreh*

Numbers

0	**cero**	*sairo*
1	**uno**	*oono*
2	**dos**	*dos*
3	**tres**	*tres*
4	**cuatro**	*kwatro*
5	**cinco**	*seenko*
6	**seis**	*says*
7	**siete**	*s-yeteh*
8	**ocho**	*ocho*
9	**nueve**	*nwebeh*
10	**diez**	*d-yes*
11	**once**	*onseh*
12	**doce**	*doseh*
13	**trece**	*treseh*
14	**catorce**	*katorseh*
15	**quince**	*keenseh*
16	**dieciséis**	*d-yeseesays*
17	**diecisiete**	*d-yesees-yeteh*
18	**dieciocho**	*d-yes-yocho*
19	**diecinueve**	*d-yeseenwebeh*
20	**veinte**	*baynteh*
30	**treinta**	*traynta*
40	**cuarenta**	*kwarenta*
50	**cincuenta**	*seenkwenta*
60	**sesenta**	*sesenta*
70	**setenta**	*setenta*
80	**ochenta**	*ochenta*
90	**noventa**	*nobenta*
100	**cien**	*s-yen*
500	**quinientos**	*keen-yentos*
1000	**mil**	*meel*
first	**primero/a**	*preemairo/a*
second	**segundo/a**	*segoondo/a*
third	**tercero/a**	*tairsairo/a*
fourth	**cuarto/a**	*kwarto/a*
fifth	**quinto/a**	*keento/a*
sixth	**sexto/a**	*seksto/a*
seventh	**séptimo/a**	*septeemo/a*
eight	**octavo/a**	*oktabo/a*
ninth	**noveno/a**	*nobeno/a*
tenth	**décimo/a**	*deseemo/a*

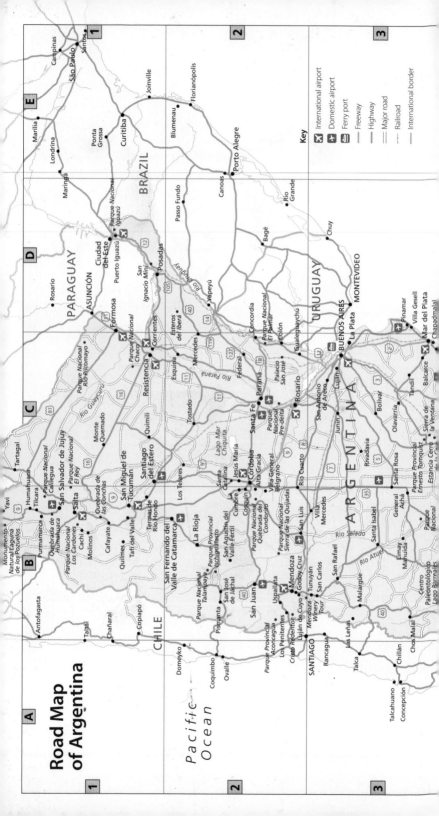